St. Clair Ave.

Davenport Ave.

nette St.

Dundas St.

Lansdowne Ave.

Dufferin St.

Ossington Ave.

Manning Ave.

Bathurst St.

3

5

Bloor St.

Grace St.

H

Roncesvalles

Keele St.

College St.

Henders

5

Dundas St.

Queen St.

Niagara St.

King St.

4

Toronto
Neighbourhoods

1. Cabbagetown and the East End
2. St. John's Ward
3. The Junction
4. The Niagara/King area
5. Italian neighbourhoods
6. Kensington Market/Spadina area

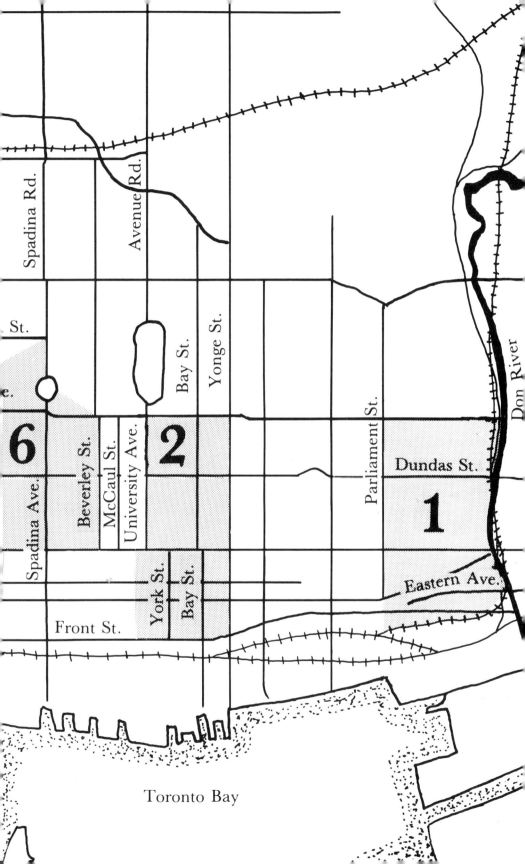

Spadina Rd.

Avenue Rd.

St.

e.

Bay St.

Yonge St.

Parliament St.

Don River

6

Beverley St.

McCaul St.

University Ave.

2

Spadina Ave.

Dundas St.

1

York St.

Bay St.

Eastern Ave.

Front St.

Toronto Bay

Gathering Place: Peoples and Neighbourhoods of Toronto, 1834-1945

Cover photo: Courtesy of the United Church Archives, Victoria University, Queen's Park, Toronto

ISBN: 0-919045-18-9 paper
      0-919045-20-0 hard
Published 1985.
Printed in Canada.
The Multicultural History Society of Ontario
43 Queen's Park Crescent East
Toronto, Ontario M5S 2C3

Studies in Ethnic and Immigration History

Gathering Place: Peoples and Neighbourhoods of Toronto, 1834-1945

edited by Robert F. Harney

1985
Multicultural History Society of Ontario
Toronto

This book was published with the assistance of a grant from the Toronto Sesquicentennial Board in honour of the 150th anniversary of the City of Toronto.

We also wish to thank the Multiculturalism Directorate, Office of the Secretary of State for its generous assistance in the preparation of this volume.

FC
3097.9
, A1
G37
1985 / 45,504

Canadian Cataloguing in Publication Data

Main entry under title:

Gathering place

Includes bibliographical references.
ISBN 0-919045-20-0 (bound). — ISBN 0-919045-18-9 (pbk.)

1. Toronto (Ont.) — Population — Ethnic groups — Addresses, essays, lectures.
2. Toronto (Ont.) — Social life and customs — Addresses, essays, lectures.
3. Neighbourhood — Ontario — Toronto — Addresses, essays, lectures.
4. Ethnicity — Ontario — Toronto — Addresses, essays, lectures. I. Harney, Robert F., 1939-   II. Multicultural History Society of Ontario.

FC3097.9.A1G37 1985   971.3'541004   C85-098155-7
F1059.5.T689A24 1985

Contents

Ethnicity and Neighbourhoods

Robert F. Harney

The sesquicentennial anniversary of Toronto has inspired the publication of a number of books on its history as a city. None, except this volume, deal with what has become the most salient feature of Toronto in its one hundred and fiftieth year, its role as a preferred target of migration for people from every corner of the globe, its polyethnic character and its reputation for tolerance of human variety.

At a time when public relations campaigns make much of the city's ethnic mosaic in order to encourage tourism and investment, and politicians seem almost to credit themselves for the growth of a civic ethos of multiculturalism, it seems useful to learn more about Toronto's ethnic and immigrant past, to examine the city's actual record, in terms of inter-ethnic encounter, tolerance and attitudes toward pluralism. The essays on ethnic enclaves and ethnocultures in the city before World War Two that have been brought together in *Gathering Place* are a first attempt to contribute to that learning.

The current celebratory mood of the city and the remarkable flowering of immigrant cultures here since the Second World War lead to a false retrospect about the history of ethnic groups in the city, one in which the past and the present are conflated into a single oversimplified story. In his superb pseudo-geography, *Invisible Cities*, Italo Calvino writes: "Beware of saying to them that sometimes different cities follow one another on the same site with the same name,

born and dying without knowing one another, without communication among themselves."[1] The lack of comprehension to which
Calvino refers is not just among ethnic groups, but occurs as well
among the various generations or migration cohorts within each
ethnic group. History as slogans and stereotypes flourishes when
serious history has not been attempted, and little or no serious
history of Toronto's different peoples and their lives in the city has
been written until very recently. We have been abandoned to labels
such as "Toronto the Good," which conjure up images of a totally
homogeneous colonial city with all its immigrants from the British
Isles. The inadequacy of that view of the past has spawned a newer
view which sees the city through the eyes of its post-World War Two
polyethnicity and assumes a Toronto past in which great numbers of
non-British immigrants were forced to hide their ethnocultures,
were oppressed or shunted aside or quickly harried into Canadian-
ness. Both views, of course, are rhetoric masquerading as history.

For Toronto, then, the past, in Marc Bloch's words, "is a given
quantity that nothing can change," but "knowledge of the past is a
thing in process." If that process is left to public relations officers
and partisans to impose upon, in an anachronistic way, it becomes
more useful as a text for reading the current struggle between
pluralists and traditionalists in the city than as a picture of the city's
past. One would think that study of the census and city directories
would answer the two basic questions: Was Toronto a mere extension of Great Britain into the mid-section of the American continent,
or had it, like equivalent American cities, received large-scale
foreign immigration? If the latter were so, was it also so that, by
what is now seen as a failure of civic virtue, the Anglo-Celtic host
society and elite chose to suppress all manifestations of other ethnocultures in the city? Behind the last question lurks the assumption
that newcomers generally wished to maintain old-world ways and
ethnic group coherence rather than seek well-being and integration
through rapid acculturation.

Both forms of retrospective falsification confuse an overwhelming statistical predominance of immigrants from the British Isles
with ethnic homogeneity. English, Scots, Irish Catholics, Irish
Protestants and Welsh did display separate ethnic identities in terms
of associational life, sometimes language, religion, culture and settlement patterns. To test the truth of this assertion, ask any Irish
Catholic who tried to break the Orange Lodge monopoly on the better positions in city government or the police, or ask any English artisan who encountered Canadian nativism whether discrimination
affected them in nineteenth century Toronto. Along with the 10 per
cent of the population that did come from "foreign lands," these
ethnic differences among immigrants from Great Britain created

patterns of separateness which foreshadowed the post-First and Second World War ethnocultures and ethnic enclaves in the city.

One can then scan the census figures for the city in the pre-World War Two period either for evidence of the overwhelming British presence, or for a glimpse of the presence of other peoples. If it is valid to ask whether Toronto the Good was a uniquely British city in North America or an incipient polyglot one like New York or Chicago a fitting predecessor to the cosmopolitan giant of today, in absolute numerical terms the answer is unequivocal. Even in 1911, after twenty years of mass migration and countless warnings by social gospellers, nativist union leaders and frightened racists about the impending inundation of the city by foreigners, the figures still show Toronto with 80 per cent of its population of British descent. About 4 per cent of the population was Jewish. Perhaps 2 per cent was of German origin, many of them long in the city and acculturated. Only the 4,000 Italians, the 1,000 Chinese and various Slavic groups — Macedonians, Ukrainians, Poles — and the Finns lived in visible concentrations of population like the Jews.

Even by 1941 the percentage of the city claiming British descent had not declined much. Then in a city of almost 700,000, there was no non-British ethnic group, which made up more than 5 per cent of the population, other than the Jews. Nonetheless, more than 14,000 Italians, 11,000 Poles, 10,000 Ukrainians, several thousand each of Finns, Chinese, Greeks and Macedonians, along with almost 50,000 Jews, did live in Toronto. They were made highly visible by their proximity to city hall and the commercial downtown or their concentration in certain industrial areas. Toronto, before 1945, had ethnic enclaves and was in certain areas a polyglot city, far more cosmopolitan than Wyndham Lewis's "mournful Scottish version of a North American city." On the other hand, it remained overwhelmingly British in terms of the origins of its people, its attitudes and, of course, the place of the English language.

While the census cannot tell us much about the sensibilities, identities and *mentalités* of ethnic groups, or about inter-ethnic encounters, it can do more than simply show us that 10 per cent of the population was non-British. Patterns of settlement record what sociologists call the residential segregation index and enable us to sense the degree of each group's dependence on immigrant ethnoculture, their "clannishness," or their exclusion from the mainstream. For instance, although immigrants from Scotland as well as those who gave German as their ancestry were almost equally distributed throughout the city's four census areas in 1911, Jews, Italians, Chinese, Ukrainians and Macedonians showed no such even dispersal through the city. Rather they were heavily concentrated in those neighbourhoods such as the St. John's Ward, the Kensington Market area, the Toronto Junction and the East End, which form the backdrop of many of the essays in this volume.

William Lyon Mackenzie King, the future prime minister, in a series of *Daily Mail and Empire* articles in 1897, made the first serious attempt to understand and study the ethnic enclaves of Toronto. King wrote:

> The presence of large numbers of foreigners in Toronto makes an inquiry into these conditions a subject as interesting as it is timely. Does their presence here portend an evil for this city such as the above statistics which have just come upon the cities of the United States, or is the class of foreigners in this city here cast in a better mould and are they likely to prove at once good citizens and a strength to the community? These are questions of more than vital moment to the city, and answers can only be found in examination of the present condition of the people, a comparative study of their numbers, occupations and methods of living, their relations to the civic, religious and industrial life, together with a retrospective glance into the past as to the causes which brought them here and a speculative forecast as to the probable increase in their numbers which may be affected in the future.[2]

King went on to write about Germans, French, Jews, Syrians and Italians among others and did so in what was a remarkably informed and fair manner for his time. He did, however, confirm a false dichotomy that remains a problem in migration studies. "The Irish, Scots, English, Americans and Newfoundlanders," he wrote, were "so nearly akin in thought, customs, and manners to the Canadians themselves . . . that in speaking of a foreign population, they have generally been disregarded altogether. For with the exception of maintaining a few national societies, their foreign connection is in no way distinctively marked in civic life."

In the more democratic and pluralistic language of our time, we would be unlikely to frame questions about immigration and ethnicity in the manner King did. Nonetheless, his agenda of study is not that far from the preliminary one necessary for a retrospective ethnography of the city now. Most of those who have followed him in commenting on "foreigners" in Toronto did so in a context in which they clearly took the presence of immigrant neighbourhoods, or "foreign quarters," to be a form of urban blight. *Missionary Outlook* in 1910 observed:

> Every large city on this continent has its fourfold problem of the slum, the saloons, the foreign colonies and the districts of vice. The foreign colony may not be properly called a slum, but it represents a community that is about to become an important

factor in our social life and will become a menace in our civilization unless it learns to assimilate the moral and religious ideals and the standards of citizenship.[3]

Any useful studies of the mores and folkways of immigrants and their children were not likely to prosper within the perimeters of the social gospel camp. From 1897 until the last half dozen years, no one, except a few evangelists and immigration restrictionists who brought a special anxiety to their work, has followed King in the effort to study the ethnic minorities and the ethnic neighbourhoods of the City of Toronto.

James Scobie observes in the introduction to his study of the city of Buenos Aires that reams of research, "on urban services, such as paving, parks, sewage, police, lighting and garbage disposal, on the location, regulation and expanse of industry, on education, public health, morality and amusements,"[4] have been produced on cities, but little is written about the people of a city. Rather than try to understand the non-British of the city, most scholars writing about Toronto have naturally enough concentrated on those whom they see as affecting power relations and the economic development of the city or as significant in the city's mainstream cultural and political life.[5]

In fact, though evangelists, city nurses, police officials, academics and teachers turned attention to the immigrant neighbourhoods of the city between 1900 and 1940, they did so without any clear understanding of what those neighbourhoods were, nor did they ask the relevant questions. Were the immigrant quarters simply stepping-stones towards acculturation, breathing spaces for immigrants and their children until they could become Canadian? Were they working-class neighbourhoods, or were they, as they were believed to be by much of their own ethnic intelligentsia, self-appointed elites and officials from the lands of emigration, stratified sub-societies and colonies within a larger diaspora? Were they new communities created by people in need of creating local ascriptive worlds within the larger, colder space of a Canadian industrial city? Did the European and Asian immigrants who gathered in ethnic enclaves do so willingly in order to preserve their old-world cultural baggage intact, or would they have been willing to embrace Anglo-Canadian ways if made welcome? Were such neighbourhoods fossils of the old world, or places of regeneration where a new ethnicity and new set of emblems, new networks of acquaintanceship and new eclectic North American ideas and values could grow up?

The terms used then and now — immigrant quarters, working-class neighbourhoods, ethnic enclaves, ghettos, Little Italies, Chinatowns, ethnocultural community — create a problem. They do not so much describe the social system and cultural life of particular groups of people in the city as they delineate the categories which such groups are supposed to inhabit. If the validity of these categories is assumed, the observer is relieved from any attempt to learn about and understand these groups. For example, all immigrants in a working-class neighbourhood may not be in the working class, and those who are may not be so in terms of their class of origin, class of destination, or *mentalités*. Moreover, ethnic enclaves are rarely made up uniformly of one ethnic group. Nor does consensus within the group necessarily follow from shared ethnicity. A sense of the variety of individual approaches to acculturation, personal and familial migration projects, senses of sojourning and settling, adjustment to the new world within the ethnic community, the persistence of sub-ethnicities, and so on, is lost when the usual nomenclature is imposed on migration and ethnicity in process.

Study of ethnicity in Canada as a North American process is best understood when integrated into a spatial, in this case an urban, frame. The obverse would seem to have equal merit. No great North American city can be understood without being studied as a city of immigrants, of newcomers and their children, as a destination of myriad group and individual migration projects. Describing city government or municipal politics, the building of an urban economy and the evolution of the city as polity obviously has value. To do so without understanding ethnicity in the city seems a bit like analysing the captain and crew of an ocean liner but not noticing the passengers, what they expect of the vessel and why they are travelling. Without knowing the networks, folkways and values of the city's immigrants, whether from the United Kingdom or not, studying the encounter between city officials and the people of the city is at best one-sided, at worst vacuous.

Since the possibility for a more deeply textured history of the city and its people exists, we must pursue it beyond the limited historiographical inheritance we have been given for the study of Toronto. The absence of traditional urban studies has spared Toronto some of the misdirection which came from the behaviouralists' emphasis on using the census, on rates of economic, social and geographical mobility as codes to measure acculturation and integration, a methodological tide which first buoyed and then set adrift urban studies in the United States.[6] Toronto's ethnic and social historians, by their late start, know that such an approach based on the host society's sources is particularly unfit as full explanation of immigrant and ethnic communities. For the most part, they would agree with Mr. Dooley, Finley Peter Dunne's fictitious Irish American bartender, who remarked on academic history in his time to a friend: ''I know history isn't true Hinnissy cause it ain't like what I see ivry day in Halsted Street. If anyone comes along with a histhry iv Greece and Rome that will show me the people fightin', gettin' dhrunk, makin' love, gettin' married, owin' the grocery man, and bein' without hard coal, I'll believe there was a Greece and Rome, but not before.''[7]

Mr. Dooley had it right. If we fail to plumb the depths of attitudes toward Canada, toward the old country, to understand ethnic identity and ethnocultures, to understand the immigrant's reactions to rebuffs or his attitudes towards his culture and those he identified as his fellows, then immigrants to Toronto — once dismissed as migrant navvies, ''sheenies,'' ''bohunks,'' ''wops,'' or just unskilled workers — will again be dismissed, this time by a generation of social, labour and urban historians who reduce them to statistics. The broad categories of social history, like the broad categories of prejudice, are conveniences for those too lazy to comprehend the complicated nature of man in the city and of individual migration projects or separate ethnocultures.

To call for an interior history of immigrant and ethnic communities in Toronto before the Second World War is not to suggest some autonomous substructure, which allows us to ignore the reality of the circumambient city. Quite the reverse; it requires that we find ways to understand all the actors in the city's history, to understand the trauma of encounter at the boundaries of identity in the classroom, the corner restaurant, the factory or at leisure on street corners.

Migration routes, projects and destinations are always in flux. The immigrant adjusts to new situations in new places, changing or resisting. With our current state of scholarship we can only wonder now why old-world styles and ideas were discarded or defiantly maintained after some calculation of the cost, or after repeated approval or disapproval by the Canadian host society. Obviously we have to know the significance of those ways and ideas for the immigrant before we can understand, not just the immigrant group itself, but the processes of acculturation and the nature of daily life in the city. If we remember that the immigrants were conscious participants in all intercultural encounters, then the study of ethnic boundaries can begin to yield up answers about identity and *mentalités* themselves — what Fredrik Barth dismissively calls ''the stuff'' inside the ethnic boundary.[8] For ethnic boundaries turn out to be penumbras of opinion, choice and situation, not just hard-edged perimeters between the immigrants and the old stock.

When, under the influence of the Irish national revival, W.B. Yeats set out to discover the common people of Ireland, he was startled to realize that their history was virtually unknown. ''Ancient map makers wrote across unexplored regions: here are lions, across the villages of fishermen and turners of the earth. So different are these from us we can but write one line that is certain: here are ghosts.''[9] Anyone who sets out in the 1980s to understand the ethnic neighbourhoods of Toronto before the Second World War may well believe, like Yeats, that Toronto's ethnic enclaves are uncharted, unexplored and little comprehended empty spaces on the map.

Separate settlement in this city, the creation of urban spaces that were somehow different from the Toronto mainstream and yet produced an ambience different from that of the country of origin, happened for a number of reasons. The sense of fellow-feeling, the in-gathering for reasons of language, both out of pride of language and out of pain produced by *diglossia,* * the need to maintain folkways and mores, the location of work, the price of housing and transportation, the need for coherence in the face of outside hostility — all these contributed to neighbourhood creation. In Toronto, the city that developed after the pioneer period increasingly took the form of a grid. Such a regular plan lent itself only grudgingly to the creation of ethnic nooks and crannies. For example, the history of the St. John's Ward, in the heart of the city, as an underdeveloped area and immigrant quarter to the west of Yonge Street and behind the city hall, was in fact very short lived. The completion of the grid with Bay Street and Dundas Street in the early twentieth century, along with the introduction of sewers, ended what had been essentially an encapsulated immigrant world. The development of commercial and public institutions followed and drove immigrants farther west into the back alleys that later produced Kensington Market and farther yet, in the case of the Italians, to the short, non-gridded streets around St. Agnes Church. At the same time, Poles, Macedonians, Finns and others settled in the small cross streets of the industrial sectors of the East End, the Niagara region, and later the Junction in the West End.

One remarkable feature of all of these neighbourhoods for the city explorer or urban archaeologist is the degree to which the sites do not now correspond to the general grid layout of the city but, if not extirpated by freeways or housing projects, have still the quality of an enclosed space conducive to close and familiar street life. Whether in Kensington Place, near Little Trinity Church in the East End, or around the Clinton Street area of the second Little Italy, there still clings a feeling that these were neighbourhoods in a very immediate and face-to-face sense.

Historical sources on immigrants in Toronto can be divided into three groups. First there are municipal records, statistical and cir-

---

* *Diglossia* is bilingualism in two languages of uneven status in society. Typically the family language, or immigrant language, is the more comfortable medium but the one valued less in the city. For immigrants from rural backgrounds, *triglossia* existed. Dialect, ethnic language and English were viewed in ascending order of value in terms of the host society, but descending order of affection by the immigrant.

cumstantial, ranging from assessment roles and city directories to pedlars' licence lists, arrest logs, police books and student cards in the various inner-city grammar schools. Such materials can be used to recreate the setting of encounter and much of the factual surroundings of immigrant life. Then there is the literature of the urban actors themselves. On the one side is the writing of those already in the land, ranging from evangelical pamphlets of the social gospel missions, reports of settlement houses, royal commissions, medical officers' reports, boards of education papers and the English-speaking press. Such sources obviously can provide a valuable picture of the interplay between perception and reality in urban history. However, to pass through ethnic boundaries to ethnic identities, the immigrant's own account of his urban experience is also necessary. For that there is oral testimony, the fragile memory of the immigrants themselves, to be used with the same caution one would apply to any kind of subjective written biography, reminiscence or memoir. There are church almanacs, jubilee volumes, the minutes of fraternal and mutual aid organizations, letters and guides to letter writing in English and in the old-country language. There are also the reports of officials, foreign consuls and intellectuals travelling from the countries of origin passing through Toronto.

The numbers of those immigrants who came to Canada before World War Two are thinning dangerously. The city's history will pay dearly if we neglect the systematic gathering of oral testimony and other ethnocultural materials which could enrich our knowledge of people in the city. As it was for Yeats, so for us the most important source of information will be the people who, as immigrants and the children of immigrants, lived in ethnic neighbourhoods and who possess in their collective memory, personal papers, or as guardians of the records of now defunct ethnic associations, the history of those places.

Immigrants need no longer be depicted either as proto-Torontonians or proto-Canadians, as people on the threshold of acculturation, or as potential fossils, living in colonies of an old country, maintaining cultural baggage which changed little until it fell away like scales from the eyes in a healing Canadian environment. Instead scholars may begin to see the immigrant colony itself as having a history, a process of development. Improved ways of observing group ethnicity may lead to more comprehension of the nature of personal ethnicity so that immigrants may come to be seen neither as simply the pre-articulate masses of Toronto, nor as Italians, Finns, Poles, etc., but as specific kinds of Torontonians — Italian, Finnish, Polish Torontonians — who underwent individually and as groups a variety of urban experiences, met a variety of receptions which affected their strategies for living here and contributed in a variety of ways to the city's growth.

The new emphasis on history from the "bottom up,"[10] along with ethnohistory's interest in analysis of culture and society, invites us to move beyond the study of the external and quantifiable to the more deeply textured and nuanced study of *mentalités*, perceptions in encounter and conflict, strategies for adjustment or persistence in relation to the changing real condition of being immigrant and for coping with a changing personal or group sense of ethnos. The task of ethnohistory should be the difficult one suggested in the phrase of Jacobo Timmerman, "to penetrate the affective world of the other." To do that, we need to look at the immigrant and ethnic neighbourhoods of the city without assuming we comprehend the intent of each person's migration project, the intensity of their ethnic networks or of their loyalties to ethnoculture.

To understand the linkage among identity, cognitive maps, psychic worlds,[11] commitment to family and friends, and then to understand how these individual commitments paralleled a continuum of place, family, work site, church, association, street-corner life, we need also to comprehend the immigrants' sense of space. We can do this by simply changing our frame of reference. The great anthropologist Oscar Lewis once lamented that anthropologists who became ethnohistorians spent most of their time talking to old Amerindians and practising a methodology they called participant observation, but rarely bothered to look at the sources of the United States Bureau of Indian Affairs or the Canadian government, since they believed that the written word represented only the view of an arrogant and ignorant conqueror of the indigenous people.[12] Historians of the city have tended to the opposite sin by thinking that they can reconstruct the reality of urban immigrant life from the writings and documents of the caretakers of the host society. Such sources leave the historian on the edge of the city's ethnocultural reality. Recreating the past from them is a bit like writing the history of British Africa or of French Indo-China from the memoirs of soldiers and missionaries alone.

Few of Toronto's ethnic neighbourhoods could qualify in the Marxist sense as "internal colonies," societies "within a society based on racial, linguistic and marked cultural differences of social class," and subject to control by "the dominant classes and institutions of the metropolis."[13] Yet the concept of internal colonies is at least as useful a model for prewar Toronto as images of homogeneity or rapid assimilation. It reminds us to look at the ethnic community as a separate place, to think of its interior life and not just its boundaries. It reminds us of what Walter Firey observed studying Boston's neighbourhoods many years ago: a neighbourhood is at one and the same time part of the city hierarchy and system and a "little homeland," a spatial corollary to a set of values, of networks, of ways of thinking and being, of ethos.[14] In Toronto some groups obviously required a "little homeland" more than others, and the result was immigrant neighbourhoods. English, Scots and Irish, except for concentrations in Cabbagetown, were not confined in enclaves. Despite tell-tale accents, they did not encounter systematic discrimination. They did, as Mackenzie King noted, form associations, from the St. George Society to the Dewi Sant and the Orange Lodge, and they did encounter enough hostility that some concepts of ethnic neighbourhood or enclave apply to them as well. Peoples' ways were shaped by living in neighbourhoods, around them, among a majority group, or indeed even by escaping from them and practising that most common third- or fourth-generation phenomenon, "weekend ethnicity": returning to the immigrant areas for religious services, food supply, haircut, or family visits only on the weekend.

Ethnic neighbourhoods can be studied as concentrated universes in two quite different ways. One is accessible to plotting by analysing factual sources, especially written city records, and by forms of social scientific measurement. Another is more notional. It is about the *mentalités* of immigrants and about the psychic worlds they inhabit.

This more complex and notional sense of the neighbourhood then as an ambience, a psychic world for the immigrants and their children and perhaps their children's children, with its moving mix of ethnocultures, part-cultures and pressures to change the mores and folkways, produced by encounter with the North American situation, is a world we must come to know. If we allow ourselves just for a moment "to surrender," in Vladimir Nabokov's words, "to a sort of retrospective imagination which feeds analytical faculty with boundless alternatives," every usage and event in the enclave becomes an intricate key for studying attitudes and identities.

Borrowing from social anthropology, we can begin to understand the value of extending and deepening our moment of observation of the immigrants and their children in their neighbourhoods.[15] Freed of the retrospective falsification that comes from fervent but anachronistic multiculturalism, and equally free from an historicism that sees all immigrants pausing only momentarily on the threshold to the house of Canadian ways, we have an opportunity to fill in the blank spots on our map of the city. We can find ways to comprehend the group's sense of group, not just the intensity and frequency of the use of neighbourhood or ethnic networks, but the changing significance, for the immigrant and each succeeding generation, of various community institutions, such as a home town club, a nationalist association, or a parish.

By learning more about the role of mutual aid societies, the ethnic press, church, drama and leisure clubs, the importance of islands of acquaintanceship within the community and the ethnolinguistic psychology which made people choose one language over another, as well as about changing symbols and emblematics of the group, we may arrive at a demotic intellectual history, a history of how the people think. If we can begin to know their attitudes about settling, or merely sojourning, about upward mobility, about social class, about other ethnic groups in Toronto, if we can learn more of the dreams they held for their children, the strategies they chose either to persist in their own culture or acculturate in Canada, we will be on the verge of being able to write a whole social and cultural history of the city.

Information and insight into all these ideas are accessible to us if we combine the little used sources generated from inside the community, such as club and church records and ethnic newspapers and print ephemera, with a more extensive and systematic use of oral testimony. The city might then have the sort of history Lawrence Levine describes as "the attempt to present and understand the thought of people who though quite articulate in their own lifetimes have been rendered inarticulate by scholars who devoted too much of their attention to less recalcitrant subjects."[16] Levine's thought parallels almost exactly that of the social anthropologist Clifford Geertz who writes, "at base, thinking is a public activity. Its natural habitat is the house yard, the market place and the town square."[17]

The convergence of the two disciplines holds special possibilities for urban and immigrant studies. Although declining and increasingly fragile, the necessary sources for the study of Italians, Jews, Chinese, Greeks, Macedonians and the many peoples and neighbourhoods of Toronto in the late nineteenth and twentieth century are still available. The equivalent of Geertz's house yard, marketplace and town square existed in each one of Toronto's ethnic neighbourhoods. Throughout Toronto there were such house yards, behind boardinghouses or rough-caste cottages in the alleys of the Ward, Kensington or the East End. They were places where kin, friends from home towns in the old country and neighbours gathered. They were also places where small-scale agriculture, commerce, industry and a bit of animal husbandry went on. There people foregathered for seasonal food processing — pickling, butchering, sausage-making and wine-making — for impromptu picnics and communal meals. They gathered to exchange collective wisdom about important decisions — sending for relatives from the old country, following work opportunities out of the city, moving out of the neighbourhood, improving a house or selling it, allowing a child to continue his or her education. The house yard was a place where hundreds of the small human decisions, which affected the city's economy, appearance and culture, were made.

The equivalent of the marketplace in Geertz's analysis were the corner stores, the factories and life on the work gangs. For the children, it was the schoolyards, playgrounds and settlement houses. Each was in a different spatial and psychic relationship to the "little homeland," the ethnic neighbourhood and the ethnic group. They were places where men and women had to negotiate their ethnicity, make those constant adjustments of style and thinking which were the milestones in the process of learning to live within the larger North American urban setting. They learned when one could trust someone from outside the ethnic group. They learned the more difficult lesson of not trusting some even within their own regional group. They had opportunity to study what was threatening and what was useful about municipal politics and city government. In this way, Toronto's ethnic groups thought, reacted and became actors in the city's history.

In the little corner stores, cafés and social clubs, animated and informed debate took place on the politics of the old country and the problems of the new. A participant observer might have seen something of ethnicity as process if he could have recorded the changing ratio of old-world talk to Toronto talk, as well as the levels of intensity accompanying each subject. Surrogate for that field work which was not done is the local ethnic press. Concordances on topics covered and on their placement in the paper give some sense of the changing concerns of the ethnic communities. In the work gangs and factories immigrants had opportunities to understand the advantages and disadvantages of ethnic cohesion in the face of an exploitive capitalist system or other ethnic groups. Encountering workers of other ethnic origins in the factories, they discovered their commonalities and differences. All of these "marketplaces" were the scenes of public discourse and decision-making which affected the city itself.

Finally and central to the neighbourhood was what Geertz refers to as the "town square." In many of the city's ethnic neighbourhoods one could reconstruct the neighbourhood outward from the church or *shul*. For usually a religious building, occasionally a secular hall, just as in the villages of origin, defined the geographic and psychic core of the immigrant neighbourhoods. That core affected even those within the ethnic group who chose to go their own way towards secularism, or who joined one of the North American evangelical faiths beckoning them toward rapid acculturation. Whether seen as friend or enemy, the church or the local hall was a part of an immigrant's map and a gathering place. It was in front of the church on Sundays, in the associational halls or home town clubs, or waiting for an ethnic newspaper to appear on a corner stand, in the streets watching children play, or shopping that the ethnic nodal point — no matter what its spatial contours — took on the context of a "town square." Corners in the Ward, in the Italian neighbourhoods to the west, in front of *shuls* or Orthodox churches, on Maria Street in the Junction, served as forums for the evolution of ethnic group thought. It was there that the reinforcing sense of the neighbourhood as ethnic enclave, as well as a sometimes irritating sense of its role as a *villagio pettegolo*, a gossipy village, emerged. Since most such neighbourhoods served as base camp for those of the immigrant groups who dared to go outside to work in the Ontario north on construction sites, to peddle, or to run fruit stores, confectioneries, dry good shops and restaurants, the "town square," especially on the weekend, had a special role in both spreading news and reaffirming the coherence of the ethnic group.

We can come much closer to understanding how currents of thought within the ethnic group affected the enclave, its culture and identity. Not understanding these things, it seems unlikely that an urban historian can paint a fair or accurate picture of the immigrant as participant in the larger city. For if we do not know, for example, whether a Catholic priest in a certain parish supported a strike action in a nearby factory, or whether immigrants from a small Balkan country were more preoccupied with the nationalist struggle at home than with their social struggle on a work site, while other immigrants from eastern Europe wrote and performed plays with titles like *Unemployed on Spadina* in order to denounce the Canadian system, we can hardly measure the impact of immigrants on the city's workforce, life and politics, or the impact of the city upon them.

Being part of an immigrant group and living in an ethnic enclave meant hearing and reading both more and less information on various subjects than those in the larger host society did. It meant receiving news with a different emphasis on almost every matter of politics and culture. What was transmitted once in the "town square" and through the ethnic press now reaches people via cable television. Toronto is a city whose populace has always been fractured, in its receipt of information, into ethnocultural groups. To take an example from outside our period, the front page of a Hungarian Marxist newspaper printed in the city in 1950 contained a picture of Ho Chi Minh and a discussion of the Vietnamese problem at a time when Ho Chi Minh was largely unknown to English-speaking Toronto and the tragedy of Indochina remote. It is remarkable that no historian of the city has studied how this multiplicity of overlapping "communication systems" in Toronto affects our political life and intergroup understanding.

In the same way that the fracturing of information is a consequence of being a polyethnic city, so too each ethnic group or immigrant cohort had a different spatial definition of the city itself. Both in the geographical sense of an enclave and in the more notional sense of ambience, the neighbourhood as a combination of individual cognitive maps and psychic worlds for immigrants and their children provided their focus and anchor in the city.

Each sojourner or settler possessed, as well as a detailed cognitive map of his world, a sense of where his fellows were in Toronto and of what parts of the city mattered to him. The immigrant's alternative atlas, of course, could not be confined to Toronto. It included key points such as his town of origin, the routes and stops on his crossing, as well as locations where his extended kin were throughout the world. The historian who tries to fit the ethnic group too neatly, geographically and psychically, into the city does damage both to urban history and to the study of migration and ethnicity itself. For example, Toronto's Ward in the 1900s served both Italians and Jews throughout the province. From it men who went to work seasonally on the labour intensive northern frontiers of Ontario, or peddled through the lonely countryside, drew supplies and cultural sustenance. Through the neighbourhood they kept in touch with other colonies of their own kind, their home town and fellow-townsmen throughout the diaspora. Through the neighbourhood passed cash remittances, ethnic goods — from tomato paste to talissim — brides, returnees and intelligence reports about travel routes, work, housing and the reception newcomers could expect in other parts of the country. In this manner the neighbourhood as an ambience was always larger than the actual enclave. On the other hand, many of the immigrants who settled or sojourned in the Ward had very little knowledge or contact with other nearby Toronto neighbourhoods. Toronto was then an urban space which, in semiotic terms, spoke to each immigrant group differently and spoke to all of them. Since their settled British and acculturated neighbours saw the city differently, they misunderstood the newcomers' behaviour.

Foreign immigrants and their children rarely developed a balanced map of the whole city. An understanding of its other people, of the use of its other spaces, or its history developed slowly. The first *Bulgaro-English Dictionary* included phrases on how to take the streetcar to King Street East "where the Macedonians live," side by side with how to find the Wabash ticket agent for trains to other Macedonian settlements near Chicago or St. Louis. It had no phrases about the Ward or Rosedale.[18] A place of work, or housing, or leisure for one group was a place seen as an unfriendly environment or simply unknown to another group. Thus Macedonians knew there was no work for them at Gooderham's even though that distillery was in the middle of their settlement. Italians knew that one needed to change one's name and hide one's origin to clerk in the big department stores, and all foreigners knew that the Hydro Commission hired only workers of British descent under the pretext, or on the grounds, that communication in English was necessary. Lithuanian men on their way from boardinghouses on Queen Street West to factories in the East End picked up box lunches paid for on a weekly basis from Chinese lunch grills near their boardinghouses. Yet they never ventured into Chinatown for a Chinese meal even though that neighbourhood lay between them and work.

For most groups, picnics and outings, even a visit to the graves of loved ones in Mount Hope Cemetery, required a trek across unfamiliar and threatening space. Leisure itself was a segregated activity for the immigrant generation, and the pattern followed them out of the city. Property owned by members of the ethnic group, by benevolent associations or parishes, usually on the outskirts of Toronto, were safe sites for planned leisure, picnics, or ethnic outings. Pontypool, east of the city, and Belle Ewart, near Lake Simcoe, were such locations for the Jews. Nearby farms served Italians, Macedonians, Chinese and Poles in the same way. In the neighbourhood, men and women built systems and networks that enabled them to survive as Torontonians and, in most instances, made it possible for their children to sally forth into the larger city to work, and to share public leisure places such as the CNE and Sunnyside. Many of the immigrants probably understood their neighbourhood and the city much in the way that Italo Calvino suggests in *Invisible Cities*. There he describes the mythical city of Vasilia — Toronto's real Junction, Cabbagetown, Ward, or Kensington Market would do just as well:

> In a city, to establish the relations to sustain the city's life, the inhabitants stretched strings from the corners of the houses, white or black or grey, or black and white, according to whether they mark a relationship of blood or trade, authority, agency. When the strings become so numerous that you can no longer pass among them, the inhabitants leave, the houses are dismantled. Only their strings and their supports remain.[19]

Good urban historians will learn how to read a narrative in those strings and their supports. It will not be easy, for few locations in the city were the exclusive neighbourhood of a single ethnic group. Kensington Market, once called the *mercato giudeo* by Italian immigrants, had by the twenties and thirties lost its exclusively Jewish character and become polyethnic. The Junction, the city's premier candidate as an ethnic industrial working-class neighbourhood, now boasts a Polish hall, an Albanian hall, a Maltese parish, a little synagogue on Maria Street, a Croatian club, an Irish club and had at one time an Italian pasta factory. The neighbourhood seems always to have been truly polyethnic.

Stores in the Junction that served Canadian Pacific Railway workers in the daytime became Macedonian hangouts at night. Separate and public schools brought children of many backgrounds together. In the battle for control of the young, it was in the playgrounds and schoolyards throughout the city where the guardians of the host society effectively took children away from the streets and from their parents' culture. In fact, if studied closely enough, the surface of neighbourhoods like the Junction give way to deeper patterns of sub-neighbourhoods. In the Junction, some streets served the workers in the stockyards, mainly Macedonians, while nearby streets housed artisans, mainly German and Jewish, from the Heinzmann piano factory, once the largest employer in the neighbourhood. Yet other streets housed mostly families which worked for the CPR, mainly Anglo-Celtic. So the ethno-histories of Maria, Mulock and Glendenan streets in the Junction diverge over time almost as much as the histories of the Junction and Kensington Market. In the East End, Cabbagetown, Corktown and the Macedonian's cognitive map of their East-End neighbourhood blurred and shared much the same space. In the same manner the Ward itself, the city's chief Jewish ghetto at the turn of the century, was also the city's Chinatown and its chief Little Italy.

If nothing else, this intimate sharing of areas by immigrant groups suggests that the usual frame of study — immigrants *vis-à-vis* a WASP or Anglo-Celtic dominant society — misses the real dynamic of encounter, exchange and competition among newcomers from many lands. The polyethnic reality reconfirms the view that the history of a great North American city can rarely be properly written unless it is also ethnic and immigration history. Unfortunately for Toronto, the history of the Junction area, the history of the Ward and the history of Kensington Market, just as the history of several ethnic groups not dealt with in this volume, who lived with high levels of residential segregation in the city before the Second World War — Lithuanians, Maltese and Hungarians, for example — have yet to be done.

Many of Toronto's newcomers had been cultural or religious minorities in their land of origin. Jews, Macedonians, Galicians, even the Catholic Irish and south Italians had had some experience in having to create and sustain their own ethnocultural institutions against regimes that were hostile or remote. Few, however, had experienced the uprooting or, conversely, the freedom to speculate about and alter identity. Although concern about a homeland or about the diaspora of one's people throughout the world persisted, such concerns themselves became elements in the forging of a new sense of group for which the neighbourhood was the territorial base. Karl Deutsch has observed that, ''an isolated minority in a strange new country might increase its efforts to recall its past and to standardize its behaviour so as to erase again and again the eroding effects of the new environment on its traditional culture.''[20] In such circumstances, the role of leaders and the nature of their status and appeal obviously calls for analysis. Reflective and ideological efforts at maintaining folkways, values and language, although themselves a long step away from primordial ethnicity, especially for those groups from the tsarist borderlands, came in logical sequence for the immigrant in North America. Each ethnoculture seemed to hold differing attitudes on the importance of group coherence. Ethnic leaders and intelligentsia encouraged different strategies for group survival, which posited roles for church, language and nationalist political party in group life.

Some of the political left in each group looked beyond ethnic persistence to a world of contact with the working class of other ethnic groups. As with those who joined North American evangelical churches, the rates of acculturation of those on the left were often more rapid, either because they came to know the larger city more quickly or found the ethnic enclave less nurturing and its leaders — priests, businessmen, foreign consuls — less acceptable. Historians have not reconstructed the degree to which, over two or three generations, ethnicity was the continuing organizer of existence in the city for many people. Some immigrants may have seen their ethnicity as simply an epiphenomenon of immigration — something of value for themselves but not their children or their children's children. Some tried to keep their ethnoculture in the form in which they brought it from the old country; others negotiated their ethnicity, altering its content or displaying ethnocultural ways selectively where they were acceptable to the host society, or when they brought them comfort or seemed right. Ethnic identity, even national feeling for the homeland, remained for most of the first two Canadian generations of any immigrant group a latent value which arose in times of crisis — such as an earthquake in the old country, an encounter with prejudice in the new, a measurement for choosing a certain politician in the city for whom to vote.

Whether experience with maintaining minority institutions in a hostile environment was long and deep, as with the Jews, or a relatively new phenomenon of national revival, as with the Galicians and Macedonians, none of the immigrant groups had faced the need to create entirely new institutions. The need to do so, in fact, was a central aspect of ethnicity as North American process. For example, when the Macedonians in Toronto decided to organize their own church in 1911, it lead them into what most Torontonians saw as visibly Macedonian national politics. On the other hand, what they did was almost entirely neoteric for them as Macedonians. People, accustomed to a village church, used to a community of elders who were just that, older and wiser, used to a priest leading them, found themselves gathering in private homes in Macedonian neighbourhoods of the city. They created a slate of immigrant delegates from thirty-one different villages of origin for the purpose of tithing one another to build a single church, not a number of village churches.

Reflecting the youth of the immigrant population, only four out of the twenty elected as village elders in Toronto were over thirty years old.[21] The condition of being Macedonian in Toronto, of being ethnic in a Canadian city, did not then replicate the old country any more than it was simply a stage towards acculturation and an Anglo-Canadian lifestyle.

This same irony existed in the creation of an Italian parish or a Polish parish. Although such parishes might appear ethnic to the larger Toronto society, or to the Irish Catholic hierarchy, they were not the "old-world transplanted." At Our Lady of Mt. Carmel, Barese, Sicilian and Venetian patron saints rubbed shoulders in a way that they would not have done in Italy. The "very Italian" feast of San Rocco seemed a melange of Canadianisms to the immigrants. The mass had an Irish celebrant, a Jewish boy from the Ward was the solo instrumentalist and "God Save the King" was played.[22] In fact, such churches were a totally new phenomenon for the people in the parish on several levels. Worshipping with co-nationals not from their home town, they encountered identities, accents and folkways they did not know. Often they developed Polish or Italian national identity together in the new world almost coincident with becoming Polish or Italian Torontonians. Moreover, Roman Catholic immigrants had to question, often for the first time, the authority and power of the church in order to gain their separate parish. Though usually viewed by the host society as an import from the old country, the national clubs, parishes and benevolent associations, which transcended home town and *landsleit* loyalties, were essentially a Toronto phenomenon and seen as such by the immigrants.

Ethnoculture is not a thing apart, merely something to which "social events, behaviour, institutions, or processes can be constantly attributed," but is rather a context within which such things can be intelligibly described. Once we see the immigrants as serious actors in the city's history, then the need to know more about their associational life, the intensity and variety of networks of acquaintanceship, the sub-economies which they created in various neighbourhoods and throughout the city, their emblems, folkways and ethnicism (ethnonationalism) becomes obvious. One of the best ways to do this is to learn how to apply the ethnographer's technique of reading "a narrative into cultural artifacts." The goal is not the rediscovery of Toronto's ethnic past, but the discovery of ways to read the significance of ethnicity in the lives of individuals, ethnic groups and the city itself.

To practise such retrospective ethnography on immigrant groups in Toronto before 1940, we need to find those "artifacts" such as cultural events through which we can read such a narrative. In special issues of *Polyphony* on the study of the immigrant press, ethnocultural theatre and religious institutions, I have suggested some ways in which sources, related to those institutions interior to the ethnocommunities, could be used to develop a more richly textured history of groups in the city.[23] Oral testimony, used more systematically, could help make the authentic voice of the immigrant in the city heard. If certain sub-groups or generational cohorts were interviewed in conjunction with a larger effort to use the census, city directories or church and school records to build a prosopographic base, then oral history would take on new value and reliability as a source. For example, one could attempt to interview and follow the lives of a single prewar class from St. Agnes school in the heart of Little Italy, or trace the careers and networks of sets of godparents from one year in the church records, or trustees from an orthodox church, or the executive from an ethnocultural association. Done well, such studies would move beyond impression and biography to become the basis of a social history, more intricate and truer than that based on quantifying gross numerical patterns in the census.

Picnics, dances, strikes, sermons, events in an association or benevolent hall, church organizations and enterprises, evenings in a café, saloon or political club are settings which provide a chance to move away from the "thin description" of mobility studies toward the "thick description" possible about the changing mores, emblems and folkways and the constant decision-making which is the process of ethnicity in a North American city and the route to understanding the many paths to being a Torontonian. A picnic organized by a *paese* club from Italy or a Macedonian village association, a dance sponsored by a socialist club among Finns or Lithuanians in the city was surrounded by emblems, organizations and sub-events susceptible to analysis. Moreover, such events had different symbolic meaning for different participants. For the immigrant generation such affairs, with their intensity of fellow-feeling, often took priority over all other social activities in their lives. For their children and perhaps even for the immigrants as they grew longer in the land, the annual associational dance or picnic had to compete with a minor league baseball game at Stanley Park or a hockey match at Maple Leaf Gardens. Analysis of the celebration of a saint's feast day, a Ward political outing, or an ethnic pamphlet brings us closer to the real sentiments and real networks of each group in the city at any given time.

For example, the organizing of an annual picnic, beyond being simply a festive event, provided a ceremonial occasion for the playing out and affirming of various obligations, networks and commitments. It was a chance to affirm membership in the ethnoculture and loyalty to group language, traditions, or liturgy. It was the occasion for the healing or confirmation of political or parochial schisms within an ethnic community. It provides us, through its changing emblems, with data which can be finely calibrated for observing ethnoculture as process. In the decision about whether the main motifs of a spring pageant will be drawn from old-country sources or highlight the new Canadian tradition of a group, of how themes of homeland and of new country are mixed, can be read the history of identity. Through such descriptions we might discover real rather than stereotyped differences in predisposition among groups. For example, one benevolent society might respond to labour problems by raising money for strike funds, another might censor members for speaking back to a foreman in a factory and thus threatening the reputation and well-being of the whole ethnic group.

Materials as apparently neutral as those about the running of a credit union can be used to reconstruct the associative, coercive and moral commitments which held an ethnic group together. For example, by studying patterns of those granted loans in a Slavic credit union, dominated by a clergyman, we might discover subtle efforts to impose endogamy on the group by denying loans to those who marry out. Such credit unions could use the need to enforce political orthodoxy, denying, as they did in some instances, credit to those who did not either pay lip service to ethnic associations or practise the predominant religion of the ethnic group; or denying it to those who were too far to the political left in the eyes of the mainstream ethnic leadership. Institutions continually redefined the boundaries and values of the group, yet they have not been the subject of serious socioeconomic or political analysis.

Recently the good urban historian's task has been likened to that of a traffic cop standing at a busy intersection where two main avenues, one the history of the nation and the other the history of migration processes and of the various groups entering the city, meet.[24] There are also side streets into the intersection which carry the traffic of labour history, women's history, ecclesiastical history. In Toronto not just the streets of the grid, but even more the sidewalks, the blind alleys and the side streets were crowded, before World War Two, with people of many backgrounds about to become actors, or launch their children as actors, in the drama of the city.

Each of the eleven studies of ethnic groups in this volume shows a sense of urban space, understands that there was an intricate relationship between the reasons why people migrated to Toronto, where and how they settled in the city and how they were received. In turn, some of the studies show that the patterns of ethnic settlement reflect not just ethnicity but also the reality of the ethnic neighbourhoods as "little homelands," ambiences which were neither simply fossils of the old country nor fully of the new. Such little homelands were the settings for evolving identities, for sub-economies and ethnocultures constantly in process. No one who reads the pages which follow should ever again be content with monochromatic histories of city politics and politicians or class analyses of our urban past that lack comprehension of the city's ethnocultural variety.

Notes

1. Italo Calvino, *Invisible Cities* (New York, 1972), p. 30.

2. W.L. Mackenzie King, "Foreigners Who Live in Toronto," in *The Daily Mail and Empire*, 25 September 1897.

3. *Missionary Outlook* (Toronto), XXX, no. 12 (December 1910), p. 267, a special issue on the Fred Victor and other city missions. For secular views of the immigrant quarter as an urban pathology, see *What Is the 'Ward' Going to Do with Toronto* (Toronto: Bureau of Municipal Research, 1918) and Margaret Bell, "Toronto's Melting Pot," *Canadian Magazine* XXXVII, no. 8 (July 1913), pp. 234-42.

4. James Scobie, *Buenos Aires. Plaza to Suburb, 1870-1910* (New York, 1974), p. viii.

5. J.M.S. Careless, *Toronto to 1918. An Illustrated History* (Toronto, 1984), effectively incorporates the lives of the Anglo-Celtic common people in his history of the city. On the non-British, see R.F. Harney and H. Troper, *Immigrants: A Portrait of the Urban Experience 1890-1930* (Toronto, 1976) and S. Speisman, *The Jews of Toronto. A History until 1937* (Toronto, 1979).

6. An attempt to apply behaviouralist and mobility measurements to a Canadian city is M. Katz, *The People of Hamilton, Canada West. Family and Class in a Mid-Nineteenth Century City* (Cambridge, Mass., 1975). Studies which use mobility rates analysis specifically to understand ethnic differences are Stephan Thernstrom, "Immigrants and Wasps: Ethnic Differences in Occupational Mobility in Boston, 1880-1940," in S. Thernstrom and R. Sennett, eds., *Nineteenth Century Cities: Essays in the New Urban History* (New Haven, 1969) and T. Kessner, *The Golden Door. Italian and Jewish Immigrant Mobility in New York City, 1880-1915* (New York, 1977). A good critique of the methodology is James Henretta, "Study of Social Mobility — Ideological Assumptions and Conceptual Bias," in *Labor History* 18, no. 2 (1977), pp. 165-78.

7. Finley Peter Dunne, *Mr. Dooley on Ivrything and Ivrybody* (New York, 1963), p. 207.

8. See Fredrik Barth, *Ethnic Groups and Boundaries* (Boston, 1969).

9. William Butler Yeats, "Village Ghosts," in *Mythologies* (New York, 1978), p. 15.

10. The first historian to develop the idea of "history from the bottom up" is Jesse Lemisch. See his "The American Revolution Seen from the Bottom Up," in B.J. Bernstein, ed., *Towards A New Past: Dissenting Essays in American History*

(New York, 1968), pp. 3-45. The idea is attributed to B.A. Botkin's *Lay My Burden Down. A Folk History of Slavery* (Chicago, 1945), C. Joyner, "Oral History as Communicative Event: A Folkloristic Perspective," *The Oral History Review* (1979), pp. 47-52.

11. For the concept of cognitive maps, see Kevin Lynch, *The Image of the City* (Cambridge, Mass., 1960).

12. Oscar Lewis, "The Effects of White Contact on Blackfoot Culture," in *Anthropological Essays* (New York, 1970), pp. 138-39.

13. M. LaGuerre, "Internal Dependency: The Structural Position of the Black Ghetto in American Society," *Journal of Ethnic Studies* 6, no. 4, pp. 29-44.

14. Walter Firey, "Sentiment and Symbolism as Ecological Variable," *American Sociological Review* 10 (1945), reprinted in Scott and Ann Greer, eds., *Neighbourhood and Ghetto. The Local Area in Large-Scale Society* (New York, 1974).

15. A good sample of this literature can be found in James L. Watson, ed., *Between Two Cultures. Migrants and Minorities in Britain* (Oxford, 1977).

16. Lawrence Levine, *Black Culture and Black Consciousness. Afro-American Folkthought from Slavery to Freedom* (New York, 1977), p. ix.

17. C. Geertz, "Thick Description: Toward an Interpretive Theory of Culture," and for specific reference to the "social nature of thought," see "Person, Time and Conduct in Bali," in C. Geertz, *The Interpretation of Cultures. Selected Essays* (New York, 1973), pp. 3-32 and pp. 360-61:

> A cultural artifact — whether suttee among Balinese or baseball in America — is analogous to a dream or Freudian slip. While it may have material cause and practical ends, the artifact is ultimately a nexus of significance, a potential narrative which the anthropologist is called on to decipher. If properly addressed, it will tell an important story about the collective mental life of the people among whom it is found.

With the appropriate changes of detail this description of Geertz's idea of a cultural artifact can be applied to ethnohistory or retrospective ethnography in a city like Toronto. The description appears in P. Robinson's review of C. Geertz, *Local Knowledge. Further Essays in Interpretive Anthropology* (New York, 1983), in the *New York Times Book Review* (25 September 1983), p. 11.

18. D. Malincheff and J. Theophilact, *The First Bulgarian-English Pocket Dictionary* (Toronto, 1913).

19. Calvino, *Invisible Cities*, p. 76.

20. K. Deutsch, *Nationalism and Social Communication. An Inquiry into the Foundation of Nationality* (Cambridge, Mass., 1966), p. 121.

21. *50th Anniversary SS. Cyril and Methody Macedonian-Bulgarian Orthodox Cathedral, 1910-1960* (Toronto, 1960).

22. *The Ward Graphic* (Toronto, n.d.), p. 14. An occasional publication of Central Neighbourhood House, copy in the Multicultural History Society of Ontario collection.

23. *Polyphony: the Bulletin of the Multicultural History Society*, vol. 1, no. 2 (Summer 1978), religion and ethnocultural communities; *Polyphony*, vol. 2, no. 2 (Winter 1979), benevolent and mutual aid societies in Ontario; *Polyphony*, vol. 4, no. 1 (Spring/Summer 1982), the ethnic press in Ontario; and *Polyphony*, vol. 5, no. 2 (Fall/Winter 1983), immigrant theatre.

24. The image is borrowed from Arthur Goren's appreciation of Moses Rischin's study of New York's Lower East Side. See A. Goren, ''The Promise of the Promised City: Moses Rischin, American History and the Jews,'' in *American Jewish History* LXXIII, no. 2 (December 1983), p. 173.

The Emergence of Cabbagetown in Victorian Toronto

J.M.S. Careless

Like many another urban neighbourhood, Cabbagetown has gone through various transitions since it first took shape in the later nineteenth century. Set at the eastern end of the original city of Toronto and extending to the Don River, the area was scarcely occupied before 1850, for the main thrusts of expansion had moved westward along the harbourfront or northward around Yonge Street, the central route inland.[1] Hence the easternmost city territory for a considerable time had stayed little more than a fringe of humble cottages and vegetable plots. But that changed with the growth of a railway and industrial Toronto from mid-century. The area increasingly became a populous residential district for urban workers, bordering a new rail and factory complex at the Don end of the harbour, which offered jobs, soot and smells together. Thus Victorian Cabbagetown characteristically developed as a domain of small, cheap houses on minor streets. It had little in common with the handsome estates of Rosedale rising beyond Bloor Street on its north, or with the big mansions on Sherbourne and Jarvis to its west. And the poor, the working class and lesser members of the middle class who filled this unadorned preserve stemmed overwhelmingly from the flow of Anglo-Celtic immigration. Consequently the community that had consolidated there by the late nineteenth century was all but homogeneously English-speaking, pre-eminently Protestant (though with a sizeable Catholic Irish minority), and highly British, and Orange, in feeling and tradition.

This was the historic Cabbagetown to be examined here. Yet one may go on, briefly, to note later transitions. Around the First World War, as still newer areas arose in the enlarging city, aspiring residents began moving from the district. Poorer elements crowded into its houses, sometimes two or more families in each. These flimsily constructed, largely rented homes readily leaked and deteriorated; and landlords found decreasing value in keeping them up. The grim years of the 1930s deepened the decline, but it no less marked a process of neighbourhood decay continually repeated across urban America. Cabbagetown's life-quality, cohesion and morale went downhill together. In due course Hugh Garner in the preface to his novel *Cabbagetown*, first published in 1950, would thus describe the locality he had earlier lived in for some three years "a sociological phenomenon, the largest Anglo-Saxon slum in North America." That is the kind of sweeping verdict that catches the eye, yet also expresses literary licence. The same licence was exemplified when Garner went on to say that "Following World War II most of Cabbagetown was bulldozed to the ground."[2] Actually, most of the area's Victorian cityscape then stayed in being, despite several big clearance projects, whereby the state and the developer erected highrise towers of sinister proportions and other handy blocks for breeding social alienation. Still, Cabbagetown went on changing from the 1950s, as an influx of newer ethnic elements brought a very different diversity, and then as gentrifiers swept in, extensively and expensively remodelling its humble houses. Again these are typical processes in urban America. In any event, today it may be said that little beyond the physical layout remains of the old Cabbagetown community. It is now scarcely more than a heritage myth, hazily invoked by real-estate agents busy merchandising quaintness.

But Cabbagetown did exist: as a working, well-knit neighbourhood of Victorian Toronto. Its community life in that era is substantially conveyed in the reminiscences of the city journalist, J.V. McAree, who was born within it in 1876 to Ulster immigrant parents, and grew up at the shop he describes in his book *Cabbagetown Store*. The account undoubtedly displays nostalgia and later, selective memory; yet allowing for these, and with corroborating evidence, one may broadly deem its picture valid. This Cabbagetown was a place of small-town family and neighbourly focuses, of mutual aid and accepted, bonding obligations. It was equally a place of arduous work, often in adjacent industries; or stringency, layoffs and all-too-frequent hardship; of contending constantly with dirt, cold and disease.[3] In fact, the record presented reads like many another urban immigrant story in a developing communal area, whatever the language spoken there, the religion or traditions upheld. At any rate, this community on the whole strove determinedly to stay decent, ordered and self-respecting. Here by no means was a slum; a haunt of degradation, social apathy and personal breakdown. Whatever it later became — and Garner's verdict surely remains an excessive overstatement — Victorian Cabbagetown was a vigorously functioning segment of the contemporary civic society, in which it played no insignificant part.

Since Cabbagetown was not an officially demarcated territory, but really represented a perception shared both by those within it and without, its recognized bounds might vary with beholders. None the less, there was, and is, a wide consensus that this community ran east from Parliament Street to the Don (not beyond it), and spread northward from Queen Street on the south to reach roughly to Bloor at its fullest extent. But points of contention immediately arise. On the south, the dwelling area below Queen and across King towards the harbour industries was intimately linked with Cabbagetown. There was a similar pattern of settlement and employment; the housing and the populace had much in common; in fact, to some extent Cabbagetown simply grew northward out of this adjoining sector. On the west the same kind of lesser streets with little homes generally extended on past Parliament to Sherbourne and its larger properties; while to the north, if some old-timer purists would hold that Cabbagetown proper just went up as far as Gerrard, others would take it on to Winchester. Yet here too the same residential setting and communal life in the time expanded virtually to Bloor. Only the eastern boundary of the Don seems beyond much dispute, for there rolling valley slopes and the wet, open flats that bordered the river at the bottom marked a plain physical limit.

Accordingly, we can merely make the best approximation of bounds which indeed were sensed, not designated. So, we will accept Queen Street on the south, but make required transgressions across it, down to King at least; will certainly endorse the Don riverline to the east, and take Parliament Street to the west — with other small transgressions. As for the north, Bloor seems the best ultimate boundary, though more precisely this was set by the grounds of St. James Cemetery that intervened before that limit, and by bigger residences that came to edge the Bloor ravine, beyond which lay Rosedale. It is also worth adding that the territory so delimited fell within one Toronto civic division, St. David's Ward, for much of the period under study, and between 1873 and 1892 was nearly coterminous with it.[4] This not only gave Cabbagetown some political framework and voice at city elections, but furnished census data on that community during its central decades of growth, because wards at that time served as urban census units. Though the neighbourhood entity and its covering city ward were not the same thing, and not at all before 1859 or after 1892, St. David's in the years between did supply the territory with a kind of municipal realization.

After 1892 Cabbagetown lay mostly in a big new Ward Two, which extended down to the harbour and up through wealthy Rosedale to new districts above. Politically and statistically, the neighbourhood was swallowed up; but socially and culturally, it certainly continued.

I

We can now turn to the settlement story of Cabbagetown. Both the initial layout of an urban community at Toronto, and the basic nature of the terrain at its eastern end had a lot to do with the way in which this area was subsequently occupied. When the city's predecessor, the little town of York, was plotted out in 1793, it scarcely reached from the harbour margin north to Queen Street (then Lot Street), and only from George to a Parliament Street (now Berkeley) on the east. East from here lay a Government Reserve, on which provincial parliament buildings were erected: thus present Parliament Street acquired its name when it was opened beyond Berkeley. And north of Lot Street, up to existing Bloor, hundred-acre "park lots" were surveyed to provide estates for government officials and, hopefully, well-to-do landowners. The first two park lots, between Parliament and the Don north to Bloor, were further reserved for government purposes, originally with an eye most likely to naval timber supplies in woods accessible from the Don. The first provincial governor, John Graves Simcoe, established his Castle Frank estate overlooking the river in the northern portion of this official tract, long to be referred to as the Park. In 1819 some of its land was granted off for hospital purposes, and later for cemeteries, then for private development. Yet this whole sector to be the home of Cabbagetown was definitely backward in being taken up. Even Parliament Street had not a house upon it before the early 1830s.

In part, this lack of growth reflected the government clamp upon the Park area. Its properties were not available to common citizens, or only through official thickets discouraging to venture. True, the parliament buildings were relocated to the western quarters of the town in the 1820s; but with them went government officers and potentially prestigious home sites, which only reduced the appeal of the Park further. Yet far more inherent in its slow development was the nature of the land itself. Through it Taddle Creek meandered to the harbour: a separate stream from the Don, it cut off the extension of Queen Street eastward for years until buried in sewers, by interposing a glum swampy area known as the Meadow. Moreover, the placid, larger Don spread still wider marshes around its mouth; while neighbouring Ashbridges Bay was similarly marsh-choked, and a fostering ground for mosquitos and fever. Nor was the area's soil that good, even where not overly wet.

In comparison with better land to westward, it was less suited to gardens and orchards than root crops and cabbages. Accordingly, physically more difficult to develop as well as none too prepossessing, the Park acquired a reputation as a backwater, despite early hopes that it would be the home ground of the provincial political elite.

After the little government and port town of York became the advancing commercial city of Toronto in 1834, its eastern growth still stayed retarded, even though construction rose vigorously west, north and centrally.[5] Yet gradually, and scarcely heralded, poorer elements in the community began to spill beyond the built-up eastern streets of original York, now a declining district where they had found cheap shelter. They spread along both sides of King Street East, and on vacant lands to northward were scattered squatters' shacks and cabbage patches. Quite probably popular tradition is right in attributing the later-received name of Cabbagetown to proliferating little fields like these, associated as the term was also with poor Irish settlers of the day, both Protestant and Catholic, who traditionally raised the humble green vegetable. Yet it should be kept in mind that such a disparaging label for a local area of low esteem was more generic than specific. Urban places in nineteenth-century North America had their full quota of similar Shantytowns, Paddytowns, Corktowns and so on. Nevertheless, a loosely applied nickname of this sort could become an enduring badge of identity for a recognized neighbourhood community: and so it had become for ''Cabbage Town'' (at first two words) by the time that title appeared in printed works on Toronto in the early 1890s. And however the name evolved, or when, it would stick; as the Park did not.

In any event, the easterly population trickle was sufficient by the 1840s to cause the establishment of a second Anglican parish in Toronto, separate from that of St. James, the church of the dominant civic elite. In 1843 Trinity Church (or Little Trinity as it has come to be known), was built on the south side of King just across from Power Street — a block east of Parliament. This attractively designed Victorian Gothic structure was funded by wealthy Anglicans such as Messrs. Gooderham and Worts, leading city millers, distillers and merchants, to serve the largely Ulster-Irish Anglican working populace of the east end.[6] Just south of Little Trinity, in 1848, the philanthropy of brewer Enoch Turner erected the first free schoolhouse in Toronto, again to help serve the disadvantaged residents of the area. And across King, north on Power Street, the Roman Catholics of the city had had St. Paul's from the late 1820s, in its case ministering to the increasing Catholic Irish lower class in this quarter. In consequence, the east end community was acquiring structuring points even before the precincts of future Cabbagetown were widely entered.

The easterly population flow swelled well beyond a trickle in the 1850s, after a fresh tide of overseas migration surged into Toronto between 1847 and 1854, chiefly from an Ireland devastated by potato blight, famine and ruthless evictions. While Irish immigrants, more notably Protestant Ulstermen, had been numerous since the 1830s in Toronto's annual intakes — together with English and Scots — impoverished Catholic Irish now formed the great proportion of the arrivals.[7] Many died tragically in the typhus and cholera epidemics that flooded with them to the city of the closing forties, and left destitute, debilitated survivors in their wake. Still, the large majority did survive and settle, engendering formidable problems of welfare, employment, social adjustment and, most simply, population pressure.[8] Inevitably, many of the newcomers collected in the poorer, eastern fringe of the city. A closely settled Irish area that was dubbed Corktown developed around the focus of Catholic St. Paul's, roughly centring between King and Queen. But many Protestant Irish, along with poorer English and Scots, also gathered further in the east end vicinity, spreading north past Queen to start the real urban settlement of Cabbagetown. Thus it was that the lands in this direction were so much in process of being occupied that the eastern wards of the city took in the former tracts of the liberties in 1859.

At the same time, the immigrant population push accorded with crucial economic developments in Toronto. From 1850 a new era of prosperity brought expanding enterprises and jobs and above all, railway building. By the 1860s, when this first rail construction boom had passed, the city had all but been transformed into a regionally dominant railway centre with track access to the Upper Lakes, across Ontario to Montreal or Detroit, and down to New York. But more than that, the steam and iron transport growth opened the way for industrialization. Rail traffic spread along Toronto's harbourfront, bringing with it engine and machine works, coal-yards, moulding and forging plants, and steam-driven factories.[9] In particular, many of these activities clustered around the southeastern edge of the city, around the harbour's end and near the Lower Don, where little-used land was cheaply available and accessibility both to docks and incoming rail lines was excellent. This growing industrial concentration in eastern St. Lawrence's Ward featured such sizeable units as the big new gas works, put up in 1855, south of Front past Parliament, the Grand Trunk Railway workshops, the truly massive Toronto Rolling Mills erected in 1857 to supply rails for that line, and the impressive Gooderham and Worts distillery, newly housed in five-storey stone buildings in 1859. Moreover, the Don as a water route had early attracted mills and small industrial concerns up its course. These grew in size and number also, so that the eastern industrial development was enlarged by other processing operations, such as wood or hardware manufactories, tanneries and meat-packing houses. Altogether, working opportunities in the city's east end by the 1860s could readily urge on its settlement, which hence began to rise rapidly north from Queen within St. David's Ward.[10]

Maps, directories or city assessment returns can demonstrate the ensuing growth in the Cabbagetown area.[11] For example, a map of 1858 shows an extensive street layout there, and the new Toronto General Hospital built on a Gerrard Street property in 1856, and St. James and Necropolis cemeteries towards the northern end of the locale. But a map of 1862 illustrates a good deal of subdivision proceeding in its southern portion, where small building lots were being parcelled out. Somewhat ironically, the low esteem in which this Park region had long been held eased the way for the creation of such a district of small residences, ones that workers could afford; though adjunct industries and packing plants no doubt helped keep up the area's poor repute. Wealthy landholders and bigger developers, who elsewhere promoted subdivisions and house plots across the park lots of an expanding city, in the main left the Park to the little men. Some improved on shacks, put up their own houses or in time enlarged them. But mostly it was minor speculators who opened streets in Cabbagetown and erected lines of utilitarian frame houses, largely covered over with roughcast plaster. Numbers of these structures were later bricked, or received a share of showy Victorian gingerbread in fretwork and cast-iron, as did more solid brick edifices like local hotels, schools and churches. Overall, however, the Cabbagetown streetscape took characteristic form as plain rows of narrow, gabled residences up to seventeen feet wide, one, or more usually, two storeys high and with attics above; perhaps as well displaying a front bay window or an added rear wing; but thinly built, lacking central heating, and boasting privies out behind. Most houses were detached, and had sufficient backyard space for vegetable patches; although there were attached terraces, notably on older, southern streets of the area. At any rate, by the standards of the time these looked desirable, practical homes to those with little money and few pretentions.

And so this neighbourhood spread onward filling up with houses from 1860 to 1890, especially as industries continued to spring up in east end Toronto. The city of the late sixties and early seventies witnessed another economic boom. Then a long period of worldwide deflation set in that brought hard times and business failures through the gloomy later seventies; but Toronto's manufacturing growth picked up powerfully in the eighties; and despite some severe downturns, in general made a major advance in scale on into the nineties. There were more, and larger, factories now to hire the people of Victorian Cabbagetown. As well, they worked as rail and civic employees, in the large stores and big press houses now prominent in the central city to the west, as cabmen, labourers and domestics, or as local artisans, shopkeepers and clerks. [12]

The development of Toronto's streetcar system — horse-drawn from 1861 to 1892, electrified thereafter — may be said to have forwarded the process of residential segregation in income-determined neighbourhoods, whereby the affluent hived off to roomier, suburban retreats opened by streetcars, and the poor collected near to downtown workplaces at lower travel costs. But the extension of carlines no less gave many Cabbagetown dwellers greater mobility in getting to jobs, and fostered the enlargement of their own neighbourhood, while knitting it up more closely. In this respect, the King Street route was carried out to the Don in 1874, when a line was also run up Sherbourne, then east along Carlton and north on Parliament to Winchester. In 1882 tracks were extended from Parliament out Gerrard to the Don, and connected with the Queen crosstown route, which in 1887 was sent on over the river. In 1889 a thriving commercial Parliament Street was double-tracked. [13] Even in the horse-car days, Cabbagetown was effectively tied into the city street transport network. The coming of the electric car in the early nineties gave it still more track extensions and much faster service.

Important also in the onward expansion of this neighbourhood was renewed immigration to Toronto in later Victorian times. The strongly Catholic Irish influx had dwindled away in the mid-fifties and was not to soar again. [14] But a migrant stream from Britain grew once more in the later sixties; and while it did not reach anything like previous flood proportions for a now far larger city, it went on, with varied fluctuations, across the rest of the period. Notably this newer intake derived more largely from England, with fewer Irish and Scots among it. [15] And those it brought were no longer country dwellers or semi-rural cottagers, but inhabitants of an urbanized industrialized Britain. Consquently they were generally adapted to city occupations, industrial and store employment — and many would move into developing Cabbagetown as a well-suited residential quarter. Along with Canadian-born inhabitants, chiefly the offspring of earlier Anglo-Celtic arrivals, they consolidated a now maturing neighbourhood, and naturally reinforced its British composition and character. Down at least to the turn of the twentieth century, there were scant non-British, non-English-speaking traces in the neighbourhood, for the smaller wave of continental European migration to the city that rose in the new century came after Cabbagetown had essentially been occupied. In any case, the later Victorian British inflow fitted into that district, continuing its motherland ties, imperialist loyalty and "Anglo-Saxonism." Furthermore, its Protestant predominance was sustained.

Anglican churches in particular arose beyond Little Trinity in the area: St. Peter's in 1866, All Saints in 1874, St. Simon's in 1888 and St. Bartholemew's by 1889. The erection of their parishes in itself illustrated the progressive filling in and structuring of Cabbagetown. Less numerous were major Methodist and Presbyterian churches, such as Berkeley Street Methodist (1871) or St. Enoch's Presbyterian (1891); while the Catholic Church of the Sacred Heart (1888) then stayed a minor focus in contrast to the strongly Catholic convergence around long-established St. Paul's in Corktown below Queen, with its big charitable House of Providence nearby (1857). Moreover, this district version of Toronto the Good, the city of churches, was decidedly evangelical in its dominant tone. Independent chapels of ardent fundamentalist faith, missions, earnest prayer meetings and outdoor revival gatherings also featured the majority Protestant community and further evidenced its outlook.

The population growth that had built up this very identifiable neighbourhood by the 1890s may be substantiated from the census records for St. David's Ward from the 1870s, in terms already noted. In 1871 (allowing for the western section of St. David's of that date which did not form part of Cabbagetown) the population of the latter locale might reasonably be estimated at around 7,000 in a city of some 56,000.[16] In 1881, St. David's, now nearly coterminous with Cabbagetown, held 11,000 in rounded numbers within a city of 96,000.[17] And in 1891, when even more coincident, it had over 22,000 inhabitants in a Toronto of 181,000.[18] The most obvious fact is the doubling of population in the Cabbagetown area over the eighties — a basic product of climbing industrialization and in-migration during the decade. Thereafter, the district's own demographic record is submerged within the new and different civic ward system implemented in 1892. For by the early nineties the Cabbagetown locale had clearly been taken up and its community had acquired firm outlines, whether or not out-migration or more crowding-in would subsequently affect its numbers. We have seen when and how it became settled during the Victorian era. It now remains instead to examine the society and life of this emergent neighbourhood.

II

One major aspect of Cabbagetown society was its religious patterning, at a time when Toronto's church ties were pervasive, whatever class ranks, and taken pretty seriously. Census statistics for the seventies to nineties affirm the area's notably Protestant complexion, yet tell more. The figures for extended St. David's in 1871 show about 7,400 inhabitants belonging to the chief Protestant denominations to some 3,000 Catholics.[19] And though it again has to be observed that this ward then still reached west to Jarvis Street and so included others besides Cabbagetowners, there is no cause to think that the religious ratio would have been greatly different if we had just the Cabbagetown section to go on. The census returns of 1881, for a St. David's reduced much more to our area, may be considered in more detail. They report 2,410 Catholics to 3,937 Anglicans, 2,095 Methodists and 1,449 Presbyterians, which (with 632 Baptists added) give a main Protestant majority of 8,113, even without other small sects.[20] Finally, the 1891 returns in a St. David's which by then virtually coincided with Cabbagetown show 3,992 Catholics to 7,166 Anglicans, 5,081 Methodists, 4,200 Presbyterians and 1,088 Baptists: or a main Protestant majority of 17,535 in a far more populous local community.[21] Three points stand out: the Catholic element had grown by less than a third over the eighties; the Anglicans had nearly doubled, and remained much the largest single denomination; while the Methodists and Presbyterians had more than doubled.

The process that in consequence produced a still more Protestant Cabbagetown can surely be linked to the relative decline of Catholic Irish immigration since the 1850s and to the continued flow of English and Scots into Toronto, even though natural increase of native-born and movement from the countryside to city jobs also affected the neighbourhood. Here we need a closer look at the ethnic origins and birthplaces of its members, and for that must focus on the 1881 census by wards. The ethnic figures for the St. David's Ward of 1871 are risky to apply specifically to Cabbagetown, while the 1891 census did what censuses too often do, change category units, rendering it of little value for a relevant comparison on nationalities.[22] At any rate, statistics for 1881, in the midst of the area's principal growth period, showed for St. David's 4,562 residents of English origin, 1,305 of Scottish, and 4,548 of Irish stock. The last-named group of course comprised both Protestant and Catholic elements. Since in that day Toronto's Catholics were overwhelmingly Irish-derived, it seems meaningful to subtract the contemporary Catholic component given for St. David's in 1881 from the Irish ethnic total, which gives a figure of 2,138. Almost certainly, this to a great extent represented the Protestant Irishmen of the ward. In other words, probably close to half the Irish residents in Cabbagetown of the eighties were of Orange rather than Green affinity. Beyond these main ethnic groups, only about 260 each of French or German origin were then reported for the area, 6 ''Russian-Polish,'' 10 Swiss, 5 Scandinavians and 18 ''Africans.''[23] There were no Italians, Jews, Dutch or Chinese listed. An Anglo-Celtic bailiwick indeed, if neither English nor Irish entity.

As for birthplaces, the English element in 1881 contained the largest number of homeland-born, 1,924 or over 42 per cent.[24] The

Irish correspondingly displayed nearly 34 per cent of overseas origin, the Scots about 32 per cent. Totalling these segments against the area majority of Canadian birth (but Anglo-Celtic stock) gives to the neighbourhood of 1881 a non-native component of around 40 per cent, still a high proportion when one considers that this comes just after the migration lull around the close of the seventies when hard times ruled Toronto. And since the city's British intake swelled again over the eighties into the nineties, it is altogether probable that Cabbagetown did maintain its large immigrant ingredient throughout the rest of the period. It remained, in short, both an Anglo-conformist stronghold and a home of migrants from the United Kingdom. That it held only 379 of United States birth in 1881 indicates that any American component was very limited. Yet it did play host to another small and rather different group of newcomers: French Canadians, about 250 by 1881, who had been brought there to work in a local tannery. They formed the nucleus of the Sacred Heart Catholic congregation, but hardly affected the ethnic nature of the community.

Another socio-cultural aspect of the Cabbagetown neighbourhood appeared in the schooling of its young, traceable from city educational records.[25] The public school system, that became free in the 1850s and compulsory in the early seventies, was naturally paramount in this Victorian quarter, where Catholic separate schools then played a very minor role. Among the main public schools of the area were Park School (1853), Parliament Street (1872), Winchester Street (1874), Lord Dufferin (1877), Rose Avenue (1884) and Sackville Street (1888). Park particularly had a tough reputation, but a survey of the school inspectors' reports shows that the most evident and endemic local school crime was absenteeism, in which Park at times ranked high for all Toronto.[26] Absenteeism, however, was a widespread problem in poorer city schools of the seventies and generally declined thereafter. It was largely ascribed to pupils being kept home through family poverty and sickness, long distances to travel to school over unimproved roads, and needs for children to supplement household earnings. More schools, streets with sidewalks, stiffer truancy measures, child labour restrictions — and, hopefully, better living standards and health services — made regular school attendance far more the rule by the 1890s.[27] In any event, Cabbagetown's schools were by no means at the bottom of the educational record. On the whole one gets the impression that our neighbourhood was hard-working and earnestly striving after respectability in education also. There do not seem to have been rowdy blackboard jungles in this morally conservative family community.

The trustees who represented the area on the city's public school board are worth some comment.[28] Two were elected annually for the St. David's Ward, until school districts replaced wards as designated units in 1892. These representatives during the period came from the locality's limited elite — professionals and business-men who maintained homes, offices or firms in the area. Three trustees who served repeated annual terms and in time became board chairmen were E.P. Roden, a newspaperman, Edward Galley, a confectioner, and the physician Dr. R.A. Pyne. Roden, in fact, held office from 1874 to 1897 while being a reporter or editor on successive city papers such as the *Leader, Mail* and *News*, and later a city hall official. The eldest son of a large family of Protestant Irish immigrants, he eventually had a school named after him. Galley, trustee from 1873 onward, was an alderman for St. Thomas's Ward just to the west through the later eighties, while Pyne, who replaced him on the school board in 1884, by the early twentieth century sat as a Toronto Conservative member in the provincial legislature, and became a Minister of Education.

This community acceptance of rule by its upper crust was plainly witnessed in municipal politics also. Those who constituted St. David's aldermen through the seventies to nineties were area business and professional men, with some industrial figures and suc-cessful artisans advancing as employers.[29] Among them were the ward's longest serving aldermen, William Adamson (1873-1885), the manager of the Toronto Tea Company, and the lawyer John Blevins (1875-1884). Others with several terms included Thomas Allen, a brewer residing on River Street; James Martin, proprietor of the Ontario Engine Works; William H. Gibbs, a painter-contractor; John C. Swait, superintendent of the Toronto Harbour Works; and Daniel Lamb, owner of a blacking and glue factory, who kept a large home on Winchester Street and sent his children to Rose Avenue school. Lamb was subsequently an alderman for Ward Two. As for Robert F. Fleming, who ran a coal and wood business on Parliament in the eighties, then moved into real estate, he rose from alderman to be mayor of the city in 1892 and 1896, and thereafter manager of the Toronto Street Railway Company. Wholesale importers and upholsterers, more manufacturers and lawyers, might be added to the list; yet it all makes plain that pro-letarian voices or labour radicals were not noteworthy in Cab-bagetown civic politics of the day. By and large, public affairs were left to a British-cast, conservative-minded (and Protestant-engrained) leadership element, which had some degree of affluence and social prestige. And if they lacked the wealth of the really rich found in other areas, their rule was not very different from that of Toronto politicos elsewhere, with whom they were well integrated.

Inherently linked both with the politics and the dominant sen-timents of this society was the Orange Order. A recent work on the Order in Canada, by Cecil Houston and William Smyth, demonstrates that its membership was widespread across later Victorian Toronto, with lowest density in the upper-class residential tracts of Jarvis Street and Rosedale, but highest in Cabbagetown. No doubt the numerous Ulster Irish in that neighbourhood had much to do with the case. Yet Houston and Smyth confirm that the Order drew widely on English and Scottish stocks also, and it had strong followings in all three major Toronto Protestant churches, Anglican, Methodist and Presbyterian, especially the first two —- which were also the largest in Cabbagetown. Smaller Protestant denominations like Baptists or Lutherans were much less evident in Orangeism, as they were also in Cabbagetown.[30] At the same time, the Order crossed class lines, and kept a substantial middle-class component, even if the bulk of its members came from the lower classes. "Orangemen were not a segregated minority confined to either economic or ethnic ghettos."[31] As much could be said of the Cabbagetowners in Victorian Toronto. Their Orange hue was markedly bright, one they shared with the Protestant city about them.

Orange lodges pervaded the district, but a main meeting place for their members was the eastern Orange Hall on Queen. Here was a forum for their views on public issues, and a headquarters for political transactions. The Orange vote in Toronto mattered, municipally, provincially and federally. Orangemen were perennial among civic politicians and plentiful in city employment, whether at city hall, the works department or in the police force, for all of which Cabbagetown residents offered a goodly quota. It is unnecessary, however, to view this as some dark conspiratorial net, a King Billy underground. Orange ties, for better or worse, operated pretty openly; and it would have been hard to impugn the respectability of the Order's stands on British loyalty and Protestant freedom to majority Toronto then. Cabbagetowners marched on the Orange celebration day, 12 July, but almost as virtuously as in a temperance or trades union parade. Granted there were fights and uproars in Toronto associated with the Glorious Twelfth or Hibernian St. Patrick's Day; still, violence chiefly occurred in more turbulent and crowded areas of the city. For our neighbourhood, Orangeism broadly implied order rather than disorder. Furthermore, it has been pointed out that Toronto's denser residential districts really contained religious admixtures, and there were no great separate, terraced confines of either Protestants or Catholics as in Belfast, mass citadels for religious warfare.[32] In Cabbagetown, assuredly, Protestants had many Catholic street neighbours; the converse was equally true in adjacent, prevalently Catholic Corktown south of Queen and on below King. There was not the same tight territorial basis for major sectarian combat. Sparring there might be, as when an Orange band trumpetted and coat-trailed into a largely Catholic street; yet this local version of "chicken" was a fairly minor fringe sport.

If the Cabbagetown community was not an ethno-religious enclave, for all its Orange display, or a politically sequestered compound, then was it set off as an economic precinct of poverty? Obviously it was one of the poorer areas of Toronto. City assessment records for St. David's Ward from the seventies to the nineties broadly show it as near the bottom in ward returns for the value of real and personal property. Nevertheless, they also demonstrate an overall rise in property worth for St. David's across the period, despite some depression downturns. Expansion of settlement and the rise of bigger industrial units in the district would explain some of this increased value; but at least the general trend was strongly upward. In 1874, the first full year after St. David's was cut back to quasi-Cabbagetown limits, it returned a real-property assessment of $1,737,646, a personal-property one of $88,005. In 1881 the respective values were $2,952,543 and $100,300; in 1891, $7,827,138 and $322,650. And the total assessment for the ward (also including land income) advanced between 1874 and 1891 from $1,857,201 to $8,195,096, a more than fourfold gain in a largely deflationary period.[33] The rise was not astronomical but it was significant. Cabbagetown was amassing dollar and tax value not declining slumward. Besides, though it was unquestionably an area of small, lower-priced houses, these were being improved, while home ownership was growing. And there were some larger dwellings, as both political and assessment records illustrate, along with a middle-class presence that was not only politically ascendant, but also widened the social context from that of a purely working-class quarter.[34] In brief, if Victorian Cabbagetown predominantly held wage-earners and many on the subsistence edge, it was not simply a proletarian conflux, but had an essentially wider economic and social make-up.[35]

Middle-class values dominated the area's schools, as they did its political life, and largely its churches and social mores. Conceivably, too, if a Cabbagetown workingman came to abhor an obdurate factory boss, he was more likely to impute personal faults than those of the economic system. He could keep up his own hopes of upward mobility when he was himself only a generation (if that) away from immigrant arrival — by which time he seemed already to have made a place in the land of opportunity, where diligence, thrift and honest toil would surely pay off. Hence conscious class conflict was no more a distinguishing feature of the neighbourhood society than was explosive religious warfare. That is not to depict it as a docile, peaceable kingdom: it had its angers, unruly spirits and share of social crime.[36] Yet it cannot be regarded as seething with deprivations and repressed discontents. It kept its own lid on, hoped soberly but rootedly, and made the best of daily living as sound Torontonians should.

Daily living meant coping with common facts of Cabbagetown existence: the drab environment blemished by industrialism, and the struggles the bulk of residents repeatedly faced against sickness and want. Drabness appeared in the monotonous little streets of box-like, meagerly built homes. Blight stemmed from the dirt, debris and fumes of factories close at hand, their industrial dumps and coal heaps — not to mention stockyards, livery stables, cow barns, and all their refuse. Some of these offences were right in the district, but other major offenders lay not too far off on the south, such as the reeking hog pens of the big William Davies Company's meat-packing plant, or the cattle herded at Gooderham and Worts to feed on used brewing mash. All these posed serious threats to area health, compounded by dangers from choked privies, overflowing cesspools and contaminated wells, in a district thinly served by the civic water system.[37]

Health conditions, however, improved from the early eighties, when Toronto's pioneer medical health officer, Dr. William Canniff, took up the tasks of sanitary reform. Deadly epidemics such as typhus and cholera had departed, in spite of a scare in the 1860s. Canniff's work checked the ravages of smallpox, though diptheria, tuberculosis and pneumonia remained killers in Cabbagetown. Still, the worst ''public nuisances'' were progressively brought under control; water mains and indoor plumbing spread (though more slowly than in better-off districts); and overall death rates curved steadily downward toward the end of the century. Pasteurized milk and civic water safe from sewage contamination had yet to be assured; but the incessant burdens of sickness were lessening.[38]

The burdens of want for most continued, with recurrent ups and downs. Nevertheless, enlarging city welfare activities, local self-help, and patterns of communal assistance gave varied but altogether valuable measure of support. Welfare agencies were more than local; but notably present for the area were the Irish Protestant Benevolent Society, the Girls' Home established on Gerrard in 1871, the Boys' Home to the west on George beyond it, and the Catholic House of Providence south of Queen, which sheltered Protestants as well.[39] The Toronto General Hospital on Gerrard, two medical schools and the Ontario Medical College for Women, built on Sumach in 1891, together afforded some doctoring and dispensary services. With regard to self-help, the neighbourhood poor all too plainly expressed it in their yearly contests with the cold: collecting firewood from the broken crates at the St. Lawrence Market, picking over the ash heaps at the gas works for stove coals, liberating more from factory stockpiles. And as to communal aid, here the small grocery stores of the locality played a crucial role. Each was a centre of neighbourly transactions, news and gossip; each had its own few street blocks of family clientele. Collectively, they sustained their customers with store credit between pay days, and often over far longer spans of illness or unemployment. Many an over-extended storekeeper certainly went down, taking his ledger losses with him; yet by and large debts were faithfully honoured by customers, with more than practical necessity as motive. Mutual help further gave comfort in times of sickness and death. The neighbours stood close: a statement of simple reality, not wishful sentiment. The joint, informal obligations were intrinsic in area living.

Community life found a relieving side in recreations. One great benefit Cabbagetown did have was ready access to the open expanses of the Don Valley on the east. Its slopes may largely have been too abrupt to build on, its bottom lands too dank, even when not subject to flood. But here still was room: bush for children to explore, flats for lacrosse and football, water reaches for summer boating and bathing, winter skating, shinny and curling. This was an unkempt parkland, but it was Cabbagetown's. Its grass and trees, its play and rambling space, offset the bleak confines of the adjoining built environment. The opening of Riverdale Park in 1880 brought lasting official designation to the tract, wherein a municipal Riverdale Zoo (fathered by Alderman Daniel Lamb) became another attraction from 1894. In any event, the outdoor engagements of the parkland, the indoor recreations of choirs, church dinners and bazaars, the Orange Hall — or many a bar and pool hall — showed that the neighbourhood did not take its leisures glumly. And festal days like the Glorious Twelfth (of course) or the Queen's Birthday on 24 May were enthusiastic mass celebrations. Austere, withdrawn Puritanism was hardly an attribute of this lively local society.

III

Where, in summary, does one place nineteenth-century Cabbage-town in Toronto's ethnic and communal development? It definitely was not some kind of a WASP ghetto. It could not be, when it formed part of the city's "social majority," and was effectively tied into the prevailing Anglo-conformity in political as well as social terms — even in its very Orangeism. It was equally not a slum, despite bleak spots of blight, or living conditions that could better be called pinched than poverty-stricken. The local populace displayed cohesiveness, vitality and confidence; they had rising property values, improving health and environmental controls, mostly separate housing; and freely attainable recreation space. Nor was this an economic enclave either. While chiefly occupied by wage-earners lacking capital, it also held influential middle-class components, and by no means functioned as a consciously proletarian district. Finally, though its immigrant origins were as apparent as its resulting ethnic and religious composition, the community was not characterized by language and cultural differences, by problems of heritage defence and adaptation, or by traits of temporary sojourning, so common to many other urban immigrant experiences in Canada and the United States.[40] What then was this Cabbagetown?

A neighbourhood. A locality with perceived limits and identity, with internal bonding, a built environment and a history of its own; thereby comprising an integral but distinctive part of the larger urban society. The study of neighbourhoods such as this one is an essential ingredient of urban history. Not least of its value is the salutary check it brings when generalizations or models applied to the urban sphere come up against local realities. The emergence of neighbourhoods, most obviously, cannot only be viewed in the light of immigrant segregation, even in a land of migrants, nor as the result alone of geographic apportionment, economic sorting or class separation. All these and other factors have their various mixes and impacts — including timing, opportunity and human evaluation. But neighbourhoods come in different shapes and weaves. The record of Toronto asserts as much; and the case of Cabbagetown decidedly illustrates the point.

This is not to conclude that particularism is everything. Common aspects of local Toronto experience surely existed also. Our specific neighbourhood was quite typically built by newcomers, the products of immigrant intake, and went on receiving them across its building years. Its Protestant churches and chapels were as focal as the homeland churches and synagogues which later arrivals established in other forming localities. The Orange lodges were its own equivalents of national and benevolent societies, while the street store-circle was as basic to local joint-survival. Still further, the community faced hard physical conditions and disparagement from outside, yet not only persisted, but also developed property-holders, a local middle class and leadership of its own.[41] No doubt European migrants slightly later in the Ward found a much rougher road ahead of them: still worse housing and living conditions, language and culture barriers, and prejudices much deeper than disparagement that attributed social evils, crime and violence to their clustering, far beyond any poor repute known to Cabbagetown. Still, the affinities were real. They were, in fact, parallel themes in the development of newer, poorer Toronto neighbourhoods. Cabbagetown does not stand unique in a story that runs from early Corktown to the Ward, to the Junction.

Notes

1. For basic background on the spatial, social and economic growth of Toronto of the period, see Jacob Spelt, *Toronto* (Toronto, 1973), esp. chapter 4; D.C. Masters, *The Rise of Toronto, 1850-1890* (Toronto, 1947); and P.G. Goheen, *Victorian Toronto, 1850 to 1890* (Toronto, 1970), chapters 1, 3, 4, 6, 7.

2. Hugh Garner, *Cabbagetown* (Toronto, 1950, reprinted 1968). The preface quoted is in the 1968 edition, p. vii.

3. The account in McAree's *Cabbagetown Store* (Toronto, 1953) may be enlarged and substantiated from contemporary newspapers, civic archival records, social statistics and city directory analysis. In drawing the picture of Cabbagetown — and throughout the article to follow — I have been much helped by the kindness of Mr. George Rust D'Eye who allowed me to read his now published work, *Cabbagetown* (Erin, Ont., 1984) in manuscript, which contains a good deal of valuable information.

4. For the history of the changing territorial limits of St. David's Ward, and neighbouring St. Lawrence's Ward, see maps and records at the City of Toronto Archives (hereafter TCA), particularly the typescript on the "Development of the Ward System."

5. F.H. Armstrong, "Toronto in Transition, 1828-1838" (Ph.D., University of Toronto, 1965), pp. 12-17, 23-30, 43-4. See also F.H. Armstrong and Gordon Pitts, *Toronto: The Place of Meeting* (Toronto: Windsor Publications, 1983).

6. Masters, *Rise of Toronto*, p. 30; Eric Arthur, *Toronto, No Mean City* (Toronto, 1964), pp. 80-81.

7. Nearly 90,000 migrants from the British Isles entered at the port of Quebec in 1847, the great famine year, of whom over 54,000 were Irish, some 31,000 English and 3,700 Scottish. See H.I. Cowan, *British Emigration to British North America* (Toronto, 1961), appendix B, table I, p. 289. By early 1848 more than 30,000 in this wave had swept on to, or through, Toronto (*British Colonist* [Toronto] 8 February 1848), when the city's resident population was then only about 23,000. Through 1853 Irish entries were greatly preponderant, though in 1854, the last sizeable year in this migration phase, arrivals at Quebec stood at approximately 18,000 English, 16,000 Irish and 6,000 Scots (Cowan, *British Emigration*, p. 289).

8. D.S. O'Shea, "The Irish Immigrant Adjustment to Toronto: 1840-1865," graduate research paper, University of Toronto, 1972, pp. 18-38.

9. See *Globe* (Toronto) 12 February 1866, for descriptions (including work forces) of major industrial establishments.

10. A map in Goheen, *Victorian Toronto*, p. 129, "Distribution of Employment in Toronto, 1860," graphically illustrates the dense clustering of chiefly industrial jobs in the southeastern corner of the city.

11. Contemporary maps and assessment records are found at TCA. Toronto yearly directories which not only show residential spread but occupations of residents,

are far more usable when they give a street-by-street treatment, as most do at least from 1868.

12. Directory information from the sixties to nineties provides the basis for this general summation.

13. L.H. Pursley, *Street Railways of Toronto, 1861-1921* (Los Angeles, 1968), pp. 7-10.

14. For example, in the migration ebb of the later 1850s, Irish landings at Quebec fell from a low 4,100 in 1855 to a minute 410 by 1861, while English entries led with 6,700 and 7,700 at the same respective dates (Rounded numbers: see *Government of Canada, Report of the Department of Citizenship and Immigration, 1860-61* [Ottawa, 1961], p. 28.) Of course Irish landings rose somewhat in the renewed phases of British migration to Canada over the late sixties through eighties, which had their own lulls interspersed. But the Irish proportion of the whole intake did not regain preponderance (ibid.)

15. Immigrant arrivals just for Toronto, as available over the later Victorian years, make the pattern evident. For instance, the numbers listed of English, Irish and Scots entrants to the city (in that order) were for 1869: 7,275, 811, 1,548; for 1874: 7,694, 1,530, 1,995; for 1878 (example of a depressed year): 2,706, 646, 979; and for 1880 (time of partial recovery): 3,982, 2,288, 1,225. (See Ontario Archives, ''Immigrants' Arrivals to Toronto, Statistical Returns, 1868-1881,'' XLVI, n.d. handwritten.)

16. *Census of Canada, 1871*, I, p. 114. The total figure for the St. David's of that year was 11,229. In view of the much older and denser development of the western, non-Cabbagetown section of this ward at that date, to assign its larger but newer Cabbagetown portion around 60 per cent of the count seems safety conservative for 1871.

17. Ibid., *1881*, I, p. 73.

18. Ibid., *1891*, I, p. 174.

19. Ibid., *1871*, pp. 114-15. If anything, the Protestant ratio for Cabbagetown alone might have been a bit higher; since the older western section of St. David's in 1871 likely held more Catholics — as is strongly suggested by the denominational charts compiled for the settled city of 1851-61 in Shea, ''Irish Adjustment,'' appendices. In any event, it is unwise to use the 1871 census figures for St. David's to convey much more than the general but sizeable Protestant ascendancy in our locale that was attained by that time. Closer applications concerning specific church numbers run into too many uncertainties of linkage between the total ward figures and the Cabbagetown community itself. The same is true regarding statistics of brithplaces and national origins: the 1871 census is not a sufficiently indicative key to them, since the fit between the St. David's of the day and its Cabbagetown content was still too loose before 1873.

20. Ibid., *1881*, I, pp. 174-75.

21. Ibid., *1891*, I, 282-83.

22. Regarding the census of 1871, see note 19 above. As for ethnic patterns later

than 1881, it could be noted that the census of 1901 did at least present "origins" by wards, and here it may be somewhat illustrative to mark the wide Ward Two that from 1892 included most of Cabbagetown. For what it is worth, the 1901 statistics for this successor ward enumerate (rounded) 15,000 of English ancestry, 11,800 Irish, 5,800 Scottish — and specifically, 1,153 "Germans," 299 Jewish, 61 "African" and 42 Italian, among other small components. But the 1881 census affords the closest analysis.

23. Ibid., *1881*, pp. 276-77.

24. Ibid., pp. 374-75.

25. The Educational Centre Archives of the City of Toronto (hereafter ECA) provide primary materials here, while H.M. Cochrane, ed., *Centennial Story: The Board of Education for the City of Toronto, 1850-1950* (Toronto, 1950), gives a secondary account of public school developments.

26. ECA, Annual Reports of the Inspector of the Public Schools, 1873-91.

27. Cochrane, *Centennial Story*, pp. 70-71, 80, 86. See also ECA, Annual School Reports which also show an improving teacher-pupil ratio for most area schools over the 1880s. Winchester, for example, went from 72 pupils per teacher in 1881 to 49 in 1892, Parliament from 62 to 38, though others altered less.

28. For trustees of the area, see Annual School Reports and biographical information available at ECA.

29. For aldermen elected in St. David's Ward over the period, and their occupations, see a convenient appendix provided on city council members in Victor Russell, *Mayors of Toronto, I: 1834-1899* (Erin, Ont., 1982), and biographical files at TCA.

30. C.J. Houston and W.J. Smyth, *The Sash Canada Wore: A Historical Geography of the Orange Order in Canada* (Toronto, 1980), pp. 108, 104.

31. Ibid., p. 106. This book criticizes the view of G.S. Kealey that the Order of Toronto was "overwhelmingly working-class" ("The Orange Order in Toronto," in G.S. Kealey and P. Warrian, eds., *Essays in Canadian Working-Class History* [Toronto, 1976], pp. 13-35), and effectively shows how it bridged classes and contained a wide occupational mix.

32. Ibid., p. 109; Shea, "Irish Adjustment," pp. 19-21.

33. TCA, Appendix, Minutes of City Council, Commissioner's Assessment Returns for St. David's Ward, 1874-92. Figures given are for original assessments.

34. This can well be discerned from city directories as examined from the later sixties to mid-nineties. For example, the house occupants listed for the streets of the locality in 1878, a well reported year (See *Toronto Directory for 1878*, Might and Taylor, Toronto, 1878), show residents who were porters, teamsters, rail and factory workers, carpenters and other skilled tradesmen, firemen, bookkeepers and so on. But also listed are commerical travellers, retailers, wholesalers and insurance agents, builders, company superintendents and factory owners, plus professionals from physicians and clerics to civil engineers. No doubt few in the upper ranks grew highly affluent, and no doubt they

gathered more on "better" streets like Winchester than, say, Sumach. Still, their local presence was widespread; and checks carried to 1895 reveal little essential change.

35. McAree notes few white-collar workers in his store's vicinity (*Cabbagetown Store*, p. 65), but also observes, "few of our customers were conscious of poverty" (p. 9). In general, his view of a community that yet showed little class polarization or worker self-awareness is borne out by George Rust D'Eye's research, and by the sources used for our study.

36. While statistical civic reports on "crime committted" are found at TCA in Council Minutes, relevant police records for the Cabbagetown area over the period have been lost or damaged. Nevertheless from what is left, but mainly through newspapers and other impressionistic accounts, one may infer that Cabbagetown did not stand out from other areas for crime and violence in the general city mind, and certainly was not regarded as a distinctive threat to public order and morality in the way that the Ward would be.

37. See Heather McDougall, "Health is Wealth: Development of Public Health Activity in Toronto, 1834-1890" (Ph.D., University of Toronto, 1981), chapters 6-7 particularly for sanitary conditions.

38. Ibid. See also H. McDougall, "Public Health in Toronto's Municipal Politics, 1883-90," *Bulletin of the History of Medicine*, LV, pp. 186-202.

39. For the significant Irish Protestant Benevolent Society see its records at Metropolitan Toronto Public Library. The main, public-aided, non-sectarian House of Industry lay in the western half of the city.

40. Cabbagetown undoubtedly took in boarders, especially after rising house prices and rents became felt in filling core neighbourhoods during the 1880s (Shea, "Irish Adjustment," p. 21). C.S. Clark's somewhat sensationalized depiction of the city's darker sides in the late nineties, *Of Toronto the Good* (Montreal, 1898), notes this trend continuing (p. 3). Yet our district evidenced relatively few boardinghouses and still less tenements in the time-span covered; while its inhabitants were more chiefly engaged in regular city employments, not the seasonal work-gangs of sojourners. Nuclear families in individual houses remained the general rule.

41. McAree's own account displays the ascent of a poor Ulster Irish immigrant family to local middle-class status. They not only ran their store (in a house with indoor plumbing), but also gained rent income from other, small store and house properties (p. 29). That certainly did not ensure economic prosperity, since their own store finally folded: another aspect of immigrant precariousness. Still, on yet another side, the rising Ulster alderman from Cabbagetown and subsequent mayor, Robert Fleming, was McAree's uncle — but not an Orange Conservative; instead, a relative rarity, a Toronto Liberal who reached top civic office. Here, too, the particulars of history both confirm and qualify generalizations on immigrant and neighbourhood development.

Peasants in an Urban Society: the Irish Catholics in Victorian Toronto

Murray W. Nicolson

The large group of Irish Catholic peasants who entered Toronto after the Irish famine of 1846-47 shattered the Protestant consensus in the city. For decades prior to their arrival, small groups of partially assimilated Irish Catholics were scattered throughout the city and its unincorporated areas surrounding it, known as the liberties. However, the new urban peasantry attempted to retain a distinctive culture in direct defiance of the assimilative and secularizing forces of the Protestant urban container. Survival was difficult. Not only did the famine Irish have to face an unfriendly milieu, but also had to contend with a physical environment foreign to them. Victorian Toronto, like other urban areas, was a "demographic parasite," requiring constant immigration to maintain numbers and growth. The Irish immigrants were diminished through disease, and therefore ethnic growth depended upon a high birth rate and constant immigration; both conditions essential to accommodate it declined in the remaining decades of the century.

The Irish Catholic immigrants had been an abused people in Ireland. Disease-ridden, superstitious, uneducated and untrained, they quickly formed a section of the lower-class, labouring population and, consequently, the urban poor. Living on the periphery of society, they were despised as human vermin, an "obsolete people" fit only for absorption or extinction. To them, the city was a "Hollow Town," for they were excluded from social participation in its cultural life, restricted from remunerative work and political preference. As outsiders looking in, the city was an animate object with all the attributes of their old English enemy. Nevertheless, those Famine Irish Catholic survived in various areas of concentration and, with the aid of their church, developed a new urban culture.[1]

I

To date, Irish Catholic in Toronto and other Canadian urban centres have received little historical attention. Perhaps one major reason for this can be attributed to the fact that historians tend to avoid the use of religion as a variable when studying ethnic minorities. Possibly the nature of available sources and the various misconceptions in the growing Irish-Canadian literature may have dictated that studies combine both Protestants and Catholics in an unified approach. Certainly, the early census and municipal reports exclude the identification of Canadian-born Irish descendants and fail to stipulate religious affiliation which makes it difficult to isolate each group in order to assess the individual economic and social differences. Moreover, there is a paucity of manuscript sources left by the Catholic Irish, for that peasantry, denied education in Ireland, remained voiceless urban nomads for decades. A general self-consciousness over the poor living standards and social conditions of their ancestors has produced a generational ethno-religious privatism in the descendants of the immigrants, making them evasive as sources for familial information.[2]

Generally, when historians examine Irish Catholics, they accept the theory of a "folk urban continuum" in which peasants, following a period of adjustment, assimilate quickly into the charter group culture. Consequently, there are writers who believe that Irish assimilation into a generalized Catholic subculture was hastened by the lack of any articulated tradition of the famine or past treatment in Ireland. This concept leaves blank areas in nineteenth-century urban and social history when the Irish Catholic could be described as the "white nigger" in Victorian Toronto.[3]

Irish Catholic adjustment carried a burden from Irish history. When attempts are made to confirm this, the authors are labelled "racist" on the presumption that the famine was the fault of the Irish Catholics who had adapted a monoculture and who procreated themselves to death. And to discuss British brutality in that period has been considered "evil." Furthermore, the argument is presented that the Irish were not ghettoized in Toronto, for that was not a Canadian urban phenomenon, that tenements and boarding-houses were uncommon in the city, and the Irish, having had considerable occupational mobility, posed no economic threat to the charter population.[4] This concept, that the Irish "were not ghettoiz- ed . . . not even chiefly urbanized," seems to be an attempt to sup- plant the American urban model with a Canadian rural one on the premise that Irish culture developed in rural Ontario. And when this concept is further expanded by a belief that Irish Catholics received fair treatment and showed considerable social mobility,[5] the Toron- to Irish Catholic urban experience is distorted. There is no argu- ment against the position that pre-famine Irish were dominantly rural dwellers. However, the bulk of famine Irish were urban dwellers, not by choice but by necessity. Many had been itinerant spalpeens or navvies in England, supporting families at home in Ireland. As penniless labourers they found it difficult to adjust from immigrant, to farm labourer, to farmer. By 1851 most of the good farm land in central Ontario had been occupied. Furthermore, the observation has been made that by 1871, in the County of Peel, Irish settlers no longer arrived, but rather, previously established Irish households have been reduced by 44 per cent.[6] Actually, the famine Irish were transient, moving from one urban centre to another, in Canada and to the United States, from city to rural area and back to Toronto several times throughout their lives. That mobility is demonstrated clearly in an examination of cemetery records, Irish newspapers and family histories.[7]

With the rise of Irish Catholic institutions after 1850, Toronto became the cultural focus for the Irish in Ontario. It was from the areas of Irish Catholic concentration, with their interacting parish networks, that a distinctive culture arose and spread to the hinterland. Urban-rural ratios made little difference, for Irish Catholic culture was urban-born.[8]

Finally, we are led to believe that the Orange Order laid the framework for an unified working class when common issues emerg- ed, while the Catholic church delayed the formation of an unified work force. When the church played its role as urban actor and eas- ed the entrance of its members into unions, it is believed that Irish Catholics were submerged in a working-class culture and their distinctive identity was neutralized.[9]

However, if one recognizes the Irish as an ethnic group and the fact that they, in absolute numbers, were the Catholics of Toronto, that particular ethno-religious identity broadens the scope of manuscript sources to include the archives of the church and religious orders, the press and a considerable oral history. In re- searching these sources it becomes evident the "folk urban con- tinuum" cannot be applied to the Irish in Toronto. Rather, the sources point to a reinterpreted peasant culture and the emergence of a refurbished ethno-religious urban identity not previously noticed, for it had been masked behind a form of ethno-religious privatism.

II

It is possible that some Irish Catholics attached to the British regiments entered York at its founding. But an examination of the church census for the mission of York in the Home District shows slow growth. In 1805 there were 6 Catholics in the mission, increasing to 46 in 1817, to 260 by 1822, and to 335 in 1826. The lists of those Catholics are composed chiefly of Irish names, interspersed with a few English, Scottish and French.[10] With the construction of St. Paul's Church in Cabbagetown in 1822 and the subsequent arrival of a permanent Irish priest, William J. O'Grady, the population in the mission rose to 1,275 in 1830 and to 3,500 in 1834. O'Grady, a controversial figure, began to instil ethnic solidarity, the need for educational institutions and reform politics in his fellow countrymen.[11] But they were a transient population, difficult to enumerate, aid or control:

> . . . as a large proportion of the Catholics of this province consists of Immigrants who have arrived within these few years past in the country and such of them have not yet acquired permanent places of residence, are moving about from one part of the province to another, it is next to impossible to ascertain correctly the number in each mission.[12]

Prior to the arrival of the famine immigrants, the Irish lived throughout the city in which there was little segregation by class. Among them was a slowly growing middle sector of journalists, skilled tradesmen, professional men and minor entrepreneurs, including the Scollards, McSherrys, Kings, Hughes, Bergins and Collins. But the vast majority of Toronto's Irish were unskilled labourers, carters and transient workers employed in public works on a seasonal basis. For part of the year, they left their wives and children in Cabbagetown near St. Paul's Church, on the waterfront, in the St. Lawrence Ward, in the liberties, over the Don River in Slab Town, and over the Humber in Corktown and Irish Town — all areas of Irish concentration.[13] None of those areas could be considered ghettos in the traditional sense.

The problems encountered by the pre-famine Irish were insignificant compared to those of the famine immigrants, for the equation that being Irish, in Toronto, equalled being Catholic had not yet been formulated. The French-Canadian hierarchy labelled the Irish the "scum of the population,"[14] an unwanted race who were disloyal and radically anti-British in a period when the French church sought British sanction.[15] Bishop A. Macdonell of Kingston, the first Roman Catholic bishop of Upper Canada, regarded them as lukewarm, semi-barbarous Catholics in comparison to his own

Scottish Canadian countrymen in Glengarry.[16] But York had been a neglected mission. The Irish who settled in its environs had been detached, in part, from the church by generational denial of religious rights in Ireland. Although they were given St. Paul's Church, it had to serve a large area and was not assigned a resident priest until the late 1820s; even then, the priest was frequently absent ministering to the needs of those in its vast hinterland. As a result, Irish Catholics married before available Protestant clergymen. They persisted in their superstitious beliefs and failed to practise a religion that was almost unfamiliar to them. Generally, they interacted well with their Protestant neighbours, but, in nationalistic fervour, were prone to violent outbursts against the Orange Order and to faction fighting. Lacking institutions to assist them, they remained, for the most part, unskilled and untrained.[17]

The few upper-class members of the Catholic community in Toronto were a section of the Family Compact which included the Babys, MacDonalds, Elmsleys and the Catholic wives of prominent figures of the Protestant elite. And it was that Catholic Compact clique which set the values for the lesser orders of society. They married in both the Anglican church and before Catholic clergy to ensure their marriage vows were valid and sacramental in the eyes of the state and their church. In many cases, the compromise was to raise sons as Anglican and daughters as Catholic. Many belonged to the Masonic Order and were resentful of clergy who demanded a strict Catholicism or introduced cumbersome devotions and rituals. Although they tended to be self-centred, utilizing power to enrich themselves, they assisted the progress of the Catholic church through gifts of land or the provision of support in governmental circles. Bishop Macdonell met with them as equals in the Legislative Council and looked to them for his power base in his official connections. They were his right arm in the administration of St. Paul's Church as appointed lay vicars with authority to act on his behalf regardless of whether a priest was there or not, arrangements which earned them the hatred of the Irish.[18] Ultimately the Irish, led by William O'Grady, were pitted against Bishop Macdonell. They seized their church only to have it placed under interdict; O'Grady and other Irish leaders of the revolt were removed and excommunicated. O'Grady joined forces with William Lyon Mackenzie, becoming a central figure in the reform movement, still influential in the political sphere over his former Irish Catholic parishioners. Like Robert Baldwin, O'Grady opposed violent action as a solution to political problems and withdrew himself and his Irish followers from the reform movement prior to the Rebellion of 1837.[19]

In 1834, St. Paul's Church in Cabbagetown served a mission area of 729 square miles which included Whitby, Pickering, Scarborough, Markham, York and Whitebridge. At that time, it had

3,500 members of whom 700 to 800 attended mass at the church. By 1836, the membership increased to 4,644 of whom 2,119 attended mass. In 1838 the mission area was reduced to 240 square miles serving an estimated 1,500 Catholics; however, no figures are available for the proportion of that population which attended services. The reduced area did not necessarily promote any bond between the Tory bishop, Macdonell, and his Irish laity in Toronto,[20] even though he, not O'Grady, was credited with keeping the Irish out of the rebellion. The British government was anxious to retain the continued loyalty of Catholic subjects and welcomed the proposal of additional ecclesiastic supervision in Toronto which had been the centre of the political upheaval.[21] It thereby granted Rome permission to establish a new diocese in Upper Canada, dividing from the diocese of Kingston all that lay west of the District of Newcastle. And in 1842, Michael Power, a Canadian-born Irishman from Halifax, was consecrated bishop of the diocese of Toronto, with Toronto the seat of his see.[22]

During the episcopate of Power, the church began to organize in its traditional mode through the establishment of synods and deaneries. However, Power had become bishop in an era of social and political change. The movement towards democratic representation through the union of the Canadas left him with an uncertain power base and, therefore, he was hesitant to become involved in public disputes which might compromise his office. In fact, he inadvertently gave episcopal approbation to the new public school system by heading it, a system which would later become the antithesis of his church and his ethnic group. He concentrated his efforts on the external signs of episcopal presence by building a cathedral and a palace, structures which left a burden of debt when Power died a martyr to the disease unleashed in the city by the famine Irish.[23]

Before 1847 the city took little notice of the Irish, for they did not disturb the Protestant consensus. The Protestant churches operated or controlled the few charitable institutions which hastened the proselytism of what seemed to be an acculturating group. Certainly there were no strong signs of Irish ethnic or religious proclivities through institutional development. With one church and a school, no religious orders and no longer any press, they posed little threat. The building of St. Michael's Cathedral on the periphery of the city and the voluntarism involved in its construction raised a few eyebrows. As yet the Orange Lodge was a seminal institution, as unpopular with the Protestant elite as it was with Irish Catholics. The city was mildly anti-Catholic, but not particularly anti-Irish. However it, like the church, was ill prepared to deal with the influx of famine Irish after 1847.[24]

III

That migration changed the ethnic nature of Toronto. From a pre-famine estimate of 2,000, by 1851 the Catholics formed 25.8 per cent of the population, or 7,940 of whom over 90 per cent were Irish; and within the Irish national group, Irish Catholics were 70 per cent. By 1860 Catholics increased to 27.1 per cent, or 12,135 of the population. But by 1880, they had fallen to 18.2 per cent, or 15,716. At that time Irish were still 85 per cent of the Catholic population but only 48 per cent of the Irish national group. At the turn of the century, Catholics had fallen to 13.9 per cent 28,994; however the Irish still formed 80 per cent of the Catholic population, but had dropped to 37.9 per cent of the Irish national group.[25] There was very little inter-ethnic conflict in the Catholic community because other ethnic groups were small and unorganized. The German Catholics shared St. Patrick's Church with the Irish; the French, concerned about assimilation, were isolated in a single, ethnic parish; and the Italian population was still too small to form a national parish.[26] Throughout the period the Irish, by sheer numbers, were the Catholics of Toronto. In order to evade the negative Irish stereotype that arose from the disrupting influence of the famine migration on the city, Ulster or Orange immigrants abandoned the old, unified Irish organizations, and often listed themselves on the census as English or Scots. Therefore to be Irish was to be Catholic.

The famine Irish poured into old Cabbagetown, east of Sherbourne Street and south of Winchester, where the substandard housing was cheap, and into the liberties and over the Don where residents were not allowed to vote but also were exempted from paying taxes. In that whole area, peasant culture had survived with its shebeen shops, wakes and wild wedding celebrations. Control measures were exercised by the Irish Brotherhood which guaranteed customary law over that of the civil law of the city. With the abolition of the liberties in 1859 and the continued increase in Irish immigration to 1870, the Irish were forced to expand and their movement was related to certain criteria. In the central core, factories encroached upon living space and, being unskilled labourers, the Irish were compelled to seek housing in proximity to job oportunities. Therefore the boundaries of the Irish ghetto became fluid, if ever they had been fixed, and tenure within old neighbourhoods was often short. It could be said that, not only did the Irish create ghettos, they moved them in the city. Although most of the former areas of concentration became working-class ghettos shared with other ethnics, within them there were pockets that were absolutely Irish. In those circumstances the Irish were segregated by class from the rest of the city and internally by their ethnicity and religion.[27]

In increasing numbers, the Irish pushed into St. Lawrence Ward and the adjacent St. George and St. Andrew wards which culminated in a heavy concentration in the west, particularly around St. Mary's Church erected in 1852 in what had been the old Garrison Reserve. In addition, they moved north into St. Patrick's Ward where St. Patrick's Church was established in 1861. The Irish followed the growth of new industries and railroad yards in the west end of the city. The church accommodated Irish patterns of concentration and established parish nuclei accordingly: St. Helen's, Brockton, 1875; St. Joseph's, Lesleyville, 1878; Our Lady of Lourdes in the northeast, 1886; Holy Rosary in Irishtown, 1892; St. John's in Norway, 1893; St. Cecilia's in the Junction, 1895; and St. Peter's in Seaton Village, 1896. By the turn of the century, the waterfront and the Junction were the most heavily populated areas of Irish concentration but, in advance of the street railway, the Irish had spread throughout the city. [28]

IV

For generations, Irish Catholics retained a peasant life style in Toronto. The lack of any assistance beyond that of their own community resulted in poor housing and improper methods of sanitation, factors which suited a dispersed cottage life as common in Montreal or American cities as in Toronto. The accommodations of those living in lower Cabbagetown, by the wharves and on the Don flats were surrounded by cabbage patches and shared with pigs and chickens; some kept cows in sheds attached to their homes. Those arrangements sustained the famine immigrants. But the central core around Yonge and King streets, particularly Stanley Street, became notorious as an Irish ghetto and was an embarrassment to the city. In that area with its overcrowded, ramshackle buildings, shebeen shops and boardinghouses, Irish society was at its worst. Some immigrants were successful enough to gain employment which allowed them to move into the major and minor areas of Irish concentration where they rented, bought or built homes. But many, with minimal job opportunities, forced to pay rent beyond their means, and with no prospect for future savings, were locked into slum existence. Although economic stratification kept them there, there were the benefits of familiar surroundings, hotels and friends. [29]

Irish girls usually left home in their mid-teens and most were gone by twenty-two. In the later suburban concentrations they tended to stay with their parents to an older age. In the first decades following the famine, many of them became domestic servants, living in the homes of their employers or boarding in lodgings nearby. As the city diversified industrially, they found additional employment opportunities in laundries, bakeries, tailoring establishments, and as dressmakers, shopgirls and waitresses. A number found security by entering the religious orders. Because of the dominance of nuns in the separate school system, the lack of a Catholic hospital until 1892 and few Catholic firms in the city, teaching, nursing and office work was effectively closed to Irish girls.[30]

Generally, Irish Catholic girls worked until they married and then withdrew from the job market. They married between the ages of 19 and 27, with the average age of 23 climbing to 25.4 years by the 1880s. In the early decades after the famine, there was a slight disproportion in the ratio of males to females; but that adjusted with increased immigration. Irish married Irish, often selecting a mate from the same district in the old country. Although Irish females had a high fertility rate which was better in the later decades under improved living conditions, they did not breed like rabbits as has been commonly implied. The average family had 2.5 children for various reasons: high infant mortality rate; transient husbands who frequently abandoned wives; high death rate among heads of household; and late marriage age. During the period of child-rearing, many Irish women took in boarders, usually kin. That raised the average occupancy rate per household from 5.5 to 8.5 people. Irish households were patriarchial, with women deferring to their spouses. However, they managed the economics of the home and, with their children, sought means to supplement the family income. They took in laundry or went back to domestic service, leaving the younger children in the care of older siblings or a grandparent. Their work often became a major element in survival when the husband was unemployed. While the men interacted independently in the shebeen society, Irish wives interacted in the home and in the church with their families, friends and relatives. By age 40, the children were gone and boarders were no longer a necessity to augment income. However, between 50 and 70 years they often reverted to the practice as a source of companionship, or they moved in with their grown children to help with the rearing of a new family.[31]

In a similar fashion, young Irish men who had close family relationships left home between the ages of 18 and 26. They lived in boarding houses and took what jobs they could find to assist the family in raising younger siblings and to contribute towards the purchase of a house. They tended to marry between 22 and 29 years of age, with the average age 26 but increasing to 29.2 by 1880. Most were occupationally stratified in labouring or unskilled trades and depended upon kin or friends to find jobs or housing accommodation. Those that were able worked until aged 70. Property ownership which became more common in the suburbs does not seem to be related to skilled or unskilled employment. It was closely related to the financial assistance received from grown children or from the availability of work for wives. Most elderly widowed males lived with kin or children, selling their homes or utilizing them as generational residences.[32]

V

The famine Irish Catholics arrived in Toronto as pre-industrial peasants whose society was already in the process of change. Much of their peasant culture, agrarian in nature, was destroyed in the famine and, in fact, decades before it. What they were attempting was to preserve and adapt the remainder. Although they lived in specific areas in Toronto, the Irish ghetto went beyond the perimeters of physical borders, for from it they carried mental conceptions that moulded them in a distinctive fashion. Experiences within the Irish milieu dictated a *Weltanschauung*, or world view, and created a selective attitude or "dearcha," an outlook that included perceptions of self, the group, the city and the world. Whether they lived in an area of Irish concentration, returned to it or passed through it, the signs of community were strongly apparent. The church was a central feature in the area and latterly, with rectory, convent, school and hall, became the focus for the parish-oriented group. From those nuclei came the priest as friend and natural leader, the nuns who taught, nursed and begged in the city, and the development of most Irish social and cultural institutions. The familiar steets marked the coming and going of friends and relatives, the journey to school and to work, the rites of passage in life from birth to the grave.[33]

Irish neighbourhoods contained Irish grocery and merchandising shops, bookstores where Irish newspapers were sold, shebeen shops in which the home brew "poteen" could be bought, and hotels where political issues were discussed. In some areas, where no church hall was available, the community banded together to rent a hall for concerts, plays, dances, St. Patrick's Day celebrations, bazaars, Irish nationalist speakers, or for church social, charitable or cultural societies. The activity and interaction within the neighbourhood formed the Irish world. Familiar scenes of the priest carrying the sacrament to the dying, members of the St. Vincent de Paul Society visiting the homes of the poor, beggars, drunks, newsboys, parades, singing, dancing, keening, fighting — saints and sinners together — contributed to the pattern. Continued Irish pride was accentuated while a new, urban identity was born, defined and promoted in conjunction with the church. The urban areas became the centre of a cultural network that spread throughout central Ontario. Those that lived apart, participated in it through parish and kin communication linkages. Outside the neighbourhood, the Irish might have been perceived as alone and isolated; but that was an illusionary perception for they masked their personal, emotional and psychological outlook in an ethno-religious privatism — a mental ghetto.[34]

Many cultural adjustments had to be made before the typical "dearcha" developed which consolidated the Irish Catholic community in Toronto. The famine Irish attempted to preserve and reinterpret the best elements in their declining peasant culture to allow for their survival as a distinct urban group. Additionally, they brought with them a number of defence mechanisms which had evolved as a response to English suppression and brutality, mechanisms that were unacceptable to both the church and the Protestant majority in Toronto. Having been denied the right to practise their religion during penal times, Irish peasants were ignorant of its laws and theology. In that vacuum, older belief patterns and practices re-emerged and melded with traditional Catholicism to form a syncretic vehicle. The belief in changelings and fairies made them appear a superstitious lot. Their fear and reverence for the dead was demonstrated in the extravagant and pagan trappings attached to wakes, wherein the corpse was honoured with drinking, lewd games and fights. Funerals were on a grand scale with horse-drawn glass hearses, keeners, the rental of mourning clothes and the erection of costly grave monuments, practices the Irish Catholics could ill afford.[35] The poverty of the famine Irish immigrants to Toronto was no different than those in other urban centres where, having arrived poor, circumstances kept them poor. Huddling together in overcrowded substandard living conditions was the method for survival of the untrained, unskilled group. Furthermore, family resources were drained by the remittance of money to less fortunate kin left behind in Ireland. In many cases, pauperism became inherent.[36]

For several decades, marriage as the institution for perpetuating family life was under stress. In the pre-famine period, confusion over what constituted a legal marriage initiated the practice of Catholics having their marriages witnessed by an Anglican priest; and uncertainty over which church law applied in mission areas encouraged the practice in Upper Canada. Because of the lack of priests in rural areas, Irish married before Methodist ministers, and the constant movement from rural to urban centres brought a number of Irish who had apostated unwittingly through that practice. Too, the lack of privacy in overcrowded housing and the lack of moral direction by priests had allowed for the continuation of "handfast" marriages, concubinage, abandoned wives and children.[37] The illegitimacy rate was high. In 1858, infants whose parents were unknown or registered without paternity composed 9.53 per 100 births; by 1878 the rate dropped to 7.17, and to 2.94 by 1898. In that last decade, most city parishes reported none; however illegitimate births occured in the central core where most social institutions reported them to the nearby St. Michael's parish.[38]

Alcoholism among the Irish was almost genetic. Alcohol had served as an escape from despair and as a stimulant in the face of a harsh and cold environment. Drinking was institutionalized in the Irish shebeens which sold poteen, manufactured in the Don Basin and as far away as Peterborough and carted to Toronto. Although the shebeen society was an early focus for Irish identity, it also became the centre for gambling, fighting and prostitution. Operating from it were old regional secret societies imported from Ireland, like the "Shamrock." However, because of the minority position of the Irish in Upper Canada, old Irish regional loyalties dissipated and were replaced by ethnic solidarity in the form of the Irish Brotherhood. That vigilante group had its own code and attempted to redress wrongs with violence, inside and outside the Irish community. The highway man, Captain John Fluke, and the notorious pickpocket, John Larney, commonly known as Molly Matches, supposedly worked out of Toronto's shebeen society.[39] Generally, drinking and its associated violence was responsible for a high crime rate among both Irish males and females. In 1863, 58.7 per cent of those arrested in Toronto were Irish, as were the 59.5 per cent incarcerated in the jail. Although not all of those figures represented Irish Catholics, their numbers were high enough to prompt Bishop John Lynch to write a pastoral letter on "The Evils of Wholesale and Improvident Emigration from Ireland." One should realize that, at that time in Toronto, the Irish had little protection from the law. Unlike the urban centres of the United States where the police forces were made up of large numbers of Irish Catholics, Toronto's policemen were Protestant and were accused of arresting Catholics while Protestants might be warned for the same offence. Judges arbitrarily sentenced Irishmen if they were residents of any Irish Catholic area in the city, particularly if they lived in the central core.[40]

A high mortality rate was another problem the Irish of Toronto encountered. An examination of the burial records at St. Michael's and St. Paul's for 1855 indicates that males accounted for 60 per cent of the deaths compared to 40 per cent for females. Of those who died, 39 per cent were under one year of age, 15 per cent had not reached the age of 10 years, and 22 per cent were less than 30 years; the remainder varied to age 70. The number of deaths was lower in June, peaked in July, declined in August and rose again in January and February. Among adults the chief causes of death listed were consumption, bowel complaint (or dysentry), pneumonia, child birth, smallpox, exposure and, in epidemics, typhus and cholera.

Children and infants died from conditions listed as inflammation, teething, croup, scarlet fever, whooping cough, measles, convulsions, bowel complaint, consumption and water on the brain. Most diseases were water-born or communicated through coughing. Confined living, poor personal hygiene, incorrect disposal of food, garbage and human waste, consumption of contaminated water, a faulty diet — all the results of poverty — contributed to the spread of disease.[41] Seen as plague carriers, the famine Irish tended to hide disease from unsympathetic city authorities, augmenting the problem. With minimal change in methods of sanitation and housing, their condition remained static for several decades. Death left widows and orphans for kin to support in a society unequipped to do so. Many, too poor to pay the expenses, were buried in pauper graves. The high rate of early infant deaths and stillborns was probably associated to the poor health of the mothers; but it might possibly be related to the superstitious, peasant belief in changelings. In that concept, sickly or deformed children were left by the Sidhe, or fairie, and therefore were neglected by the mother and buried in cabbage patches.[42]

VI

As labourers, the bulk of the Irish Catholic population formed part of the working class in the city. In the Pre-famine period many found employment in public works and the lumber trade, while others were engaged as labourers in different urban centres, on farms and in the construction of the canals. The small middle sector of Irish which had formed to serve the needs of that population were not accepted as middle class in the city and therefore, with little distinction, were as isolated as the common workers.

It was the building of St. Michael's Cathedral that provided Irish labourers with opportunities for advancement under the direction of the architect, William Thomas. Thomas (although buried as a Protestant in St. James' Cemetery because of some later altercation with the church over the acceptance of his design for St. Michael's steeple) was a Catholic and, in the voluntary manner of the workers he directed, monetarily contributed towards the roofing of the cathedral. More importantly, under him the Irish learned skilled trades which prepared them as building contractors. Forming partnerships, Irish Catholic contractors were utilized in the building program of Catholic churches, schools and social institutions that burgeoned after the arrival of the famine Irish. In a similar fashion, Irish merchants opened up shops to supply the needs of the cathedral and thereby were established to serve the needs of the new immigrant group. From that thrust there evolved a group of prosperous Irish Catholics whose sons entered the professions as doctors, lawyers, dentists, priests and undertakers to service the whole Irish community. [43]

The famine Irish immigrants created a surplus in the labour market of the city and were considered a threat in the belief that they would hire themselves out at cheaper wages than Protestant workers. Within the emerging economic metropolis, they were forced to a peripheral position. As a minority group in the labouring population, they faced the attitudinal standard that "No Irish Need Apply." Many, adopting the old practice of transient employment, left Toronto to find jobs but, unlike past practice, most failed to send money back to assist their families. As a result abandoned wives and children increased the economic strain on the community. The streets were filled with Irish Catholic youths who joined forces as "Street Arabs," becoming newsboys and boot-blacks. In the factories, Irish Catholics were at the mercy of lead hands and foreman — last hired and first fired. [44] As late as 1869 the *Irish Canadian* reported that Irish Catholic immigrants:

> . . . will find out through bitter experience, that whether as a day laborer, an artizan, or parlor-maid, their prospects are damped, their chances are curtailed, and the openings of employment lessened, because of their religion . . . once let fall a hint of your Catholicity, and immediately can be observed a marked change towards you; you are not wanted; your services are not needed; you don't answer the requirements. [45]

The journey to work was harzardous and Irish Catholics worked in isolation from their Protestant counterparts. There were few fights in the work place, for Irish Catholics had developed a new cultural defence mechanism. Ethno-religious privatism dictated that religion, ethnicity, family or politics were not discussed. In that way the mental ghetto encompassed the work place. Violent outbursts between Catholics and Protestants occurred, but they were related specifically to incidents wherein Irish Catholic workers demonstrated publicly their attachment to their religion through parades and to their national heritage by inviting Irish speakers to the city. One of the most notable confrontations was the Jubilee Riots of 1875, when Irish Catholic men, women and children were attacked by an Orange mob. The Irish workers, no longer confined by the strictures of the work place or restrictions of privatism, turned upon their attackers in an outburst of ethno-religious rage and fought back, an emotional catharsis for generational, differential treatment. [46]

The struggle to retain some of the positive and negative aspects of peasant culture delayed the cohesive organization of the Irish Catholic urban community. It was not until the church became the central institution in their lives that survival became a holy cause. Although there had been some sense of Irish pride and ethnic consolidarity in the early Irish community, majority Protestant attitude towards the famine immigrants forced the Irish into a new urban identity in which certain traits stood in the way of rapid progress for the working class. Voluntarism among them, as displayed in the construction of St. Michael's Cathedral, was a positive trait that would be utilized to develop the social institutions to save the group; but self-interest was seemingly looked upon as a tainted thing. Christian forebearance predicated acceptance of their lot and, therefore, generalized urban violence was not considered a justifiable means to bring about change, unless they were under attack for the practice of their religion. Sermons were anti-commercial, anti-work ethic. The church preached that there was no stigma attached to poverty or to failure in the work place and the social realm; degradation arose from failure to maintain morally acceptable standards and values. As a result, there were few social levels among the Irish Catholics — just a general middle-class aspiration.[47]

Although the church provided clerical leaders in the spiritual realm, the Irish needed a lay leadership to direct them in the secular city. In the pre-famine period, journalists like Francis Collins, James King and the ex-priest, William O'Grady, had been genuinely interested in the small Irish community. But their effectiveness as ethnic leaders dissipated because of their quarrels with each other and their conflict with Bishop Macdonell and the Catholic Compact clique. A number of entrepreneurs, like William Bergen, had gained financial success and attained recognition as wardens at St. Paul's Church. But, by making extreme monetary demands for pew rents and by utilizing their positions for private gain, they were ostracized and never gained a leadership role in the impoverished Irish community.[48] From the union of the Canadas to the early 1850s, the Catholic converts, John Elmsley and S.G. Lynn, among a few others, struggled to keep the Catholic community viable during the influx of the famine Irish and the death of Bishop Power. Those men assisted Bishop Armand Charbonnel when he arrived in Toronto in 1850 to reorganize the disrupted diocese. During Charbonnel's tenure, priests began to direct Irish life, a practice which was strengthened under the jurisdiction of Charbonnel's successor, John Lynch, when the priesthood drew numerous candidates from the Irish-Canadian community. Meanwhile, journalists, like Patrick Boyle of the *Irish Canadian* and George Moylan of the *Canadian Freeman*, stirred disputes over support for Thomas D'Arcy McGee, Irish nationalism, the Fenian question, Catholic representation in the political sphere, and lay control of separate schools — issues which divided the Irish community in Toronto. Some men, like Frank Smith and J. O'Donohoe, were successful enough to form part of the "Lace Curtain" Irish clique in the city, but they used the Irish Catholic community for private gain and political preference and thereby lost their trust. It was not until the late 1880s and 1890s that men like J.J. Foy, Senator F. O'Connor, E. O'Keefe, Hugh Ryan, Timothy Anglin, the unionist Daniel O'Donoghue, and Patrick Hynes, who, through their selfless actions, earned respected leadership roles among the ethno-religious group and influence outside it.[49]

VII

Prior to the famine migration there had been nominal pressure on the Irish Catholic community to assimilate. Although they differed on theological principles, there was a strong feeling of camaraderie between the Anglican Bishop John Strachan and Bishop Macdonell. As Compact Torys, both believed in loyalty to the crown and an episcopal form of church government. Certainly, the scattered groups of French, Scottish and Irish Catholics in Upper Canada posed no threat to the position of the Anglican Church, particularly in York. Although the unruly Irish had been responsible for an interdict in 1832, Bishop Macdonell subdued them effectively. The creation of the new diocese of Toronto under the jurisdiction of Michael Power was no cause for alarm because, at that time, the Catholics had one established parish and were burdened with the debt of the cathedral and palace. Having no institutions and few priests, they were viewed as just another small sect. Furthermore, relationships between Catholics and Protestants were open and friendly. Power and Egerton Ryerson cooperated in the establishment of an acceptable public school system. The Anglo-Irish joined together in a single society with their Catholic brethren to celebrate St. Patrick's Day. The Orange Lodge, as yet a benevolent society, had labelled Bishop Macdonell a good and loyal Tory. Granted, there was antagonism between the Irish Catholics and the Orange Lodge, but generally, the influential Protestant community distrusted the secret oaths of the order and resented its introduction of old world hatreds to Toronto. The Maynooth Endowment in 1845, which increased public funds to train priests in Ireland, fomented riots in England but went almost unnoticed in Toronto where "popery" was not yet considered a threat.[50]

With the influx of so many diseased, dirty, poor famine Irish, past traditions in the city ended and were replaced with racial and religious hatreds. Depicted as apes in clothing and labelled with ethnophaulisms, like "Dogan", "Mick", "Tague", the famine Irish precipitated a Protestant crusade that lasted for almost eighty years.[51]

One of the proponents of that crusade was George Brown, a

staunch Presbyterian. He epitomized the Protestant nature of the city and, as the owner and editor of the *Globe*, set the anti-Catholic, anti-Irish tone of the press that lasted decades beyond the time he, personally, had come to terms with both the church and the Irish. Brown equated Catholicism with the worst qualities of the Irish and attacked both in a singularly abusive manner. With vicious statements like ". . . the Irish papists come in swarms on the whole to do us evil . . . . They increase taxation for the poor. They render necessary a strong police . . . ,"[52] Brown encouraged the development of a derogatory stereotype which made Irish and Catholic synonymous. He drew attention to the growing strength of the Roman Catholic church in Toronto, made visible through the rapid increase in churches, convents, social institutions and the separate school system which, in his evaluation, are an extention of papal aggression.[53]

George Brown did not support Egerton Ryerson's policies on what he considered a watered-down religious education in the public school system, but he did agree with Ryerson's attitude towards the Irish and the demands for a separate system of Catholic schools. Ryerson's pronouncements discriminated against the Irish and fuelled the feelings of hatred and the perpetuation of a negative stereotype. Calling them unfortunate, idle paupers filled with vice, Ryerson was convinced that the status of the Irish would improve through public education in common schools. But fearful that a large influx of socially deprived Irish Catholic children might contaminate students in the public institutions, he conceded and allowed the establishment of some separate schools in the city to split the Irish Catholic student body. In his analysis, that part attending common schools would be absorbed gradually; the other, attending poorly financed, separate schools, would become disillusioned with the inferior quality of education in their system and would abandon it in favour of the public one. But Ryerson did not understand that his subjective view and personal efforts to limit the separate system stirred the Irish resolve to perpetuate it. Because of that thrust, Ryerson believed Catholics had no right to complain about the application of the restricted phrase, "No Irish Need Apply"; they had placed themselves at a disadvantage by insisting upon an institution which isolated them in an inferior educational culture and left them ill-prepared to compete in the secular city.[54]

The Orange Lodge was a nativistic organization, vehemently opposed to Roman Catholicism. Its position strengthened after the famine migration for two reasons. Ulster Irish immigrants to Toronto increased its membership, but it also gained credibility among the general Protestant population because the growth of Irish Catholic institutions posed an alien threat to the Protestant consensus. Belonging to many Protestant churches, but not a majority in any one, the members of the Orange Lodge participated in the Protestant crusade of the 1850s and supported the Equal Rights Association and the Protestant Protective Association in the last decades of the century. As an organization, the Orange Lodge held Victorian Toronto in its grasp like the maw of a shark. Through its membership it controlled the militia, the police, civic employment, city hall, ward politics and the work place. In his work on Toronto, J.E. Middleton cited H.C. Hocken, MP and former municipal politician, who boasted:

> From the early days, also, the Orangemen have exerted almost a dominating influence in the municipal administration. Since 1834, when the City was incorporated, only thirteen men who were not Orangemen have been elected to the mayor's office. . . . The administration of the Public School system has, from its inception, been carried on by elected trustees, the majority of whom have been Orangemen. . . . The spirit of this institution has been stamped upon the Public Schools through the men who have directed the primary education of the population either as trustees or officials.[55]

Jointly, the Orange Lodge, Egerton Ryerson and George Brown, though differently motivated, succeeded in turning the city against the Irish Catholics. Their institutional church, their demand for schools and their separate existence were a menace to Protestant conformity. And it was Bishop Charbonnel who embodied the antithesis.

VIII

The former French count and monk, Bishop Armand Charbonnel, arrived in Toronto in 1850 and became a catalyst for change. His spirituality and administrative ability was closely aligned to the mode of Giovanni Maria Mastai-Ferretti, Pope Pius IX and, like him, Charbonnel has been considered a political failure. Nevertheless, giving his family fortune to the Irish poor of Toronto and adopting the lifestyle of a beggar, Charbonnel formed a growing partnership between the church and the Irish laity of his diocese. That partnership culminated in the creation of a strong eccleciastical organization, social development, and a new, urban-based, ethno-religious cultural vehicle, Irish Tridentine Catholicism, which sustained the group as a distinctive entity.

Charbonnel was no stranger to the conditions of the famine Irish, for he had been situated in Montreal on their arrival. Because of illness, he returned to his native France and subsequently was called to Rome to be consecrated Bishop of Toronto. The task appointed him was not an easy one for he spoke English with great difficulty and, as a Frenchman, was considered a foreigner in Toronto. On a return visit to Europe to make further arrangements for his diocese, Charbonnel wrote the following quatrain for the benefit of friends who had never heard of Toronto:

> Venio de Toronto
> Apud Lacum Ontario
> In populo barbaro:
> Benedicamus Domino.[56]

Regardless, on taking charge of his see, Charbonnel quickly set in motion the administrative machinery developed by Power which had fallen into abeyance during the period of interregnum. That included a system of deaneries, a synod of priests, a seminary to train priests, and strict fiscal accountability with the introduction of the dime to pay off the cathedral debt. Above all, when economically feasible, he built new parishes in the city. Ideal was the parish establishment at Clover Hill where, surrounding St. Basil's Church, there developed two colleges, a convent and a school, Church, rectory, convent, school and hall became the standard unit, a focus for the Irish locked out of social interaction in the city. Priests were sent from established parishes to set up mission stations in other areas of the city until financing allowed for the erection a permanent church structure. To reduce the span of control, Charbonnel succeeded in having his one diocese divided to form three: Toronto, Hamilton and London. By 1870, Toronto became an archdiocese with two suffragans, making it the Irish Catholic capital of Ontario.[57]

In conjunction with the centralization of the diocesan communication network, Charbonnel initiated a system of social institutions that continued to expand long beyond his tenure. By utilizing the internal communication linkage available to him, Charbonnel ascertained the needs of his Irish laity and then, through the external framework of the universal church, obtained personnel, funds and models to fulfill them. By 1852 the Sisters of St. Joseph, the Brothers of the Christian School and the Basilian Fathers had come from France, each called for a specific purpose. By the time the Sisters of St. Joseph arrived to assume control of the orphanage on Nelson Street, Charbonnel had already organized the few prominent Catholic laymen in the St. Vincent de Paul Society whose purpose was to serve the poor as friends, not as social observers. It was through the efforts of those two organizations, complemented by the work of Catholic lay women, that a corporate system of Irish Catholic social action began. Beginning simply with outdoor relief for the provision of food, clothing, shelter and human caring, the programs expanded to encompass a total welfare system. Basic needs were never neglected, but methods, such as a savings bank, a fuel cooperative, the distribution of tools to workmen and the establishment of an employment agency, were used to direct Irish Catholics towards means of self-help.

Institutions such as the House of Providence were constructed to give care to the aged, the infirm, the destitute, the sick and the orphans which provided the Sisters with versatility.[58] Bishop Lynch had suggested that the precarious financial position of the Toronto General Hospital might be improved if the domestic management of the hospital was placed under the care of the Sisters. The board of directors declined the offer in the belief that such an arrangement would not ensure the general support of the whole public. The General Hospital faced a period of bankruptcy and its doors were closed for almost a year.[59] It was not until 1893 (after the Sisters of St. Joseph had responded to the request of city officials to nurse diptheria patients in the Isolation Hospital on Broadview Avenue when others refused) that St. Michael's Hospital opened under the auspices of Archbishop John Walsh.

Beyond orphanages and the St. Vincent de Paul Children's Aid Society to protect the religious rights of Irish Catholic children, the orders established the St. Nicholas Home for newsboys and apprentices, Notre Dame des Anges as a boarding home for girls, an agricultural college and an industrial school for boys in trouble with the law, St. Mary's Industrial School for girls and the Refuge of the Good Shepherd to assist with the rehabilitation of wayward women. By the end of the century the church had duplicated or penetrated every proselytizing public institution in the city and offered assistance to all, regardless of religion or ethnicity.[60] Charbonnel had uplifted the spirit of the famine Irish and stirred their voluntary nature. Although the orders he imported to Toronto were French and the St. Vincent de Paul Society initially non-Irish and elitist, the selfless manner in which they and the bishop interacted with the Irish poor filled the people with feelings of self-worth. And in the process, the personnel of religious orders and lay organizations shortly became Irish and working class.

In Charbonnel's evaluation, providing basic human needs was one measure to retain the famine Irish as Catholics; but a system of separate education which encompassed a Catholic philosophy was the method to socialize and secure the future generations. In the face of overt bigotry, Charbonnel fought to attain for the Irish children in Canada West parity with the minority rights of Protestants in Canada East, a goal which pitted him against the Protestant population of the city. And by making use of the legislation in every way he could, Charbonnel advanced his position on behalf of the Irish Catholics. Within the separate system Irish children were sheltered from degradation of their nationality and their religion, even though the journey to school through the city's streets was often hazardous. The academic subjects taught by the Sisters and Brothers were much the same as those offered in the public system. Catechism was utilized to teach Irish children the practice of their religion and good morals. But it had to be related to the urban milieu and in that sphere it was the socializing vehicle employed to teach cleanliness, politeness, obedience, respectful deportment, generosity and group sharing. The pupils learned to uphold their Irish heritage presented by way of a nostalgic and subjective approach to Irish church history, an idealism to which they and their parents responded enthusiastically.[61]

In many cases, children were absent from school because they lacked sufficient clothing or were needed at home; in others, it was because parents were too absorbed in their own misery to care what happened. Under Charbonnel's prompting, the St. Vincent de Paul Society volunteered members to act as the first attendance and truant officers in the city and, with other charitable Catholic agencies, supplied food, clothing and shoes to the children, which helped to alleviate the truancy problem to a degree.[62]

In his struggle to save his flock from absorption into the secular city, Charbonnel perpetuated an Irish Catholic identity. That ethno-religious solidarity often reflected an Irish nationalism which made the Church's position untenable. The Irish press, which had played a role in the creation of a Canadian Irish identity, tended to divide the community and to embroil the church in the politics of Ireland. It was not until the 1890s, when conditions had improved in Ireland, that the church was able to replace the ethnic press with a Catholic one. By that period Irish identity was cohesive enough to abandon ties with the old country.[63]

Similarly, the church had difficulty controlling Irish politics and voting preference. For a decade, Charbonnel tried to convince the Irish that they held the balance of power. However, the Irish wasted their franchise, voting for candidates who promised much but delivered little. Through the Catholic Institute, Charbonnel laid the basis for the organization of the Catholic League in the late 1860s which forced John A. Macdonald's guarantee that religion would not enter federal politics and that Catholics would receive a fair proportion of political preferment. At the provincial level, Archbishop Lynch was able to make accommodation with Oliver Mowat's Liberal government; but it took until the first decade in the twentieth century for the Conservative party to realize that Catholics did in fact hold the balance of power Charbonnel had recognized. J.J. Foy was instrumental in delivering the Irish Catholic vote and, in return, received the promise that religion had no place in Ontario's politics. But, within the Orange city of Toronto, Irish Catholics had no power.[64]

The problems of the Irish labourer were of concern to the church. Its fear of oath-bound, labour organizations, with rituals similar to other secret societies under condemnation by the church, prohibited Irish labourers from joining them. With the rise of the Knights of Labor and Archbishop Lynch's stand on their behalf, Irish Catholics were given the opportunity to join labour unions. The church could not enter the work place; but it controlled the culture Irish Catholic labourers carried into it. They were isolated by ethno-religious privatism but, at the same time, were protected by their silence. The Irish position improved with the arrival of new ethnics and visible minorities who became the new scapegoats in what many labour historians consider an unified working class.[65]

IX

Quite clearly the Irish immigrants who arrived in Toronto after 1848 broke the Protestant consensus. In the view of the city's establishment, those Irish who carried a peasant culture into the urban milieu were an obsolete people and were to be assimilated culturally and religiously to charter group standards. By sheer numbers, they formed the Catholic population of Toronto and the church was committed to act on their behalf. To attend to the immediate needs of an impoverished people, physically, spiritually and intellectually starving, the French Bishop Charbonnel reorganized a diocese that had been in disarray. Through the development of a complex ecclesiastical system, Charbonnel organized the Irish and precipitated the formation of a new cultural vehicle for urban survival, Irish Tridentine Catholicism. It was a mixture of reinterpreted Irish custom and traditional religious practice that took shape in the Irish ghettos of Toronto and was masked in a form of ethno-religious privatism. It spread with the expansion of the urban parish system and through the communication network to all of English-speaking Ontario. Although the Irish Catholics were never fully accepted, they were tolerated eventually and formed another side of Victorian Toronto society — the first ethnic side.

Notes

1. For the city as a demographic parasite see: Patricia Herlihy, "Death in Odessa. A Study of Population Movements in a Nineteenth-Century City," *Journal of Urban History*, vol. 4, no. 4 (August 1978) pp. 417-42. Ethnic obsolesence is described in: Samuel F. Yette, *The Choice: The Issue of Black Survival in America* (New York, 1972), pp. 13-15. For the concept of Hollow Town see: Clifford Geertz, *The Social History of an Indosenian Town* (Cambridge, 1965), p. 4. The city as an animate object is discussed in: Richard G. Fox, *Urban Anthropology. Cities in Their Cultural Settings* (Englewood Cliffs, N.J. 1977), pp. 21-2.

2. Dorothy S. Cross, "The Irish in Montreal, 1867-1896," (M.A., McGill University, 1969) provides a good example of an unified study. The urban nomad is described in: Fox, *Urban Anthropology* pp. 13-14. My concept of ethno-religious privatism is a variation of that presented by S.B. Warner in *The Private City: Philadelphia in Three Periods of its Growth* (Philadelphia, 1971), pp. 3-4. For the evasiveness among Irish see: R. Gabriel, *The Irish And Italians, Ethnics in City and Suburb* (New York, 1980), p. xi.

3. A good example of Irish social disruption can be found in: Michael Cross, "The Shiners War: Social Violence in the Ottawa Valley in the 1830s," *Canadian Historical Review*, 54 (March 1973), pp. 1-26. The model for the "Folk-Urban Continuum" is described in: Robert Redfield, "The Folk Society," *The American Journal of Sociology*, LII, 4 (1947), pp. 306-8. The supposed lack of any articulated tradition of the famine is documented in: John Moir, "The English-Speaking Catholic Church in Canada in the Nineteenth Century," *The Canadian Society of Church History Papers* (1970), p. 10; and T. Suttor, "Catholicism and Secular Culture: Australia and Canada Compared," *Culture* XXX, no. 2 (June 1969), pp. 93-113. For the Irish Catholic as "Nigger" see: Michael Katz, "Irish and Canadian Catholics: A Comparison," *The Canadian Social History Project*, Report no. 4 (1972-73), pp. 35-36.

4. D.H. Akenson in "Ontario: Whatever Happened to the Irish?" D.H. Akenson, ed., *Canadian Papers in Rural History*, III (1982), pp. 204-56, labels the works of a number of authors as racist for their descriptions of Irish life. The attack is directed against: H.C. Pentland, *Labour and Capital in Canada 1650-1860* (Toronto, 1981); K. Duncan, "Irish Famine Immigration and the Social Structure of Canada West," *The Canadian Review of Sociology and Anthropology*, (1965) pp. 19-40; and Cross, "The Shiners War." Furthermore, see D. Akenson, "Review of Paddy's Lament," *Globe and Mail* (August 1982) in which he supports his thesis for the success of the Irish in Canada and labels the work of the author "as evil": Thomas Gallagher, *Paddy's Lament: Ireland 1846-1847. Prelude to Hatred* (New York, 1982).

5. Akenson, "Ontario: Whatever Happened to the Irish?" p. 225.

6. L.A. Johnson, "Land Policy, Population Growth and Social Structure in the Home District, 1793-1851," *Ontario History*, LXIII (1971), pp. 41-60; D. Gagnon, H. Mays, "Historical Demography and Canadian Social History: Families and Land in Peel County, Ontario," *Canadian Historical Review*, 54, no. 1 (March 1973), pp. 27-47.

7. Archdiocese of Toronto Archives (hereafter ATA), Cemetery Records of St. Michael and St. Paul.

8. For cultural consolidation and its transference see: Nicolson, "The Irish Catholics and Social Action in Toronto, 1850-1900," *Studies in History and Politics*, 1, no. 1 (1980), pp. 30-55; and "Ecclesiastical Metropolitanism and the Evolution of the Catholic Archdiocese of Toronto," *Social History*, XVI, no. 29 (1982), pp. 129-56.

9. G. Kealey, *Toronto Workers Respond to Industrial Capitalism 1867-1892* (Toronto, 1980); and "The Orange Order in Toronto: Religious Riot and the Working Class," G. Kealey, P. Warrian, eds., *Essays in Canadian Working Class History* (Toronto, 1976), pp. 13-34.

10. ATA, Bishop Macdonell Papers, Various Church Census 1805 to 1838.

11. To date, little published material is available on this controversial Irish priest. See: Nicolson "The Catholic Church and the Irish," and "William John O'Grady, Rebel Priest" (Unpublished manuscript).

12. ATA, Macdonell Papers, A Return of the Catholic Population for the year 1834.

13. ATA, Pew holders, St. Paul's Church; Records of Burial, St. Paul's Cemetery; Sundry Books and Records for various years.

14. J.O. Plessis to J.N. Provencher, 6 April 1823 reprinted in G.L. Nute, ed., *Documents Relating to Northwest Missions, 1815-1827* (St. Paul's, 1942), p. 398.

15. ATA, Macdonell Papers, A. Macdonell to J.J. Lartrique, 7 April 1821.

16. Ibid., A Macdonell to Major Hillier, 23 March 1823; and to Bishop McEachern, 3 April 1829.

17. ATA, Macdonell Papers, Bishop Power Papers and the Papers of the Interregnum.

18. For identity and function of the Catholic Compact see: Nicolson, "The Catholic Church and the Irish," and "Identifying the Catholic Compact in Early Toronto" (unpublished manuscript).

19. ATA, Macdonell Papers.

20. Ibid. Church Census 1834-1838.

21. ATA, Power Papers, Monsignor Power to Lord Stanley, 27 September 1841.

22. *The Cross*, 23 October 1847.

23. See, in general: ATA, Power Papers.

24. ATA, Macdonell and Power Papers prove the paucity of Catholic institutions.

25. Canada, Board of Registration and Statistics, *Census of The Canadas 1851-52*, I, pp. 30-31, 66-67; *Census of the Canadas 1860-61*, I, pp. 48-49, 128-29; Canada, Department of Agriculture, *Census of Canada 1880-81*, I, pp. 174-75, 276-77; and Canada, Census and Statistics Office, *Fourth Census of Canada, 1901*, I, pp. 218-19, 222-23.

26. There is little written about the early German Catholic population of Toronto. In 1884, at Archbishop John Lynch's request, the Redemptorist, Fathers, German-speaking priests renowned for mission work, took over the administration of St. Patrick's Church where Germans mixed with the predominant Irish. See: ATA, Lynch Papers; and St. Vincent de Paul Minute Books, St. Patrick's Church. It was not until 1982 that a German ethnic parish was constituted. The early French population is examined in: T.R. Maxwell, *The Invisible French. The French in Metropolitan Toronto* (Waterloo, 1977), pp. 19-26. For information about the Italian experience see: J. Zucchi, *The Italian Immigrants of the St. John's Ward, 1875-1915* (Toronto, 1980), pp. 1-43.

27. In particular, see: ATA, Church Census for 1850 to 1860; D.S. Shea, "The Irish Immigrant Adjustment in Toronto: 1840-1860," *Canadian Catholic Historical Association Study Sessions*, no. 39 (1972), pp. 53-60; P.G. Goheen, *Victorian Toronto 1850-1900* (Chicago, 1970); W.B. Hambly, "Cabbage Town," *The York Pioneer Centennial Edition* (1969), pp. 33-44; D. Ward, *Cities and Immigrants, A Geography of Change in Nineteenth Century America* (New York, 1981), pp. 105-124.

28. *Sadlier's Catholic Almanac and Ordo* (New York) for the Years 1864-1900.

29. *Globe*, 25 November 1859, 26 July 1866; *British Colonist*, 23 July 1847; *Toronto Daily Telegram*, 21 May 1866.

30. ATA, Records of Births, Marriages and Deaths. The information was expanded from data gathered through interviews with Irish octogenerians who had vivid recollections of family histories.

31. Ibid.

32. Ibid.

33. Ibid.; ATA, General Correspondence sections in the Charbonnel and Lynch files. In addition, much material was taken from: *The Irish Canadian*; and *The Canadian Freeman*.

34. Ibid.

35. The reinterpretation of older religious practices when Christianity has been removed or restricted is described in: W. Kolarz, *Religions in the Soviet Union* (London, 1961), pp. 101-103. For the nature of the Irish belief patterns see: D. MacManus, *Irish Earth Folk* (New York, 1959); S. Ó Súilleabháin *Irish Wake Amusements* (Dublin, 1967). This cultural pattern was checked through interviews with the descendants of the famine migrants.

36. ATA, Records of St. Vincent de Paul Society, 1851-70.

37. For the difficulties encountered in trying to get the Irish laity to accept the laws of the church regarding marriage, see: ATA, Power Papers, Charbonnel Papers and Lynch Papers.

38. ATA, Sundry Books and Records, Registration of Births for the City Parishes. These figures were checked by the late Rev. J. McGivern, archivist, ATA.

39. City of Toronto Archives, Statistical Report of Crimes Committed in the City of Toronto 1850-1890; ATA, Minutes of the St. Vincent de Paul Society 1865-1880.

40. ATA, Lynch Papers, For the Clergy of Ireland Only, "The Evils of Wholesale and Improvident Emigration from Ireland."

41. ATA, St. Paul's and St. Michael's Record Books, and the Cemetery Records of the Archdiocese of Toronto.

42. Ibid. In addition, oral history gives evidence of child destruction in Toronto and

its environs. A similar incident which occurred in Ireland in this century is noted in: K. Briggs, *A Dictionary of Fairies* (London, 1976) pp. 70-72. For a habit of destroying unfit children to gain insurance, perhaps with the approbation of superstition, see: British Parliamentary Papers, Question 12585 (ed. 2M5) XXX, II, p. 462, cited in J.W. Nicolson, "Factory Inspection and Legislation in Ireland, 1878-1914" (Ph.D. thesis in preparation, University of Guelph).

43. ATA, St. Michael's Cathedral File, various lists of tenders and workers. That William Thomas, "as being a member of that Church" was a Catholic, see: ATA, St. Michael's Papers, William Thomas to the Building Committee of the Catholic Cathedral-Toronto, 5 June 1845.

44. Most of this information was gathered from oral history and the Irish newspapers printed in Toronto during the period.

45. *The Irish Canadian*, 29 September 1869.

46. For a description of the Jubilee Riots see: M.A. Galvin, "The Jubilee Riots Toronto, 1875," *Canadian Catholic Historical Association Report*, no. 26 (1959), pp.

47. See: E. Hoffer, *The True Believer. Thoughts on the Nature of Mass Movement* (New York, 1966), pp. 21, 33.

48. ATA, Macdonell Papers, W.J. O'Grady to Bishop Macdonell, 14 July 1832.

49. See, in general; Nicolson, "The Catholic Church and the Irish."

50. ATA, Macdonell and Power Papers.

51. For a description of the Protestant Crusade see: F.W. Walker, *Catholic Education and Politics in Ontario* (Toronto, 1976).

52. *Globe*, 11 February 1856; and *Canadian Freeman*, August 1869.

53. For the growth of Catholic institutions in Toronto, refer to *Sadlier's Catholic Almanac and Ordo* (1860 to 1880).

54. *Remarks on the New Separate School Agitation by the Chief Superintendent of Education for Upper Canada* (Toronto, 1865).

55. J.E. Middleton, *The Municipality of Toronto. A History* (Toronto, 1923), pp. 788-99.

56. Wm. Perkins Bull, *From Macdonell to McGuigan. A History of the Growth of the Roman Catholic Church in Upper Canada* (Toronto, 1939), p. 278.

57. Nicolson, "Ecclesiastical Metropolitanism."

58. Nicolson, "The Irish Catholics and Social Action in Toronto, 1850-1900."

59. *Globe*, 6 December 1865; *Toronto Leader*, 9 March 1867; and *Canadian Freeman*, 6 August 1868.

60. Nicolson, "The Irish Catholics and Social Action."

61. Nicolson, "Irish Catholic Education in Victorian Toronto: An Ethnic Response to Urban Conformity," paper given for The Canadian-American Urban Development. A Comparative Urban History Conference, University of Guelph, August 1982.

62. Ibid.

63. Nicolson, "The Catholic Church and the Irish."

64. Ibid.

65. Nicolson, "Six Days Shalt Thou Labour: The Catholic Church and the Irish Worker in Victorian Toronto," paper prepared for the Canadian Historical Association Conference, Vancouver, June 1983.

The Blacks in Toronto

Dan Hill

The white man first became aware of the site of Toronto — an Indian name usually interpreted as "meeting place" — when Etienne Brûlé, led by Indian scouts to the mouth of the Humber River in 1615, looked out over a sweeping tree-lined bay sheltered from the open waters of Lake Ontario. Blacks arrived nearly two centuries later, in 1793, as slaves and servants to British officials and officers charged with building a town that would become the permanent capital of Upper Canada.

When the British party led by the first provincial governor, John Graves Simcoe, surveyed the site from the bay, it was almost in its original natural state. Before Simcoe's arrival, the British authorities had purchased the area from the Mississauga Indians. Simcoe decided the splendid harbour, distant from the United States frontier, was well suited for a military and naval base to meet the threat of invasion from the south. He set up his governor's "mansion" — a series of tents — on the lakeshore near the present foot of downtown Toronto, and renamed the place in honour of the Duke of York, son of George III. Work then got under way to build dwellings along the shore and a building where the government and legislature could meet.

Black history in Toronto, then, originates with the Town of York in 1793. The first Black residents aided their masters in the mundane and demanding labours required to establish a principal town on virgin land. By 1797, the year after Simcoe returned to England leaving his Inspector-General, Peter Russell, to administer the new province, the population of York was 241, and in 1800 it was 403. The first brick house was built in 1810. York grew slowly until after the War of 1812, when a trickle of immigration, primarily from the British Isles, grew to a flood.

In 1814, York's population was just under 1,000. It was incorporated as a town in 1817 and ten years later, in spite of what turned out to be its most dominant natural feature after the bay — muddy streets — the population was 1,800. In the 1830s, York mushroomed in size and importance and in 1834, with a population of 9,000, it was incorporated as a city and its original name, Toronto, was restored. It was the third-largest city on the Great Lakes, after Rochester and Buffalo, cities it would later outgrow, and the corresponding boom in industry, commerce and finance created a voracious demand for skilled tradesmen and labourers and opportunities for merchants and other businessmen.

The time was ripe then for the first wave of Black immigrants. Word filtered into the American states that there was work to be had in a growing new frontier town. For Black freedmen it was a journey within easy reach, and for escaped slaves it was far enough from the border to be out of reach of their former masters. Toronto, the message went out, was free, safe, and a place where a person could live and prosper. In time, it would be a major haven for runaway American slaves.

Among the early Black residents in Toronto were the slaves of some of the most important men in the province: Peter Russell, who held positions in the Executive and Legislative Councils and then became administrator of Upper Canada; Secretary William Jarvis, and Colonel James Gray, Upper Canada's first Solicitor General — these and many other distinguished persons were slave owners. Russell is said to have brought his slaves with him from England.

Fifteen Blacks were counted in York in 1799, with no distinction between freedmen and slaves. In the same year, a free Black, Peter Long, and ten members of his family lived east of the Don River outside the town limits.[1] The first Black businessmen were two contractors, Jack Mosee and William Willis, who "undertook to open a road [in 1799] from Yonge Street, York, westward through 'the Pinery'; and although at first the senior surveyor of the province found the road too narrow and improperly cleared, in time it was completed satisfactorily."[2]

In 1802, eighteen free Blacks were living in York, including six children. Several Blacks from York fought in the War of 1812, including Sam Edwards, a member of Captain Runchey's Coloured

Corps and Solomon Albert, a gardener, who served earlier as a private in the 10th Regiment.

In 1837 there were at least fifty families of Black refugees settled in Toronto. Many were from Virginia where they had been engaged primarily in service occupations, such as waiters, barbers and cooks. Others were tradesmen — blacksmiths, carpenters, painters and shoemakers — who brought sufficient means to start small businesses and buy homes. They built churches and established benevolent societies and fraternal organizations. William Lyon Mackenzie remarked about the affluence of some of these early Black families during a visit to Philadelphia in 1832:

> They speak of equality in this country [the U.S.], but it is in Upper Canada that it can be seen in all its glory. There is a man of colour, a barber and hairdresser in our town of York, named Butler; he is married to a coloured woman and they are respectable, well behaved people in their line, and punctual in their dealings; they have, of course, a black family and (hear it, ye slave-trading, equal rights and independence people) they keep white men and women servants from Europe to wait upon them and their black children. This is turning the table on the Southerons, and fairly balancing accounts with the ebony-hearted slave-holders.[3]

W.H. Edwards also operated a successful barbershop at 102 and then 77 King Street as early as 1839 where he had rooms set apart for ladies and children for perfuming and barbering. He advertised that he used, "Vegetable Extract, for Renovating and Beautifying the Hair, cleansing it from all Dandruff, Dust, etc. and giving it a beautiful glossy appearance without the slightest injury to the Hair or Skin."[4] Early accounts also referred to Thornton Blackburn as the town's first cab man and Richard Gray, another Black, as one of the early storekeepers.

Probably the most successful Black businessman in Toronto was Wilson Ruffin Abbott. Born in Richmond, Virginia, in 1801 of free parents, he was apprenticed to a carpenter but ran away from home at fifteen and went to Alabama where he worked in a hotel. He later worked as a steward on a Mississippi steamboat where he had an accident that took a fortunate turn. Ellen Toyer, a Black maid travelling on the same boat, saw a cord of wood fall on Abbott. She nursed him back to health during the voyage. Abbott married Ellen Toyer and they settled down in Mobile, Alabama, where he opened a general provisions store. His wife taught him to read and write, but Abbott had natural mathematical ability and could calculate large sums mentally. Abbott was successful in his business and he was known to help slaves purchase their freedom. His business ability, combined with activities on behalf of the city's slaves, eventually angered local whites. The city council passed an ordinance requiring all free Blacks to produce bonds signed by two white men as evidence of good behaviour and to wear badges showing they were under bond. Incensed by the city's action, Abbott refused to comply with the ordinance. He then received an anonymous letter warning him of a plot to attack and destroy his store and advising him to leave the city immediately. Abbott, believing the information to be reliable, withdrew his money from the bank, put his wife and children on a steamer for New Orleans and followed the next day. His store was ransacked. He never returned to Mobile but did attempt, without success, to get a settlement for his property.

Abbott moved with his family to New York, but "finding the feelings toward coloured men no better in the North," he decided to settle in Toronto, arriving in 1835. In 1837, when the brief rebellion led by William Lyon Mackenzie broke out, Abbott along with other Toronto Blacks took part in the defence of the city as one of Captain Fuller's Company of Volunteers.[5]

Abbott started in business as a tobacconist but when that enterprise failed he turned his energies to real estate. He quickly prospered in buying and renting houses, warehouses and business offices and by 1875 he owned over seventy-five properties in Toronto, Hamilton, Dundas and Owen Sound. As his fortunes grew, Abbott participated in community life and became active in the Coloured Wesleyan Church, the Anti-Slavery Society of Canada and in the political life of St. Patrick's Ward, where he lived. Ellen Toyer Abbott founded the Queen Victoria Benevolent Society which provided relief to the Black refugees who were entering the city in large numbers.

The Abbotts raised a family of five daughters and four sons, including Anderson Ruffin Abbott who became Canada's first native-born Black medical doctor and a surgeon for the Union Army during the American Civil War. For a short period the Abbott family moved to the Elgin Settlement near Chatham in order to give the children a classical education at the famous Buxton Mission School. The elder Abbott died in 1876 at the age of seventy-five and was buried on a hillside in the Necropolis, overlooking the Don Valley.

Practice of the Baptist faith began in Toronto in 1826 when a dozen slaves who had fled to freedom in Canada met on the shore of Toronto Bay and prayed. Elder Washington Christian, a native of Virginia who came to Toronto in 1825, organized the Black worshippers into a congregation which became the First Baptist Church. Christian had been ordained in the Abyssinia Baptist Church of New

York in 1882 and heeded the call to serve the refugees in Canada West. He established Baptist churches in Toronto, St. Catharines and Hamilton, and toward the end of his career he pastored in the town of Niagara.

Christian was a firebrand preacher with a vivid style that drew large crowds of followers. One demonstration of his popularity is given in a description of a Sunday service in Whitby in 1837. News had spread that Elder Christian would be preaching at 10 a.m. Worshippers assembled hours in advance. Two "emergency" ministers had to be called upon to address the large numbers who thronged outside the packed church. "While he was preaching," a witness reported, "every eye in the house was fixed upon him and while truth fell from his lips it reached many hearts and suffused many eyes with tears."[6]

The Toronto Baptists, worshipping at first outdoors where the Toronto docks are now located, grew in number until, in 1827, they leased the St. George's Masonic Lodge for Sunday meetings. Noting the significance of this Baptist group, historian John Ross Robertson stated: "A few coloured people sixty years ago by organizing themselves into a Baptist Church, stimulated a few white people that attended their services to start out for themselves; from the latter, the old Bond Street church originated and from that the present Jarvis Street edifice started."[7]

From 1834 to 1841, services of the First Baptist Church were held in a building on Richmond Street and for a number of years the church continued to grow and increase in membership and influence. Late in 1841, the congregation built a frame structure on the northeastern corner of Victoria and Queen streets on a lot donated by the family of Squires McCutcheon. After the new church was built in 1843, Elder Christian left for Jamaica and returned in 1845 with funds obtained from Baptist colleagues to pay off the mortgage. The First Baptist Church has the distinction of being Toronto's oldest Black institution and is situated today at D'Arcy and Huron streets.

Blacks and whites worshipped together in many of the city's churches. James G. Birney, a white American visiting in Toronto during the summer of 1837, gave an illuminating account of Toronto Sunday worship:

> On Sunday I attended, in the morning the "English (Episcopal) Church". I saw here *several colored people sitting promiscuously with the whites*. In the afternoon I went to a Baptist Church, the pastor of which is Mr. Christian, a colored man, a native of Virginia, and formerly a Slave. The Congregation, which was larger than the building could well accommodate, was composed of about an equal number of whites and colored

persons. There was no distinction in seats, nor any, the least recognition, so far as I could discern, of a difference made by complexion or any other cause. There is a considerable number of the members of the Church that are whites. I never saw a better looking, or a more orderly Congregation assembled. In their persons they were neat — in their attention to the services decorous and exemplary.[8]

Birney commented further that any Black "of good health and steady conduct" could succeed in Toronto and Upper Canada, since the laws were just and impartially administered without regard to race.

In 1840, three years after Birney's visit, a Toronto census showed a total of 518 Blacks, most of whom were Baptist. Eighty-six family heads indicated they were Baptist, 47 Methodist, 4 Church of England, 2 Roman Catholic and 1 Presbyterian.

Several other Black churches appeared between 1830 and 1847. Property situated on Richmond Street near York was purchased for £125 from John Cawthra and James Leslie on July 7, 1838 and deeded to W.R. Abbott and two other Blacks who were considered founders of the Coloured Wesleyan Methodist Church of Toronto. Starting with a congregation of forty, the Coloured Wesleyan movement seems to have arisen from the indignation of some of its original members concerning the city's white Wesleyans who were in fellowship and union with pro-slavery churches in the South. By 1850, the Coloured Wesleyans claimed over one hundred members, and the church continued to function until 1875 when the death of many members and the loss of others to the United States brought an end to the Coloured Wesleyan movement.

The African Methodist Episcopal (AME) Church — a branch of the American denomination founded in Philadelphia in 1796 — was formed in Toronto in 1833 with a church on Richmond Street, east of York Street. A few years later a split developed when some members, wishing to drop the American connection in favour of a closer identification with British ideals and government, established the British Methodist Episcopal (BME) Church in 1844. There was also a practical reason for the British identification. Newly arrived Blacks, mostly fugitives, fel they would be safer from American slave hunters, who frequently roamed Canada, if they had a church with a British name that was serving British subjects.

The Toronto AME congregation numbered 128 persons in 1851 and by 1852 at its yearly conference, it was the third-largest of six reporting districts, including Sunday School classes of fifty pupils and six teachers. Over the years the congregation had several downtown locations on Elizabeth, Sayer and Elm streets, and finally moved to its present address on Soho Street.

Birney's view of "decorous and exemplary services" in Black churches was not shared by all observers. In the 1850s, a biting criticism of Toronto's Black churches and their ministers was made by Rev. Samuel Ringold Ward, a former slave, a Congregational minister and journalist. He castigated the AME church in the following bitter description:

> Should you come here and go to the Bethel Church, African Methodist, up street and hear a man named Taylor harangue his audience in what he calls a sermon; should you listen to his disgusting, abusive and indecent language and witness his semi-theatrical gestures and should you see a large number of colored people of this city if not a majority of them, seemingly approving if not admiring it, you would join me in saying that such things bedarken our prospects.[9]

Despite Ward's gloomy prediction, Black churches thrived between 1840 and 1860. The leaders of the community recognized the strong allegiance of the refugees to the Black Baptist and Methodist churches in the city — denominations familiar to them during their former slave days. But the city's Blacks noted, as well, that the major support in terms of teachers, missionaries and material resources for the newly arrived Blacks was coming not from Baptists and Methodists, but from the Presbyterians, Congregationalists and Anglicans. An article in the November 10, 1855 issue of the *Provincial Freeman* commented:

> It is a fact that the colored people of Canada are almost entirely of the Baptist or Methodist persuasion and nearly all the teachers sent among them have been either Presbyterian or Congregationalists. No one would wonder at their failure since Black people have conscientious conviction of their duty as well as white ones. We thank our Presbyterian and Congregationalist friends for what they intended to do for us. They meant well! But we must admonish our Baptist and Methodist friends, that they are sadly in fault since they neglected their duty and done but little or nothing for us, when they have been earnestly entreated to do something; nor are our "Free Mission Baptists" friends to be excused, in this case.

In time a decided drift would appear, especially among affluent church members who began to feel that Black churches impeded the goal of integration into the city's institutions. The split in the AME

Church and the ultimate demise of the Coloured Wesleyans prompted W.R. Abbott and others to join St. George the Martyr Anglican
Church on John Street in later years.

The earliest wave of black refugees was getting established by
the 1840s. They had built churches, added their number to the
growing trades and business class, provided a new source of unskilled labour, and had begun to settle in the city's west end. Several
Toronto city directories and private surveys made during the 1840s
provided breakdowns — not always in agreement — of the number
of Blacks, their residence and occupations during this period. Frequently, however, Blacks were listed as white, or whites as Black,
and at times some were not listed at all, as in the case of W.R. Abbott and several others. Nevertheless, a general pattern of Black
socioeconomic development does emerge from early records.

The survey of 1840 enumerating 528 Blacks showed that the
largest single occupational group was unskilled labour, but an equal
number of Blacks were occupied in skilled trades or private business:

Cook	6	Mason	1	Shoemaker	2
Baker	2	Seamstress	1	Hair Dresser	3
Plasterer	3	House Painter	3	Cordwainer	5
Cooper	2	Barber	4	Tobacconist	4
Inn Keeper	2	Musician	2	Grocer	4
Labourer	73	Carter	3	Carpenter	13
Tailor	2	Dyer	1	Blacksmith	5
Tanner	1	Hatter	1	Widow	10
Pauper	1	Baptist Minister	2	Retired from business	3

Unskilled, 73; Skilled, 60; Businessmen, 13; Others, 13. Total, 159.[10]

Another survey was conducted in 1841 at the request of Bishop
Strachan. It was carried out by a young Black, Peter Gallego, a stu-
dent at Upper Canada College who later graduated from the
University of Toronto and became active in defending the rights of
Blacks. Gallego's survey found 525 Blacks in Toronto. The majority
were labourers, but Gallego found there were also Black carpenters,
shoemakers, grocers, tailors and masons working in the city.
Gallego also provided details on a number of prominent Blacks. Mr.
Ross, a carpenter, owned "200 acres in the Gore of Toronto . . .
more than half under good cultivation, with extensive buildings,
plenty of fine stock, besides several little houses in the town."[11] He
reported that Abbott owned and rented five or six houses and that a
Mr. Lafferty, a cart driver, also owned properties on King Street.

One of the wealthiest Blacks in Toronto during the 1840s was

James Mink, owner of the Mansion Inn and Livery on Adelaide Street. Mink was born in Upper Canada. His parents were brought as slaves from New York with the Herkimers, a Loyalist family that settled in the Kingston area around 1800. He was the eldest of eleven children and was described in the *Anti-Slavery Reporter* of 1858 as "a fine example physically of a pure Black man; in countenance good humored, open and sensible, stout in figure and inclined to obesity."

Mink opened additional stables at 6-7 Teraulay Street and on Queen Street. His stage coaches, carrying passengers and the mails, ran from Toronto to Kingston where his brother George operated a similar service. For many years Mink's livery stables and carriage services were used extensively by the city council. Minutes of council meetings record numerous instances of payments to Mink, including one entry on February 20, 1854, when seven accounts for carriage hire were presented for payment approval. One account was for the use of Mink's vehicles at "the swearing in of the mayor." On other occasions Mink hitched up four-horse teams and went to Kingston for prisoners, generally at a cost to the city of £32, 10s.

Mink appeared before council frequently to petition for services and amendments to existing cab laws. It appears that Mink was in favour at city hall, as his Mansion House was used as a polling place in the St. James Ward for municipal elections in January 1847 and 1848.

Numerous stories are told of Mink's eccentricities. He had difficulty marrying off his daughter, Minnie, so he offered $10,000 for a "respectable white husband." A local cabman from Yorkshire, James Andrews, married Minnie, took her to the United States supposedly for a honeymoon, and promptly sold her into slavery. Months later Mink discovered his daughter's plight and paid considerably more than his original sum for her return to Canada. The Grand Trunk Railway is said to have broken up Mink's stage lines, causing him to lose the greater part of his fortune. He retired to a mansion in Richmond Hill and little was heard of him thereafter.

Although the Blacks constituted a new refugee class settled primarily in a working-class area, the community seemed to be neither indigent nor a drain on the public purse. Earlier, in 1837, James Birney had observed that the city's Blacks were "exempt from pauperism, from intemperance and from the grosser forms of vice . . . . The gentlemen from whom I had this testimony more especially were of the radical party in politics, and as such were opposed by the colored people generally who belong to the Government party. The testimony therefore, is the more valuable."[12]

John Dunn, Receiver General for Upper Canada at the time, stated in a letter to an American abolitionist: "Negroes ask for charity less than any other group, and seem generally prosperous and industrious.''[13] In Kohl's *Travels in Canada*, an old man named Robertson, "while complaining that his fellow Negroes would not help him, [said] that there were of Negroes who were well off not a few in Toronto.''[14] Later, the writer Benjamin Drew observed while travelling through Upper Canada that most Toronto Blacks owned their own homes, and some had acquired valuable property.[15]

The Toronto City and Home District Directory of 1846-47, published by George Brown of the *Globe*, lists 36 labourers; 34 skilled tradesmen (e.g., shoemakers, carpenters, waiters, tailors, barbers and bricklayers); six proprietor-businessmen, including three inn-keepers and restaurant owners, one tobacconist and two store-keepers; a miscellaneous group of five including two ministers, a cabman, one sailor and a teamster. Some of the Black-owned restau-rants were: Rescue Inn, Prince Albert Recess, Tontine Coffee House and Epicurian Recess.[16]

In an analysis of the early distribution of Blacks in Toronto, Professor F.H. Armstrong states:

> How can one explain this population distribution? Leaving out those Negroes connected with what might be called down-town businesses on King Street (10 in all) nearly all the rest lived in two areas: one running north from York (55 listed), and the other around Church/Queen East/Victoria (9 listed). These areas do not correspond entirely to the less affluent sections of the city: some of the most thickly populated poorer areas, such as Stanley Street, had no Negro inhabitants. Aside from business reasons one obvious explanation is the location of the churches. We have already noted that a third of the Negroes in the east probably lived near the Baptist church, and the Negro population on York Street, plus two on Adelaide Street West, may have located for convenience near the African Methodist Church, which had been built on Richmond, just east of York, about 1833 . . . .[17]

City directories from the 1840s onward show most of the Blacks located farther west of Yonge Street, on Elizabeth, Chestnut, Sayer and Teraulay streets and Centre Avenue, between the present University Avenue and Yonge Street. (The area is to the north of the present city hall; some of the streets have disappeared.)

The Queen Victoria Benevolent Society was established by the Black women of the city (led by Mrs. Ellen Abbott) to assist refugees in adjusting to their new milieu.

The *Globe* of December 11, 1847, printed a letter sent to the

Honourable W. Badgely, Attorney General of Canada East, by W.R. Abbott and forty-five other Blacks to thank him for his assistance to American abolitionists seeking support in Canada:

> We the undersigned coloured citizens of Toronto and vicinity, loyal and dutiful subjects of Her Majesty's just and powerful government, take pleasure in availing ourselves of this opportunity to express to you our sincere thanks for the courteous and Christian-like manner in which you have recently received our late kind and worthy friend, the Rev. Samuel Young of New York, who is known to have been deeply interested in the protection and welfare of our afflicted brethren in the U.S.A. especially as evinced in the case of the innocent and grossly injured and persecuted man who has lately found his way to this asylum, from the midst of republican despotism and slavery.
>
> (Signed) W.R. Abbott and 45 others)

There are records of Americans kidnapping former slaves and of racial discrimination in Toronto during the 1840s. Peter Gallego expressed concern about American slave-owners who were tracking their "property" into Canada in the hope of kidnapping or having them extradited. A report appeared in the *Toronto Patriot* of July 3, 1840, that:

> Two persons, Irishmen we believe by birth, but Yankeefied by habit, were charged on Thursday last, before Aldermen Gurnett and King, with an attempt to kidnap a coloured man whom they asserted to be their slave, and with drawing bowie knives on another person.
>
> The parties after being suitably reprimanded by the sitting Aldermen for the brutal and cowardly practice of carrying bowie knives, and made aware that under Monarchical Institutions and British Laws, there existed no excuse for wearing such weapons, were severally fined Five Pounds, and held to bail for their future good conduct.

The community reacted to kidnapping attempts by forming vigilance committees and publishing notices warning all newcomers that slave-owners had their agents in the city. In the meantime, Gallego continued to be active, writing to the Queen and arguing that it would be wrong to extradite runaway slaves on criminal charges since they would not obtain a fair trial or justice in American courts. He also protested against the presence in Canada of Americans who, he claimed, frequently brought their racial prejudice with them.

Indeed, Gallego faced some of these difficulties himself. While making a voyage between Toronto and Kingston, he was told to stay out of the captain's dining room. Defiantly he entered and was attacked by the Captain whom he knocked down. He then proceeded, undisturbed, to eat his meal. When the ship reached Kingston the Captain charged Gallego with assault and Gallego, in turn, charged the captain with denying him his natural rights. The case went to court where both were fined, Gallego £5 and the captain £20.[18] By 1841 Gallego had concluded that Blacks stood a better chance in the West Indies and he campaigned, unsuccessfully, for Canadian Blacks to move there. He left Toronto shortly thereafter, presumably to settle in the West Indies.

The indefatigable W.R. Abbott appeared before city council on numerous occasions, primarily concerning business matters, such as the paving of streets and permission to build cellars and obtain gas lights. However, in July 1840 he led a major deputation to city council on a matter concerning the welfare of the Black community. Abbott and other citizens had become weary of white American actors coming to Toronto and performing plays and skits that ridiculed Black people. They also objected to circuses and "freak shows" that featured Blacks. Despite the apparent harmony between the races in Toronto, there is some indication that such American theatrical and musical groups, using so-called Black dialect and caricatures, were popular, as noted in the *British Colonist*:

> The following is taken from the *Hamilton Express*: "The two White Negro boys, which were exhibited here during the week are great natural curiosities, and attracted much attention during their stay. They are perfectly white, with Negro features, white wooly heads, hazel sleepy eyes, and are the offspring of black parents. They are six and eight years old, and afford much amusement by the manner in which they dance and sing à la Jim Crow." They are now exhibiting in Toronto.[19]

Abbott and his colleagues argued that these performances caused the Black population "much heart burning and lead occasionally to violence." The petition included the signatures of practically all the city's fledgling Black business community as well as that of George Brown: fifteen in all.

Council's first reaction was that it had no authority to prevent such performances. However, the following month the city enacted a by-law providing for licensing of travelling theatrical groups and circuses. The protesting deputations and petitions became a yearly pattern. There is no record of council's response to them until July 1843, when the mayor, with council backing, refused to let a travelling circus perform in Toronto without a guarantee that it would not sing "Negro songs" or perform acts that would hurt the feelings of "the gentlemen of colour." Whereupon one Toronto citizen complained that the mayor had not stopped the Orangemen from walking and parading, which would have "gratified a more respectable and larger portion of the community."[20]

During the 1850s the second wave of refugees came into the city, swelling the existing Black population to approximately one thousand. This influx was unquestionably related to the passage in the United States of the Fugitive Sale Act in September 1850.

On September 10, 1851, an historic convention was held in the newly built St. Lawrence Hall. The North American Convention of Colored Freemen, whose leaders included H.C. Bibb, Josiah Henson and J.T. Fisher, having debated the feasibility of meeting in a northern city or in the Windsor area, decided to gather in Toronto. The convention leaders felt Toronto was the safest place for such a meeting. Hundreds of colored freedmen converged on the city from the northern United States and England. The convention resolved to encourage American slaves to enter Canada instead of going to Africa, since Canada was the best place to direct anti-slavery activity. After discussing the problems of resettlement in Ontario particularly, the convention leaders stated "that the British government was the most favourable in the civilized world to the people of colour and was thereby entitled to the confidence of the Convention."[21]

Blacks were concentrating in the southernmost cities and towns of the province and by 1851 there were at least thirty-five thousand refugees in Canada West. The *Colonist* of June 17, 1852, noted that every boat arriving in Toronto harbour from the United States seemed to carry "several fugitive slaves, men, women and children as passengers." Clearly apprehensive about the influx of Blacks, the *Colonist* later commented:

> Large numbers of slaves continue to escape into Canada daily from the United States. One of the Detroit papers tells us that on the 15th instant no less than eighteen of them crossed the river into Canada. We fear they are coming rather too fast for the good of the Province. People may talk about the horrors of slavery as much as they choose; but fugitive slaves are by no means a desirable class of immigrants for Canada, especially when they come in great numbers.[22]

The *Provincial Freeman* replied in militant fashion, attacking the *Colonist* for dishonouring the numerous Blacks who had succeeded in their adopted country, and noting that there were no objections to poorer European immigrants who had yet to make their contribution to the welfare of the province. Nevertheless, the *Colonist* received support from Colonel Bruce, a member of Parliament for Essex, who introduced a bill in the provincial legislature to impose a tax on the head of every fugitive slave coming into the province. The bill did not receive public approval and failed to reach third reading.

Perhaps the best reply to the *Colonist* and Colonel Bruce came from crime statistics for the period. In the mid-1850s Toronto had a population of about 50,000, of whom 1,200 or so were Black. Chief of Police Samuel Sherwood reported a lower crime rate for Blacks than for whites. In 1856, 5,346 persons were arrested by the police in Toronto and of these only 78 — 70 males and 8 females — were Black.[23]

In 1854, writing in the *Provincial Freeman*, W.P. Newman observed:

> The accession to our numbers have been great during the winter past, at this, and other points west of us. Nearly all who have joined us have been directly from the south, fugitive slave bill and bloodhounds to the contrary notwithstanding. Those who have reached this point have been mostly from the "Old Dominion" and I assure you that some of them are not only "the dare-devils of the South" but also the choice sons and daughters of Virginia's best blood.[24]

Bounty hunters continued to operate in Toronto, searching for runaway slaves. "Negro vagabonds," through subterfuge and coercion, sought financial gain by preying on the fugitives. Starting on March 24, 1855, the *Provincial Freeman* printed the following warning in each edition:

> CAUTION
>
> From information received from reliable sources, we learn that parties are at present in Toronto endeavouring to induce coloured persons to go to the States in their employ as servants. From the character of the propositions, there is reason to believe 'foul play' is intended. Possibly that Constable Pope's designs on the fugitive and others are being carried out.
>
> Individuals have proposed to women to go to Detroit to live in their service, and another party under circumstances of great suspicion to a boy, to go as far south as Philadelphia. We say to our people, listen to no flattering proposals of the sort. You are in Canada, and let no misplaced confidence in this or the other smooth-tongued Yankee, or British subject either, who may be mercenary enough to ensnare you into bondage by collusion with kidnappers in the States, deprive you of your liberty.

Because of the favourable social atmosphere in Toronto,

Newman wrote, "Here there is no difference made in public houses, steamboats, railroad cars, schools, colleges, churches, ministerial platforms, and government offices. There is no doubt some prejudice here, but those who have it are ashamed to show it. This is at least true of Toronto."[25]

S.R. Ward, an editor of the *Provincial Freeman*, commented frequently on the relatively secure economic position of Toronto's fugitive slaves as well as on the lack of serious racial problems in the city. He was particularly satisfied that there were no Black schools (which were developing in other areas of the province) and that churches and other institutions were open to all without regard to colour. "If we are asked how it [racial equality] affects them," Ward said, "we answer that a more intelligent, enterprising and independent class of coloured people, we have yet to see."[26]

Nevertheless, early Black settlers confessed some uneasiness about the newcomers, fearing that their social and economic position would be jeopardized by the influx of refugees and that all their past efforts to gain public sentiment and good will for their small community might be wasted. Despite these concerns, the established Black community continued to assist the refugee group. In 1856 the Liberating Association, established "to assist the weary and worn out fugitive that may reach our shore," reported that Blacks were coming in steadily at the rate of "nine, seven, two" at a time. Incoming Blacks were also assisted by the Society for the Protection of Refugees, the Ladies Coloured Fugitive Association, the Ladies Freedman's Aid Society, and church groups. The annual report of the Toronto Ladies' Association for the Relief of Destitute Colored Fugitives for 1853-55 stated:

> During the past inclement winter, much suffering was alleviated, and many cases of extreme hardship prevented. Throughout the year, the committee continued to observe the practice of appointing weekly visitors to examine into the truth of every statement made by applicants for aid. In this way between two and three hundred cases have been attended to, each receiving more or less, according to their circumstances."[27]

How much money was disbursed during the year is not stated: the amount of subscriptions and donations for the year was a little more than £160.

The major centre for anti-slavery activities and community meetings throughout the 1850s and 1860s was the St. Lawrence Hall (newly built in 1850), which the Toronto city council made available without cost to groups working in behalf of the city's new Black population. Benefits, recitals and concerts were held featuring noted abolitionists, including Frederick Douglass.

The Toronto Anti-Slavery Society was formed on Feburary 26,

1851, with George Brown of the *Globe* as one of its founding members. The *Globe* reported: "The largest and most enthusiastic meeting we have ever seen in Toronto was held in the City Hall last night. His Worship the Mayor in the chair . . . . The meeting was called to enable the citizens of Toronto to enter their protest against the manifold and unspeakable iniquities of slavery."[28]

The main function of the Anti-Slavery Society was to assist the numerous Blacks who were drifting into the city, destitute, dazed and disoriented from the weeks and months spent in planning and executing their escape. The society was dedicated to caring for the fugitives, obtaining educational and employment opportunities and advancing their well-being.

At this inaugural meeting, the society had the support of some of Toronto's leading citizens. Mayor John G. Bowes was chairman and the opening prayer was given by Dr. Michael Willis, principal of Knox Presbyterian College, who was elected the society's first president. Rev. William McClure, a Methodist minister, was named secretary and Captain Charles Stuart, originally of Amherstburg, was appointed corresponding secretary. A number of resolutions were passed at the opening meeting and a platform was approved that proclaimed: "Slavery is an outrage on the laws of humanity [whose] continued practice demands the best exertions for its extinction." The society further declared that it would fight slavery by every lawful means and would manifest sympathy for and assist the many "houseless and homeless victims of slavery flying to our soil."[29] A powerful committee was set up to conduct the business of the association, including George Brown and Oliver Mowat.

Samuel Ringold Ward was appointed an agent for the society to go across the province lecturing about slavery. Ward succeeded in forming numerous branches and auxiliaries of the society throughout Canada West. He commented on the strong anti-slavery sentiment that existed in Toronto and vicinity:

> Toronto is somewhat peculiar in many ways, anti-slavery is more popular here than in any city I know save Syracuse . . . . I had good audiences in the towns of Vaughan, Etobicoke, Markham, Pickering and in the village of Newmarket. Anti-slavery feeling is spreading and increasing in all these places. The public mind literally thirsts for the truth and honest listeners, and anxious inquirers will travel many miles, crowd our country chapels and remain for hours eagerly and patiently seeking the light.[30]

During the first year a women's auxiliary raised nearly $1,000 from benefits with which three hundred refugees were clothed, fed and housed. In 1857 the society reported raising $2,200 to assist four hundred escaped slaves.

The Toronto Anti-Slavery Society's most spectacular case was in the defence of John Anderson. In 1853 Anderson, whose real name was Jack Benton, killed Seneca T.P. Diggs, a friend of his Missouri master. Diggs and three other whites were beating him, trying to prevent his escape, when Anderson stabbed Diggs to death and fled. He went at first to Chatham, later settling in Brantford. In 1860 a fellow Black became angered with Anderson and reported to the authorities that he had committed murder in Missouri, whereupon Anderson was arrested and brought before Chief Justice Robinson and the Court of Queen's Bench.

The verdict of the judges, delivered before a packed court room and with crowds waiting outside, was for Anderson's extradition. However, Mr. Justice Richards dissented, arguing that Anderson did no more than any other man would have done under like circumstances. His master had kept him in unrequited toil the better part of his life and then tried to have him killed when he sought freedom. Judge Richards insisted that Anderson was justified in defending his freedom even unto death and "in doing so he exhibited a heroism of which we all might feel proud."

The city's Blacks were keenly aware of the injustice to Anderson. Dr. A.R. Abbott, W.R. Abbott's son, expressing the community's mood, wrote: "There was slavery and cruelty before them, outrage and injustice behind them and on either side, doubt and uncertainty. They could then realize the anguish of our Saviour when he exclaimed, 'Foxes have holes, birds of the air have nests but the son of man has nowhere to lay his head.'"[31]

Seeking the support of the Canadian people, the Toronto Anti-Slavery Society and the *Globe* attacked the decision. D'Arcy McGee also spoke on Anderson's behalf. On February 16, 1861, Anderson's counsel, Samuel B. Freedman, led an appeal before the British Court of Common Pleas where it was found that there was a flaw in the original indictment against Anderson. The court ruled he should have been charged with manslaughter since, under British law, a slave could not be accused of a crime if it could be shown to be a necessary part of the act of escaping. Anderson was freed. Support for the Anti-Slavery Society rose throughout the Toronto community.

George Brown used the influence of the *Globe* to support the city's anti-slavery activities, but his brother Gordon was considered a more zealous abolitionist, and further to the left of his brother in aiding the cause of Blacks. Fred Landon, a Western Ontario University historian who conducted extensive research on Black history in Upper Canada, commented on George and Gordon Brown's abolitionist activities:

> Reference has been made to the support given the society by the *Globe*, of Toronto. For this George Brown was given the

credit but it must be said in justice that no small share of the credit for the *Globe*'s attitude should go to the lesser known brother, Gordon Brown, who was regarded by many as really more zealous for abolition than George Brown. This was tested during the Civil War period when the turn of sentiment against the North in Canada brought much criticism upon the *Globe*. There was a disposition on the part of George Brown to grow lukewarm in his support of the North, but Gordon Brown never wavered and is said to have threatened on one occasion to leave the paper if there were any more signs of hauling down the colors. When the war was over American citizens in Toronto presented Gordon Brown with a gold watch suitably inscribed, an indication possibly of the opinion of that day with regard to his services.[32]

Many refugees broke away from the more stereotyped, menial tasks to which freedmen in the United States were frequently confined. Blowden Davies, in stating that the first ice company in the city was started by a Black "who drew his stock from the mill ponds beyond Bloor Street," was probably referring to T.F. Carey and R.B. Richards, who operated four ice houses in the city during 1854, which they claimed in advertisements ". . . are filled with pure and wholesome spring water ice, from Yorkville. . . . The ice will be conveyed by wagon, daily, to places within six miles of Toronto."[33] Carey also operated a barbershop at 88 King Street West, to which he invited "all who wish to be operated upon in the line of either hair cutting, shaving, hair curling or shampooing."[34] In May 1885, Carey moved to Front Street east of Church Street, and added a bath house ("warm and cold baths at all hours") to his barbering establishment. Other businessmen whose advertisements frequently appeared in the newspapers included T. Smallwood, who operated a hardware store at 35 Front Street. Another advertisement read:

Central Medical Hall
A.T. Augusta
Begs to announce to his friends and the public generally that he has opened the store on Yonge St. one door south of Elm Street, with a new and choice selection of
DRUGS, MEDICINES,
Patent Medicines, Perfumery, Dye Stuffs, etc. and trusts, by strict attention to his business, to merit
a share of their patronage.

> Physicians' prescriptions accurately prepared
> Leeches applied
> Cupping, Bleeding, and Teeth Extracted
> The proprietor or a competent assistant,
> always in attendance.[35]

A.T Augusta was a native of Virginia, but had lived for a number of years in Philadelphia. Finding that Blacks were barred from medical schools in that city, he came to Toronto and entered the Faculty of Medicine at Trinity College, University of Toronto, and graduated in 1860. He was later appointed physician to Toronto's poor house. The *Anti-Slavery Reporter* said of Augusta, "He both talks and writes well and is generally respected throughout the city." Augusta returned to the United States before the outbreak of the Civil War, joined the Union army and was commissioned a captain in the medical corps. He did not return to Toronto. His wife had been the only Black businesswoman of the period. She operated a "New Fancy Dry Goods and Dress Making Establishment" on York Street between Richmond and Adelaide, "where will at all times be found the latest Paris and London patterns."[36]

The Provincial Freeman was founded in Windsor on March 25, 1853, and moved to Toronto one year later. It moved once again to Chatham in June 1855, with the last issue of the paper appearing in September 1857. The newspaper followed a militant editorial policy and included vivid descriptions of church, business and abolitionist activities and it was the community's outstanding achievement. Although plagued by subscription and management difficulties, it nevertheless reflected the problems, aspirations and gratitude of a new refugee group in a strange but usually friendly land. The motto on the paper's masthead read: "Self-Reliance is the True Road to Independence."

The paper's guiding genius and most colourful writer, later its first full-time publisher, was Mary Ann Shadd, well known for her sharp tongue and biting editorials. She was born of free parents in Wilmington, Delaware, on October 9, 1823, the first of thirteen children of Abraham and Harriet Shadd. Since the education of Blacks was forbidden in Delaware, her parents sent her to a Quaker school in Westchester, Pennsylvania. The passage of the Fugitive Slave Act prompted the Shadd family to leave for Canada, and within the year they had moved to Windsor, then settled in Chatham. In 1853, with the backing of several Black businessmen, Mary Ann Shadd established the *Provincial Freeman*. She married Thomas Carey, the ice house entrepreneur who was a part-owner of the newspaper. In August 1863 she was appointed a recruiting officer for the Union army and at the war's end she studied law at

Howard University in Washington, D.C., practised there for a
number of years before becoming principal of a school in the District
of Columbia. Although a naturalized British subject, she lived the
balance of her life in Washington, where she died in 1893.[37]

Mary Ann Shadd is acknowledged as the first Black newspaper-
woman in North America and the publisher of Canada's first anti-
slavery newspaper. She was also perhaps the first woman publisher
of a newspaper in Canada. In her final article as editor, in the June
30, 1855 edition, she wrote: "To colored Women we have a
word — we have broken the 'Editorial Ice' whether willingly or not
for your class in America, so go to editing as many of you who are
willing and able and as soon as you may, if you think you are
ready."

The *Provincial Freeman* in its first issue claimed that its goal was
to "represent the 40,000 Negroes, freedmen, fugitives, wealthy and
poor, recently arrived in Canada; encourage 'the right class' to enter
Canada by publishing an account of the country and its advantages;
and develop in Canada a society to deny all assertions regarding the
Negro's inability to live with others in civilized society."[38] Basically
integrationist in its policy, the newspaper bitterly fought Black colonization schemes and what were felt to be dubious refugee aid
societies:

> Our tour satisfied us abundantly that the coloured people
> of Canada are progressing more rapidly than our people in the
> States — that the liberty enjoyed here makes different men of
> those once crushed and dispirited in the land of chains — that
> along with the other poor classes who come here and improve
> themselves in wealth and status, the black people will also arise
> in some cases very rapidly, but generally slowly, though
> surely — that the day is not far distant when we shall put to
> shame the selfish, systematic charity seekers who go to the
> States, and some of them to the south, to beg partly for fugitives
> but chiefly for their own pockets — that more money has been
> begged professedly for Canadian blacks than said blacks ever
> did, or ever will receive, by a thousand fold — that unless per-
> sons going to the States begging for us are the accredited agents
> of some duly organized society, with honest, unselfish men at
> its head, our friends should hold them at arms' length — that
> what the recently arrived fugitive most needs is not land buying
> societies, not old clothes, not any substitute for labour, but
> stimulation to self-development.[39]

The *Provincial Freeman* urged refugees to avail themselves of
training and exhorted them to enter business, agriculture or the professions. Occasionally it goaded the community. Under a heading,
"Lectures," it said:

One great subject of regret is that the colored citizens of Toronto should so seldom attend lectures, whether the meetings are called by those of their own number, or others. It would be well for them to meet oftener, to look in the face the cause of present discords and former antagonisms, and endeavor to do away with the just imputation of "division, ignorance, disunion, love of menial occupation and the like" that however much we regret it, can be and is brought against them with so much force every day. Why with the abundant opportunites surrounding us — the schools, churches, associations and lectures — need the sad spectacle our people here present be persisted in by them?"[40]

Despite the editor's comments, there was considerable cultural activity in the Black community. Blacks were among the first to be enrolled in the University of Toronto, and others attended the local normal school (for teacher training). In 1855 Miss Emaline Shadd received top honours and the first prize of £5,10s. along with her first-class certificate from Toronto's Normal School. Mention is made of an organization called the Young Men's Excelsior Literary Association. Miss E. Greenfield, an American artist referred to as "The Black Swan," sang frequently in Toronto and received enthusiastic reviews in the local press. The *Toronto Daily Patriot* on May 11, 1854, described her as a "stout, good-looking coloured lady possessing a sureness of tone and a most marvellous compass of voice."

On August 9, 1854, the Provincial Union Association was established, setting out a broad program for Ontario's refugees:

To promote harmony — not based on complexional differences — among Her Majesty's subjects.

To encourage and support a press — The *Provincial Freeman* particularly.

To remove the stain of slavery from the face of the earth — and check its progress in America by all legitimate means.

To encourage the rising generation in literary, scientific and mechanical efforts.[41]

Thirty-five Blacks from Toronto and other areas, such as Chatham, Hamilton, Dresden, London and Amherstburg, held executive positions in the union. Although S.R. Ward was elected first president *in absentia*, he declined when the news reached him in England, and leadership devolved upon such stalwarts as W.R. Abbott and T.F. Carey. Little news was carried of the organization's activities after the *Provincial Freeman* shifted its headquarters to Chatham in August of 1855, but each issue of the paper carried a roster of the union's officers and district representatives, and the names of the fourteen women constituting the Ladies' Committee.

The Toronto Directory of 1859-60 lists a "Moral and Mental Improvement Society (African)" with the following description: "This Society has for its object the improvement of its members by means of essays and debates; it meets every Monday evening in the upper part of No. 120 Elgin Buildings in Yonge Street at 8 o'clock during the summer and 7½ during the winter."[42] Among the officers of this organization were: R.P. Thomas, F.G. Simpson, E.G. Bailey, W.H. Taylor, J.W. Cary, and G.W. Squirrel.

The most important social event every year was Emancipation Day, organized by white and Black citizens to celebrate the abolition of slavery throughout the British Empire in 1834. Toronto records show that this celebration took place as early as 1840. Plans for the 1854 activities were carefully laid several months in advance at the First Baptist Church, where the gathering passed the following resolutions:

> Resolved, that we celebrate that glorious event which took place in the Year of our Lord 1834, when the British Nation did honour to itself and justice to 800,000 of her coloured subjects in the West Indies;
>
> Resolved, that we meet in the Second Wesleyan Chapel, Richmond Street at five in the morning to offer up devout Thanksgiving to Almighty God for his past mercies and to engage in fervent prayer for the utter extinction of slavery throughout the United States and other parts of the world where the evil now exists;
>
> Resolved, that we meet at 9:00 at the Government House, King Street West, form in procession and proceed from thence to Yonge Street Wharf, to meet our friends from Hamilton; thence to St. James Cathedral, King Street East, to listen to a sermon at 11:00 from the Rev. J.H. Gassett after which the procession will proceed through the principal streets of the city to the Government grounds to partake of a Dinner provided by the Committee of Arrangements at two o'clock.[43]

In another version of this important annual event, Dr. A.R. Abbott wrote:

> It was the custom of the members to turn out in procession on the first of August to celebrate the emancipation of the slaves in the British colonies. On one occasion within my memory they provided a banquet which was held under a pavilion erected on a vacant lot running from Elizabeth Street to Sayre Street opposite Osgood Hall, which was then a barracks for the 92nd West India Regiment. The procession was headed by the band of the Regiment. The tallest man in this Regiment was a Black man, a drummer, known as Black Charlie. The proces-

sion carried a Union Jack and a blue silk banner on which was inscribed in gilt letters "The Abolition Society, Organized 1833." The mayor of the city, Mr. Metcalfe, made a speech on this occasion followed by several other speeches of prominent citizens. These celebrations were carried on yearly amid much enthusiasm, because it gave the refugee colonists an opportunity to express their gratitude and appreciation of the privileges they enjoyed under British rule.[44]

On March 28, 1857, during the last months of the *Provincial Freeman's* existence, H.F. Douglass, then editor, stressed the importance of Blacks becoming British-oriented. In an article headed "The Duties of Colored Men in Canada," he said:

> What are the duties of colored men in these provinces, who have been forced here from American despotism and oppression? . . . We owe everything to the country of our adoption and nothing to that miserable, contemptible despotism and government of the U.S. . . . Colored men should become as thoroughly British as they can. We are opposed to all separate organizations, whether civil, political or ecclesiastical, that can have no other effect than that of creating a line of demarcation; fostering if not creating a spirit of caste here, such as colored men are compelled to suffer in the U.S. Separate schools and churches are nuisances that should be abated as soon as possible, they are dark and hateful relics of Yankee Negrophobia, contrary to that healthy, social and political equality recognized by the fundamental principles of British common law, and should never be permitted to take root upon British soil.

Despite its faith in British justice, the *Provincial Freeman* reported numerous cases of discrimination. In 1854 a meeting was held to oppose a plan presented by the Colonial Church and School Society, Church of England, to establish a normal school for coloured people in Toronto (presumably to train Negroes for teaching in Africa). Meeting on September 20, 1854, in the Wesleyan Church, the coloured citizens of Toronto rejected the plan and later published three resolutions to deal with the situation, the second and third of which read:

> Resolved — That should such schools be opened, and efforts made by the Colonial Church and School Society contrary to our expressed wish and interest, we cannot consistently, and will not, as coloured citizens, give them our support.
> Resolved — That we caution our people throughout the province to be careful as to how they give their influence and support to institutions and efforts whether established and made by friend or foe, white or black, that tend to make distinc-

tion on account of colour and to destroy the foundation of our liberties.[45]

And in 1857 the city's Blacks found themselves engaged in a series of mass meetings to protest derogatory remarks by Colonel John Prince, a member of the Legislative Council and formerly in charge of a company of Black soldiers in Chatham. Among other comments, Colonel Prince had been quoted as saying:

> Of the coloured citizens of Toronto I know little or nothing; no doubt some are respectful enough in their way, and perform the inferior duties belonging to their station tolerably well . . . . I believe that in this city as in some others of our Province, they are looked upon as necessary evils, and only submitted to because white servants are so scarce. But I now deal with these fellows as a body and I pronounce them to be as such the greatest CURSE ever inflicted upon the two magnificent counties which I have the honour to represent in the legislative council of this Province . . . . It has been my misfortune and the misfortune of my family to live among these blacks (and they have lived upon us) for twenty-four years.[46]

Other Toronto papers, the *Colonist* and the *Toronto Times*, condemned Colonel Prince for his remarks. Following a report on criminality among local Blacks, the *Toronto Times* stated: "We refuse, positively, the communications [Prince] made on the subject. The coloured people of Toronto are an example in point of industry, sobriety and morality, to their white neighbours.[47]

Nevertheless, Colonel Prince had some support, including a Black master-builder who employed both whites and Blacks in his business. He derided his fellow Blacks for "their improvidence, their love of finery, their disposition to shirk hard work," and concluded that he preferred hiring whites since "they required as a rule less looking after."[48]

George Brown also voiced concern over racism in the city. When Brown was a candidate for Parliament in Upper Canada, 150 people signed a paper stating that if he would agree to press for a law to exclude Blacks from the common (public) schools and put a head tax on those coming into Canada, they would vote for him; otherwise they would back his opponent. Disgusted by this action of fellow Torontonians, Brown commented: "There were 150 men degraded enough to sign such a paper and send it to me."[49]

But the prejudice against Blacks that existed in Toronto was not pervasive. There was no deliberate segregation and an atmosphere of "live and let live" prevailed.

The Black community had reached its apex in the decade of the 1850s and began to decline after Abraham Lincoln's Emancipation

Proclamation freeing the slaves took effect in the United States in January 1863. A listing of Black residents appeared in the 1864-65 city directory. Of the 141 Black persons listed, 129 were in the following occupational groups: 57 labourers, 60 skilled tradesmen (including 17 waiters); 10 businessmen and proprietors (including four restaurateurs and two tavern owners); the balance included a minister, a law student, and individuals with unspecified occupations.

Although the population was in decline, those Black families determined to remain in Toronto formed a small but stable community, integrated within the predominantly white society. They lived well and were comfortably situated, most owning their own homes. A few Black businesses flourished, including a shoe repair shop owned by Levi Lightfoot, whose two sons eventually became a dentist and a doctor. Philip Judah was a tobacconist and for many years proprietor of a large fruit market on Queen Street near Augusta. The second generation of the earliest arrivals from the South, Canadian-born, was becoming established by the mid-nineteenth century and two of its members, Anderson Ruffin Abbott and William Peyton Hubbard, were to distinguish themselves in two fields not usually associated with Blacks at that time, medicine and politics.

Abbott, the son of W.R. Abbott, was born in Toronto in 1837. Hubbard, whose family of freedmen, like the Abbotts, had moved to Canada to escape persecution and discrimination in the United States, was born in the city in 1842. Abbott, one of eight Black surgeons in the American Civil War, wrote the following biographical sketch:

> My name and title in full is Anderson R. Abbott M.D. I was born in the city of Toronto April 7th in the year 1837 . . . . I was married in Aug. 9th 1871 to Mary A. Casey daughter of T.P. Casey — a Canadian born in St. Catharines Ont. I received my elementary education in private and public schools afterwards at the Toronto Academy in connection with Knox's College . . . . A.M. Lafferty, Samuel R. Ward and myself were the only Colored students in attendance — I remained at this school about three years and was very successful in carrying away either prizes or honors in all my classes — I afterwards attended school in Oberlin, Ohio, remained there about three years. On returning home I matriculated in medicine in the University of Toronto and studied medicine for four years under the care of the late Dr. A.T. Augusta M.B. Trinity College, and passed the primary examination for the degree of Bachelor of Medicine at the Toronto University in 1857, also the Medical Board of Upper Canada for a licence to practice in

1861 — I graduated in medicine when I was 23 years of age. In 1863 I was appointed a surgeon in the U.S. Army and . . . was placed in charge of [Camp Baker and Freedman's] Hospitals in Washington . . . until my resignation April 5th 1866. I then resigned, returned home, was married in 1871 and went into practice in Chatham, Ontario. In Chatham I held the following positions: President of the Wilberforce Educational Institute from 1873 to 1880, Coroner, County of Kent, 1874, . . . President of Chatham Literary & Debating Society, President Chatham Medical Society in 1878. In 1881 I removed from Chatham to Dundas. Appointed Doctor for Dundas Mechanics Institute in 1881 . . . . I removed from Dundas to Oakville in 1889, and in 1890 removed to Toronto — In April 1890 I was elected a member of Jas. S. Knowlton Post No. 532 Grand Army of the Republic and on Nov. 21st 92 appointed Aide de Camp on the Staff of the Commanding Officers Dept. of N.Y. . . . On resigning I was presented with Sword, Sash and Belt by the officers and Comrades of the Post. I was also honored by being presented with a Shepard Plaid Shawl which Mr. Lincoln wore on his way to the 1st inauguration and which formed part of a disguise which it is alleged he wore on that occasion to escape assassination — The shawl was presented to me by Mrs. Lincoln after the assassination of the President.[50]

Abbott was also an active member of the York Pioneers and of the Canadian Institute. In 1894 he became Medical Superintendent of Provident Hospital in Chicago, where he remained for several years before retiring to Toronto. In later years he wrote articles for the *Chatham Planet*, the *Dundas Banner* and the *New York Age*. He was a leader of the Toronto Black community and attacked prejudice and discrimination wherever he found it.

W.P. Hubbard, whose father was a Virginian, was raised in a cabin in "the bush," now the bustling Bloor Street — Brunswick Avenue area, well northwest of the centre of Black population of the 1840s. His father worked as a waiter at the Cataract Hotel in Niagara Falls. Young Hubbard was sent to the Toronto Model School where he learned the trade of baker, which he enjoyed throughout his life. Hubbard was a livery man in his uncle's business during his youth, and while riding his rig down the Don Mills Road in the 1860s, is reputed to have saved George Brown, who was a passenger in the cab, from plunging into the Don River. Brown hired Hubbard as a driver, befriended him and urged him to go into politics.

Hubbard, a baker for sixteen years, invented an oven which was sold through a company called Hubbard Ovens. In 1874 he married Julia Luckett, who had been teaching in Washington, D.C.

They raised a family, and finally, in 1893 at age fifty-one he entered civic politics, a career that would span nearly twenty years. Hubbard was first elected an alderman in 1894 in the affluent Ward 4 where he lived, and was re-elected in thirteen consecutive annual elections. In 1897 he topped the polls for the first of many times and his gift for oratory earned him the title, "the Cicero of Council." From 1898 to 1907 he was elected to Board of Control, first by his fellow aldermen, then by the citizens at large; and from 1904 through 1907 he was vice-chairman of the Board of Control, second in rank to the mayor. He was acting mayor of the city on numerous public occasions.

Hubbard often worked for the little man. When rich laundry owners tried to drive the small Chinese laundries out of business by demanding exorbitant municipal licence fees, Hubbard instead got a gradual increase in fees, which the Chinese laundrymen could meet without hardship. In his early years he had fought a tough battle to retain public ownership of Toronto's water supply, so it was natural for Hubbard to become an uncompromising champion of cheap, publicly-owned electric power. He fought for this goal alongside Adam Beck, who founded Ontario's hydro-electric system. Beck later said he regarded Hubbard "always an ally." Hubbard's chairmanship of a special power committee consumed most of his time and interest and he led the effort to win provincial legislation enabling the city to generate, develop, produce and lease electric power — a move that established the Toronto Hydro-Electric System. The time and energy that he put into establishment of Ontario and then Toronto Hydro — to which many voters at the time objected — contributed to his defeat in 1908. Ironically, in later years it was known as his greatest achievement for the city and a significant contribution to the future of Ontario.

Following his defeat, Hubbard moved to Ward 1 east of the Don River, where he built a fourteen-room house at 660 Broadview Avenue overlooking the valley. He was back on city council representing that ward in 1913, but he retired at the end of the term because of the serious illness of his wife. Before he retired, Hubbard was honoured in a gala ceremony in the city hall chamber, where Adam Beck presented council with a large oil portrait of the controller. The portrait hung for many years in the broad, marbled corridors of what is now the old city hall, and in 1976, long after it had been taken down, it was rediscovered in good condition.

Hubbard's son Fred, whose house was next door to the family home, served as general manager of the Toronto Street Railway Company and later became commissioner and then chairman of the Toronto Transit Commission.

W.P. Hubbard retained a strong attachment to the city's Black community with membership in the Home Service Association and the Musical and Literary Society of Toronto. He was a close friend of Dr. A.R. Abbott; his son Fred married Abbott's daughter, Grace, and Abbott chose to live out his final years in W.P. Hubbard's home on Broadview Avenue. Abbott and Hubbard shared a concern for the place of Black citizens in Canadian society. "I have always felt," Hubbard wrote on one occasion to Abbott, "that I am a representative of a race hitherto despised, but if given a fair opportunity would be able to command esteem."[51]

Abbott was concerned as well with the very survival of the Black community in Toronto. The American Civil War, the supposed benefits of the Reconstruction Period, a desire to reunite broken families, and a belief that greater economic opportunity in general lay south of the border, all combined to weaken the structure of the community, not only during the 1860s, but thereafter. While estimates of the community's population during the 1850s had been placed at nearly one thousand by 1861 only 510 Blacks lived in the city — a figure that barely fluctuated for the rest of the nineteenth century. The exodus of the Black population from Toronto during the 1860s was a reflection of the decline in the rest of the country. The census of 1871 reported a decrease from the original estimate of thirty-five to forty thousand in 1851, to an enumerated figure of 21,394. The *Provincial Freeman* was no longer available to give an account of the dwindling Black population during the 1860s. Nevertheless, sporadic reports regarding Toronto Blacks appeared in local newspapers, indicating that the community, though smaller, maintained some degree of cohesiveness. For example, the *Globe* of January 1, 1864 reported a meeting of Black voters in St. John's Ward who objected to the use of the term "nigger" by one of the city councillors. The incident evidently started a furor among Black voters and public officials.

The last great manifestation of anti-slavery sentiment occurred in April 1865, after Abraham Lincoln was assassinated. The shock felt by Torontonians was manifested in the closing of businesses during the funeral; the observance in churches, Black and white, of funeral services with capacity throngs attending; and a mass meeting held by Black citizens. In many cases, "people of colour" in the community wore an arm band or some other symbol of mourning for eighty days.

The city's Black population in 1871 was 551. It remained at about that size until 1911 when it dropped to an all-time low of 408. Between 1904 and 1913, just prior to the First World War, 1,633 Blacks had emigrated from Canada to the United States. And between 1914 and 1920, shortly after the war, an additional 2,232 Blacks had left for the United States. In 1905 Dr. Abbott analysed the trend in an article written for a New York newspaper:

The constant drain to which our population has been subjected since the close of the Civil War precludes the possibility of any very great increase in wealth or numbers. Our youth evince a strong disposition to cross the border line as soon as they acquire sufficient knowledge and experience to make a living. In this way we are impoverished and you [Americans] are correspondingly benefitted. By the process of absorption and expatriation the color line will eventually fade out in Canada.[52]

Abbott died in 1913. He was not able to anticipate the influx of West Indian and American Blacks who were recruited and brought to Canada during the First World War by railroad and industrial interests. Hubbard was to witness this development. He lived in retirement to the age of ninety-three and became known in the press as Toronto's Grand Old Man. He could be counted on to make good copy, and each of his birthdays in the last years of his life was covered in the newspapers. When he turned ninety-three he told a reporter: "Too much leisure makes a man languid. His organs stop functioning as they should and complications develop. It is written that man shall earn his living by the sweat of his brow."[53]

Only thirty years later, thousands of new arrivals from the West Indies and the United States would once again begin to swell Toronto's Black community, some to make their mark on public life. But few would know the debt of gratitude owed to the bright, tough and progressive Black leaders who, years before, had surmounted all barriers of race and left for them a legacy of public accomplishment.

Notes

1. Ontario Department of Planning and Development, *Don Valley Conservation Report* (Toronto, 1950).

2. OPA, Crown Land Papers, General Correspondence: agreement between Mosee, Willis and Thomas Ridout, Feb. 2, 1799, and between Parker Mills and David William Smith, Surveyor-General, Jan. 13, 1799, and Reports, 3, 5; Ontario Department of Lands and Forests, History Branch, Survey Records, Letters Received: W. Chewett, Senior Surveyor, to Smith, Feb. 11, June 22, 1799, pp. 396, 621, as cited by Robin Winks, *The Blacks in Canada* (New Haven: Yale University Press, 1971), p. 47.

3. W.L. Mackenzie, *Sketches of Canada and the United States* (London: Effingham Wilson, 1833), p. 19.

4. *British Colonist*, 10 May 1842.

5. Abbott Papers, Baldwin Room, Metropolitan Toronto Library Board.

6. Haldimand Baptist Association, Minutes (1837), pp. 5ff as cited by James K. Lewis, "Religious Life of Fugitive Slaves and Rise of Coloured Baptist Churches, 1820-1865, in What Is Now Known as Ontario" (M.A. thesis, McMaster Divinity School, 1965), p. 32.

7. John Ross Robertson, *Landmarks of Toronto: A Collection of Historical Sketches of the Old Town of York from 1792-1837 and of Toronto from 1837-1904* (Toronto: J.R. Robertson, 1904), pp. 471ff.

8. *Letters of James Gillespie Birney, 1831-1857* (New York, 1938) I, pp. 395ff.

9. *Voice of the Fugitive*, 10 July 1852.

10. "Number of Coloured Persons Resident in Toronto, 25 July 1840," Metropolitan Toronto Library Board.

11. "Report on the Toronto Negroes for Lord Sydenham by E. St. Remy, 5 April 1841," Cross Cultural Centre, University of Western Ontario.

12. *Letters of James Gillespie Birney.*

13. W.R. Riddell, "Interesting Notes on Great Britain and Canada with Respect to the Negro," *Journal of Negro History*, XIII (1928), p. 201.

14. J.G. Kohl, *Travels in Canada* (London: George Manwaring, 1860) II, p. 110.

15. Benjamin Drew, *The Refugee* (Boston: John P. Jewett and Company, 1856), p. 94.

16. F.H. Armstrong, "Toronto Directories and the Negro Community in the Late 1840's," *Ontario Historical Society*, LXI, 2 (June 1969), p. 115.

17. Ibid., p. 118.

18. D.G. Simpson, "Negroes in Ontario from Early Times to 1870" (Ph.D. thesis, University of Western Ontario, 1970), p. 437.

19. *British Colonist*, 10 June 1840.

20. Adam Wilson to Robert Baldwin, 12 July 1843, Baldwin Papers, Metropolitan Toronto Library Board.

21. *The Provincial Freeman*, 10 September 1851.

22. *British Colonist*, as cited by *The Provincial Freeman*, 5 May 1855.

23. *The Provincial Freeman*, 22 March 1854.

24. Ibid.

25. *Anti-Slavery Reporter*, 1 April 1858.

26. *Voice of the Fugitive*, 8 October 1851.

27. Drew, *The Refugee*, p. 238.

28. *The Globe*, 1 March 1851.

29. Ibid.

30. *The Provincial Freeman*, 26 February 1852.

31. Abbott Papers.

32. Fred Landon, "The Anti-Slavery Society of Canada," *JNH*, IV (1919), p. 39.

33. *The Provincial Freeman*, 3 June 1854.

34. Ibid., 16 March 1854.

35. Ibid., 14 April 1855.

36. Ibid., 11 January 1854.

37. Hallie Q. Brown, *Homespun Heroines and Other Women of Distinction* (Xenia: Aldine Press, 1926), p. 94.

38. *The Provincial Freeman*, 25 March 1854.

39. Ibid., 11 January 1854.

40. Ibid., 17 March 1855.

41. Ibid., 19 August 1854.

42. PAO, *Directory for the City of Toronto, 1859-60*.

43. *The Provincial Freeman*, 3 June 1854, 29 July 1854. The event was followed by a soiree and fireworks display with the accompaniment of a cornet band. The statute of 1833 abolishing slavery took effect August 1, 1834.

44. Abbott Papers.

45. *The Provincial Freeman*, 25 March 1854.

46. Ibid., 20 June 1857.

47. *Toronto Times*, as cited by The *Provincial Freeman*.

48. *Anti-Slavery Reporter*, 1 April 1858.

49. Samuel Gridley Howe, *The Refugees from Slavery* (Boston, 1864), p. 43.

50. Abbott Papers.

51. Ibid.

52. Ibid.

53. *The Evening Telegram*, 27 January 1933.

St. John's Shtetl: the Ward in 1911

Stephen A. Speisman

St. John's Ward, a district bounded roughly by Yonge Street, University Avenue, Queen and College streets, was one of the first speculative developments on park lots in Toronto. Originally called "Macaulay town," it was already subdivided by the middle of the nineteenth century, most of the buildings standing sixty years later being one- or two-storey stuccoed frame cottages dating from the 1850s and 1860s. Typical of developments of this sort, many of the streets were short and close together, punctuated by alleys and laneways bearing names such as Cuttle Place, Foster Place and Price's Lane.

"The Ward," as it was popularly known, was considered a slum from the beginning, its status confirmed by the placing of the local poor house — the House of Industry — at Elm and Chestnut streets in 1848. Centre Street (later Centre Avenue) was considered a red-light district until late in the century.[1] The population of the area was largely English-speaking, but the Ward was destined to become a major immigrant reception area by the turn of the century, and the principal component of its population would be East European Jews.

The earliest Jewish residents in Toronto — English, Germans and those from Quebec — had settled farther east along King Street, in the commercial centre of mid-nineteenth century Toronto, and when they grew prosperous enough to live separately from their places of business, they continued to be found east of Yonge Street. These individuals never lived in a bloc; they did not succeed in creating, nor did they seek to build, a Jewish enclave within the larger community. The last two decades of the century, however, saw a transformation in the Jewish population of Toronto, indeed of all North America, as large-scale emigration from Eastern Europe resulted in an influx of thousands, escaping the persecution and economic difficulties of their homelands. Until immigration was curtailed temporarily by the outbreak of the First World War, the Jewish population of Toronto grew dramatically, from a little over three thousand in 1901, to about nine thousand in 1907. By 1911, there were over eighteen thousand Jews in the city.[2]

Almost without exception, those who arrived from Eastern Europe in this period gravitated to St. John's Ward. First to appear were the Lithuanians and Galicians, whose livelihoods had been threatened by the advent of the industrial revolution. Then came Jews from Russia and Russian Poland, seeking to avoid the restrictions of the May Laws and the hazards of the pogrom. The latter, impoverished by comparison to many of the Litvakim and Galicianer who were able to bring some financial resources with them, soon constituted a majority of the Jews living in the city.[3]

The earliest East Europeans came as individuals, hoping eventually to bring their families, or themselves to return to Europe. By the end of the century, however, emigration of entire families was the rule. They came in search of the *golden medine*, the golden land, and that certainly was not Toronto. Some settled here because they had run out of money on the way to some locality in the United States, perhaps Chicago. Nevertheless, once there was a nucleus of Jews here, urging their relatives and *landsleit* to come, often sending back photographs of well-dressed Toronto Jews which bore little resemblance to reality, emigrants began to set out bound specifically for Toronto. Certainly by 1900, this was the case.[4] Most of those who arrived prior to the turn of the century settled to the south of what would become the core of St. John's Ward, along Richmond Street between Yonge and York and on York Street itself. Some of the more substantial families (relatively speaking) did, however, settle north of Queen Street; the Lithuanian synagogue, the first permanent East European congregation in the city, opened at University Avenue and Elm Street in 1883.

By the late 1890s, however, increasing numbers of Jews were moving north and west of the intersection of Queen and Yonge, until by 1900 Jews outnumbered all others in the Ward, the first time they were to do so in any district in the city. Over the next decade, they would create, in these few square blocks, a miniature Jewish civilization in the heart of Anglo-Saxon Toronto, reaching its peak in the half-dozen years prior to the outbreak of World War One.

They did not set out to create a ghetto, but many soon discovered the advantage of reconstructing, as far as was possible, the amenities and the security of the shtetl.

Jews settled in the Ward initially because they had little choice; they needed inexpensive accommodation close to steady employment immediately upon their arrival. The European experience had taught them the value of living adjacent to the commercial centre of the city, and in St. John's Ward the right conditions obtained. Few had skills that could be used in North America. Restrictions upon Jews in Eastern Europe had limited the crafts into which they were admitted. Most had some mercantile experience, but even the most petty enterprise demanded some small amount of capital. Even peddling required at least credit. The alternative was to find employment in the factory.

It was in the field of ready-made clothing that the Jews found employment here as in other North American cities. The reasons for this phenomenon have been detailed sufficiently elsewhere and need not be elaborated here.[5] Suffice it to say that the Ward was in convenient proximity to this industry. In the early years of the twentieth century, the major clothing firms, the Lowndes Co., Johnson Brothers and others were located on Front Street, Wellington Street, Church and Bay. By 1910, the T. Eaton Company, which would become the largest single employer of Jews from St. John's Ward, had established an enormous manufacturing complex in the streets bounded by Teraulay (now Bay), Albert, Louisa and James.

Factory operatives preferred to live close to their places of employment. They worked long hours and wanted to minimize travelling time; they sought to avoid spending money on streetcars by walking to work; they needed a variety of employment opportunities, for although day-hiring was rare, the introduction of the piecework system reduced the skill required for specific tasks and so heightened competition for jobs. Seasonal layoffs and strikes made employment even more precarious. St. John's Ward, therefore, developed as an immigrant reception area adjacent to the central business district, in much the same way as similar areas appeared throughout the continent. While all Jews certainly did not work in the factories, it was their presence, combined with the availability of relatively inexpensive housing, that drew Jewish immigrants to the Ward.[6]

Working conditions in Toronto factories nowhere approximated the appalling situation that existed in the Lower East Side of New York or even in Montreal. Indeed, by the standards of the time the atmosphere at Eaton's, for instance, was very good. Orthodox Jews could take Saturday mornings off without fear of dismissal and one could earn a little extra by informally instructing boys sent by their parents to learn the trade. And in general, because rents were not excessively high in the Ward prior to the First World War, few had to engage in homework.[7] Nevertheless, a significant number of Jews avoided the factory if they could, and for a variety of reasons. Some simply were uncomfortable working for non-Jews;[8] the major firms were still not in Jewish hands. Others would not work on Saturday mornings, when a majority of the establishments remained open and would make no provision for Sabbath observance. Still others could not abide the restriction of set working hours, preferring to continue the European tradition of morning and evening synagogue attendance and religious study.

If the solution was to strike out on their own, their choices were limited. They had virtually no capital and in many enterprises they had not the traditional skills to compete with non-Jewish immigrants. Consequently, independent Jewish "businessmen" were generally to be found in the salvage trades, as rag-pickers, bottle collectors, used furniture dealers, or as peddlers. Peddling and the salvage trades were low on the scale of occupational prestige — a factor which lessened competition from other groups — but they had the advantage of allowing the Jew to maintain his independence and, indeed, his dignity within the Jewish community. Status, prior to the First World War, still depended largely upon piety and learning rather than upon wealth.[9] By 1916, Jewish rag-pickers, alone, would number six hundred in Toronto.[10]

The ultimate in independence, of course, was the occupant of the retail or artisan's shop: the barber, shoemaker, grocer, restaurateur, pawnbroker, second-hand or drygoods dealer. Such enterprises abounded in the Ward, serving the local population, but so many businesses of similar type were compressed into so small an area that competition was fierce and often the storekeeper could neither support his family on this endeavour alone nor employ his own grown children. Members of the family, therefore, engaged in a variety of occupations, some tending the store, others engaging in peddling or working in the factories. Others, still, did contract work in their homes for the large needle-trade firms.

Living conditions in St. John's Ward in the first decade of the twentieth century were not nearly as bad as those in immigrant districts in other large cities in the United States,[11] but by Toronto standards, they were deplorable. In 1911, there were eighty-two people per acre, a higher density than in any other part of Toronto except the predominantly Anglo-Celtic Cabbagetown;[12] and in view of the smaller buildings in St. John's Ward, the density per room, if not per acre, could be as high as elsewhere. On the average, there were six to eight people per building — the overwhelming majority of these, it will be recalled, were cottages — but some housed as many as ten to fifteen. Most structures had three to five rooms, with the amount of living space being diminished by the presence of the workshops and sewing machines of home industry. Few barracks-like tenements appeared in the Ward; in 1911, there were only eight such structures, as well as several hotels converted into boarding houses. Jews appear to have avoided these, primarily because their rents were exorbitant. The municipal authorities imposed no limit on the number of people who could inhabit a given structure and consequently large families crowded into the cottages, together with *landsleit* from Europe and boarders taken in to supplement the family income. Most of these cottages in the early years of the century appear to have been rented from non-Jews.

While the moral tone of the Ward improved as the population became predominantly Jewish, physical conditions deteriorated rapidly. The occasional prosperous Jewish investor attempted to improve conditions in the area by erecting modern brick row houses on Chestnut and Armoury streets about 1908-1909;[13] these efforts were too few to make much difference. Large numbers of Jews arrived from Europe and settled in the Ward between 1905 and 1912; the demand for housing increased, rents soared and landlords, hoping to make a substantial profit as the commercial and administrative sector of the city expanded westward, neglected to improve their properties. Dr. Charles Hastings, the Medical Health Officer, reported in 1911 that 108 houses in the Ward were unfit for habitation, yet most were occupied. Some barely kept out the elements. One structure housed three families in five rooms, one of which contained two sewing machines as well. Another cottage, rented for an astronomical $20 a month, had four feet of water in its basement. Almost a third of the structures had no plumbing or drainage; waste was simply thrown into the yards.[14] Conditions in the rear cottages — that is, those built in the laneways behind cottages fronting the streets, by landlords attempting to maximize the profits from their properties — were the worst. Surrounded by stables, privies and yards full of garbage, the occupants found the odour so foul that they hesitated to open their windows even in summer.

By 1911 congestion had reached alarming proportions and was aggravated by the encroachment of the Eaton complex and the municipal buildings on the residential portion of the area. In that year, a large block of land at College and Elizabeth streets was expropriated and cleared as a site for the new Toronto General Hospital and, to make matters worse, the city would soon expropriate the area bounded by Louisa, Albert, Elizabeth and Chestnut to make way for a new Registry Office.[15] Rear tenements demonstrated the worst conditions, each divided into dwellings of six dark and tiny rooms. Yet these commanded exorbitant rents; in some cases families living in one room had to take in boarders to help pay them. One three-storey structure on Teraulay Street, specifically mentioned in Hastings' *Report*, had a factory on the top floor, while the outhouse adjacent to the building was shared by thirty residents and the forty employees of the factory. In winter it was generally frozen. Behind the row was a privy which had been overflowing for some time, but was rented to the occupants of a front house for the outrageous sum of $10 a month. Jews tended to avoid such accommodation; but at the time the *Report* was compiled, some Jews were living in this particular tenement, although they were gone within several months.[16] It should be noted that none of these tenement rows or converted hotels was owned by Jews.

Jewish householders in the Ward, as the assessment rolls indicate, tended to be young as compared to non-Jewish residents. In the case of the latter, women were widows and men were over fifty. This suggests that many were long-time residents, having arrived before the advent of the Jews. The relative youthfulness of the Jewish householder, however, does not mean that there were few elderly Jewish residents, but immigrant ghettos, in general, do exhibit a higher proportion of young to old than do districts inhabited by the native-born. Jewish families tended to emigrate when the father was in his twenties or early thirties; the elderly often refused to leave Europe until they were persuaded to come at a later time or until the family was financially capable of supporting them. Once here, they lived with their children and consequently do not often appear on the assessment rolls. The youthfulness of the population was reflected also in the large number of children under the age of fourteen. Even married children continued to live under their parents' roof, the extended family being typical of the immigrant ghetto throughout North America.

By 1911, the Ward, together with the few blocks between University Avenue and McCaul Street, had become virtually a self-contained community as regards Jewish services and cultural, religious and educational facilities. A rich variety of service and retail shops, run by Jews and generally catering exclusively to them, operated throughout the area. Some, like Dworkin's News Agency on Elizabeth Street, the offices of the various Jewish steamship agents, or the multitude of *kosher* restaurants, became important social and political centres for the area. At Dworkin's, for instance, one could read copies of the Yiddish press imported from New York, and discuss the latest philosophies of social change or the efforts of labour unions throughout the continent. Once the local Yiddish-language paper, the *Yiddisher Zhurnal*, began to publish in 1912, Dworkin's became its major distribution centre. Of less cosmic significance, but nevertheless important, were institutions such as Halpern's seltzer factory, which perpetuated the comforts of the shtetl on Chestnut Street. The seasoned observer could always spot the establishments which claimed superiority, be it in the field of food, laundry or plumbing; they were invariably signified by the designation "New York."

After 1909, a Jewish day nursery and a free dispensary were available on Elizabeth Street south of Agnes (Dundas). The former enabled mothers who had to work outside the home to do so with relative peace of mind. The dispensary was a direct attempt to counter missionary activities, especially those of the Presbyterians, who provided such facilities in order to attract parents and children into the missions. Presided over by Dora Goldstick, a young Toronto midwife trained in Ohio, and Abe Hashmall, the first Jewish graduate in pharmacy at the University of Toronto, the dispensary would eventually grow into Mount Sinai Hospital.

Formal entertainment was to be had in the institution of the Yiddish theatre, at first at the National in the former Lithuanian synagogue on University Avenue and later at the Lyric which, after 1909, occupied a former Methodist church at the northeast corner of Agnes and Teraulay (Dundas and Bay). Local companies and those from New York and Detroit were popular attractions whose repertoire ranged from riotous and occasionally risqué comedy to Shakespeare and tragedies of heartrending capacities. The latter served a dual purpose; in the absence of a psychiatric service, the tragedy provided the struggling immigrant, especially the overburdened housewife, an inexpensive opportunity for catharsis. However much *tzores* one had, the character on the stage had infinitely more, and for a few pennies, one could go to the theatre and have a good cry. Productions too large for the Lyric could be staged at Massey Hall, within easy walking distance of the Ward.

The most ubiquitous institution in the Ward, however, was the synagogue. By 1911 a majority of Toronto congregations were still located in the Ward where they had been founded. A few, such as Goel Tzedec on University Avenue (the Lithuanian synagogue, opened 1907) and Machzikei HaDas on Teraulay Street (A Galician synagogue established in 1906) were housed in spacious structures built for the purpose; indeed, Goel Tzedec, the largest such building in the city with a capacity of twelve hundred, was modelled on the Roman Catholic Cathedral of Westminster. Other congregations occupied converted churches (e.g., Shomrai Shabbos, Chestnut Street) or remodelled stores or cottages. Each ethnic grouping or group of townsmen as a rule insisted upon its own synagogue, where the peculiar customs of its European locality could be meticulously observed. So numerous had they become that Centre Avenue, only a few blocks long, had four major congregations on it in 1911 and probably also several "shtiblach" (cottage synagogues) which do not appear in the municipal records. The synagogue was the anchor for the majority of Jews living in St. John's Ward, providing a social and cultural centre as well as a place to pray. Facilities for charity organizations and social gatherings were provided, as well as opportunities for religious education for adults and children alike. The latter were still informal in 1911. Efforts to establish congregational schools in the East European synagogues would not come to fruition until 1914.[17]

Formal Jewish education for children in the Ward was still, in 1911, provided on four levels: by the incompetent "siddur melamed," usually someone inept at business, who hawked whatever little knowledge he had door-to-door; by the capable private teacher who either set up a "cheder," a one-room school, in part of his own home or taught in the homes of individual pupils; by the congregational school at Holy Blossom on Bond Street; or by the community schools. Of the last, there were two in 1911, one religious and one secularist; both were located on Simcoe Street, on the western periphery of the Ward.

The Toronto Hebrew Religion School, or Simcoe Street Talmud Torah as it was usually known, had been established in 1907 through the efforts of Rabbi Jacob Gordon, the spiritual leader of the Lithuanian and Russian communities, together with the lay leaders of both of his congregations, University Avenue and McCaul Street. Its purpose was to provide education on a high level, in contrast to the abominably low standards tolerated by the employers of most of the private teachers and the bare minimum of traditional subjects taught at Holy Blossom. The intention was to attract the children of all Jews regardless of ethnic origin or religious position, but by 1911 it had come to be viewed essentially as the Lithuanian *talmud torah*. The Polish Jews, and many of the Galicians, were alienated by its modernist approach: its approval of secular subjects (although none were yet taught), its Zionist leanings, and the fact that the language of instruction was Hebrew rather than Yiddish. The dissidents, under the leadership of Rabbi Joseph Weinreb, the rabbi of the Galician community, and Rabbi Judah Rosenberg of the Polish community, who would arrive in 1912, did not yet have the resources to set up a school of their own. It was not far off, but in the interim, private tutoring continued to be the rule.

The extreme orthodox were not alone in their opposition to Simcoe Street. Toronto now had a sizeable minority of secularist Jews, many having escaped after the abortive Russian revolution of 1905. These wanted a Jewish education to promote the idea of peoplehood, without the religious trappings which they considered irrelevant to their lives. Their ideologies were varied: socialist, territorialist, anarchist, communist. But they had a common bond, a sympathy for the working class, and a belief in the necessity of perpetuating Jewish culture through the Yiddish language and of bridging the gap between immigrant parents and their children. To this end they founded the Jewish National Radical School in September 1911, under the leadership of dedicated individuals such as Isaac Matenko, who held down a factory job during the day and taught in the evenings.

A final Jewish institution in the Ward deserves mention: the mutual benefit society. In a system in which public welfare was virtually unthinkable, both on the part of the government and on the part of the potential recipient, a mechanism had to be found to help the immigrant over the difficult times following his arrival and to assist him in bringing other members of his family from the old country. For many, the synagogue provided these services: moral support, interest-free loans, credit to purchase merchandise or a wagon, contacts to employment. For others, however, secular organizations were preferred, some cutting across ethnic lines (e.g., the Toronto Hebrew Benevolent Society, founded 1899, and the Pride of Israel Sick Benefit Society, founded 1905). Still others organized *landsmanshaften*, composed of individuals from the same locality in Europe. Too numerous to mention individually, these organizations provided emotional and often economic stability to the Jews of St. John's Ward. They were perhaps the strongest link between life in Toronto and the shtetl of Eastern Europe.

By 1911, therefore, Jewish society in St. John's Ward was virtually self-contained. One ventured forth to work for non-Jews in the factories, to gather junk in the city or to peddle in the hinterland, but for most it was only out of necessity. Few residents of the Ward dared yet consider themselves a part of the larger Toronto society. Fewer still would have ventured to support a Jew for municipal office, let alone stand oneself for election. Those who did so in the first decade of the century were not taken seriously.[18] Granted, there were political concerns. One would like to feel he had a friend at city hall when peddling licences were necessary, when gas rates had to be guaranteed or when one ran afoul of the law by stabling a horse illegally. But the consensus was that a Jew would be isolated at council and that the most advantageous course lay in cultivating the Orange establishment.

In 1911, Toronto Jews still had no Yiddish newspaper that would serve, as the *Forward* was doing in New York, to urge participation on the political scene. Nevertheless, over the previous decade, political awareness had been growing in the Ward, for the mundane issues just mentioned, but also out of a genuine desire to understand and participate in the Canadian political process as befits the citizens of a democratic society. Indeed, the residents of the Ward demonstrated surprising enthusiasm and interest in the federal election that year. As one observer remarked, "every man, woman and child in the ward was a politician . . . ."[19] Under these circumstances, the potential for corruption was great, as ward heelers were not above purchasing the votes their candidates required with favours and dollars. Some of the more acculturated and politically astute Jews, therefore, had established the Hebrew Ratepayers Association in 1909, not only to lobby for Jewish interests, but also to channel this growing political awareness, through education, to "a higher standard of citizenship."

While the Hebrew Ratepayers professed to be non-partisan, urging support of the best candidate regardless of affiliation, there existed in the ward, as early as 1910, a Hebrew Conservative Association, which was considered a force worthy of attention by local members of Parliament. By 1911, the residents of the Ward were beginning to have enough confidence to support Jewish candidates, these being especially numerous — although unsuccessful — in the municipal elections of 1913. Eventually, in 1914, Louis Singer, a scion of the East European community, albeit now a member of Holy Blossom, would be elected alderman in Ward 4, representing the area west of University Avenue.

Social status and social mobility operated in the Ward on two levels: community leadership, either religious or secular, and in the area of economics. Rabbis Weinreb and Gordon, representing the Galician and Lithuanian communities respectively, still exerted considerable influence among their followers; members of the Goldstick family took the lead, for instance, among secularist intellectuals; the major Jewish employers — Mendel Granatstein, for example, who operated a waste-processing concern at Agnes and University — unpopular as they may have been, were nonetheless considered to have made it. Most residents of the Ward, however, were not concerned with their status in the total Jewish community; they concentrated on improving themselves economically and on providing the best possible living conditions for their families.

The assessment rolls indicate that by 1911, an increasing number of Jewish residents of the Ward, indeed of Ward residents generally, were owners of their properties. About half of the buildings in the area by this time were owned by residents of the Ward and half of these by their occupants. Jewish owners were not necessarily self-employed craftsmen or storekeepers as one would expect; "operators" appear frequently among the lists of property owners and peddlers, too, were not absent, although a majority of these did continue to rent. There seems to have been some correspondence between length of residence in the city and ownership, but it is not improbable that some of the prosperous preferred to invest their money elsewhere in expectation of greater profit or were saving to bring relatives from Europe.

There is evidence of hierarchies among members of particular occupations; a peddler could make his living with anything from a backpack to a handcart or a horse-drawn conveyance. The nature of the goods he sold often determined his status as much as his means of transporting them. And some peddlers, through good business sense or the luck of having on hand goods in demand, did exceedingly well.

By 1911 one can discern the presence of Jewish owners of Ward property living outside the area, usually between University Avenue and Bathurst Street, south of Bloor. But almost invariably, they had lived in the Ward during the previous decade. For Jews in the Ward, removal west of University Avenue was indicative of achievement. In some cases, the move was accompanied by changes in occupation, demonstrating upward mobility. For instance, Israel Greisman was a peddler living on Chestnut Street in 1905, whereas in 1911 he was a *rentier* living on what is now Dundas Street near McCaul; another peddler, Simon Rabinovitch, also living on Chestnut Street in 1905, had moved to Beverley Street by 1911 and was listed as having been engaged in real estate. Nevertheless, for those living outside the Ward, upward movement had not been rapid; most had been living in Toronto prior to 1895. Only shortly before 1911 did relatively large-scale movement out of the Ward begin to take place.

It is difficult, on the basis of such a limited study, to say much with accuracy about the speed of upward mobility of those Jews remaining in the Ward in 1911. Since the actual census documents are still closed to researchers, it is impossible to determine, for example, when each resident arrived in Canada. Although the assessment rolls indicate that virtually every Jewish householder held the municipal franchise in 1911, this required only three years residence under the act of 1906. One can say something, however, about physical mobility. The rapidity with which occupants of particular dwellings changed is striking; there was often a complete turnover in the few months between the compilation of the city directory and that of the assessment rolls. Indeed, there was probably even greater movement than the assessment rolls suggest, since they do not take into account the non-taxpaying lodger.

In total, one can discover three types of movement among Jews of the Ward in this period. One group moved several times within the Ward, a sign of economic difficulty. It was not unusual for such people to leave the city within five years. A second category consisted of those who moved out of the Ward but to areas of the same character, for instance to the slums of Niagara Street, near the municipal abattoir. All movement out of the Ward, therefore, did not demonstrate improved social and economic status. Finally, there were those who moved westward toward Spadina Avenue in the half-dozen years following 1911. These constituted a majority, the upwardly mobile who followed the prosperous Jewish professionals and entrepreneurs who had moved west of University Avenue prior to 1911. As was the case with the latter, the move was often accompanied by a change in occupation; grocers became real estate agents, tailors clothing manufacturers and carpenters contractors. Most appear to have retained their occupations but to have achieved a measure of success in them. For this last group, especially, a minimum period of eight to ten years in Toronto seems to have been a prerequisite for such a move. As a rule, elderly shopkeepers remained in the Ward while their children moved westward. A similar pattern is evident among elderly non-Jews as well, but it would appear that Jews over the age of fifty were more mobile than non-Jews in the same age group.[20]

By 1911, the Ward had achieved the apex of its development as a Jewish area and had generated enough inertia to maintain itself as a self-contained community, even as many of its residents were economically capable of leaving it. The presence of Jewish institutions, retail shops and other amenities, coupled with the secure Yiddish-speaking atmosphere, was a powerful cohesive. Nevertheless, the seeds of the Ward's disintegration as a Jewish district had been sown as early as 1904, when a catastrophic fire destroyed a major segment of Toronto's manufacturing district. Many of the ready-made clothing factories which employed residents of the Ward had been located in the heart of the area devastated by the fire. When these firms resumed production, they chose new quarters to the west, often along Wellington, Richmond and Adelaide streets between York Street and Spadina Avenue. The pattern of disruption for Jewish factory workers would have been considerably greater, and consequently would most certainly have been accompanied by westward residential movement, had not Eaton's been unaffected by the fire. Indeed at this very period, Eaton's was expanding its operation adjacent to the Ward and so contributed to the stability of the area.

It was the Eaton strike of 1912 that fractured the artificial shell of inertia that had been maintaining the Ward for almost a decade. It came at a period of increased population and consequent overcrowding in the Ward; it came also at a time when economic expectations were rising among local Jews and when the confidence of the younger generation was coming to fruition. It propelled some Jewish employees into business for themselves, when perhaps otherwise they might have been content to remain. The municipal expropriations for the General Hospital and later for the Registry Office accelerated the process, as did the outbreak of the First World War, which gave new opportunities for contracts to smaller manufacturers, and unexpected profits to practitioners of the salvage trades, who suddenly found themselves in possession of quantities of scarce metals, glass and cloth. The "golden land" west of University Avenue now looked more inviting than ever and had at last entered the realm of reality.

Notes

1. J.E. Middleton, *The Municipality of Toronto: A History* (Toronto: Dominion Publishing Co., 1923), I, p. 402; C.S. Clark, *Of Toronto The Good* (Montreal: Toronto Publishing Co., 1898), p. 89.

2. Louis Rosenberg, "Population Characteristics of the Jewish Community of Toronto" (Montreal: Canadian Jewish Congress, 1955); Louis Rosenberg "Jewish Mutual Benefit and Friendly Societies in Toronto. The First Fifty Years 1896 - 1945" (typescript, 63 pp., ca. 1947, Toronto Jewish Congress Archives).

3. See Bernard D. Weinryb, "Jewish Immigration and Accommodation to America" in M. Sklare, ed., *The Jews: Social Patterns of an American Group* (Glencoe, Ill.: Free Press, 1958).

4. J.B. Salsberg, personal interview, Jan. 15, 1973.

5. See Stephen A. Speisman, *The Jews of Toronto: A History to 1937* (Toronto: McClelland and Stewart, 1979), p. 73; and Maldwyn A. Jones, *American Immigration* (Chicago: University of Chicago Press, 1960), pp. 219-20.

6. For comparable patterns of ghetto formation, see David Ward, "The Emergence of Central Immigrant Ghettoes in American Cities: 1840 - 1920," Association of American Geographers, *Annals*, LVIII (June 1968), pp. 343-59; Moses Rischin, *The Promised City: New York's Jews, 1870 - 1914* (New York: Corinth Books, 1964); and Louis Wirth, *The Ghetto* (Chicago: University of Chicago Press, 1964), p. 202.

7. Samuel Charney, "From Rags to Riches," *Masada* IV, 2 (Oct. 1972), p. 11; David Green, personal interview Apr. 9, 1973; Ida Siegel, personal interview, Dec. 23, 1971. For sweatshop conditions in Montreal, see *The Jewish Times* (1903), p. 73.

8. Even when manufacturers engaged Jewish managers, as was the case with Sigmund Lubelsky at Eaton's, these were acculturated individuals with whom the East European Jew felt, often with justification, that he had little in common.

9. Weinryb, "Jewish Immigration," pp. 4-22; J.B. Salsberg, personal interview, Jan. 15, 1973; Harry Korolnek, personal interview, Dec. 26, 1972. For a contemporary description of Jewish occupations in the 1890s, see *Mail and Empire*, Sept. 25, 1897.

10. *Daily Star*, May 30, 1916.

11. See e.g., Charles N. Glaab and A. Theodore Brown, *A History of Urban America* (Toronto: Macmillan, 1967), p. 162.

12. Dr. Charles D. Hastings, "Report of the Medical Health Officer dealing with the recent investigation of Slum Conditions in Toronto 1911" (Toronto: Dept. of Health, n.d.; Folio No. 5, City of Toronto Archives).

13. One of these was Henry Greisman, a Galician manufacturer of suspenders. His houses were built as investment, not philanthropy, but he did rent them at a reasonable rate.

14. Hastings, *Report,* pp. 4, 8, 9, 12, 10-11.

15. See Canada, Bureau of Statistics, *Fifth Census of Canada, 1911* (Ottawa, 1913) esp. II, p. 158; *Globe,* June 21, 1911; *Evening Telegram,* July 17, 1913.

16. Hastings, *Report,* pp. 5 ff.

17. See *Jewish Times,* Apr. 11, 1913, p. 28; Feb. 21, 1913, pp. 28-29; Sept. 6, 1912, p. 20; June 20, 1913.

18. Ibid., Dec. 14, 1906; Jan. 8, 1909.

19. S.B. Rohold, *The Jews in Canada* (Toronto: Board of Home Missions, Presbyterian Church in Canada, 1912), pp. 13-14.

20. See *Assessment Role for City of Toronto made 1910 for 1911,* Ward 3, Division II; *Assessment Roll for City of Toronto made 1911 for 1912,* Ward 4, Division II.

Italian Hometown Settlements and the Development of an Italian Community in Toronto, 1875-1935

John E. Zucchi

The peasants who emigrated to Toronto from many villages in Italy left their country not as Italian nationals but as people of their hometowns. While the unification of the peninsula and the subsequent period of consolidation instilled some sense of national consciousness in the Italian peasantry, the primary affections and loyalties of the emigrant were directed at their *paesani* or fellow townspeople. These allegiances were not totally sentimental, for a townsgroup met specific economic needs as well. The peasant looked to his townspeople to provide capital and information for emigrating from the isolated *paese* to Toronto. The chain from the town might depend on the good will of a group of townspeople in Toronto, or even on a labour agent from the hometown operating in the Ontario capital. On the other hand a labour agent in Toronto or Montreal who obtained labourers from many Italian towns might be responsible for getting the sojourner to Toronto. Even in that case, however, the emigrant relied on his townspeople to get in touch with the network of agencies and sub-agencies which eventually would lead to a job and cash.

In Toronto each hometown group developed its own community, although this did not necessarily mean that each group lived on the same street or even in the same neighbourhood. At the same time the process of settlement influenced the development of an Italian community in Toronto and of distinctively Italian neighbourhoods. This paper examines the development of both types of communities in Toronto between 1875 and 1935, and more specifically, the physical, distinguishing features of each community. Marriage registers of the three Italian Catholic parishes in Toronto and city directories were most helpful in reconstructing the communities of each townsgroup and of the Italian community as a whole. With these two sources it was possible to trace the principal boarding houses for each significant Italian townsgroup in the city.

One useful way of examining the formation of a Little Italy and understanding what constitutes the residential area that goes by that title is to examine the features which attract its inhabitants. In *The Image of the City*, Kevin Lynch argues that in order to come to terms with the confusion of the urban world a citizen develops his own mental maps of what he considers the important locations or "nodal points" in the city. Those nodal points heighten the individual's sense of the morphography of his habitat. Later in this chapter a study of the nodal or focal points of some of the hometown groups in Toronto and of the city's "Italian" immigrants between 1885 and 1935 will give us an indication of the nature of a Little Italy and of some of the reasons behind its evolution.[1] This approach will give us some sense of the early settlement of each hometown group and of how the community as a whole affected the old world local and national loyalties of the immigrants.

In tracing the genesis of a Little Italy one must bear in mind the three forces responsible for its settlement: 1) the precursors or *girovaghi* (itinerant workers) who established an Italian presence in the city. These included fruiterers from the province of Genoa, plaster statue-makers from the province of Lucca, and street musicians from the provinces of Genoa and Potenza. The *laurenzanesi* (street musicians from Laurenzana, Potenza) and some Genoese would emerge as early leaders in Toronto's Italian community; 2) the padrone system, that is the network of labour agents who brought many immigrants from diverse Italian towns and villages to North American industry, railroad, and other outdoor construction projects; and 3) chain migration, the mechanism by which the members of respective villages were ensured a job and lodging in their destination in the new world. Each of these routes was functional in helping the prospective immigrant move out of his hometown and into a North American city. By relying on a padrone or on a fellow townsman for his sojourning venture, the immigrant placed himself in a set of patron-client relationships, in a new series of social alliances. The method by which the padrone or the fellow townsman provided for the sojourners' needs shaped to a great extent the nature and physical structure of a Little Italy.

The mid-nineteenth century Italian immigration to the city can be divided into two types — early men of letters and soldiers of fortune until the 1850s, and northern Italian craftsmen and peddlers until the 1880s. Among the early Italians in the city were the Roman-born British imperial officer, Philip De Grassi (mid-1820s) and a Piedmontese professor of modern languages at the University of Toronto, James Forneri.[2] They were followed by northern Italian, mostly Genoese, craftsmen, peddlers, and service tradesmen, such as Francesco Rossi, Toronto's first confectioner and icecream-maker, and the Canessa brothers, Nicholas and Peter, brush-makers.

The early settlement of Toronto following the arrival of the Genoese was very much determined by labour agents in the city ánd elsewhere who acted as middlemen between Ontario capital and Italian immigrant labour. At least from the early 1880s Toronto was host to those padroni and their clientele of stonecutters, unskilled outdoor labourers, and/or railway navvies. The shape of Toronto's early Italian neighbourhood was very much a product of their agencies and of the transient labourers' sojourning way of life.[3] Boardinghouses along Elizabeth Street or Centre Avenue in Toronto's Italian and Jewish immigrant neighbourhood, the Ward, filled in the winter as many navvies returned from their outdoor work sites. In 1897 Mackenzie King observed that "As a rule, a good percentage of them [Italian immigrants] are absent from the city during some months in the year," working on the railroads near Hull, Muskoka, and Niagara Falls; on the Peterborough canals or on the Ottawa and New York railroad bridge near Brockville.[4]

The Italian population in Toronto's first Little Italy in the Ward, bounded by Queen, Yonge and College streets, and University Avenue, was to a great extent settled by single, male sojourners from many hometowns whose work and lodgings were provided by labour agents. Toronto's two other Little Italies were also very much the product of the padrone system. However, in both of those settlements, most of the early Italians were brought there by less important padroni from their own villages. Street and railroad construction attracted the early residents to those new settlements. Mansfield Avenue, near College and Grace Streets, had been a receiving centre for many of the destitute Irish of the 1870s and 1880s.[5] The Italians eventually replaced many of the Irish who settled in that western part of Toronto. Almost all of the early Italian immigrants who settled in that area were from the towns surrounding the city of Cosenza in Calabria, particularly from San Vincenzo la Costa and San Sisto la Costa. The earliest Italian on Mansfield Avenue was Salvatore Turano, a grocer from San Sisto; he was most likely the earliest padrone and boardinghouse keeper in the area.[6]

Meanwhile, further north and west along Dufferin Street near Davenport Avenue a new Italian neighbourhood emerged in the 1890s. At its western fringe, the junction of the Northern Railway and the Ontario and Quebec District line of the CPR formed the eastern boundary of the West Toronto Junction. Railroad labourers and construction labourers were the earliest migrants in these areas, working at railway maintenance, sewer installation projects and the macadimization of dirt roads. In 1905 Canadian General Electric initiated production in its new Canada Foundry plant at Lansdowne and Davenport avenues, and workers moved into nearby homes. Many Italian moulders, especially from Terracina, settled there after bitter walkouts at the plant in 1903-5. They replaced many of the strikers who moved to the United States.[7]

The annual winter influx of labourers before the First World War shaped the quality of life as well as the physical structures of the three Italian neighbourhoods, but especially of the Ward because it was the prime receiving centre for Italian sojourners in Toronto. The discrepancy between official census population figures and unofficial estimates gives us some idea of the enormous impact of the transient sector on the Italian population. One travelling emigration inspector from Rome estimated the city's Italian population in 1902 at 4,000, only one-quarter of whom were permanent. In 1913, another inspector from the same organization estimated that 5,000 of Toronto's 14,000 Italians were sojourners. Between 1910 and 1913 population estimates ranged from 4,873 to 14,000. In 1911, the census recorded 1,475 Italian males and only 609 Italian females within the federal electoral district of Toronto Centre, where the majority of the city's Italian population resided.[8] Even in 1906 when the Italian population stood at about 5,000, the *Globe* "stated on good authority that the overcrowding this winter is chiefly among the Jews. Between 2,000 and 3,000 Italians have gone home to Italy for the winter, and in this way the Italian element is not so strong in the overcrowded districts as it might have been."[9] The population was therefore fluid and many of the immigrants were single males sojourning in the city for a number of years or winter seasons, before returning to their hometowns in Italy, or moving on to another Little Italy on the continent.

Not all of the Italian residents in Toronto, of course, were single males. Some of the earlier settlers either arrived with their wives or eventually sent to the hometown for their betrothed. By the 1890s most of the *laurenzanesi* who had arrived during the previous twenty years were living in family units and not as single boarders. The same was true of many of the immigrants from San Sisto and of some of the immigrants from Termini Imerese, Sicily. The influx of male labourers created many opportunities for these familes in the Ward to rent out a room or two to the migrants. Lodging and boarding influenced living conditions, the family economy and family privacy. In 1897 Mackenzie King reported that "During the winter season there have been as many as forty or fifty Italians living in a single house on Chestnut Street.[10] In 1910 another writer for the *Globe* observed that Italian women in Toronto cared for their families or even shops, "and often for ten or a dozen or even twenty boarders in addition." Almost ever household in the Ward, and later, in the other two Little Italies put up at least one boarder at some point before the First World War.[11]

The practice of placing sojourners in one's home affected social conditions and relations among the city's Italian immigrants as well as the family economy. The lodgers were a source of income to the family willing to let its rooms — $2 a week per boarder, at the turn of the century.[12] Besides cultural mores, renting rooms gave the housewife an additional incentive to work at home. The padrone became a patron not only of the sojourners but also of many of the families which kept lodgers as an additional source of income. In that way, the attention of a majority of the Italian population of the city was focused on a few individuals: the padroni. Because the interests of most temporary and permanent immigrants in the city were so intently centred on this small group, the newcomers from many towns in the peninsula became aware of their common circumstances and dependence on the labour agents. In the aftermath of the Messina earthquake in December 1908, some Sicilians and Calabrians consulted the consular agent, Victor Giannelli, for information regarding next-of-kin in Italy. However, to achieve results, "a meeting of Italians was held in the office of Dini Bros., York Street, where a cable message addressed to the mayors of the five different cities of Calabria and Messina asking . . . for information was sent off."[13] In moments of crisis or need such as the Messina earthquake, Italians turned to their padroni for aid or direction. This shared experience of dependence was translated by the immigrants into a shared identity and helped prepare the basis for the development of a Toronto Italian identity.

From the 1870s until the Second World War many, perhaps most Italian immigrants came to Toronto through migration chains from their respective hometowns or with the help of a labour agent from the hometown living in Toronto. Others were brought to the city under the auspices of one of the important Italian padroni in Toronto, either directly or after having sojourned in other work camps or Little Italies on the continent. Once in Toronto they continued to identify with their townspeople living in the city. These *paesani*, however, also had allegiances to the mother country, and upon their arrival in North America they felt some affinity to other immigrants from the peninsula, as opposed to other British or Eastern European immigrants. If nothing else, the simple condition of living outside their hometown disposed them to associate with other Italians in the city. Between 1875 and 1935 immigrants from the various Italian hometowns came to identify with an Italian immigrant population and to a great extent, as we have indicated, the padrone system was responsible for that. The labourers came from a myriad of villages and towns in Italy but were all thrust into the same economic process controlled by middlemen. Navvies from different towns worked together during the open season on job sites, ate meals in common, joined in protest against their employers, showed respect or deference to the same padroni. The sojourning experience gave many of the *paesani* their first glimpse of "other" Italians.

Upon their return to Toronto in the winter the sojourners interacted with other immigrants from different hometowns who had arrived in the city through the migration chains of their respective hometowns. More important, the annual re-entry created the first truly Italian physical focal points of the emerging community. The boardinghouses were owned by labour agents — those of James Palma on Elizabeth Street in the 1880s; the Glionna Hotel (built in 1885) owned by Francesco Glionna on Chestnut and Edward streets; Michael Basso's grocery on Chestnut Street in the 1880s and 1890s; Albert Dini's agency on York Street after 1900; Francesco Nicoletti's, Giuseppe Izzo's, or the Trentadue brothers' agencies, all on the corners at Centre Avenue and Elm Street, between 1900 and 1915. The street-crossing remained the commercial centre of Toronto's Italian community until the early 1930s. Glionna's Hotel, built in 1885, was also the first saloon for Italian sojourners in Toronto. Salvatore Turano's grocery on Mansfield Avenue was the earliest boardhouse/agency in the College Street and Grace Street Little Italy. Before 1910 John Martello, a grocer from Lanciano (province of Chieti), ran a boardinghouse on Dufferin Street near Davenport Avenue for moulders and labourers from his hometown who worked at Canada Foundry. These large boardinghouses owned by labour agents and/or grocers, and the large labour agencies, such as Glionna's saloon, were the first outward signs of a Little Italy and the only physical structures of Toronto's Italian community until after the turn of the century. Those functional, nodal points became the catch signs of the Toronto community for both the sojourners who wintered in Toronto and the permanent Italian residents of the city. As important components of the immigrant's mental map of Toronto, they influenced to a great extent the newcomers from the various hometowns of the peninsula to develop an Italian immigrant identity in the city.[14]

The patterns of settlement of the permanent residents of Toronto's Italian population, however, was a function not only of the padrone system, but also of the migration chains from specific villages. Some of the chains were in fact dependent on minor labour agents such as John Martello of Lanciano or Salvatore Turano of San Sisto la Costa, who functioned as padroni only for their *paesani*. To be sure, a permanent Little Italy was always built up around labour agencies and boardinghouses for migrants.[15] Nevertheless, a close analysis of the street in an Italian neighbourhood reveals that one's decision to settle in a particular location was more complex than simple economics or convenience, for cultural factors were also involved; indeed the three were often intertwined.

The immigrants who had left the towns of rural Italy under the auspices of their town's migration chains chose specific destinations in the new world.[16] In Toronto and in other Little Italies, the chain provided the new arrivals with temporary lodgings, a job, and an immediate community. It arranged for other needs by introducing the townsman to particular shops, professionals, mutual aid societies perhaps even a larger circle of acceptable friends. In other words the migration chain formed by the *paesani* of a particular town to any destination was an intricate socio-economic system. Because the chain was functional it caused the migrant to continue identifying with his *paesani*, or with immigrants from the cluster of towns surrounding his hometown, long after he had arrived in the North American city. In order to understand how each hometown chain provided for the settlement of its members it is essential to know the most prominent hometown groups and their respective populations in Toronto.

One method of gauging the population of some of these groups, or of provincial or regional groups from Italy in Toronto, is to examine the marriage records from the Italian parishes in conjunction with estimates of the Italian population in Toronto for the mid-1920s. The marriage registers at Our Lady of Mount Carmel, St. Agnes and St. Clement parishes usually included the hometown of each marriage partner. In all 1,836 men and women who married at one of those three parishes between 1908 and 1935 had their hometown in Italy listed in the "place of baptism" column. Table 1 records the numbers of immigrants from the most representative regions and provinces in the marriage registers of the three Italian parishes. Sicily, Abruzzi Appulia and Calabria were the home regions of most of Toronto's Italian immigrants — over 50 per cent between the four of them. Trapani and Palermo (Sicily), Foggia (Appulia), Cosenza (Calabria), and Isernia (Campobasso) were the most prominent provinces of origin. A few of the townsgroups claimed a very high proportion of the city's Italian population. The Sicilian towns of Termini Imerese (province of Palermo), Vita (Trapani), and Pachino (Siracusa) accounted for over 15 per cent of the city's entire Italian population, while Pisticci (Matera), Modugno (Bari), and Monteleone di Puglia (Foggia) claimed over 10 per cent.

By correlating the proportional representation of each region, province, and town listed in the marriage registers from 1908 to 1935 with estimates of the Italian population of the city between

Table 1: Italians in Toronto, 1908-35

Region Province	population sample from marriage registers	%
Sicilia		
Palermo	113	
Trapani	140	
Siracusa	86	
Messina	18	
other	26	
Total	383	20.9
Appulia		
Foggia	124	
Bari	78	
Lecce	5	
Total	207	11.3
Abruzzi		
Teramo	78	
Chieti	88	
Aquila	38	
Pescara	3	
Total	207	11.3
Calabria		
Cosenza	123	
Reggio Calabria	61	
Catanzaro	21	
Total	205	11.2
Lazio		
Roma	60	
Latina	21	
Frosinone	55	
Total	136	7.4
Basilicata		
Matera	71	
Potenza	43	
Total	114	6.2
Campobasso		
Isernia	111	
Total	111	6.0

Region Province	population sample from marriage registers	%
Campani		
Caserta	68	
Benevento	8	
Avellino	18	
Salerno	18	
Total	112	6.0
Friuli	96	
Total	96	5.2
Veneto		
Treviso	32	
Venezia	7	
other	3	
Total	42	2.3
Le Marche		
Pesaro	21	
Macerata	7	
Ascoli Peceno	33	
Ancona	6	
Total	67	3.6
Piemonte		
Torino	40	
Alessandria	7	
Asti	1	
Total	48	2.6
Toscana		
Lucca	27	
Total	27	1.5
other regions and provinces	83	
Total	1,836	100.0

SOURCE: marriage registers, Our Lady of Mount Carmel Parish (1908-35), St. Agnes (1913-35), St. Clement (1916-35) Roman Catholic parishes.

Table 2: Prominent Italian hometown groups in Toronto

Town	no. married in 3 Italian parishes, 1908-1935	%
Vita, Trapani	121	6.6
Termini Imerese, Palermo	97	5.3
Pachino, Siracusa	86	4.7
Pisticci, Matera	69	3.8
Modugno di Bari, Bari	69	3.8
Monteleone di Puglia, Foggia	55	3.0
Boiano, Campobasso	39	2.1
San Sisto la Costa, Cosenza	33	1.8
Total	569	31.1

1917 and 1934 [see Table 1], we can formulate a rough estimate of the population of each sub-community in the mid to late 1920s. Accouting for biases, the following figures in tables 3 and 4 provide an estimate of the population of Italian regional groups in Toronto, and of specific hometown groups.

As we indicated earlier, the Italian sojourners who worked for the more significant padroni in the city created mental maps of Toronto according to functional nodal points. Each group of townspeople also charted its own map with its particular points of convergence. A boardinghouse was required for young men arriving from the village. Bachelors who had sent home for their betrothed

Table 3: Estimated population of Italian regional groups in Toronto, 1925-1930

Region	Population
Sicilia	3,800
Abbruzzi	2,000
Calabria	2,000
Appulia	2,000
Lazio	1,350
Basilicata	1,200
Campania	1,100
Campobasso	1,100
Friuli	500
Piemonte	500
Le Marche	350
Veneto	250
Toscana	250

Table 4: Estimated population of Italian hometown groups in
Toronto, 1925-1930

Hometown	Population
Termini Imerese	750
Vita	650
Pachino	475
Pisticci	400
Modugno	400
Monteleone di Puglia	300
Boiano	200
San Sisto	200

had to place them in reputable lodgings (preferably with a widow) apart from male boarders before the marriage. The pioneers of the town's chain to Toronto had to be consulted occasionally either out of deference or because of authentic needs. The homes of the pioneers and the boardinghouses became the central features of each townsman's mental map and it was around those nuclei that each community of *paesani* settled.

Between 1875 and 1930 each group established itself on particular streets within one or two of the three little Italies and even outside those neighbourhoods.[17]

The first recognizable group of townspeople in the city was the street musicians from Laurenzana. The chain to Toronto was pioneered by Giovanni Glionna and his brothers in 1874. Glionna had been charged in New Haven with having imported four child street musicians into New York for mendicant purposes and soon after the charge ended up in Toronto. There he was followed by his brothers and other townsmen who had lived in the same tenements with him on Crosby Street in Manhattan. Originally they lodged in or rented houses on Chestnut Street, and they eventually settled at Chestnut and Edward streets. In the early 1880s the Glionnas, who by then had made a small fortune, completed the construction of eleven brick buildings on the northwest corner of Chestnut and Edward streets, including the Glionna Hotel. The corner remained the centre of the city's *laurenzanese* community until the First World War when Francesco Glionna, the patriarch of the townsgroup, died, and the hotel closed its doors with the introduction of prohibition.[18]

The early immigrants of San Sisto la Costa, San Vincenzo la Costa, Montalto Offugo, Cerisano, and other towns surrounding Cosenza were fruit traders who opened shops along Queen Street West. In the 1890s Salvatore Turano, who married a *laurenzanese*, moved to Mansfield Avenue where he invested in a grocery store. It was most likely a boardinghouse and labour agency for his townsmen working on road and street railway construction, for within a few years many Italians, but especially immigrants from near Cosenza, had moved to the neighbourhood. At the turn of the century the groups from the towns surrounding Consenza had two focal points: one was Mansfield Avenue where the early fruit traders from San Sisto lived. Most prominent among them were Sal Turano and Raffaele Bartello, both of whom owned stores on Mansfield Avenue. At 92 D'Arcy Street just west of the Ward, Vincenzo Muto from Cerisano kept many lodgers from his town, most of them tailors in his tailoring shop. Muto moved the business to College Street near Grace Street around 1910 and some of his employees lived above the shop. In the 1920s two more addesses became important as boardinghouses for bachelors — Carmine Spizziri's home at 30 Mansfield Avenue, and Pasquale Molinaro's house at 19 Gore Street. Molinaro's address became a centre of this Cosenza sub-group in the 1920s when he began a long association with the New York–based *Progresso Italo-Americano* as its part-time Toronto correspondent. Like a number of other *san sistesi*, Molinaro was a motorman for the Toronto Transit Commission. By the early 1930s the townsgroups from the Cosenza area had settled primarily in the College and Grace streets Little Italy and especially on Bellwoods Avenue (between Plymouth and Mansfield avenues); on the east side of Clinton Street; on Mansfield Avenue, north side; on Gore Street, south side; and on the east side of Manning Avenue. A handful of families lived in or just outside the Ward. A small but significant group also settled in the Dufferin Street and Davenport Little Italy.

The townspeople from Monteleone concentrated on York Street in the 1890s but by the turn of the century had settled on what would remain the centre of the *monteleonese* colony until the 1930s — Walton Street and Elm Street in the Ward. The most prevalent occupation among those immigrants from the Puglia region was boot-blacking. From the first decade of the century the shoeshiners of Monteleone opened parlour after parlour in the business district of downtown Toronto. Some also became barbers while still others moved into the laundry business. From before the First World War, sojourning bachelors from this town had a choice of living with relatives on a *monteleonese* street, or in one of the large boardinghouses run by their townsmen. At 72 Gerrard Street West (between Elizabeth and Terauley streets) Frank Casullo and Mike Volpe, shoe polishers, ran a boardinghouse, probably for employees of their parlours on Queen Street West and on Victoria Street. In the immediate postwar period, Louis Colangelo, a labourer, operated a boardinghouse at 32 Walton Street. The two most important homes, however, were those of two grocers (and probably padroni) in the Ward, Michael Circelli and Antonio Volpe. Circelli's residence at 71 Elm Street housed migrants from Monteleone and also from Modugno di Bari; both towns were in Puglia but relatively distant from each other. By 1920, a *modugnese*, Onofrio Giovanielli, purchased the grocery. Betrothed women who had just arrived in the city were usually sent to Antonio Volpe's boardinghouse at 64 Edward Street unless a relative had a spare room to offer.

During the 1920s the townspeople of Monteleone began gradually moving out of the Ward but they did not settle in either of the other two Little Italies. Some moved to the Dufferin Street and Eglinton Avenue district, especially on Gilbert Street. Mortimer Avenue and Nealon Avenue became the two most popular streets for Monteleone's emigrants well into the 1950s.

Many of the immigrants from Modugno di Bari were like the *monteleonesi*, involved in the barbering and shoeshining trades but also in other occupations — in small and large industry and construction. The centre of the colonia *modugnese* continued to be the Ward until the 1950s, if for no other reason than because Mount Carmel Church, the Italian national parish, housed the statue of St. Rocco, which they shared with the *monteleonesi* for their treasured annual feast-day processions. From soon after the turn of the century the *paesani* from Modugno lived near the townspeople from Monteleone on Gerrard, Walton, and Hayter streets in the Ward. There was also a small pocket on Centre Avenue just north of Elm Street. Before 1915 immigrants from Modugno had begun settling in the College and Grace streets neighbourhood, along Manning Avenue, especially on the east side; along the north side of Henderson Avenue; on Gore Street; and on Clinton Street just north of Henderson Avenue. Others lived in the East End in the Danforth and Donland avenues and Danforth and Pape avenues districts (Ravina Crescent, Stacy Street), and further south, especially on Booth Street (near Queen Street and Carlaw Avenue) and Bright Street (near Queen Street and Broadview Avenue).

Most of the large boardinghouses for *modugnesi* remained in the Ward until the 1920s. One of the early important lodging houses for the group belonged to a musician from Laurenzana, Egidio Donofrio, at 62 Elm Street. Donofrio's daughter in fact married the patriarch of the *modugnese* colony in Toronto, Nicola Majorana (at 218 Chestnut Street). As noted earlier, Salvatore Turano, one of the leaders of the immigrants from San Sisto la Costa, had also married a *laurenzanese*. By marrying into Toronto's pioneering hometown groups, these individuals enhanced their own prestige among their townspeople and helped broaden the Italian ethnic awareness of their *paesani*. Majorana and Turano were leaders of their respective groups. By marrying Italian women from outside their hometowns they most likely provided an additional stimulus to their townspeople to identify with the city's Italian community.

In the 1920s some homes in the other smaller *modugnese* settlements could put up the occasional boarder. Sal and Maria Vitale at 128 Booth Street (Queen and Broadview) or Teodoro Zambri at 175 Drayton (Danforth and Coxwell) rented out their rooms to a few bachelors.

The immigrants from Boiano lived mostly in the second Little Italy at College and Grace streets, although some settled in the West Toronto Junction; others lived in apartments over their stores on Adelaide Street West. Most of the immigrants from Boiano were involved in the city's banana trade as peddlers, retailers, or wholesalers. A large basement would be a main attraction for these small entrepreneurs, for banana bunches must be ripened on hooks attached to the ceiling joists. The most concentrated settlement of the wholesalers, jobbers and peddlers was Markham Street, between College and Dundas streets (about ten families in the 1920s and 1930s). Number 105 Markham Street was the central home among the *boianesi*, for many bachelors roomed there before their marriages. Originally the home belonged to the Scinocco brothers, Mark and Michael, banana peddlers; later, after the First World War, it was sold to Antonio Janetta, a prominent fruiterer who had moved to Toronto from Hibbing, Minnesota.

The early skilled labourers from Friuli's towns and villages originally lodged in some of the large boardinghouses in or just outside the Ward. A small settlement also opened up in the Coxwell Avenue and Greenwood Avenue area in about 1905. The latter residents were employees of Toronto Brick Company, and all came from one village. Friulan brickmakers also settled alongside brick companies in Port Credit, Mimico and Cooksville. Their residences at the latter resembled a veritable shantytown of tar sheds. Just before the Second World War the *friulani* began moving out of the Ward. Luigi del Negro, a bricklayer, ran a large boardinghouse, probably for his own employees, at 591 Dufferin Street, near Dundas Street. By the early 1920s a mosaic, marble and tile contractor, John Gasparini, had purchased the home. The site remained Toronto's most concentrated residence of tile-setters until the mid-1920s. In the meantime many *friulani* moved into what would become the centre of their community until the 1960s: the area bounded by Dufferin Street, Davenport Avenue, Wallace Avenue, and the West Toronto Junction. By the 1930s the Italian population of that district was composed almost exclusively of skilled and unskilled construction labourers. Streets in the area were filled with boardinghouses owned by *friulani*, and by the immigrants from the towns surrounding Chieti — Lanciano, Fossacesia, and Rocca San Giovanni — and from Terracina. Boardinghouses for the two latter groups were located on Dufferin Street just south of Davenport Road. Chieti's immigrants were heavily concentrated on Beaver Avenue (and also on the corner of Manning and Henderson avenues in the College and Grace Little Italy). At first, immigrants from Friuli settled on Symington Avenue and later spread northwest to Wiltshire Avenue and northeast to Chandos Avenue. During the 1930s the move northward continued. The *friulani* were involved in the construction of their new homes on Hartley Avenue and other streets in the Keele Street and Eglinton Avenue area, in Fairbank.

The barbers and labourers of Pisticci (province of Matera) lived in the Ward from the 1890s, on Walton Street between Terauley (now Bay) and Yonge streets, and on Terauley just above Queen. Some of the more established barbers moved up to Robert and Major streets during the 1930s. The main area of settlement for the townspeople, however, was the College and Grace streets neighbourhood, especially Henderson Street and Manning Avenue, and Euclid Avenue below College. About one-quarter of the group was dispersed throughout the residential areas east and west of the downtown commercial district. In the 1920s a number of *picticcesi* homeowners on Henderson or Clinton streets let rooms to fellow townsmen. Down in the Ward, before the First World War George Abate, a *laurenzanese* at 65 Elm Street, kept many boarders from Pisticci. Two of these men married the daughters of immigrants from Laurenzana.

Most Sicilians did not reside in the common areas of Italian settlement in Toronto. Because they were fruit traders, most immigrants from Termini Imerese, Vita and Pachino settled along the main thoroughfares of the city — Queen, Yonge, Parliament and Bloor streets, and Danforth, Eglinton and St. Clair avenues. New immigrants from Vita and Termini Imerese in western Sicily generally boarded with their kin, but each hometown group depended on at least one major boardinghouse run by a widow. From just before the war, Agata Lamantia, a widow from Termini, put up both men and women in the apartment above her store at 103 and later, 894 Queen Street East. Among the *vitesi* (or as they would call themselves, *u vitalori*), the homes of Peter Catania (1018 Queen West), Vito Leo (1608 Queen West), and Sam Leo (311 Danforth Avenue) were important addresses for single men and women who required lodging facilities. Francesca Simone's home at 18 St. Paul Street (in the Queen Street East and Sackville Avenue neighbourhood) was the largest boardinghouse for this group. Many immigrants from Pachino in eastern Sicily also boarded at her home, since other *pachinesi* also lived in that neighbourhood. During the war a number of brides-to-be lived at Mrs. Simone's house but she kept bachelors there in the 1920s — six men in two shifts.

The other Sicilian hometown group in the Queen and Sackville district was the immigrants from Pachino, who were mostly involved in the fruit trade or in heavy industry in the East End. Almost the entire population of that group lived east of Yonge Street outside any of the city's Little Italies. Many of them also lived on farms contiguous to those of the *termitani* and *vitesi* in West Hill — on Midland Avenue between Eglinton and Lawrence avenues where they operated market gardens.[19]

Each Italian hometown group in Toronto, therefore, developed its own particular map with specific focal points within the city. None of the streets in the three Little Italies was dominated by any one group and none of them lived entirely on one street. The key residential areas or streets of the *paesani* — the boardinghouse for sojourners and betrothed, the homes of the prominent men of the community — were all components of those mental maps, and were the products of the chain migration of the townspeople from their homes in Italy to Toronto. The chain itself, the respect one paid to the notables of the town, and the network of boardinghouses, however, were functional and not only sentimental. Thus to a great extent they perpetuated the loyalties of the immigrant to his townspeople in the city and allegiance to townspeople was maintained by the pragmatic or expedient aspects of group cohesion. Loyalty did not mean simple fellow feeling, for it also embraced obligation and debt to intermediaries between the immigrant and his lodgings, job, or future wife. The more a greenhorn was "processed" through a boardinghouse, a job, and perhaps small enterprise by his *paesani*, the more likely were his loyalties to orbit around his townsgroup.

One way of gauging the loyalties of the townspeople is to study their marriage patterns. As some scholars have hypothesized, a high rate of endogamy among immigrants from the same hometown would seem to suggest a very cohesive hometown group. Similarly, extensive endogamy between immigrants from the same province or region would seem to indicate a cohesive provincial or regional group. In her study of Slovaks in Pittsburgh, June Alexander found that between 1895 and 1914, 65 per cent of the marriages at Slovak parishes were contracted between immigrants from the same county in northern Hungary. William De Marco discovered that in a sample of 1,582 marriages at the two North End Italian parishes in Boston, 87.1 per cent of the marriages between 1899 and 1929 occurred between co-regionalists. In 82 per cent of the cases, partners were from the same province; and 60 per cent of the marriages were between mates from the same hometown in Italy. In the smaller Italian settlements of Rochester, Utica and Cleveland, John Briggs found that just under 40 per cent of 2,005 marriages between 1903 and 1917 were contracted between partners from the same hometown.[20] A survey of the marriage registers in Toronto's Italian parishes reveal lower endogamy rates than the above examples. Of 1,195 marriages between 1908 and 1935 — and these include marriages in which the hometown of at least one partner was recorded

by the officiating priest — only 237, or 19.8 per cent were endogamous. The endogamy rates for the larger groups in the city
were not particularly high either.

These data by themselves, however, shed little light on the
loyalties of the immigrants for a number of reasons. First, one-third
of the Italians in the marriage registers were born outside Italy, and
in most cases we do not know the hometown of their parents. Of
1,551 marriages at the three parishes between 1908 and 1935 involving 3,102 partners, we have a hometown listing for only 1,836 partners. About 75 per cent of the remaining 1,266 husbands or wives
were children of Italian immigrants but were born outside Italy (the
remaining 25 per cent either were not Italian, or their birthplaces
were illegible). The statistics in tables 5 and 6 did not include the
children of fellow townsmen under the category of "endogamous by
town" because it would be impossible to determine the hometown
for all second-generation partners. Because the immigrants from
Termini Imerese, Palermo, were so numerous, I was able to infer
from the names of the marriage partners' parents whether or not
second-generation Italians (that is, children of Italian immigrants,
born outside Italy) were from Termini Imerese. Of 109 marriages
involving immigrants from Termini, or their children, 61 marriages
were endogamous to the group. If we were to exclude the children of
the *termitani* (born outside Termini) from the sample, we would
tabulate only 25 endogamous marriages. In fact, in 9 of the 61 endogamous marriages the bride and bridegroom were both children
of *termitani* but born outside the hometown. A similar knowledge of
other hometown groups would certainly produce a higher rate of
group endogamy.

A second problem with marshalling data from the marriage
registers to estimate endogamy rates is the assumption that people

Table 5: **Endogamy rates by parish for all marriages in which
the hometown of at least one partner appears in the
register, 1908-1935**

Parish	Endogamous (town)	%	Total marriages
Mount Carmel	158	22.9	690
St. Agnes	78	17.5	447
St. Clement's	1	1.7	58
Totals	237	19.8	1,195

SOURCES: Marriage registers, Our Lady of Mount Carmel, St.
Agnes and St. Clement Roman Catholic parishes,
Toronto, 1908-1935.

Table 6: Endogamy rates for particular towns, and their intermarriage rates with home provinces, regions, and country

Town	Total marriages	Town	%	Province	%	Region	%	Italy	%
Modugno di Bari	46	14	30.4	16	34.8	19	41.3	39	
Monteleone di Puglia	30	22	73.3	24	80.0	27	90.0	29	
Boiano	21	11	52.4	14	66.7	14	66.7	19	
Pisticci	49	22	44.9	22	44.9	29	59.2	48	
Terracina	7	7	100.00						
Fossacessia	17	4	23.5	5	29.4	6	35.3	17	
Sora	26	9	34.6	11	42.3	11	42.3	25	
Apricena	12	3	25.0	3	25.0	5	41.7	11	
San Sisto la Costa	21	8	38.1	11	52.4	11	52.4	19	
San Vincenzo la Costa	8	2	25.0	5	62.5	5	62.5	7	
Montalto Offugo	9	2	22.2	6	66.7	6	66.7	9	
Totals	246	104	42.3	117	47.6	133	54.1	223	90.7

from hometowns in Italy married only people from their hometowns. In the old world village, endogamy did not by itself infer loyalty to the hometown; what *did* infer loyalty regarding marriage was either marrying within the hometown group *or* into a group outside the town yet approved by one's own group. In many districts in the old world one's sphere of action was not limited to the hometown but also to the surrounding towns. For example, the villages surrounding Susa (Piemonte) — Gravere, Meana, Montepantera, and Venaus — were involved in the fruit export trade with France so there was much contact between the villages. This resulted in intermarriage between different villages. As a result, immigrants from various towns from the Susa district also intermarried in Toronto. Of the 16 men from Susa who were married in Toronto's Italian parishes between 1908 and 1935 (they came from four villages), 7 married women from their respective hometowns. However, 8 of the remaining 9 bridegrooms married brides from other towns in the Susa district. The same was true of immigrants from the Friuli region, and from towns surrounding Cerisano in Cosenza — San Sisto la Costa, San Vincenzo la Costa, and Montalto Offugo. Only a handful of men from Friuli married women from their hometowns; between 1908 and 1935, however, 52 of 66 men, or 79 per cent of *friulani* men in the Italian parish marriage registers, married wives from Friuli. Fifty-eight of 66 men, or 88 per cent, married wives from Friuli or from the contiguous province of Treviso (Veneto). During the same period, 15 of 43 immigrants from San Sisto la Costa, San Vincenzo la Costa, Cerisano and Montalto Offugo married immigrants from their respective hometowns. However, 26 of 43, or 61 per cent married women from their respective hometowns or from towns in the district of Cerisano.

Furthermore, a careful examination of the marriage registers reveals that immigrants did not marry mates only from towns approved by townspeople in Italy; they also developed new marriage alliances with other townsgroups in the new world. Probably because of the dearth of available mates from the hometown, some groups in Toronto sanctioned the new alliances. To a certain extent, the leaders of each group were instrumental in directing the attitudes of their townspeople. When the leaders married outside their hometown group, their *paesani* would tend less to regard exogamy with opprobrium. As we saw earlier, the pioneers of three townsgroups — Modugno di Bari, Pisticci (Materia), and San Sisto la Costa (Cosenza) — married into families from Laurenzana and thus helped give that practice a stamp of legitimacy for their townspeople. Some hometown groups formed marriage alliances more readily with particular groups than with others. For example, four men and women from Pisticci (Materia) married mates from Laurenzana (Potenza, in the same region of Basilicata); four *modugnesi* took spouses from Monteleone di Puglia, and three other immigrants from Modugno took spouses from Pisticci. The Sicilians from Vita (Trapani), Termini Imerese (Palermo), and Pachino (Siracusa) intermarried almost to the exclusion of other Italians. It seems that some hometown groups felt an affinity to other groups because of shared experiences in Toronto — either boarding, working or participating in the same enterprises. The early sojourners from Modugno or Monteleone, for example, lived on the same streets and in many cases in the same boardinghouses in the Ward (especially 71 Elm Street). Furthermore many immigrants from each town were involved in the similar trades of shoe-shining and barbering. Four marriages were recorded between these two groups before 1935.

As the above figures on Sicilian marriages suggest, the immigrants from those towns identified strongly with their island; however, regionalism was not the only reason for the high rate of endogamy among immigrants from Pachino, Termini Imerese and Vita. The three groups shared similar work and enterprise and lived on the same streets. All three of the groups were involved in fruit and vegetable peddling, retailing and market gardening. In West Hill, gardeners from all three towns owned contiguous farms. Many immigrants from Pachino and Vita lived on the same streets in the Queen and Sackville neighbourhood. As a result many marriages were contracted between the three groups. Only two marriages occurred between *pachinesi* and a non-Sicilian. In both cases, the outside spouse was from San Sisto la Costa, a hometown which claimed many of the city's early fruit traders. Two immigrants from Vita married non-Sicilians from Boiano, another town which sent Toronto many of its early banana peddlers, and later, wholesalers. Marrying outside the hometown group, therefore, did not indicate disloyalty towards one's *paesani*. Rather the group itself approved marriage alliances with groups it felt had shared important experiences in the migration process — boarding, occupation, enterprise. Thus the townsman in Toronto was influenced by his own townspeople to look beyond the pale of his own group and identify with a larger Italian community in the city.

Loyalty to the hometown group therefore did not preclude loyalty to the larger Italian population of the city. Each group did not segregate itself from other groups but rather lived among them. When marriage partners could not be found within the hometown group in Toronto (or in the hometown) the group itself eventually approved marriages to other groups. It was through the hometown that the immigrant began to identify with an Italian community in the city.

An Italian community emerged in Toronto from at least the early 1880s. By an Italian community we mean not the three

Table 7: Endogamy and exogamy among immigrants from Termini Imerese, Vita and Pachino, Sicily, 1908-1935

town origins of one partner		Termini Imerese	%	Vita	%	Pachino	%	same prov.[a] as partner	%	Sicily[b]	%	other	%	totals
Termini Imerese	Mt. Carmel	45		5		8		7		10		9		84
	St. Agnes	16								2		4		22
	total	61	57.5	5	4.7	8	7.5	7	6.6	12	11.3	13	12.3	106
Vita	Mt. Carmel	5		26		6		5		6		12		60
	St. Agnes			14		2						5		21
	total	5	6.2	40	49.3	8	9.9	5	6.2	6	7.4	17	21.0	81
Pachino	Mt. Carmel	8		6		14		7		2		3		40
	St. Agnes			2		2				2		3		9
	total	8	16.3	8	16.3	16	32.7	7	14.3	4	8.2	6	12.2	49
Totals						162		19		22				236
						A		B		C				D

origins of other partner

Total marriages endogamous by town [A/D]   = 117 (49.6%)
Total marriages endogamous by province [(A + B)/D]   = 157 (66.5%)
Total marriages endogamous by region (Sicily) [(A + B + C)/D]   = 179 (75.9%)

[a] where only one partner is from Vita, Termini, or Pachino
[b] where partners are from different provinces and only one partner is from either Vita, Termini, or Pachino

physical Italian neighbourhoods which would emerge in the 1890s nor do we mean the sum of the distinctive hometown groups. Rather, an Italian community was based on the sentiments of immigrants from Italy, on the belief that they belonged to a group of people with a shared background and shared interests. The emergence of an Italian community and its institutions was strongly influenced by four factors. First, although the immigrants from Italy had arrived in Toronto as people of their villages, they also shared a fellow feeling for their old world countrymen, especially since they lived in a foreign environment. Secondly, shared experiences prepared the immigrants to identify with each other. Informal bonds developed between Italians in many situations — on the street, at a church, on the job, or in enterprise. In the 1880s, for example, fruit peddlers in Toronto were primarily from small towns surrounding Lucca and Genoa, and from Laurenzana and San Sisto la Costa. These men met at the crack of dawn as they loaded their carts on the market railyards on the Esplanade.

Thirdly, the growth of the Italian population of the city encouraged the development of a community. Institutional organization among Italians was more viable in 1901 when the population stood at 4,000, than in 1891 when it numbered only a few hundred. Fourthly, the rate of growth also influenced the development of a Toronto Italian community. Between 1897 and 1901 the population more than quadrupled from under 1,000 to about 4,000. After the recession of 1907-8, the population rose dramatically from 5,000 in 1908 to about 14,000 in 1913. The effect of this rapid growth was to consolidate the older members of the community: they felt that they had shared experiences in the city, had formed their own clubs, had pioneered the Italian community of Toronto, and that the greenhorns must approach them with deference. Many of the young men from Modugno di Bari and from Lucca who had arrived during the ten years preceding the First World War felt that they were barred from holding offices in the older organizations; in 1916 these young men organized the Circolo Columbo, a socio-recreation club tied to Mount Carmel parish. In fact it was during periods of rapid immigration that many of the institutions and clubs of the colony were formed. The first Italian mutual aid society, the Umberto Primo, was initiated in 1888 by immigrants from Laurenzana and a few Genoese. During the large migration at the turn of the century, two more important mutual aid societies were organized, the Vittorio Emanuele III and the Circolo Operai dell'Ontario, in 1902 and 1903. Many members of those two societies were from Calabria. In 1907, with the backing of the Conservative party, many of the city's wealthy Italians, especially those from Lucca and San Sisto la Costa and Cerisano formed the Italian National Club, a posh socio-recreational centre on D'Arcy Street. Meanwhile, the socialists established a branch of the Italian Socialist party. The Sicilians maintained a distance from the community. Rather than join the three main mutual benefit societies, they formed their own Grand Lodge in 1909, but only one of their societies, the Trinacria, survived, and was reorganized in 1913. By the First World War, therefore, the institutional bases of an Italian community in Toronto had long been developed.[21]

The institutional development of the community was paralleled by the growth of visible Italian focal points in each of the three Little Italies. By 1916 all three neighbourhoods boasted a Catholic church and a Methodist meeting place. Centre Avenue and Elm Street became the commercial centre of the entire colony. Louis Puccini, Francesco Nicoletti, Virginio Zincone, Angelo Petti and others operated their food-importing businesses in conjunction with their banking services and steamship agencies. Smaller grocery stores served specific hometown groups: Joseph Polito catered to the immigrants from Termini, Jim Farano's wife on Elm Street geared her store to the *modugnesi* of the colony, while Michael Circelli's clients were mostly fellow *monteleonsei*. Some professionals and entrepreneurs (often it was difficult to distinguish the two) began posting their signs in the Ward also. A university-educated immigrant from Bologna, Harry Corti, operated the Italian Publishing Company on Centre Avenue near Elm Street. Starting in 1907 the firm published the *Tribuna Canadiana*, Toronto's third and most successful Italian newspaper. The Conservative party backed that venture.[22] Small pasta manufactories, Italian cigar-making shops, real estate agencies, and a law office also operated in the Ward.

The College and Grace streets neighbourhood saw its first steamship agency in 1916: Francisco Tomaiuolo's on Clinton Avenue. Angelo Lobraico, the son of a *laurenzanese*, soon moved to the area and opened a real estate agency on Manning Avenue. A few small grocery stores dotted the neighbourhood, including Dominic di Stasi's, which catered to the many *pisticcesi* in the district. On north Dufferin Street, the churches and Methodist kindergarten were the most important focal points.

Each Little Italy developed a sense of neighbourhood. A *friulano* on Beaver Street in the north Dufferin area might deposit his pay cheque at Nicoletti's bank in the Ward, and might even look for a bride in the small *friulano* community in Port Credit; however, he also felt a sense of loyalty towards Italians in his own neighbourhood. In 1924 when the Fratellanza (Brotherhood) Mutual Benefit Society was formed, virtually all its members were (and remained) skilled labourers from Chieti (Abruzzi) and Friuli who lived in the Dufferin and Davenport district. Although they came from different regions, the two groups had the common bonds of occupation and neighbourhood. Indeed, very few Italian immigrants moved from one of the three Italian neighbourhoods to another. Prejudices developed towards each Little Italy. The Ward was considered a slum by the other two neighbourhoods. The Ward residents found the College-Grace district a rough neighbourhood. Meanwhile those two neighbourhoods found the north Dufferin Little Italy downright dangerous.[23]

Between 1885 and 1915 Toronto's Italian immigrants identified with a number of groups — their townspeople, their neighbourhood, and ultimately with the city's Italian community. They operated on two levels, what Robert Harney has called the "chiaroscuro" of old world local and national loyalties.[24] By the First World War the migrants from the peninsula had expanded their attachments to townsmen and associated with an Italian population in Toronto. The new horizons had originally opened up in the home village where prospective migrants first heard about their nation. They expanded in the early settlement and work experiences of the sojourner, and under the guidance of the emerging community's elite. The chiaroscuro image, however, would remain with the migrant throughout the prewar years. Unlike the day he first arrived in the city, however, the immigrant who had settled even temporarily in a Little Italy could understand that while his little universe, his idea of Italy, might revolve around his *paese*, a larger body of Italians did exist and he *could* identify with them.

Notes

1. Kevin Lynch, *The Image of the City* (Cambridge, Mass.: The M.I.T. Press, 1960), ch. 3, esp. pp. 72-77.

2. See R.F. Harney, *Italians in Canada*, Occasional Papers on Ethnic and Immigration Studies (Toronto: Multicultural History Society of Ontario, 1978), p. 3, and A.V. Spada, *The Italians in Canada* (Ottawa and Montreal: Canada Ethnic, 1969), p. 265. Philip De Grassi's papers are in the University of Toronto Archives. On James Forneri, see John King, *McCaul: Croft:/Forneri: Personalities of Early University Days* (Toronto: Macmillan Co., 1914). Also, Julius Molinaro, "Giacomo Forneri (1789-1869): From Turin to Toronto," *Mosaico* (September 1975), pp. 14-16.

3. The Montreal Italian Padrone system is described skilfully in Robert Harney, "Montreal's King of Italian Labour: A Case Study of Padronism," *Labour/Le Travailleur*, 1979. The Toronto press occasionally reported cases of exploitation of Italian labourers by padroni. See, for example, "Italian Labourers," *Globe*, 14 Nov. 1883, p. 1, and "Those Deluded Italians," *Toronto Empire*, 9 August 1888, p. 8.

4. "Foreigners Who Live in Toronto," *Daily Mail and Empire*, 2 October 1897, p. 10.

5. See, for example, "Poverty Stricken Immigrants," *Globe*, 17 November 1883, p. 8.

6. Turano's fellow townsman, Luigi Spizziri, was the banker/padrone responsible for bringing many Calabrian immigrants to Chicago during the 1880s. See Rudolph J. Vecoli's "Contadini in Chicago. A Critique of the Uprooted," *Journal of American History*, 51 (December 1964), pp. 404-17.

7. "A Day in the Works of the Canada Foundry Company," *Globe and Mail*, 2 March 1907, p. 10. Wayne Roberts, "Toronto Metal Workers and the Second Industrial Revolution, 1890-1914," *Labour/Le Travailleur* 6 (Autumn 1980), pp. 49-72. In July 1903 iron workers were shipped from Scotland as scabs; these included sixty Scottish moulders who had been brought to Toronto on misrepresentation. When they discovered they had been hired as strikebreakers they protested and fifty of the moulders refused to work. *Toronto Star*, 19 July 1903, p. 1. Information on the Terracina moulders was obtained by cross-referencing city directories with marriage registers (which give the hometowns) from Our Lady of Mount Carmel Italian National Parish.

8. Egisto Rossi, "Delle condizioni del Canadà rispetto all'emigrazione italiana," *Boll. Emig.* no. 3 (1903), p. 9; "Notiziario: Informazioni sulle condizioni dell'emigrazione italiana nella Provincia di Ontario (Canadà), *Boll. Emig.* no. 14 (1913), p. 74; *Census of Canada*, 1911, which estimated the Italian population at 4,873; Emily Weaver, "The Italians in Toronto," *Globe Saturday Magazine*, 10 July 1910, p. 2, estimated the city's Italian population at 10,000.

9. Forced to Live with Crime and City Lands are Vacant," *Globe*, 21 December 1906, p. 10.

10. "Foreigners Who Live in Toronto," *Daily Mail and Empire*, 20 October 1897.

11. Weaver, "Italians in Toronto," p. 2.

12. See University of Toronto Library, Thomas Fisher Rare Book Room: Ms. Coll. 119, James Mavor Papers; Box 70 Arc 19.

13. "Messina Earthquake," *The Evening Telegram*, 30 December 1908, p. 1.

14. *Might's City Directory of Toronto* was indispensable for re-creating the neighbourhoods, and tracing the labour agents/grocers.

15. For two excellent studies of the immigrant boardinghouse see R.F. Harney, "Boarding and Belonging," *Urban History Review* 2 (October 1978), pp. 8-37; A. Vazsonyi, "The Star Boarder: Traces of Cicisbism in an immigrant community," *Tractata Altaica* (Wiesbaden, 1976), pp. 695-713.

16. John S. and Leatrice D. Macdonald, "Chain Migration, Ethnic Neighbourhood Formation and Social Networks," *Millbank Memorial Fund Quarterly* XLII (1964), pp. 82-97; Frank Thistlethwaite, "Migration from Europe Overseas in the Nineteenth and Twentieth Centuries," XIᵉ Congrès International des Sciences Historiques, *Rapports, Vol. V: Histoire Contemporaine* (Stockholm: Almquist and Wiksell, 1960), pp. 32-60.

17. Information on settlement patterns was obtained by cross-referencing data in marriage registers with addresses in city directories and oral testimony.

18. On the *laurenzanesi* in Toronto before 1905, see John Zucchi, "*Paesani* in a Toronto Neighbourhood: Italian Immigrants in the 'Ward', 1870-1940," (M.A., Department of History, University of Toronto, 1979), ch. 1. On Glionna, see Giovanni Florenzano, *Della emigrazione italiana in American comparata alle altre emigrazioni europee* (Naples: Giannini, 1874), p. 167n.

19. In addition to city directories and church registers some oral interviews with immigrants or their children were helpful in analysing the settlement of townsgroups: for the *laurenzanesi*, Mr. Michael Glionna (15 November 1978); for the Modugnesi, Mr. Jim Farano (18 December 1978); for the *boianesi*, Mr. Michael Chiovitti (2 October 1981); for the *friulani*, Mrs. Albina di Clare (9 March 1980) and Mr. Luigi Piccoli (23 May 1980); for the *vitesi* and *pachinesi*, Mrs. Rose Catalano (31 January 1982). Similarly, the immigrants from Sora and the towns surrounding Susa had their own clusters; those from Sora lived along Claremont Street and Manning Avenue, while those from Gravere and Meana di Susa lived mostly on Beatrice and Grace streets. For the latter group, interviews with Mr. and Mrs. Attilio Bonavero (8 February 1982) and Mr. Fred Peirolo (18 December 1981) were very helpful.

20. William M. De Marco, *Ethnics and Enclaves: Boston's Italian North End* (Ann Arbor, Mich.: UMI Research Press, 1981), pp. 35-44, and John W. Briggs, *An Italian Passage: Immigrants to Three American Cities, 1890-1930* (New Haven: Yale University Press, 1978), pp. 73-94. Among Slovaks, see S. June Alexander, "The Immigrant Church and Community: The Formation of Pittsburgh's Slovak Religious Institutions, 1880-1914," (Ph.D., University of Minnesota, 1980), ch. III, pp. 158-208.

21. Information on all the mutual benefit societies can be found in the annual report of the Registrar of Friendly Societies, in the annual report of the Inspector of Insurance, *Sessional Papers* of the Ontario Legislature, 1896-1940. The incorporation papers and charters of the Vittorio Emanuele III, Italian National Club, and later for the Vitese Mutual Benefit Society, can be found in the Business and Partnership Registry, Ministry of Consumer and Commercial Affairs (Government of Ontario), Toronto. On the Grand Lodge of Sicilian Mutual Benefit Societies, see Giovanni Oranova to Bonomelli, SDA president, 7 July 1913, SDA.

22. Toronto's first Italian newspaper, *Lo Stendardo*, was published by Joseph Saporita between 1898 and 1900. Saporita was also president of the Italian Workingmen's Circle Mutual Benefit Society in 1902 and financial secretary from 1903 to 1905. See Duncan McLaren, ed., *Ontario Ethno-cultural Newspapers, 1835-1972* (Toronto: University of Toronto Press, 1973), pp. 107-10; also annual reports of the Registrar of Friendly Societies, 1900-1905. Interview with Mrs. Iglesias, daughter of Harry Corti (9 May 1978, MHSO).

23. Father A. Scafuro, pastor of St. Clement's Church in the Dufferin-Davenport neighbourhood noted in 1924 that "Years ago it was not safe to pass by Beaver Avenue and Dufferin Street." Scafuro to Archbishop McNeil, October 10 1924, "National Parishes," McNeil Papers, ATT.

24. R.F. Harney, "Chiaroscuro, Italians in Toronto, 1885-1915," *Italian Americana* I:2 (1975), pp. 142-67.

The Chinese in Toronto

Dora Nipp

Toronto's historical, social and political evolution has, for the most part, focused on prominent individuals or as a celebration of events and institutions. Until recently the participation of ethnic groups throughout Toronto's various stages of development has unfortunately been overlooked. Curiously, the city's very social fabric, its ability to sustain a multiracial, multicultural ambience unique to a Canadian metropolis, requires that the collective experience of its residents be examined. Only then can one truly appreciate Toronto's historical development. The Chinese, in common with the many immigrant groups who settled in Toronto at the turn of the century, came in search of economic betterment. These early pioneers subsequently laid the foundation from which the skills, labour and knowledge of succeeding generations could be incorporated into this continuously expanding urban centre.

A vigorous and vibrant community, Toronto's Chinese population is the largest in Canada. This, however, is a postwar phenomenon. From the beginning, Chinese immigration was almost completely restricted to British Columbia. The exact date of their appearance on the west coast is a point of contention for many historians, but 1858 is generally viewed as the year in which the first Chinese community was established in Victoria.[1] The majority of these early immigrants had come north from the gold fields of California. As the mines were slowly depleted and Asiatic xeno-

phobia increased, Chinese miners joined thousands of other pro-
spectors in the trek northward to the most recent gold find in the
Fraser River canyon. By 1860 news of "mountains of gold" and
precious jade had encouraged some four thousand Chinese to sail for
what was to become British Columbia in that year alone. Rather
than prospecting, many Chinese supplied unskilled labour, and
entered into such services as cooking and washing. The sudden
swelling of the population had left a vacuum of necessary services
which could not be met and thus the Chinese filled the demand.

The second largest influx of Chinese came a number of years
later with the construction of the Canadian Pacific Railway from
1880 to 1884. The lack of available labour to complete the final
western section of the transcontinental system created deep rifts between the Dominion and the provincial government of British Columbia. The province had entered Confederation in 1871 with the
understanding that the CPR, linking east with west, would be completed within ten years. The decade elapsed, however, with no sign
of construction beginning in British Columbia. When the Dominion
government alluded to the possibility of resorting to Chinese labour,
the Legislative Assembly vociferously attacked the suggestion, for
while British Columbians clammered for the railroad, they were not
prepared to tolerate competition from Chinese labour. Nevertheless,
Andrew Onderdonk, chief contractor for this portion of the CPR,
with Prime Minister Sir John A. MacDonald's concurrence, over-
rode the opposition and in 1880-81 contracted for fifteen hundred
Chinese navvies from the United States. The following year an additional two thousand men were recruited through Hong Kong. Over
the next three years, until it was completed, approximately fifteen
thousand Chinese labourers worked on the construction of the
railroad. Once the terminus was completed, their terms of service
also ended and they were discharged. The resultant effect was to ex-
acerbate labour competition in an economy on the margins of a
depression. As no provisions had been made for their welfare,
thousands of unemployed Chinese found themselves scattered
among small towns which had grown up next to the tracks or in Victoria, then the largest centre on the west coast. A small number,
however, decided to travel eastward to the prairies, while others
went farther on to Toronto.

In the 1880s, Toronto was undergoing unprecedented industrial growth coupled with a population increase that a decade
before had initiated its metamorphosis into a major urban centre.
For the many, primarily transatlantic, immigrants arriving during
this period, Toronto held glowing opportunities. The city's rapid
economic ascension depended heavily on an efficient railway network not only for the distribution of goods, but also to accommodate
the increasing demand for a constant labour supply. Toronto had its

first steam railway by 1860,[2] but it was with the completion of the
CPR that its potential in both domestic and international markets
blossomed. The CPR transported more than just products, it
facilitated the transportation of settlers re-establishing themselves in
various parts of the country. Thus, as European immigrants made
their way west, a small group of Chinese migrated eastward against
this current.

It is probable that Chinese began moving east even before the
CPR's completion.[3] The earliest official record of the Chinese in
Toronto is found in the 1877-1878 city directory. Included were two
laundries, that of Sam Ching and Company at 9 Adelaide Street
East, and Wo Kee, located at 385 Yonge Street close to Gerrard.
These were two of fifteen laundries appearing that year. According
to city assessment rolls, Sam Ching was the lone proprietor in the
two-storey building.[4] A 15.6 by 28 foot roughcast building that occupied a 15.6 by 60 foot lot, its total value at the time was $2,310.
Also on the same street was a machinist, a blacksmith and oil merchants and bookkeeper.

Two years later Sam Ching moved a few doors over to 15
Adelaide Street East. His new operation was set up in a three-storey
brick building and its property value was considerably greater than
the former shop. By this time, three more laundries had appeared
but in no discernible pattern. Sam Lee was located at 42 Jarvis
Street, Sam Sing was at 133 1/3 Queen Street West, and Tan Gee
was found at 121 Yonge Street. This scattered settlement remained
until 1900, when economic considerations drove rents up, anti-
Chinese agitation from the west was finding its way to Toronto, and
an increasing number of new Chinese arrivals acted in concert to encourage the establishment of a so-called Chinatown. In his detailed
historical study of Toronto's Chinese community, Paul Levine notes
that "the pattern of Chinese settlement has historically followed the
city's growth proportionally."[5]

The nature of their occupation was also a determining factor in
establishing these businesses. Unlike either Victoria or Vancouver,
Toronto's Chinese were rarely engaged in mining, the canning industry, construction, or in small merchant businesses. Instead, they
were mostly employed in secondary occupations of which laundries
predominated. By 1881, there were an estimated twenty-two
Chinese in Ontario. Ten of those enumerated lived in Toronto and
all operated laundries. Seven were found in the St. James Ward
area. In St. Andrews Ward there were three such establishments.[6]

By 1882 a few of the pioneer operations had done well enough
to move into larger premises. Sam Lee, formerly of 42 Jarvis, was
now found at 44 Jarvis. Sam Sing was relocated at 135 Queen Street
in a former furniture store. Sue Hong opened his shop at 355 1/2
Yonge Street, and one of the earlier laundries operated by Tan Gee

is no longer listed. Concurrently, a new business, run by Sam Wing, reopened at 9 Adelaide Street.

After the first laundries were established in 1878, within five years seven more appeared. Three of these were located at 40 St. George Street, 91 Queen Street East and 208 King Street East. The only other occupations listed in the city directory included Alexander Chin, a barber at 105 York Street; Robert Chin, a bartender who boarded at 171 York Street; and William Chin of 24 Grange, a butler. Within the next five years, of the forty-four laundries enumerated, fifteen were known to be operated by Chinese.

The areas the Chinese chose to set up their businesses in were decided by the cost of rent and the proximity to their clientele. Most, such as Chue Thomas who established his shop on Queen Street, had for their neighbours a number of small businesses such as a barber, a second-hand store, a tailor and a small fruit market. Over at 119 York, Kee Sam had in his neighbourhood a lodging house, pawnbroker, dyer, shoemaker and a restaurant.[7] These businesses, many of which changed proprietors yearly, catered to a transient population. The somewhat fluid nature of these areas was thus fairly receptive to domestic services such as eating places and laundries. Moreover, as their customers were essentially non-Chinese single families and individuals, access to some form of transportation was necessary for pick-up and delivery of clothing.

There are two possibilities as to why Chinese pioneers entered secondary occupations. The city's rapid growth created demands for domestic services that surpassed the supply. Small businesses, including laundries, not only met these demands, but virtually ensured that new arrivals would have employment. If the operation was large enough to employ more than one worker, it was generally a family affair. The initial capital needed was not so large as to create a severe loss should the owner decide to sell the business. The assets could be quickly liquidated or passed onto others.

By the 1890s the settlement pattern had changed slightly and there were now hints of a discernible Chinese sector of the city. While there is not distinctive side-by-side grouping there is a noticeable increase in the number of launderies along Queen Street. In the 1890 directory thirty of the sixty-nine launderies listed were Chinese-operated. Seven were found along Queen Street West. The newest entry was a Chinese and Japanese fancy goods store, Wing Tai and Company of 405 Yonge Street. These earlier laundries were established in predominantly Jewish neighbourhoods, mostly along Parliament to Church streets, and Yonge along Queen Street East to Elizabeth Street. Years later when the Jewish residents shifted northwestward to the present Kensington Market area, their stores and buildings were occupied by the Chinese.[8]

For the many Chinese pioneers who arrived in Toronto, their

Railway man George Cane and his sons arrive from Kent, England, 1911.
Courtesy: City of Toronto Archives.

636 Queen Street East, rear view, 1912.
Courtesy: City of Toronto Archives.

CLASS OF '86.
St. Michael's College, Toronto.

St. Michael's Hospital, Toronto, Canada

1900.
Courtesy: Ontario Archives.

Jackson family, c. 1897. One of the children (Richard) was a jeweller in a store at College and Lippincott Street.

C. 1917.

The immigrant Ward in the shadow of City Hall, c. 1911.
Courtesy: City of Toronto Archives.

Jews walking to services in the Ward, c. 1911.
Courtesy: Central Neighbourhood House.

Italian labourers working on Toronto street railways, c. 1912.
Courtesy: City of Toronto Archives.

Italian Reservists marching off to the First World War, Yonge and Dundas streets, 1915.
Courtesy: Public Archives of Canada PA 91104.

Chinese physical training and boy scout groups in High Park, 1919.
Courtesy: Public Archives of Canada PA 83876.

Elizabeth Street, 1937.
Courtesy: City of Toronto Archives.

Macedonian boardinghouse, 1913.
Courtesy: City of Toronto Archives.

Convention of Macedonian Political Organization (MPO) held in Toronto, 1929.

The Lindala and Ranta families, founding members of the Toronto Finnish community, 1895.

Finnish maids on Augusta Avenue, c. 1933.

An excursion to Lambton Park for a Toronto Polish language school, 1925.

Polish Alliance of Canada, Branch No. 1, and their new flag, 1931.

St. George Greek Orthodox Church youth group participating in Toronto centennial celebrations, 1934.

Greek Bonita Restaurant, 1935.

Blessing the cornerstone of St. Josaphat's Church by Bishop Budka, 1913.

Vasile Avramenko's Ukrainian School of Ballet, Toronto, 1926.

migration was a continuation of the journey that had first brought them to British Columbia. Most of these immigrants originated from the Pearl River Delta area of Guangdon province in southern China. *Si-yi* or the "4 Districts" sent out the largest number of emigrants, followed by *San-yi* or the "3 Districts." Of those who came, by the late nineteenth century 73 per cent were from *Si-yi*, which included the countries of Tai-shan, Xin-hui, Sun-duc, En-ping and Kai-ping.[9] Of these counties, Tai-shan people predominated in the early period. Up until the 1960s and the flow of immigration from Hong Kong, the Caribbean and Southeast Asia, the Tai-shan dialect was the lingua franca of Chinese Canadians. Today only the older generation still speak it.

With very few exceptions, only men emigrated from China. Legal sanctions, historical tradition and social customs discouraged women from going abroad. The complexities of emigration, and the economic demand for only male labour also contributed to an unbalanced outflow. This was one reason for the increasingly anti-Chinese editorials that found expression in Toronto newspapers by the 1880s. Reflecting the prevailing opinions of the west, the *Toronto Telegram*, the *Toronto World*, and the Toronto *Globe* called for restrictions on the entry of Chinese labour. With the support of the newspapers, politicians and various labour groups succeeded in pressuring the Dominion government into enacting the Chinese Immigration Act of 1885.[10] The first of four restrictive acts, it placed a $50 head tax on all Chinese entering Canada, exempting only members of the diplomatic corps, government representatives and consular agents, tourists, merchants, men of science and students. The bill immediately resulted in a considerable drop in immigration. These regulations, however, only proved effective for five years. In 1886 the number of arrivals dropped to 212, a dramatic change from the thousands entering during the previous years. But by 1890, the trend had reversed and an increasing number of emigrants sailed for Canada.

Fed by fears of an "Oriental invasion," pressure groups in British Columbia campaigned for total exclusion. The Dominion government was in a difficult position. On one hand it recognized western Canada's anxiety over these unwelcome immigrants, but it was hesitant to harm Anglo-Chinese relations. Although Canada was no longer under British rule, it still followed Great Britain in its foreign policy. Thus, in order to appease discontented western politicians and labour groups, the Dominion government raised the head tax to $100 in 1900 and then increased the amount to a phenominal $500 in 1904. The Chinese immigration bills were introduced in effect to deter further entry of Chinese. Opportunities in Canada, however, were so attractive that many Chinese found ways to pay the tax in order to come over. Canada's Chinese population responded in various ways to these laws. Ghettoization of the community in Victoria and Vancouver for economic and social reasons contrasted with Toronto's Chinese immigrants. Here, there was no self-segregation but both the Chinese and the larger society made greater attempts to establish contact and interact with one another.

Toronto's Chinese were well received by, and responded favourably to, missionary workers. Indeed, the church had a major influence in the development of the community. This is evident in their involvement in Chinese activities. Toronto also had the largest Chinese Christian settlement in Canada. By 1941, 40 per cent of Canada's Chinese Christian population was in Ontario. Their association with the church helped the community identify more readily with Canadian society.

As early as May of 1882, the Toronto Young Men's Christian Association weekly bulletin from Shaftsbury Hall, located at the old YMCA on 30 Queen Street West, mentioned the presence of Chinese in the city:

> It is probably unknown to most of our friends that a Chinese class is held in our rooms every Sabbath afternoon, at three o'clock. Mr. D. McLaren has been led by the Lord to take a deep interest in this work and has met with much encouragement in his labours. The men fully appreciate those efforts for their advancement. Many of the U.S. Associations have flourishing classes and Sunday Schools for Chinamen.

A later bulletin notes the class's favourable progress exceeding the expections of the teacher:

> The gentleman who has assumed charge has spared no effort toward securing the attendance of the pupils and it speaks well for the interest taken when we find that out of some sixteen Chinamen in our city, nine attend the class. An organ has been purchased by the chairman and a number of Chinese and other mottoes are being prepared to adorn the walls of the Bible Parlour in which the class meets.

Financial assistance for maintaining the classes seems to have been through the generosity of the chairman, Mr. McLaren. Ther services of the YMCA were interdenominational, for the churches had not yet developed an interest in the Chinese. The Presbyterians and Methodists, who were active in British Columbia, were comparatively slower to respond to these new immigrants arriving in Ontario.

Actually missionary work among the Chinese did not begin until 1894, under the auspices of the Christian Endeavour Society, Cooke's Presbyterian Church.[11] Attempts to proselytize the Chinese were hampered by a language barrier, and so Sunday schools provided English lessons. This was viewed as the most constructive and effective means of reaching the Chinese. On August 12, 1894, J. Henderson, superintendent of the Chinese Sunday school, invited the Reverend R.P. McKay, Foreign Secretary of the Presbyterian Church, to meet with the teachers and the class at the church's annual social in the parlour of the Young Men's Christian Association.[12] A month later, as a follow-up to this meeting, McKay wrote to Henderson expressing his concerns about the Chinese:

> I am sorry to say I cannot speak with any confidence as to the number of Chinese in the city. I have understood that they may number about 50. We have in our school . . . about 15 to 17 and I think at the Metropolitan Church they have an equal number. I think more must be done if we had workers who had more time at their disposal to visit the men at their shops although they do not like to be interrupted in their work too frequently and they are industrious and hard working.[13]

Understandably, the missionaries employed English classes as a tool for conveying religious teachings and instilling Christian values. Long hours at their shops, however, meant that many could not make full use of these opportunities. McKay reflects on the current situation:

> The work we do in teaching English at first, is very slow, necessarily so, since we have only one day in the week in which to do anything in this way and therefore a pupil may be a long time in the class, before such a knowledge of English can be acquired by him, as to enable him to understand even very simple and elementary gospel truth.[14]

Prior to the spring of 1895, there had been a concerted effort by the Presbyterians of missionary work among the Chinese.[15] It was only after J.C. Thompson's sermon delivered at the morning service of Cooke's Church that the congregation turned its attention to the Chinese. Their initial response was one of enthusiasm, and the Christian Endeavour Society offered to supply enough teachers so that each student had his personal instructor. The classes were well attended and the missionary workers made fair progress in attracting pupils. Eighteen ninety-nine was a hallmark year for Christian work, for by this time five Chinese Sunday schools had been organized in the city. Within a year Cooke's, which played a key role in facilitating such programs, had an estimated sixty-five men on its enrolment list. The Metropolitan Church and the YMCA both had forty registered. West Church had twenty-five and Oak Street Church had a class of fifteen. Thus the estimated total number of Chinese in church-sponsored English classes was 185.[16]

In the same year, Mrs. William Patterson, one of the language teachers at Cooke's, organized the Chinese Christian Endeavour Society. Established on December 11, 1899, the executives of the society were all Chinese. The elected president was Hong Woo; vice-president, Wong Foo; secretary, Joe Leong, and the convener of the music committee, Mah Tang.[17] Meetings were held regularly at six o'clock every Sunday evening. Discussions, with the exception of reading the Bible lesson, were conducted in Chinese.

Within a year, the classes proved so popular that students were travelling in from Toronto Junction to attend. The church then decided to accommodate those who lived farther from the city centre in an evening class at West Church. To their credit, the missionaries, in addition to Canadianizing the Chinese by first turning them into good Christians, also realized that if they attempted to accelerate the acculturation process they ran the risk of alienating the Chinese. Rather than demanding that their pupils sever ties with China, mission workers encouraged the Chinese to maintain contact through their association with the church. The students were asked to contribute to "help persecuted and famine stricken sufferers in their own land," and to donate to the support of a Chinese missionary worker in British Columbia.[18]

Missionaries were essentially of two minds in their decision to work among the Chinese. There is little doubt of their concern for the social well-being of these new immigrants, but contrasting sharply with the spirit of humanitarianism was a fear of allowing the entry of an unassimilable and alien people who threatened the Christian ethics of Canadian society.[19] Peter Ward has noted that, ". . . at the heart of missionary thought lay an unrecognizable conflict between evangelical humanitarianism and ethnocentric nationalism."[20] Yet this apparent ambivalence did not detract from the positive influence church work had on the community's sociopolitical development.

By introducing these new immigrants to Christianity the churches were not only Canadianizing the Chinese; their efforts also helped to prepare a new generation of community leaders. In February 1910, Knox Presbyterian Church arranged a meeting at 70 Duchess Street for some of its Chinese students. From this gathering came the idea of forming a Chinese Christian Association, also known as the Young Men's Christian Institute (YMCI). One of the nine founders was E.C. Mark. Shortly after it was established, the association moved into a house at 134 Church Street. No less than 450 (or 43.6 per cent) of Toronto's Chinese were at that time attending Sunday school classes in several of the city's churches.[21]

Another of the founding members was Reverend Ma T.K. Wou, who became the YMCI's minister. A 1908 graduate of the Toronto Bible College, he and his wife Anna Ma were extremely active with the Chinese Christian community. When the original house could no longer accommodate the expanding YMCI, larger premises were purchased in 1914 at 187 Church Street. The monthly rent was an affordable $85. The ground floor was used for worship and the second floor maintained a Chinese school. The cellar served as a library and reading room. The YMCI invited Mr. T.C. Mark from China to act as the school's principal. By autumn the congregation included between twenty and thirty men. In her memoirs Anna Ma recalled a "typical Sunday programme":[22]

10:00 a.m.	Sing Song
11:00 a.m.	Service
2:00 p.m.	Bible Class led by minister & school principal
3:30 p.m.	Open air meeting in Chinatown
5:00 p.m.	Evangelical meeting
6:00 p.m.	Dinner (9n the basement, prepared by Reverend Ma)
7:00 p.m.	Evening Service

In 1917, the YMCI held the first conference of Chinese students in Canada. Reverend Ma was instrumental in organizing this event. The following year, as membership increased and the current building was no longer big enough for the many functions scheduled for the future, the association moved to 474 University Avenue. From here the YMCI served as a community centre, where "young people could meet" as well as a boardinghouse for an increasing number of visiting students from China. It continued teaching Chinese language to children and, in addition, operated a nursery school for the neighbourhood families. The YMCI's involvement in a variety of activities reflects the gradual changes taking place in the internal structure of the community.

Because of their ability to speak English, and through their contact with the missionaries, Chinese Christians had greater access to resources outside their community. From this background there emerged articulate and capable men who were seen as spokespersons or leaders of "Chinatown." Individuals such as Reverend Ma and T.C. Mark served as links between the Chinese and Canadian society at large. This group was recognized by many as representing the community, particularly in the eyes of government officials. Yet while they assumed a position of authority, the Chinese Christians did not have the mandate to exert control over those groups and organizations which dealt primarily with internal concerns. Clan, district and fraternal organizations had their origins in China and evolved independent of church influence. The male-dominated society required special social needs which these groups attempted to meet. They offered information and assistance in dealing with migration, payment of immigration taxes, help in seeking employment, as well as providing leisure activities such as gambling and cultural interests, welfare services, the arranging of loans and settling of disputes.

Clan associations were based on surname affiliations, and district organizations depended on one's county of origin. In Toronto, the small number of Chinese led to a relatively slow growth of both district and clan associations. Indeed, it was not until the 1920s that clan associations were readily identifiable. By that time the city had a number of such associations, including the Wong Kung Har Tong (the Wong Association), the Lem Si Ho Tong (Lem Society), and the Lee, Chin, Ing and Mark clans. Sometimes surname groups joined together under an umbrella group such as the Lung Gong brotherhood consisting of the Liu, Quon (Kwan, Quan), Chung and Chu families, or the Gee Duck Tong which represented the Hum, Tom, Hoy and Tse families.[23]

The oldest fraternal organization is the Cheekungton (CKT), also known by its English name of the Chinese Freemasons. Established in 1876 in Quesnel Forks in the interior of British Columbia, the organization originally consisted of workers and middle and small merchants.[24] While it also offered members social assistance, its main objectives were intrinsically related to the political cause in China. This meant the overthrow of the ruling Manchu government and the re-establishment of Chinese rule. The first mention of the CKT in Toronto appeared in the 1905 city directory. Listed as the Chee Swing Tong, Might's Directory incorrectly noted it as a laundry, but this mistake was rectified the following year. Located at 192 York Street, the CKT occupied the second floor of a building which also housed a restaurant.

The time of the CKT's arrival coincided with an increase in the number of Chinese establishments. Toronto's Chinese population had been growing substantially so that by 1900 the community supported ninety laundries, and two dry goods and vegetable stores. During the next five years expansion continued rapidly. In 1905 there were 228 laundries, a number of grocery stores and restaurants, and some fifteen or more merchants.[25] Thus, by the beginning of 1906, the city had a Chinese community substantial enough to require the services of, and to support, associations such as the CKT.

Another association which comes under none of the above classifications was the Chinese Benevolent Association (CBA). As a community organization which had no specific qualifications for membership, it enjoyed much support from the Chinese in both Vancouver and Victoria but was less popular in the eastern provinces. Although it professed to speak for all Chinese Canadians, it actually represented only those in the west. Part of the CBA's inability to generate support in Ontario was due to the influence of the Chinese Christian Association. Not only was the YMCI well established before the arrival of the CBA, but from its inception the Chinese Christian Association had involved itself actively in community affairs. It was the YMCI, not the clan, district or fraternal organizations that represented Toronto's Chinese at North American Chinese meetings held in eastern Canada and the United States.[26]

The organization most involved in the politics of China was the CKT. It was essentially through the network of the Chinese Freemasons that Chinese Canadians were kept informed of the political situation at home. Before the Nationalist Chinese Revolution broke out in 1911, Toronto hosted a number of prominent political figures who visited major Canadian cities soliciting financial aid. Li Hung Zhang was the first important individual to tour Canada. In 1896, he paused briefly in Toronto before heading out to the west coast. During his stopover, he brought news of China's defeat by the Japanese.

China had suffered a great loss of face at the hands of the Japanese, exposing not only the Imperial govenment's weaknesses but also the urgent need for reform. There emerged a group of intellectuals who advocated radical reform of the Chinese government, economy and the military. In 1898 two of the leading reformers, Kang You Wei and Liang Qi Chao, under the emperor's patronage, issued a series of edicts, hoping to bring about reforms through a constitutional monarchy. Within three months, however, the Empress Dowager had overthrown the young emperor and re-established herself. Reformers such as Kang and Liang were sent into exile abroad. Although they were banished from political involvement in their home country, they carried their movement to the overseas Chinese. Southeast Asia and North America, both of which had substantial Chinese nationals, were obviously potential power bases. Canada was a major target not only for the constitutional reformers, but for those who sought changes through revolution as well. The most notable of the revolutionaries was Dr. Sun Yat-sen.

Kang visited Canada on three separate occasions. In 1899, he formed the Emperor Protection Association (Bo Wong Wui). The objectives of this association are more correctly reflected in its English title, the Empire Reform Association. Kang came again in 1902 and 1904 seeking both financial and political support and met with a favourable response, particularly from the CKT. At the conclusion of his last visit, the Empire Reform Association could claim affiliation with twelve CKT branches across the country. The Toronto local was established in 1903, shortly after Kang's arrival earlier in the year.

When Sun Yat-sen turned to Canada he actively sought the support of the CKT for his proposed revolution. The Chinese Freemasons in all urban centres contributed generously to the revolutionary cause. For its part, the Toronto branch mortgaged its building and donated $10,000.[27] In fact Sun was fund-raising in the city when the abortive Huang Hua Kang uprising took place in Canton on March 29, 1911. His visit had considerable impact on the Chinese. Large crowds turned out to hear him speak in Victoria Hall. A skilful orator, Sun appealed to the Chinese nationalism of his audience. Sun's charisma and revolutionary spirit aroused an increasing interest in China's current political and social situation. His influence is evident in the growing political activity within the community, and two associations appear for the first as pro-nationalist organizations — the Chinese Christian Association and the Chinese Empire Reform Association. Both were "prototypes of organizations aimed at institutionalizing a wider political life among the members of the Tongs (associations) and Hung Men (larger political body of the CKT)."[28]

According to Levine, who offers the closest examination of Chinese organizational development in Toronto:

> 1911 is not only a significant year for the growth of the Chinese community in Toronto, but also the year of the National Chinese Revolution. From 1908-1911, nationalist forces are combining within Toronto to change the nature of the community, so that after 1911 political and social life within the Chinese community began to change drastically.[29]

Sun's Nationalist Party, the Kuomintang (KMT) rapidly established itself as a political party in Toronto. By 1917, it had its own newspaper, the *Shing Wah*, which was used to promote the party line. One year after its operations began, however, the Canadian government banned all so-called dissident parties, including the KMT. This move was possibly made at the request of then president of China, Yuan Shikai, who feared the potential power of overseas-based opponents. Ten of the KMT members who were responsible for the *Shing Wah* were arrested in 1918, and publication ceased. As a result, the KMT was forced underground and did not re-emerge again until 1919. In 1922, the newspaper was revived and appeared on the streets as the *Shing Wah Daily News*.

There is no question that Toronto's Chinese community had a vested interest in China's affairs, but this is not to imply that they ignored what was happening in Canada. The 1904 Chinese Immigration bill which imposed a $500 tax on incoming Chinese did not have the desired effect of limiting the number of arrivals. In 1901 there were an estimated 17,043 Chinese in Canada, with 758 in Ontario. By 1921 the population had increased to 36,924, and Ontario's Chinese also increased proportionally to 5,394. Throughout this period white British Columbians persisted in their demand for complete exclusion. In 1923, the Canadian government finally acquiesced. The Chinese Immigration Act in effect prevented the entry of Chinese immigrants. Although the bill made allowances for specific classes, its passing was thought to signal a slow death for Chinese Canadian communities. Despite attempted negotiations between the Chinese and Canadian governments to find a more equitable means of regulating immigration, the talks proved fruitless. The threat of the impending regulations and their ramifications had circulated through the Chinese population in most Canadian cities and towns. Committees were struck to defeat the act, or failing that, to seek possible amendments. But the speed with which the bill was introduced and passed through each reading left little time to organize or develop strategies. The time factor placed considerable constraints on generating support from outside the community, necessary for an effective lobbying campaign. The Immigration Act was introduced in the House of Commons in March 1923, passed in May and assented to June 30. Ironically, it was officially enacted on July 1, Canada's Dominion Day. For Chinese Canadians it was not an occasion for celebration; instead it was black-marked as "Humiliation Day." Understandably, for years afterwards Chinese across the country refused to participate in Dominion Day festivities.

The Chinese were not sitting idle as the act was being passed. Within this brief period communities had consolidated their efforts and established a general headquarters from which to direct and determine their course of action. Toronto's proximity to Ottawa, the presence of ready leaders, and the substantial Chinese population, made the city the most practical centre for the offices of the Chinese Association of Canada. Its executive committee consisted of representatives from the major Chinese communities of Victoria, Vancouver, Winnipeg, Toronto and Montreal. Because the association was based in Toronto, the city's spokesmen played a central role in formulating directives and organizing the various groups involved. The YMCI served as the national headquarters. The president was T.C. Mark; vice-president, Reverend Ma T.K. Wou; English-language secretaries, Ing S. Hoon, George P. Mark and E.C. Mark. All of these individuals were leaders of the Toronto Chinese Christian Association.[30] As in the past, certain of Toronto's missionaries demonstrated support for the Chinese, the most notable being Reverend Noyes, executive secretary of the Eastern Canada Mission, Dr. MacKay, secretary of the Presbyterian Church of Canada, as well as several prominent members of the Methodist and Anglican missions. They all urged amendments to the bill.

The threat of this exclusion policy left the Chinese community with little choice but to consolidate their forces as quickly as possible. The interval between the act's introduction and its implementation pressured the Chinese into manoeuvres they had hitherto not undertaken. So long as the bill did not receive official sanction and loomed menacingly in the background lobby groups believed there was a chance to influence the outcome. But once the Immigration Act was enacted the pain of defeat and humiliation resounded throughout the Chinese communities, and the enthusiasm which the Chinese community demonstrated at the onset was soon absorbed by the constraints of everyday living. While they did not totally resign themselves to their present situation, the leaders and supporters realized that amendments would not be achieved quickly. The Chinese Association of Canada simply could not sustain the energy required for a long-drawn-out battle.

In the face of political opposition and social criticism of their presence in Canada, the Chinese did, nevertheless, establish communities in various provinces. The common stereotype of the bachelor societies, while true to a degree, belies the group's efforts to create a familial environment. In addition to nuclear families, they tried to duplicate the social organizations of villages and towns at home. Dramatic and music societies were formed, mothers' group sprang up, as well as such Canadianized activities and interests as scout troops, hockey teams and Canadian Girls in Training (CGIT). Thus while the Immigration Act signalled the end of future immigration it also ensured that Canadians were diverting their attention away from the Chinese "threat." The community virtually disappeared from the pages of the newspapers, and was expected to die a slow death. But the Chinese had been confronted with adversity before, and although the 1923 act was the most devastating of the legislated measures, it did not prevent the intended victims from participating in a society which they also considered theirs.

Based on statistics from the census of Canada, prior to the Immigration Act, Toronto's Chinese population numbered 1,616, with the largest concentration in the Centre Ward area. In the 1911 census 1,036 had been enumerated. This meant an increase of approximately 50 per cent over ten years. The majority of these were male, many were single, but others were married with their families still in China. The occupations open to unskilled labour included laundry work, cooking, domestic services, or establishing grocery stores or small businesses.

Laundries were generally run by individuals or close relatives. They were family affairs operated by a father and son, brothers, or male cousins. Dr. George Lee came to Toronto as a boy in 1905 and helped out at a laundry set up by his father and uncle at 1132 Yonge Street. Harry Lem, founder of the Lichee Gardens, also started out in a laundry which his father and uncle, along with two helpers, ran in the Danforth area. Further examples of a family-based business are Mark Kwong Ping, who worked with his cousins at College and Beatrice, and Kam Hong Chong who, after arriving in the city in

1922 at the age of fourteen, lived with his uncle at a laundry located near King Street East and Sackville.[31]

The initial output required to set up a laundry was approximately five to six hundred dollars. This was a manageable amount for most prospective operators. In many cases, relations or friends from the same village or district pooled their resources to invest in similar businesses. If, however, one did not have such connections, assistance was often given by one's association or organization. One of the reasons the investment was so low was because most of the work was done by hand. Machines, at least in the earlier days, were unavailable or not required to accomplish the task. As Tom Lock recalls, the Chinese were known for the fine hand-finish of their wash:

> To make the linens white, we used to put the soiled clothing in a big square steel tank 4' x 4' x 6' deep on top of the coal stove. We would feed the tank using a hose and add bleach stirring the washing with a big stick. After, Ma would stand on a stool, reach into the boiling water and drag out the clothes with the stick. She would then drop them in a pail and transfer them to the washing machine.[32]

The actual machine used for washing was cylindrical in shape. The older models were constructed of wood, but were later changed to metal. It moved in a rocking motion with two huge cylinders, one inside the other. To rinse the clothing the water first had to be drained and then refilled. Before clean water could be placed in the washer, it had to be locked in a still position. Once the cycle had been completed and the clothes clean, they were starched and hung on a rope that stretched across the drying room. The temperature of this room was constantly kept hot so that the clothes would dry more quickly. Generally speaking, the laundries restricted their business to single families and unmarried individuals. The size of their operations and thus the absence of machinery to speed up service and take in large quantities prevented the laundries from dealing with hotels and restaurants.

In Toronto, laundry operators provided pick-up and delivery service. One interviewee recalled how in 1915 he used to go out at night with his father to pull an ''artillery-cart'' along Yonge Street, dropping off clean laundry. In common with many other immigrant families, children were expected to contribute to the support of the family as best they could. When Dorothy Soo was growing up in the mid-1930s she and her brother ''used to pick up and deliver the laundry by sled or wagon, then by bikes until the family could afford a car.''

Customers could also bring in their own clothing. Laundries

were open until eight or nine o'clock in the evening. The shop served as both residence and business for the workers so the long hours were made slightly more tolerable by the proximity of home. By living and working in the same premises there was no need for transportation costs or time spent travelling between two places.

Laundries had a very serious limitation, however. Regardless of the amount they took in, not enough hands and the lack of larger facilities severely restricted the monthly returns. With maximum output, a laundry operator might produce a return of $150 a week. "Around the mid-20s laundries were charging 12¢ a shirt, 15¢ a sheet, 5¢ a collar and 3¢ for hankies."[33]

The laundrymen worked an average of twelve hours a day and six and a half days a week. This left little time for leisure activites. On the half-day off, usually a Sunday, some men would attend Sunday school English classes. "We often took Sunday off to go to Church where we would learn English. Every student had a teacher. My teacher was Miss Moore and she taught at St. James Chinese School at Gerrard and Yonge."[34]

Although the profits from laundries proved to be lower than from other business, they were still a fairly secure investment. During economic slumps the laundry business did not necessarily fluctuate with the changes. Tien-fang Cheng, in his thesis on Oriental immigration in Canada, stated that "people could save by eating at home, but all men, except labourers had to change their shirts and collars no matter how bad business conditions may be."[35]

During the period from 1910 to 1915, a discernible Chinatown area emerged in Toronto. The Chinese referred to the block bounded by Dundas, Queen, Church and Yonge Street as "Tong-yen Gai" or "Hua-fau." An excerpt from a 1971 study on the development of this area describes the settling of Chinatown:

> As more and more Chinese moved into the community, businesses were set up to provide services to the residents; such as Chinese grocery stores, which specialized in Chinese foods imported from China, or British Columbia. The community's proximity to a warehousing station and port enabled the proprietors to bring in speciality goods for sale with relative ease. The community was close to a large market area both by day (commercial areas to the south and west). It was also close to the old city hall and the Parliament Buildings where information on immigration and the head-tax and related legislation could be obtained.[36]

Chinese restaurants started relatively late compared to the establishment of laundries. The first appeared in the city in 1901 or 1901 at 37½ Queen Street West. The Sing Wing Restaurant, then operated by Sing Tom, was later changed to Kong Yee Teas. It is not known why this restaurant was so short-lived. The operator may have left Toronto, or found the demands of running such a business too great. According to one restaurateur, staff used to work up to sixteen hours a day. There were three categories of restaurants. The highest grade were those established with a capital of $12,000 to $20,000 which catered mainly to a business clientele including both Chinese and non-Chinese. A second-class restaurant invested less in decor and had poorer quality flatware and dishware. The third or "C" class establishments served mainly local Chinese labourers or, in later years, students. While these categories reflect the differences in restaurants, it is unlikely that the early places were so classified. It is only in the 1920s and 1930s, when an increasing number of Chinese opened eateries, that such grading was noticeable. By this time there were restaurants serving a variety of clientele.

Tea companies were also popular. In 1902, Quong Ying Yune Company had a tea shop at 69½ Queen Street West. A year later it was known as Wah Lung Company Teas and in 1903 the name had changed again to Shing Yuen Teas. There were two tea companies side by side on York Street: Lee Chong Lung at 154 York and Yee Quong Teas at 156¼ York. There was a shop at 85-87 Queen Street East known as Kwong Yoot Loy. The frequent name changes, as in the relatively high turnover rate for laundries, indicate the transient nature of Chinese businesses of the time.

Two restaurants existed on Elizabeth Street around 1918-1920. Hung Fah Low catered mostly to Chinese. The other was Jung Wah, located at 12½ Elizabeth Street. Jung Wah served Chinese-style food, and had a capacity of about forty to fifty people. The clientele was, understandably, Chinese, with a few outside patrons, mostly Jewish. Some of the missionaries also came here to eat as did the vaudeville actors who played at Shea's on Bay Street or at the Casino on Queen.

Chinese-run restaurants outside of Chinatown did not serve Chinese food. Instead they catered to a largely Canadian clientele who preferred Canadian-style dishes. A full-course meal then cost about 20 cents. And as one patron recalled, "Where else could you get food so cheap?"

With few exceptions Toronto's early Chinese settlers were single men or "married bachelors" whose families remained in China. While there is little need to challenge the preponderance of men in pioneer Chinese communities, it is incorrect to believe that there were neither women nor families in Toronto. For example, although all hand work in laundries was done by men, when wives did arrive from China, they assisted husbands in the shop. Besides helping with the wash, they also did the cooking and sewing:

My mother helped for many long hours in the laundry. She did not go out even to shop. She worked the longest. My father worked six days and also Sunday. We worked until 8 or 9 each night. There were eight children in our family and we had two to three helpers. Sometimes she had to cook for thirteen. She was too busy to belong to any group. She didn't go to China-town, besides, she didn't know the way.[37]

In 1927, the Ontario government attempted to reintroduce an earlier prohibition on the hiring of white women by Chinese restau-rateurs. Section 30 of the Factory, Shop and Office Building Act read: "No Chinese person shall employ in any capacity or have under his direction or control, any female white person in any fac-tory, restaurant or laundry." Toronto's Chinese restaurant oper-ators formed an association to oppose the regulation. The restriction threatened not only the livelihood of the operators who depended on the waitresses to serve non-Chinese clientele, but also the women who lost their employment because of the ban. One proprietor of a Queen Street cafe stated that:

He had recently engaged a young woman who had worked for him before her marriage and had come to him to ask for work when her husband lost his job. He had given her work in his cafe but was forced to dismiss her by police orders. Later, he said he was called by the police commissioner and told by Mayor McBride that he would either employ no female help or receive no license. He was given no chance, he said, to explain the circumstances which he had in employing the girl.

In a study conducted on Toronto's early Chinatown from 1917 to 1933, the researcher found that by 1933 there were thirteen known Chinese families in the Chinatown area. Of these, three of the women were teachers trained by missionaries in China. One was a minister's wife, three were brought to Canada to be married, and one woman arrived with the family to join her husband.

As of 1916, four of the original families were involved with the church. In that year, four Chinese families joined Knox Presbyte-rian Church. Women's meetings were held separately from that of the men as it was not socially acceptable for the sexes to mix freely. The minister's wife assisted at these gatherings by reading the Bible and explaining biblical stories.[38] These four ladies were Mrs. W.L. Mark, Mrs. Lock Kwong, Mrs. Mark Park and Anna Ma, Rever-end Ma T.K. Wou's wife.

The occupations of the male head of the Chinese families in Toronto represented a cross sample of the community. There were:

2 merchant/herbalists
1 professional gambler

1 CNR agent, agent Elias Coal and later manager of a local
   newspaper
4 merchants selling groceries and laundry supplies
1 minister/herbalist
1 laundry
1 CPR agent/merchant
1 seasonally employed on lake boats
1 wholesale tobacco

All of these families lived in or near the Chinatown area,
generally in rented premises. The stores would be on the main floor
and the families occupied living quarters above the shop. Several of
these lived on Elm or Chestnut Street, as well as Elizabeth Street.

Women rarely went to Chinatown, but they did go shopping at
Eaton's, Simpson's and the St. Lawrence Market. Most of the food
was purchased by the husbands so there was no need for women to
go into this area. When it was inconvenient for the men to buy
groceries the children were sent to the stores. For the wives and
mothers who lived in Chinatown, much of their time was spent in
the family store, keeping a close eye and ear on the children in their
living quarters upstairs.

As most businesses in Toronto were run by members of the extended family, it was not uncommon for them to live together. Some
places had two or three bachelors living under one roof, including
men whose wives and children were still in China. Women were
thus kept busy helping out in the store or shop, caring for the
children, cooking and washing for their immediate and larger family.

In the laundries, women mended socks and turned shirt collars
and cuffs. On Sundays, most of the mothers went to church with the
children. Some managed to attend a weekly Bible class on Wednesday afternoons organized by the minister's wife. These were aug-
mented by ''cottage'' meetings when the women met in each other's
homes. Here they had a chance to discuss the week's activities, as
well as engage in handicrafts for the Christmas holiday season. It is
quite likely that these social contacts were the focal point of their
week. One mother whose husband's business was quite profitable,
did not have to help as much, so she devoted her attention to Knox,
Cooke's and the Chinese Presbyterian churches, the Bay Street Mission and the Baptist churches. Another mother helped teach the daily primary Chinese class at the YMCI after school. Two of the
mothers eventually had to work outside the home. After the death of
her husband, one found employment as a waitress at a Chinese
restaurant on Spadina Avenue; the other supplemented her husband's earnings by working in a laundry in Chinatown.

When the 1923 Immigration Act cut off future arrivals from
Hong Kong and China, thousands of Chinese men many of whom

were then middle-aged, were separated from their families for an indefinite period of time. The exception were those fortunate enough to have brought their wives and children over before the bill was enacted. By 1921, Toronto's Chinese population included 1,947 males and 88 females. Of this number, 55 per cent of the women over twenty-one were naturalized. It was not a matter of women acculturating at a faster rate, but rather the need to be a citizen if one were to join one's husband. According to the 1921 census figures, 11 females and 24 males under twenty-one had been naturalized. Among the thirteen families, there were 31 girls and 38 boys. Three of the boys came to Canada with their mother and a fourth was born in China. Hence, a total of 31 girls and 34 boys were Canadian-born.

All of the local Toronto Chinese children were born at home. Delivery was assisted by a doctor and one or two of the neighbourhood ladies. One of those who was present at the deliveries was Mark Luk Sim (literally sixth aunt) who served as a community midwife. She was a widow and sister-in-law and aunt to one of the families. Mrs. Houston, a registered nurse and a deaconess, was also often in attendance.

The children who lived south of Queen Street attended York Public School while those west of University went to Ogden or McCaul. The majority of the children, however, were enrolled at Hester How School located between Chestnut and Elizabeth, south of Gerrard. After regular school hours, the children would attend Chinese classes at the YMCI for two more hours before returning home for dinner.

After school and when the family business took a day off, the children had time to participate in outside activities. The girls often joined Brownies at the Bay Street Mission and/or the CGIT. Some of the boys became scouts, and one became an excellent gymnast at the Central Y where the rest were taking swimming, calisthenics and playing basketball. In 1935, the Chinese boys' basketball team won the championship for the city of Toronto.

Most of the neighbourhood boys and girls regularly went to Sunday school. At first they attended classes at Cooke's, but in later years the Y also had Sunday school teachers. For those living away from the Chinatown area, cars were sent each week to pick up the children. The highlight of the year for the Chinese Christian community was the annual church picnic held yearly on July 1 at Exhibition Park, High Park or on Centre Island. Although organized by the church, the event was essentially a Chinese affair, for this data coincided with the Chinese "Humiliation Day."

Generally speaking, family outings were not common, as many of the businesses were open six or seven days a week. The children, restricted by both distance and parental orders in how far they could go wandering, often turned the city streets and public buildings into their playground. They played hide-and-seek behind the columns of the Registry Building on Chestnut Street. This street was ideal for games because it was a dirt road and seldom used on the weekends. Elizabeth was not so suitable as it was occupied all day long by the streetcars. One of the favourite spots, however, was Hillock's lumberyard between Elizabeth and Chestnut, and south of Albert. It was closed on weekends and according to one interviewee, "easy to get into." It proved to be a wonderful place for children to let their imagination loose. Everybody played hide-and-seek, and follow-my-leader. While the games were fun, the choice of playground often proved somewhat tenuous, especially for the adventuresome. One boy, while playing follow-my-leader, followed those in front him out of a second-floor window on Elizabeth Street and fell through the sky-light of the adjacent building at 66 Elizabeth into the barbeque pit below.[39]

The adults also had diversions from their daily work. In addition to schools, religious groups and recreation associations, dramatic societies were an integral part of organizational life in the community.

The Chinese United Dramatic Society and the Ship Toy Yuen Dramatic Society are two of Toronto's longest established theatre troupes. What initially began as a social get-together soon evolved into amateur groups that performed traditional Cantonese operas for their own entertainment. Unlike the clan or district associations, which had prerequisites for membership, the dramatic societies were open to anyone who wished to participate. During the 1930s, one recently arrived immigrant to Toronto, Mr. D.J. Lumb, found participating in the activities of the clubs an interesting way to spend his free time. He learned to play a few instruments and, with coaching from former actors, he was taught to sing. Eventually, Mr. Lumb took on acting roles; but as women were still relatively few in-number, he was assigned to play the female characters. Ironically, when Jean Lumb, his wife, started acting, she portrayed men. "Nobody wanted to play the bad characters," she explained, "so I was chosen for those parts. We performed together at the Casino Club on Queen Street."

By 1935 there were three Chinese opera houses in Toronto. The Chinese United Dramatic Society, the Ship Toy Yuen Dramatic Society and a third (now the Hung Lok Club) were located in old Chinatown. The Ship Toy Yuen had its headquarters on Dundas Street and a theatre at 126 Elizabeth Street, where the Kwong Chow Restaurant is today. The Chinese United Dramatic Society (Lun Kiu) was further down the block. When the Holiday Inn on

Chestnut Street was built in the 1970s, the dramatic society moved to its present location at 350 Dundas Street West. Local performances were also held at the old Victory Theatre on Spadina Avenue.

Now and then troupes from Hong Kong would tour Canada presenting Chinese headliners. One performance entitled *One Word Often Relieves the Difficulties of a Nation* captivated Toronto audiences in March 1940. The drama, which boasted local and visiting artists, performed three to four times a week at the Gee Gung Hong Clubroom on Elizabeth Street. The play would begin at 7:00 p.m. and run until midnight — without intermission. Tickets ranged from fifty cents to fifteen dollars for those who wished to support the theatre. Quite often the more seasoned playgoers did not arrive until the middle of the evening when the tempo of the story and the acting had reached a high point of interest.

From 1935 to 1949 the Chinese community was actively involved in the dramatic arts. During the depression and later throughout the Sino-Japanese and Second World Wars, local talent performed regularly for fund-raising benefits. It was also at this time that the drama associations enjoyed an influx of visiting stars as the war drove many performers to North America. The Chinese United Dramatic Society and the Ship Toy Yuen Dramatic Society brought over two professional troupes with about twelve members each. Some, like Ming Sing Loo, stayed temporarily, but other members remained and established themselves in the city. Lim Mark Yee, director for the Ship Toy Yuen, was considered one of the finest instructors on the continent in the ancient art of Chinese sword and spear dancing. Chong Yung, who came at a much earlier time, directed the Sing Kew Theatre in Vancouver and later became very active in promoting Chinese theatre in Toronto. On V-J Day, August 1945, a huge celebration was held in Toronto's Chinatown. "The Chinese were able to put on a huge parade because of the three dramatic societies. Each of the societies had a float, and they dressed in their opera costumes."

Many believed that after two or three generations Chinese drama in Toronto would disappear, and indeed this was almost the case in the 1960s and 1970s. Although the dramatic societies were still in existence, they no longer performed. Some of the members branched out into musical associations such as the Cantonese Music Club, formed approximately seventeen years ago. A former actress with the Ship Toy Yuen Dramatic Society assisted in establishing a Chinese dance group. "She was a tiny actress, her costumes fit an eight-year-old girl. With the old outfits and the costumes we had found in a trunk at Lun Kiu, left over from former days, we altered them for the girls," recounts Jean Lumb, founder of the group. With the help of the Chinese Canadian Association, skirts and jackets were fashioned in the style of the original theatre costumes.

Concurrent with the present-day revival of traditional drama, Chinese Canadians are expressing an increased interest in the performing arts as a whole. CanAsian Artists, a newly formed umbrella group for Asian Canadian performing artists, had recently produced *Yellow Fever*. Written by Toronto playwright R.A. Shiomi, *Yellow Fever* has given undiscovered Asian Canadian actors and actresses their first opportunity to perform in a major production. Drama within the Toronto Chinese Canadian community is very much alive.

The period from 1937 to 1947 proved to be probably the most exciting decade in the community's history to that date. Although the Chinese still lived in the shadow of the 1923 Immigration bill, they became increasingly involved in both home and overseas affairs. It was during this time that the Canadian Chinese made their most dramatic contribution to both China and Canada. Beginning with the Sino-Japanese war of 1937, Chinese in Toronto and other centres saw their patriotism for their country of origin flow into the support demonstrated for Canada when the Second World War broke out. Not only were China and Canada allies in that war, but Chinese Canadians fought with the Allied forces.

When the Sino-Japanese war broke out, China, as it had previously done, called upon its overseas nationals for financial support and assistance. Chinese communities across the country organized aid for their home districts, and campaigned to buy ambulances and airplanes. They collected donations to purchase winter clothing for soldiers and medical supplies. Through the selling of war bonds and other activities Chinese Canadians contributed an estimated $5 million to the war efforts. [40]

Vancouver served as the collection centre for the west coast, while Toronto was the base for the eastern provinces. The influence of the KMT, which was more evident here than in either Victoria or Vancouver, assisted in unifying the various organizations with surprising speed and efficiency. As the city lacked a functioning Chinese businessmen's association, the thrust of the war efforts came from the Chinese Christian Association, and increasingly from the Chinese Patriotic Federation of Ontario. Established as early as 1938, the CPF included in its membership those from the Chinese Christian Association, the Kuomintang, the Chinese Freemasons as well as other organizations and associations.

The involvement of Toronto's Chinese was further encouraged by the arrival of the KMT central committeeman, Liu Wei-chih. He began organizing in the Lung Kung-so, one of the wealthiest in Toronto. The head of this association, who was later known as the "unofficial mayor of China," was Chong Ying, a powerful local KMT member.

With the assistance of Chong Ying, Liu established the Chinese Patriotic Federation. Linking all Toronto associations and having contact with most others in Ontario, the CPF held its first meeting on September 4, 1938. Over two thousand people crowded into the Carr Cinema on Queen Street at 1:00 p.m. Two days later, the meeting was officially closed at 11:00 p.m. The Toronto-based federation maintained its position as the single unifying fund-raising body in Toronto, and it was through this centre that over $2 million was directed to China during the war against Japan.[41]

Through the war years, the CPF had few changes in leadership. Two of the prominent members were Chong Ying and E.C. Mark, at that time the secretary of one of the federation's major subcommittees, the Chinese War Relief Fund. Organized on the initiative of non-Chinese, the Fund was set up by a group of prominent white Canadians who sympathized with China. The Canadian government recognized the Relief Fund under the War Charities Act. From its inception in December 1941 to December 1946 over $4 million was raised, mostly by white Canadians.[42]

Toronto's Chinese women, under the auspices of the Chinese Patriotic Federation of Ontario, and local church organizations put on shows to help raise money for Chinese war victims. Funds raised through Rice Bowl Festivals at Convocation Hall and bazaars at the Chinese Christian Institute as well as tag days were also sent to Britain for the Allied forces. Among the groups actively involved in fund-raising were the Chinese Young People's Society of Toronto, the Chinese Ladies' Auxiliary of the Young Men's Chinese Institute, and the Bay Street (Chinese) Women's Association. Madame Chiang Kai-shek visited Toronto and Ottawa in the spring of 1943. Speaking to both Chinese and non-Chinese audiences, she acknowledged the generous support of Chinese Canadians, and drew greater sympathy from the larger society for China's efforts. Increasingly, Canadian attitudes toward the Chinese community became more favourable.

The war had a number of effects on Toronto's Chinese. First, the Chinese had cooperated with Canada both locally and internationally as an ally. Moreover, during the period of exclusion, although no new immigrants were permitted entry, the Chinese Canadian-born population grew considerably. Seventy-five per cent of Chinese Canadian youths were born in Canada. This made a difference to the degree of assimilation this generation, with its English-speaking and Canadian-educated young men and women, was able to achieve. The very visible and active participation of the Chinese as patriotic Canadians coupled with the United Nations Charter acted in concert to alter former biases against the community.

In 1946, Toronto and other centres began to agitate for the repeal of the 1923 law. The drive in Toronto was, as before, a joint Chinese and non-Chinese effort. Such individuals as Reverend W.D. Noyes and Reverend A.E. Armstrong, both extremely vocal in the 1923 protest, were again part of the struggle. Of the seventy-one names appearing on the letterhead of the Committee for the Repeal of the Chinese Immigration, 80 per cent were not Chinese.[43] The legal advisor and spokesman was Toronto attorney Irving Himel. From the Chinese community came Dr. S.K. Ngai, a local surgeon, Chong Ying of the KMT and *Shing Wah Daily News*, Wong Yick, editor of the CKT publication *Hung Chung She Po*, Professor C.C. Shih of the University of Toronto, and K. Dock Yip, in 1945 the first Chinese Canadian called to the bar.[44]

The Committee for the Repeal of the Chinese Immigration Act was formally organized by the end of November 1946. Shortly after it began sending delegations to Ottawa to meet with the Minister of External Affairs, the Minister of Mines and Resources (responsible for immigration) and the Director of the Immigration Branch. The committee also generated further support for their cause from Chinese and non-Chinese organizations across the country. These were supplemented by briefs and letters presented to local government officials. They received support from the Protestant and Catholic churches, the Council of Women, several members of Parliament, the Canadian Congress of Labour and the Toronto Trades and Labour Councils.[45]

The act, after much deliberation by Ottawa and hesitation on British Columbia's part, was repealed in May 1947. The Chinese, however, did not gain equal footing with other non-Asian immigrants. Instead they, like the Japanese and South Asians who were citizens, could now bring their families to Canada. The repeal made it easier for Chinese to obtain citizenship, but special regulations governing Asian entry were to continue.

The revival of Toronto's Chinatown came slowly, as the repeal did not create a sudden influx of immigrants. Chinatown gradually shifted northward along with the centre of the city. Its business sector was bounded by Elizabeth, Bay, University and Dundas streets. But in 1955, plans for construction of the new city hall in the centre of this block forced the community to move once again. Residential and commercial dwellings were now found farther north and westward. Slowly, the Chinese also sought housing in the former Jewish neighbourhood bounded by Spadina, University, Dundas and College streets. Here a second or ''new'' Chinatown was established.

The decline of the Chinese Canadian population was arrested with changes in the immigration regulations in 1962, and again in 1967. In 1950, there were approximately 2,900 Chinese in Toronto, but by 1971, census statistics record 15,700. Today there are four areas recognized as Chinatowns by the number of restaurants and food stores which cluster together serving a predominantly Chinese clientele. Changes in the physical characteristics of these areas reflect changes in the social characteristics of the Chinese community as well.

Those arriving in Toronto are no longer the perceived ''sojourners'' of a pioneer community. Instead, Chinese from the West Indies, South America, Southeast Asia and Taiwan now constitute a considerable percentage of the Chinese Canadian community. The number of recent immigrants has also created a need for social service agencies to serve these people in their own language. Groups and associations active in fostering greater understanding between the Chinese and non-Chinese community, in promoting and maintaining Chinese Canadian interests have also emerged. The Chinese Canadian National Council and the Ontario Council of Chinese Canadians are concerned with such areas as race relations, developing a resource centre on Chinese Canadian history, ensuring the rights of all individuals. As with most other ethnic groups, the Chinese are far from homogeneous politically and this is reflected in the number of associations and organizations which exist and are often in conflict with one another. Much of this inconsistency is due to the different parts of the world Toronto's Chinese come from as well as differences in the cultural background of Chinese.[46]

For example, recent arrivals include ethnic Chinese from Vietnam and a large number of ethnic Chinese students from Hong Kong, Taiwan and Southeast Asia.

The diversity within the community has led to the emergence of interest in Chinese culture — particularly among Canadian Chinese. The Chinese Instrument Group, whose name explains its activities, consists entirely of Canadian-born Chinese. Dance troupes, such as the Toronto Chinese Dance Workshop, has a number of local-born members. The recognition of one's identity as Chinese in Canada led the University of Toronto and the Chinese Businessmen's Association to establish a scholarship for graduate work in Chinese Canadian studies.

Today there are approximately 120,000 Chinese in Toronto. The city boasts the largest community in Canada and the third-largest in North America.

Throughout their years in Canada, Toronto's Chinese have withstood numerous obstacles. The hopes and aspirations of the early pioneers have been realized in the succeeding generation. It has been nearly four decades since the Immigration bill of 1923 was repealed, and within this period, the community has many significant accomplishments and achievements to its credit. Today Chinese Canadians are found in virtually every section of Toronto's political, social and economic life. Yet behind this scenario of relative success, difficulties that the settlers encountered are perpetuating themselves one hundred years later. Recent immigrants still face the problems of adjustment, a language barrier, access to resources and the lack of employment opportunites. Financial constraints prevent social service agencies from fulfilling their objectives. The transition from one's home environment to a foreign one has taken its toll on many new Canadians. Behind the neon lights of restaurants, tea houses and small eateries, the grocery stores and arts and crafts shops, women are working for under minimum wages doing piecework at home or in the sweat shops along Spadina for the garment industry. The increase in the number of family breakdowns and the rise in juvenile delinquency indicate the weakening structure of the nuclear family.

Yet, in contrast to what seems to be a repetitive cycle for all newcomers to Canada, another aspect of Chinese Canadian culture is emerging. Out of Toronto has come the Asian-Canadian Resource Workshop in 1978. Producing a quarterly magazine, as well as organizing seminars and participating in Asian-Canadian conferences, the workshop is the first of its kind to bring together Canadians of Asian descent. The CanAsian Artists Group draws together Asian-Canadian artists and promotes their talents to the larger and often unreceptive Canadian public. The Chinese in Toronto are not represented only by what one sees in Chinatown. A stroll down Dundas or along Broadview offers only a small glimpse of a diverse community. At once very much mainstream yet also still foreign in the eyes of the larger society, the Chinese cannot by typecast in either direction. For whether they are new Canadians or descendants of the first pioneers, they have remained active agents of their lives in Toronto.

Notes

The author wishes to thank Valerie Mah for her assistance in the preparation of this article. Mrs. Mah is a special education teacher at King Edward Junior and Senior Public School. She is a Toronto Chinese community historian and treasurer of the Mon Sheong Foundation which administers a home for the aged.

1. Two other dates also figure here; one is 459 A.D. when Chinese Buddhist monks, according to Chinese records, sailed across the Pacific Ocean and arrived in the legendary land of Fusan. From descriptions of their travel this seems to be the west coast of British Columbia. The second year in question is 1788 when Captain John Meares crossed the Pacific with a crew that included approximately fifty Chinese artisans. Upon landing at what later became Nootka Sound, the crew built the first fur-trading posts in North America. It is not

known what eventually became of these men, but it is believed that they gradually assimilated into the local native population. Neither group, then, established a continuous community.

2. Peter Goheen, *Victorian Toronto 1850 to 1900: Patterns and Process of Growth* (Chicago: University of Chicago, 1970), p. 115.

3. Paul Levine, "Historical Documentation Pertaining to Overseas Chinese Organizations" (M.A., University of Toronto, 1975), p. 78.

4. Valerie Mah, "The 'Bachelor' Society: A Look at Toronto's Early Chinese Community from 1878 to 1924" (Unpublished paper, Toronto, 1978), p. 6.

5. Levine, "Overseas Chinese Organizations," p. 79.

6. St. James Ward was bounded by Yonge, Jarvis, King streets and the northern city limits. St. Andrews Ward was bounded by the western city limits, the east side of Yonge, King Street to the south and Queen Street to the north.

7. Mah, "The 'Bachelor Society'," p. 77.

8. Levine, "Overseas Chinese Organizations," p. 79.

9. David Lai, "An Analysis of Data on Home Journeys by Chinese Immigrants in Canada, 1892-1915," *Professional Geographer* 29 (November 1977), p. 362.

10. The bill was enacted upon the recommendations of the 1885 Royal Commission Reports on Chinese Immigration.

11. Cooke's Presbyterian Church Year Book, 1899, p. 28.

12. Correspondence, United Church of Canada Archives, 1894, Box 1 file 32.

13. Ibid., May 5, 1894.

14. Ibid.

15. Cooke's Presbyterian Church Year Book, 1898, p. 24.

16. Correspondence, United Church of Canada Archives, July 25, 1900, Box, file 33.

17. Cooke's Presbyterian Church Year Book, 1899, p. 24.

18. Ibid., 1901, p. 39.

19. Peter Ward, "The Oriental Immigrant and Canada's Protestant Clergy, 1885-1925," *B.C. Studies*, 22 (Summer 1974), p. 42.

20. Ibid., p. 41.

21. S.S. Osterhout, *Orientals in Canada* (Toronto: United Church of Canada, 1929), p. 127.

22. Memoirs of Anna Ma, unpublished, p. 58.

23. Mah, "The 'Bachelor' Society," p. 52.

24. Stanford Lyman, *et al.*, "Rules of a Chinese Society in British Columbia," *Bulletin of the School of Oriental and African Studies*, 27 (1964), p. 330-31.

25. Levine, "Overseas Chinese Organizations," P. 82.

26. Edgar Wickberg, *et al.*, *From China to Canada* (Toronto: McClelland and Stewart, 1982), p. 107.

27. Ibid., p. 103.

28. H.C. Tam, "Secret Society and Revolutionary Politics. A Study of the Chih-Kung T'and (Triad)," Paper for distribution at the Canadian Society for Asian Studies Convention (Toronto, Summer 1974), p. 12.

29. Levine, "Overseas Chinese Organizations," p. 30.

30. Public Archives of Canada, RG 76 file 827821, part 9, Chinese Association of Canada to King, 12 July 1923.

31. Mah, "The 'Bachelor' Society," p. 23.

32. Interview with Tom Lock, recalling his boyhood in the laundry from 1925 to 1950.

33. Ibid.

34. Mark Kwong Ping, 76-year-old resident Mon Sheong Home for Aged, to V. Mah.

35. Tien-fang Cheng, *Oriental Immigration in Canada* (Shanghai: Commercial Press, 1931), p. 188.

36. Kwan-Seng Mok, "A Study of the Spatial Development of the Chinese Community in Metro Toronto," 1971, p. 9.

37. Interview with Dorothy Soo, 1977.

38. Memoirs of Anna Ma, n.p.

39. Mah, "An In Depth Look at Toronto's Early Chinatown, 1913-1933," Unpublished paper, 1977, p. 35.

40. Wickberg, *From China to Canada*, p. 189.

41. Levine, "Overseas Chinese Organizations," p. 94.

42. *Shing Wah Daily News*, 3 December 1946.

43. Wickberg, *From China to Canada*, p. 205.

44. *Globe and Mail*, 30 December 1946.

45. Ibid.

Sojourner and Settler: the Macedonian Presence in the City, 1903-1940

Lillian Petroff

As a people Macedonians have always continually moved beyond the confines of their villages. They learned early and well that the only way they could live as Macedonians was to leave the homeland. *Meisters* (master builders) and carpenters from the villages of Zhelevo, Besfina and Gabresh, for example, actively plied their trade far from their villages. They took their skills and willingness to work to their neighbouring settlements, the Bitola district and other areas of western Macedonia, Turkey, Serbia, the city of Athens and the Greek islands. The men left seasonally, polyseasonally and finally for good, chiefly because of the influx of cash into the economy and the subsequent emergence of money earned outside the village life and society. So despite a chronic shortage of good arable land, rising expectations — the desire not only to subsist and survive but to improve and make better — affected everyone in the villages. If the economy and social conditions were the trigger, the political background, first of Turkish then of Greek oppression, and the constant warfare, was a backdrop that made leaving even more attractive.

The turn of the century saw many of these experienced sojourners leave their families and homesteads yet again, as they quickly joined the growing number of southeastern Europeans who went to ''America'' in search of greater economic opportunity. The new world had finally been discovered as a lucrative migratory stop.

Pay packets that had been sent or brought back by the pioneer migrant returnees created and spread the news throughout Macedonia that in Canada one could earn more than in any other country.

The overwhelming majority of Macedonians who came to Toronto before the First World War did so intending to make the best of it, to live frugally and to earn good money as industrial labourers. These men saw their future squarely in terms of the old country, return to their families. Cash obtained in the new world would be used to maintain or enhance the village way of life and to consolidate or expand more homesteads. Thus Toronto came to be regarded as a source of upward mobility, but upward mobility at home in the village and not in North America.

The sojourners and activists who came to North America hailed primarily from the provinces of Kostur and Lerin, areas which were once important *vilayets* of the Ottoman Empire but are now identified as portions of northern Greece. Few came from western Macedonia or from towns and cities. "Hardly anybody emigrated" to Toronto from the districts of Prespa, Bitola, Prilep or Skopje according to the 1916 church National Calendar "because there is more agricultural land and most of our people cultivated the land owned by the beys." Significant exodus from that area began in the post-depression years and gained momentum in the aftermath of the Second World War.

Few Macedonians were in the city before the years 1903 and 1904. The compilers of the 1916 Macedonian church National Calender could, in retrospect, state that "their number was so small that it could be counted on your ten fingers." By 1940 readers of various political and nationalist almanacs learned that there were upwards of twelve hundred families in Toronto, making it the site of the largest Macedonian community in Canada and probably in North America.[1]

The purpose of this paper is to document and understand the presence of a little known people in Toronto in the period before 1940. Until recently, social and urban historians have generally ignored the presence of immigrants, especially the southeastern Europeans, in Canada's city centres. Toronto historical studies have acknowledged this early non-Anglo presence only within the context of urban ills and difficulties. For example, in *The Municipality of Toronto*, chronicler Jesse Middleton saw the Ward and Niagara Street as salient examples of the fact that slum areas and the foreign presence often went hand-in-hand. But sojourners and settlers were never studied for and of themselves.[2]

This paper is largely a product of oral history; the reconstruction of historical detail about early Macedonian settlement and community life is taken from tape — recorded reminiscences of older settlers in Toronto — and of *Might's City Directory* and the City of Toronto tax assessment rolls for the years 1903 to 1940.[3] Used together, tax assessment rolls and city directories helped chart the settlement patterns of the group, their land acquisitions and holdings. But at best, these written sources gave only rough estimates about the size of sojourner and settler households. Like those from other ethnic groups, migrants within the city and hinterland railroad navvies were under-enumerated. To judge the limits of *Might's City Directory* as a source consider the information given for 1 Eastern Place (the west side, south end commencing at Eastern Avenue) in the year 1910:

> Name: Various tenants
> Age of taxable person: —
> Manhood: —
> Freehold or tenant: —
> Occupation: Macedonians
> Name and Address of Owner or Lesee: The Canadian
>   Northern Ontario Railway
> Total Residents: 8

Nameless men pursuing unknown occupations, identified only as being Macedonians in a strange, often hostile environment.

The tax assessment listings of industrial firms sometimes included the names, addresses, job classifications and incomes of employees, including labourers, and so they can on occasion be matched with street and residence/boardinghouse listings. For example, the 1919 Ward 7 Division 1 tax assessment rolls stated that 150 Cawthra Avenue in the Junction housed ten residents. Using the 1919 industrial tax listing for Gunn's slaughterhouse, we are able to discover that at least three of the ten residents were employed as labourers by the firm and had taxable incomes that year of $414, $414 and $390 respectively.

There are limits and problems associated with the use of these urban history sources for an alien group which only oral testimony and good ethnographic sense can overcome. For example, the alphabetical listing of names in the city directories and their classified business directories/sections are hard to use. Hellenization of Macedonian names was required by the Greek government: "the names in our village (Zhelevo) were changed to 'Manou Nikolou' and 'Atanasiu,' etc. The people of Zhelevo and the Prespa district often laughed together about their long names." Macedonians, perhaps reacting to a sense that they were perceived as alien, rarely used their family names on businesses intended for a general clientele. Thus restaurant names, such as the Queen's Tea Rooms Company, Florida Tea Room and the Harbord Lunch, were as much Macedonian enterprises as the Balkan Café or Hadji Peroff's. Advertisements used in such group publications as almanacs and dictionaries helped in part to identify those Macedonian establishments not obvious from the city directories.[4]

The marriage, baptism and burial records of SS Cyril and Methody Cathedral provide limited insight into group and village settlement patterns. At best, these records should have contained such basic information as name, Toronto or Ontario hinterland address, place of birth and/or village of origin. Complete citations were rare. The omissions probably a reflection of the language and writing skills of the various secretaries and religious officials. The first priest of SS Cyril and Methody, Archimandrite Theophilact, made a conscious effort to note and acknowledge his parishioners' village of origin whenever he himself made the entries. Visiting Russian priests, who served in times when a Macedonian priest was absent, were either content to list ''Macedonia'' as place of origin on sacramental documents, or were simply incapable of more precise identification.

The group's dictionaries, guidebooks, letter-writers and political almanacs are helpful and important because they became an everyday reference tool for the men on the move as well as suggesting some of their geographic range. Sample letters about how to request a job and accommodation, forward baggage and mail, for instance, reflect the temporary, often isolated and far-flung work world and existence of the sojourners. Likewise the political almanacs' greetings and salutations for Macedonians throughout North America, the records of meetings held in various urban centres show us not just the Macedonians' nationalist spirit, but also the variety of accomplishment and space they occupied, and knew themselves to occupy, in North America.

Despite the limitations of these traditional sources they do provide the underpinning which enabled me to use oral testimony and ethnic group correspondence in an ethnographically sophisticated manner so as to obtain and understand the complexity of the Macedonian urban experience.[5]

Sojourners first came to roost in Toronto's east end. This initial settlement area was bounded by King Street East to the north; the southern boundary was formed by Lake Ontario, the industrial sites of Gooderham and Worts, the National Iron Corporation Limited, etc., and the adjacent railway areas; while the eastern and western boundaries were marked by Trinity and Cherry streets respectively. This settlement area quickly grew. In the period 1910 to 1919, the group moved above King Street, settling the area above and below

Queen Street East. After 1920 the northern boundary came to be pushed above Dundas and Gerrard streets to Carlton. In the period 1910 to 1919, the western boundary rapidly moved beyond Trinity Street to include Berkeley, Ontario and Princess streets. Movement to the Sherbourne Street area came primarily in the period after 1920. By 1919 Cherry Street had ceased to be the eastern boundary as the group settled in the St. Lawrence and River streets area. The period after 1920 proved important, as it marked the group's movement and involvement in life east of the Don River.

Two later settlements were established in the city's west end. In the period 1909 to 1919, Macedonians settled an area which came to be known as the "Niagara Street" settlement. Queen Street West formed the northern boundary while Spadina Avenue formed the eastern one. Macedonian residences present by Stanley Park on Niagara Street and Walnut Avenue helped to create the western residential boundary. Wellington Street West, the municipal abattoir, the Grand Trunk and the Canadian Pacific Railway lines made an impenetrable southern boundary. Macedonians moved into the area above Queen Street West after 1920, settling on Augusta Avenue and McDougall's Lane. Macedonians also inhabited Ward 7. Eager young slaughterhouse workers helped to establish "the Junction" — formerly the Town of West Toronto Junction before its annexation by the city in 1909 — as a third settlement area in Toronto. During the First World War, Macedonians settled an area bounded by St. Clair Avenue West to the north, Annette Street to the south, and Weston Road and Miller Street to the east; Keele Street and the Canadian Pacific Railway terminal and complex, for the most part, both formed the western boundary. After 1920 the Junction settlement rapidly expanded into the area around Jane Street and Runnymede Road and so Macedonians eventually found themselves in the suburban areas.

The Macedonians' initial and largest settlement area attracted and proved a large Macedonian labour pool for the local sheet metal industries, iron and steel foundries, slaughterhouses, leather and fur processing companies. Indeed, the group exhibited a special perverse sort of pride in their ability to endure near these "smelly" fur dressing and dyeing works. Macedonian sojourners found work at the National Iron Corporation and the William Davies Company, a Front Street East pork-packer and slaughterhouse, and at the Kemp Manufacturing Company. Macedonians were also to be found in the city's slaughterhouses, namely the Harris Abattoir Company which was located at 35 Jarvis Street and Gunn's Limited of 74-80 Front Street East. From slaughterhouses to working with hides at such tanneries and producers of staple and leather goods as the A.R. Clarke and Company, Clarke and Clarke Limited and Wicket and

Craig was a natural step. The group also worked in the various soap works in the district, especially at Taylor Soap Company and Lever Brothers.

The Junction and the Niagara-Wellington Street settlement areas were established later as the west end became the site of Toronto's meat-packing industry and new job opportunities opened up. The emergence of West Toronto Junction as a slaughterhouse centre began in 1903 with the opening of the Ontario Stock Yards on Keele Street, just north of the terminals and shops of the Canadian Pacific Railway. Stockyard officials and promoters saw the area as an ideal location for this unpleasant type of industry because it stood apart from the city itself and its residents. In the beginning the stockyards stood alone, since no packing plants were established immediately adjacent to them or in the vicinity. At this time livestock was first unloaded a block or so east of the yards and then driven along Junction Road to the pens. Later, when the stock had been sold, the process was repeated and they were driven down the street to the waiting stock-cars for shipment to the packers in the east end. In 1905 the establishment of the Levack slaughterhouse next to the stockyards signalled the end of this difficult and inconvenient method of operation. In 1907 Gunn's shifted its base of operations to the Junction; Swift's followed in 1911 and the Harris Abattoir Company came in 1912. Macedonians, especially those who were already employees with those firms, made their way to the new job sites.

The development of the third area of settlement along Niagara Street had a similar pattern. The creation of the municipal abattoir in 1912 at the site of the Western Cattle Market at the foot of Tecumseh Street helped to bring Macedonians to Niagara Street district. Men also came to the area to work at Massey Harris, the Ideal Bedding Company and the York Knitting Mills, a Queen Street West firm. F.S. Tomev argues in his unpublished "Memoirs" that in addition to work opportunities, men came after the destruction of old Union Station by fire. Fear — "the flames had reached their (boardinghouse) windows" — and the devastation in the fire's aftermath brought them from central downtown to Niagara Street.[6]

Toronto was not a city of tenements, so the Macedonian sojourners lived in two- and three-storey roughcast or frame houses. They also occupied the top floors and rear rooms of Macedonians' stores and businesses. Junction confectioner John Christo housed at least nine boarders at his St. Clair Avenue West shop during the Great War. The 1915 tax assessment rolls record the presence of a King Street East restaurateur, George Uzunoff. He was, however, also a rooming-house operator, and that year his establishment, which was located between Parliament and Power streets, served the needs of ten men.

Macedonians settled in parts of the city that were similar to one another. The average value of land and buildings was about the same in each area, with the east end having the lowest values and the Niagara district the highest. In 1910 the land and buildings at 18-20 Eastern Avenue (at Gilead Place) — the site of grocer and steamship agent H.D. Peroff's store and boardinghouse which had twelve boarders—were valued at $489 and $500 respectively. That same year, a house at 35 Eastern Avenue (at Cherry Street), which was owned by the Canadian Northern Ontario Railway and occupied by twelve Macedonians, had land valued at $168 and the building at $350. In 1915 the house and land at 6 Trefann Street — the site of another Macedonian boardinghouse — were of comparable value, $400 and $410 respectively. In the Niagara Street district, a house on Tecumseth Street had land valued at $857 while the building was assessed at $1,450 in 1919. That same year, 131 and 151 Niagara Street, which were houses between Tecumseth and Wellington streets, had land valued at $829 and $821 respectively and buildings at $800 a piece. In the Junction, 51 Dods Avenue (between West Toronto Street and St. Clair Avenue West) had a house valued at $1,000 on property assessed at $306 in 1915. In 1927, a St. Clair Avenue West restaurant/building was valued at $500 on land assessed at $750.

In all these neighbourhoods, buildings were generally worth more than the land they were on. That was in sharp contrast to Toronto's most celebrated ethnic quarter, the Ward in the centre of town. The Macedonian neighbourhoods were not slums; landlords were not speculators in search of a quick turnover; buildings were not allowed to deteriorate as their owners waited to sell out. Since they settled in areas not as valuable or central as the Ward, Macedonians probably enjoyed a greater measure of stability and better living conditions than the Jews, Italians and Chinese of the city's core. City officials did not see it that way, equating crowding, which obviously did exist in the boardinghouses, with the social disintegration characteristic of slums.

In the first decades of the century, foreign receiving and settlement areas came under careful scrutiny and study by Health Department officials and documentary photographers for the city. What the camera saw was explicated by the city's chief medical health officer, Dr. Charles Hastings, in his 1911 report on slum conditions. He found the Eastern Avenue and Niagara Street districts, among others, to be the sites of many violations of Toronto's health and housing standards. (Hastings was silent about the Junction although the area had been annexed by the city in 1909). Rooms in many houses were found to be insufficiently lighted and badly ventilated. In cellars and basements where men might bed down at night, dampness was also a serious problem. Indeed, one home in the Niagara Street district was found to have four inches of water in the cellar. Dr. Hastings also considered the problem of over-crowding. One four-room boardinghouse on Eastern Avenue, for example, provided accommodation for twelve to fifteen men. Each room, with the exception of the kitchen, had been converted into mens' sleeping quarters with three or four beds. Older respondents now remember that overcrowding vividly and acknowledge the medical reports' accuracy. Four- and five-room houses on Niagara Street, for example, were known to have accommodated as many as twenty Macedonian men at a time.[7]

What the photographs also revealed was that these men in layered and ill-fitting clothing were preoccupied with their old world commitments and responsibilities. Money needed to be saved to purchase a piece of land on return to Macedonia or for a sister's dowry. Such commitment precluded major expenditures on housing. Sojourners' sense of order and organization in the new world was functional; it anticipated temporary deprivation. The commitment to frugality was total even if the men understand all too well the degree to which their living conditions were substandard. A complex order emerged in most establishments. House rules and codes about residents' responsibility developed. In many boardinghouses cooking and other household chores were often performed by tenants on a rotating basis. The fifteen or more men who occupied a Wellington Street West boardinghouse clearly understood and performed their duties under the rotation system:

> Early in the morning, the person that was on duty for the day got up before the others, lit the stove, fried the meat in the big stew pan. After work, he prepared supper and saw to it that all the men had their fair share. He then washed the dishes after all had eaten and swept the floor. The household chores were now done for the day.

In other households, responsibilities were assigned according to age and were not egalitarian. Remembering the additional duties he performed as one of the youngest members of a Macedonian boardinghouse on Front Street East, one immigrant recalled that, ''the young fellows in the house (fourteen or fifteen years of age) were responsible for washing the older fellows' clothes.'' In his memoirs, F.S. Tomev recalls that major household tasks were performed once a week by the residents as a whole. In his West End boardinghouse:

> the floor was usually washed on Saturday afternoon or on Sunday. We used the garden hose and a brush like those used by the street cleaners to wash the floor. We then burrowed a hole in the floor in order to let the water run down to the basement (it had a dirt floor) when the washing was completed.

Most men honoured their obligations. The few who shirked household responsibilities were, more often than not, asked or forced to move out. Unclean and untidy men were also asked to leave households. Conversely, one man who "was very much in favour of cleanliness" came to be despised for his fastidious nature. As a result, he acquired a bad name among boardinghouse residents and so was "chased (driven out) from house to house."[8]

Macedonian letter-writing manuals and dictionaries provide some insight into problems of boardinghouse management. For example, the *Various Bulgarian-American Letters* instructed its readers how to summon company representatives and repairmen as well as offering a sample request to delay the payment of rent. Nedelkoff's *English-Bulgarian and Bulgarian-English Letters* offered samples of a lease agreement and a tenant's letter of complaint to the landlord. The *First Bulgarian-English Pocket Dictionary* concerned itself with food; it acquainted its readers with the system of weights and measures and offered meat, vegetable, fruit and bread item lists in translation: for example, White bread, brown bread, rye bread, stale bread, new bread. Clearly, bread was the staple. One Niagara Street boardinghouse with only male residents ordered twenty loaves a day. The bread man who delivered to the area was soon promoted to supervisor because management mistook Macedonian need for the man's sales prowess.[9]

There was also fellow feeling. The shabby physical surroundings of the boardinghouses were tempered by the warmth of human relationships strengthened by ties of language, custom and hard work. Men from the same village often shared friendships, memories and moments of light-heartedness. Residents of a Niagara Street district boardinghouse:

> celebrated all the church holidays. . . . They celebrated namedays. They sang patriotic and folk songs. They danced "horos." They talked about their places of birth, about their families and relatives about the heroic "chetnicks" [freedom fighters] and their leaders, and for the struggles of their people.

Talk was often translated into action. The men of this boardinghouse contributed not just emotion and words, but also money towards improvement of village facilities such as the building of a new bridge. Many also interfered in the religious and ethnic politics of their home villages. Believing that their village should be placed under the spiritual jurisdiction of the Bulgarian Exarcate, these men used their new status and income to influence those who stayed behind in Zhelevo to make that decision.

There was also talk about survival and success in the new world and much planning of job or work-site strategies. Men, for example, discussed how and when to ask for raises. In such moments, men who possessed a degree of literacy and an understanding of the

English language were very much appreciated. One such individual was frequently called upon to pen "Please, Boss" notes—requests for a raise. Success at work was earnestly sought and celebrated. A former tin metal worker recalled: "I was talking to the boys at the house rented among ourselves. Somebody ask me, "Why don't you ask for a raise?" I got a fifty cents raise. I comes home to the house with all the boys. I told them I got the raise. [They] all laughing so happy."

The availability of informal loans in the boardinghouses suggests a high level of mutual trust. Men from Gabresh who were residents of an east end boardinghouse had such faith in each other. One respondent remembered that no receipts were ever demanded on loans, even on those that went as high as $300.

Fellow feeling did not always prevail; the business of living together often created tension and anger in the boardinghouse. F.S. Tomev writes of the scolding he received from a fellow boarder for burning onions during the preparation of the daily stew. Tomev's father came to his defence and was soon arguing with the other residents. The young man and his father felt bound to move out despite subsequent apologies. Another father and son dealt with their disagreements and anger at each other by placing a wooden board between them—a sort of temporary partition—in the double bed they shared in a west end boardinghouse. [10]

In some boardinghouses, leadership was provided by a dominant male, usually an older, more experienced sojourner or a man of good standing in the village who presided over the affairs of the house "with seignorial authority . . . who had to be consulted about everything." In others, the equality of migrant conditions led to democracy; the consensus of the group that created each household usually sustained it. Differences in jobs and incomes did cause a natural hierarchy to emerge sometimes. For example, slaughter house labourers and butchers who shared a house in the Junction at 50 Cloverdale Road in the year 1919 showed annual taxable incomes from work at Gunn's ranging from a low of $336 to a high of $450. It is interesting to note that a butcher was collecting the lowest pay while a labourer was drawing the highest. Only oral testimony can provide any insight into whether boardinghouse status depended on income, on job skills, or on ethnic ascriptive values which had nothing to do with work. [11]

The boardinghouse was a basic sojourner tool. The twin objectives of living a frugal life and saving money were most effectively served by this institution in its many forms. At the same time, however, these establishments prepared village men for a settler existence. They helped shape the men's larger identity, that of being Macedonians in Canada. Such households offered a model and training for such future settler group endeavours as creating a community parish and nationalist political organizations.

As the initial settlement area, the east end was the site of the earliest Macedonian enterprise. Businesses which catered to sojourner needs, such as the cafés, steamship agents, grocers and bankers, first appeared on Eastern Avenue, Trinity Street and King Street before the First World War. Eastern Avenue was early a centre of the grocery stores. Men such as George Dimitry and Dimitry Peroff ran shops on the north side (at Gilead Place); George and Samuel T. Stoyanoff had a store on the south side (at Eastern Place). The east side of Trinity Street (at Eastern Avenue) was the site of two restaurants, including Jordan Belcheff's International Restaurant which quickly became a popular gathering place and a favourite for those sojourners who bought weekly meal tickets. The north side of King Street East (between Parliament Street and Wilkins Avenue) was the site of a variety of establishments and services, including restaurants, grocery stores, butcher shops and haberdasheries, such as the mens' furnishings store of proprietor and railroad labour agent Andrew D. Georgieff at No. 364.

The *First Bulgarian-English Pocket Dictionary* reflected this rapid commercial development of the ethnic group in its back page advertisements and even encouraged it. Sponsor Hadji D. Peroff informed dictionary readers of the many services that his company, which was located in Toronto at 18 Eastern Avenue, could provide: "Our firm's business is selling large and small old country foodstuffs and products, issuing ship cards with the best steamships, sending money to Bulgaria and Macedonia through express and exchanging Napoleons." Promising to serve customers "quickly, honestly and accurately," the steamship agency, Slave Petroff and Company of 457 King Street East, offered the services of a labour bureau, a post office and address bureau. The firm also sold insurance and a variety of first-aid preparations. The dictionary's compiler, Archimandrite Theophilact, directed his readers to the east end colony and encouraged patronage of those who advertised in his book.

These enterprises were the beginnings or toeholds of a permanent and stable community. Inadvertently they posed a threat to the sojourner's way of life. Habitual attendance at a café, for example, while enhancing the coffers of that business, also represented a potential threat to the order of things, for it was a first step away from the migrant's maximizing of savings and spartan life in preparation for return to the homeland. For the most part, conscientious migrants went to coffee-houses only once a week, usually on Sundays. As the major-domo of a well-run boardinghouse would ask of an impressionable young charge, "Who goes on weekdays to the coffee-house? Only the loafers, the *bumbi*."[12]

Because the Junction became a Macedonian settlement after the east end, it did not develop the same enterprise system. There was neither a Macedonian steamship agent nor banker. Junction and Niagara Street businesses did, however, both serve the sojourner and settler and the non-Macedonian residents. Macedonians in the Junction especially around Keele Street, ran diners and cafés, groceries and barber shops. Most of these businesses were established during the First World War or shortly after. By the late thirties, Macedonian establishments were lined along Keele Street between Junction Road and St. Clair Avenue West, among them the CPR barbershop and George Petroff Grocery Market Lunch, Balkan Café, Stock Yard Lunch and the Step-in Lunch.

An analysis of the clientele these businesses sought and served helps us to understand the world of immigrant enterprise. The Junction's lunch rooms, barber shops and groceries, the Exchange Hotel — a non-Macedonian venture — served primarily the farmers who came to town to strike deals with stockyard and meat-packing officials, cattle dealers, supervisors and bosses of the railways and slaughterhouses. All those engaged in livestock commerce had the money and leisure to buy their lunches or wait in the barber's chair. The labourers of Junction industries carried lunch pails and patronized the George Petroff Grocery, a place where they could buy such supplements to cold sandwich lunches as milk, pop, cigarettes, ice cream and meat pies. Nearby the Balkan Café catered exclusively and without apology to the ethnic group, Macedonian sojourners and settlers. It was a café, a meeting-place and a restaurant. Well-run boardinghouses and budget-conscious immigrant wives did limit the number of meals purchased. Macedonian restaurants and groceries in the Niagara Street-Wellington Street area had a more ethnically varied clientele. They provided meal tickets and daily lunches to carry for many of the Polish and Lithuanian boarders who inhabited that factory district.

The entrepreneurial base of the Macedonians in the Junction included a few butcher shops. This was partly because slaughterhouse employees were allowed to select and purchase meats for themselves and their friends during the course of a working day. With a network extending from slaughterhouses to many small restaurants, Macedonians became involved in wholesale meat supply and street vending, but the depression limited their mobility in this occupation. A Dundas Street West hot-dog stand proprietor summed up his difficulties by stating: "[The] hot dogs are turning green; [I] keep turning them in water. [I] throw the coffee away."[13]

Sojourners were often burdened, even frightened men. Saddled with the responsibility of paying off mortgages on farms and homesteads back home as well as providing for other family needs and planning households, they frequently bore their "birds of passage'' label uncomfortably. In Toronto at least they were not as physically mobile as one might think. Nor were they perpetual searchers and seekers of work opportunities. Happy to find a job with appropriate accommodations nearby, they fell into a pattern of surviving and enduring, not daring to risk much either entrepreneurially or by moving on. Several respondents remembered feeling locked into their first jobs — dangerous, often brutal positions in slaughterhouses and industrial concerns — for the duration of their stay. Others did challenge the group's emphasis on job security. A young east end slaughterhouse worker defied a boardinghouse rule that said: ''No one quit a job unless it was to go to another, one with higher pay, or to go back to the old country.'' He quit his job at the William Davies Company after working only a day. Hands reddened by salt and animal skins, sickened by pungent odours and handling cattle entrails, he walked away from the slaughterhouse and his more docile countrymen forever. It is probably not incidental that the young man's father was also among the sojourners, had secure work and allowed the young man the breathing space to look for more appropriate work. Few arriving migrants had such a safety net of family income.

The Macedonian peasants, no matter what their levels of education, were thinking men who established their own priorities and operated according to their own perceptions of opportunity and success. If some never left the jobs in which they were first niched, many others were in motion, constantly changing jobs and moving around the three settlement areas in the city. For example, the opportunity of employment as a butcher in a west end slaughterhouse caused a young Macedonian to give up his east end residence on Wascana Avenue and his steady job piling timber on the Toronto docks along Cherry Beach to move to Old Weston Road in the heart of the west end community. Another sojourner travelled back and forth between the east and west end settlement areas as he moved between respective labouring jobs at Kemps, an east end sheet metal producer; Massey Harris, the west end agricultural implements firm; and the Phillips Manufacturing Company, an east end manufacturer of mouldings, mirrors and frames. Oral testimony alone offers an insight into the choices involved in the decisions that led to internal migration in the city, or to clinging to the first migrant reception neighbourhood. Some men subordinated their feelings about households, living quarters and neighbourhoods to their jobs, changing residences in accordance with work opportunities. However, when the Harris Abattoir Company established itself in the Junction, a group of novice and seasoned slaughterhouse workers abandoned their Trefann Street boardinghouse and followed the company to the west end. They took up residence at Keele and St. Clair Avenue West.

Others accepted years of long and costly commuting rather than give up ethnic companions and ambience. The belief that accommodation should be in close proximity to employment was often discarded. In one case a group of young men lived with fellow villagers on Trinity Street in the east end while they held jobs at the Massey Harris plant across town. East end residents also worked in such Niagara Street and Junction industrial concerns as Gunn's Abattoir, Matthews Blackwell Limited and the York Knitting Mills. For example, among labourers at Gunn's slaughterhouse in the Junction, Anton Vasil and George Chriss lived at 418 King Street East and 82 Berkeley Street respectively. Two Macedonian spinners, who were residents of 122 Parliament Street and thus tenants of the former steamship agent and immigrant banker, H.D. Peroff, made the daily trek to the Queen Street West knitting mills. The 1919 tax assessment rolls show us a pork-packer who resided at 362 King Street East and worked at Matthews Blackwell Limited, a firm located at Niagara and Wellington Streets, the site of the municipal abattoir, the Western Cattle Market and Livestock Exchange. West end residents, in turn, worked in the east end. The William Davies Company employed the services of a Tecumseth Street butcher. These patterns prevailed even though each of the three neighbourhoods had some Macedonian presence. It may be that village ties were different in each of the three areas.

Sojourners also moved freely between the two western settlement areas. Junction resident Tony Chriss, a boarder at the Keele Street restaurant of George Aceff and Mite Todosoff, held a job as a spinner at the York Knitting Mills. Niagara Street settlement area residents also came to work in the Junction slaughterhouses. A Richmond Street butcher, Cosma Djidroff, worked at the Harris Abattoir. Labourer Argie Velcoff, a resident of the venerable Bull's Head Hotel, also came to work at the abattoir. If the majority of Macedonian men continued to live in boardinghouses close to work, then the above examples demonstrate that there were forces other than employment defining their choices about community. Bonds of family, village friendship and fellow feeling, for instance, might outweigh the convenience of living close to work.[14]

The Macedonians' commitment to a temporary stay in Toronto was altered by the end of the Balkan War in 1913. The Ottoman Empire's long-standing and oppressive domination of Macedonia now gave way to the rigours of a Greek hegemony and repressive regime. Hopes for a freer Macedonia faded quickly when Bulgarian-language schools and churches in Macedonia were ordered closed by the Greeks. Villages were forced to billet Greek soldiers who conducted comprehensive searches for the hidden rifles and ammunition of rebellious peasants. This unhappy situation in the old country convinced the men abroad that their future and that of their families lay in the new world. As sojourners, the suitors, husbands and fathers worried about survival and well-being of their women folk and children left behind. As settlers, they continued to do so; their concern inspired the decision to bring them to Toronto.

When those who were sent for began to arrive, what was their impression of Toronto? Were the Macedonian settlement areas recognizable as such to the male and female greenhorns, or was it all "America" to the new arrivals? Most of them got a rude introduction to Toronto after the clean and open spaces of the village — smoke, grime, identical squalid and box-like houses greeted them as they met urban industrial life and Canadian society head on. A new bride arriving in the west end summed up her first impressions of her new home and neighbourhood by saying "most houses look same to me, only [the] numbers are different." A woman who came to join her brothers in Toronto was appalled at having to live in a "shack on Tecumseth." In her home village of Zhelevo, she had lived in a six-room house with two balconies, appropriately paid for with money that her migrant father had dutifully earned in the new world. Female Macedonian newcomers often demonstrated a critical sense and eye to match that of the city medical health officer, Dr. Hastings. Seasoned sojourners, men who had worked in or near European towns and cities, on the other hand, accepted matter of factly the less attractive aspects of the new urban way of life.

Like all greenhorns, the newly immigrated womenfolk had little time for reflection. Each had the private task of coming to grips with mates they sometimes barely knew and an ambience totally foreign to them. They were required to adjust quickly and take their place in the family as an efficient economic unit. The coming of women had affected the bachelor households and the sojourning way of life. The boardinghouse was an unsuitable residence for newly married couples. One man's story is typical; he left a Keele and St. Clair Avenue West boardinghouse and, with his wife, found a flat on nearby Mulock Avenue. He remained close to his fellow villagers, but by taking a wife and moving into a flat, removed himself from both the migrant and bachelor ranks. On the other hand, women joining men who already ran established boardinghouses were more often than not expected to become part of the operation.

Family-run boarding establishments began to appear everywhere in the settlement areas. They varied in size, in terms of the number of boarders. Families appear to have housed anywhere from one to ten boarders at a time depending on the couple's energy, business commitment and ethnic network as well as the physical dimensions of their building. Boarders began to reside with families in four- or five-room houses on quiet side streets. This pattern began to replace the earlier sojourner pattern of renting collectively big old houses on main streets. Two boarders — one of whom was a restaurant worker, the other a Queen Street peanut vendor — shared a Tracy Street house with a confectioner's family of five. The men occupied "a little room" in the house. In contrast, a Blevins Place family of five chose to accommodate ten boarders. While family members occupied the living-room, the boarders slept in two bedrooms upstairs and on couches in the dining-room.[15]

Men were also housed in cramped upper and rear residence rooms on streets such as King and Queen Streets East, the sites of immigrant businesses and commercial enterprises. Living in a three- or four-room flat above his store, a King Street East clothing merchant and his family took in boarders too. Whether such a practice was to maximize income or from a sense of fellow feeling for the bachelors is difficult to ascertain. The profit motive was rarely absent, but the sense of ethnic fraternalism usually pervaded as well. Occupying the smaller rooms, the family chose to rent out the larger to the boarders. Boarders were also found in the larger Macedonian residences. Men occupied the third floor of a house on Wyatt Avenue in the city's east end. In the Junction, seven or eight boarders shared rooms on the second and third floors of a nine-room house on Keele Street. In the same building, barber and grocer Noe Petroff and his wife slept in the front room on the second floor — the first floor was the site of the kitchen, dining-room and barber shop — while their friends, Mr. and Mrs. Steve Gemandoff also occupied a room on the second floor.

Running a boardinghouse was a well-organized business enterprise; payment was expected and made for services rendered and understood. A variety of services were available, reflecting both the demands of the men and the priorities and responsiblities of the operators and boardinghouse keepers. Many women prepared meals for boarders, washed their clothing, provided fresh linen and frequent bed changes. One east end women also performed banking duties, depositing pay packets entrusted to her in the men's accounts. In the Junction, Gina Petroff and her friend Mrs. Gemandoff cleaned and dusted for their boarders. They also changed their linens, but they did not cook for the men. It appears that the men enjoyed doing this; they appreciated freedom in the choice and preparation of food. One resident was particularly known for his ability to pickle peppers — a treat he sometimes shared with his boarding "missus." If the system had any drawbacks, they were more often the result of crowding and pre-urban modes of thinking than of personal or economic conflict. The toilet in one house frequently blocked as a result of the men's efforts to flush away sparerib bones and other food scraps.

That boardinghouses were very much a business is reflected in the selection and choice of boarders. In the beginning, boardinghouses operated on a logical extension of village and kinship ties. An east end boardinghouse keeper and former resident of Zhelevo catered to the new world needs of her relatives and fellow *Zhelevari*. Summing up her mother's philosophy, a respondent said, "You're trying to help out so he [a fellow villager] can get somewhere too." Later on, when two women, formerly from Bobishta and Zigoricheni respectively, took on household duties for boarding men from different villages, included Vumbel, Smerdesh and Zeleniche, they did so as their contribution to their family's earning power as a unit. No other obligations of kinship or village were involved.[16]

The outlay of expenses and the integrity of the boardinghouse keepers were monitored carefully by the men. The parsimonious use of coal by an east end boardinghouse keeper was recalled by her daughter: "She didn't dare use a bit more coal because everything went halfers with the boarders." Junction men placed money under their pillows to determine whether the boardinghouse operators were honest while doing their daily housekeeping chores. Gina Petroff recalled her experiences:

> . . . we fix the bed, we put the five dollars where they been and when he come in the night time — used to work in the Swift — I say . . . it's nothing to me . . . we found 'um five dollars in your bed. We put them back over there.
>
> Next morning you gonna find some coppers on the bed. We fix the bed and leave the coppers. . . .

Disruptions or threats to the spirit and working order of the boardinghouse simply could not be tolerated. An oral respondent recalled the story of Nick Coca Cola, an unsuccessful resident of a Junction boardinghouse:

> Any way he been sleeping on the third floor. Not working. He never get up two days, just sleep and stay there day and night. . . . There's depression and nobody give work to you. So anyway they [the boarding family] they kept him for a little while over . . . and they kicked out.

Carrying a blanket, Nick established a residence in one of the larger sewers near the Swift's Canadian Company. The community, despite a sense that it was just that he should evicted, now concerned itself with this plight over a short period of time; the other men who met him at the Balkan Café humoured and cajoled him into returning to the old country.

When tenants dealt with their rent and living expenses promptly, it meant that that type of enterprise could survive and succeed as a much welcome financial asset to the boardinghouse-keeper families involved. Families often depended on this money, for example, to help with the cost of rent and mortgages — "we put so much roomers over there and we make a little rent and we pay the rent."

For all that it was business, there was also much warmth and fellow feeling between the boarders and the boarding "missus" and her family. The men who ran the integrity tests by leaving cash around were also the ones who allowed diapers to be dried in their quarters, bought Christmas presents for the children of the house and solicitously purchased old country style bread to help appease the particular food cravings of a pregnant boarding "missus."[17] But good feelings co-existed with personal tensions and human difficulties. "Older boarders were called uncle by the young women who, after marriage to a boarding boss, found themselves wives and keepers of boarders." The use of such terms was at once respectful; but it also helped in the establishment of a household decorum. The term "uncle", it is important to note, was also used by the children of the boarding operators. It was a custom that mirrored an ordering of proprieties about sexual relations. The selection of boarders was often made carefully by a young husband uncomfortable with the economic necessity which made him bring other males into his household. Recalling his father quietly sizing up potential residents, a man said, "You get a young woman into a place with ten roomers, my father would pick."

The coming of brides, wives and families brought a change to such sojourner and bachelor settler institutions as the coffee-house. The proprietors of such establishments had little choice but to accept the presence of families in the community. And so they learned to cope with it. A proprietor in Ann Arbor, Michigan, advised his customers to "keep your wife as a pet," and to continue eating at the Buffalo Lunch or to cater to it; the International Restaurant in Toronto held weekly family nights in summer. The Balkan Café in the Junction and the east end's Geneva Restaurant remained male strongholds and sought the business of the remaining bachelor settlers, new arrivals and serviced the family men on a night out. Most husbands and fathers found time for an occasional visit to their former haunts, but revelled in the establishment of normal family life. A resident in the Junction was only too happy to eat his wife's cooking after a steady diet of Balkan Café food. The proprietor's annoying habit of scooping out daily specials, such as macaroni and cheese, with his bare hands after stroking his pet cat often made dinner a less than enjoyable experience.[18]

The bachelor boardinghouse experienced a decline with the coming of families after the First World War. The period before 1940 witnessed both the heyday and decline of the family-run boarding operation. By the late 1930s the family-run establishment had outlived its usefulness. Many boarders left simply because they felt the need to start their own households. Even diehard bachelors tended to leave the boardinghouse, choosing to look for more comfortable private space with non-Macedonians elsewhere. Having made the decision to strike out on their own, to enter rooming-houses or become a single roomer often in an Anglo-Canadian or Jewish household, men found that they could turn to *The First Bulgarian-English Pocket Dictionary* for help. The dictionary, for instance, taught men how to make proper inquiries of a prospective landlord:

Good morning, lady
I want to rent a room
How much do you want per week?
Alright sir. Please come in
I would like to see the rooms
Have you a front room for rent?
rear room
quiet room
not very expensive
I want a small room
I don't like this room
I will move in tonight
Where is the water closet?
Please give me the key.

Macedonian slaughterhouse workers in the Junction, for example, rented quarters in Jewish households on Maria Street.

The availability of numbers of prospective boarders, obviously the necessary raw material for the enterprise, was severly limited by the harsh realities of life imposed by new immigration restrictions and the depression. The depression also caused the boardinghouse business to go underground, at least when the family running the establishment was also collecting relief. One respondent vividly remembered the need to "take the bed apart so they [city welfare officials] wouldn't know we had a roomer" each time a welfare worker was seen making his way up towards the house on Adelaide Street West. Those who had kept successful boardinghouses changed their housing and income pattern as the business declined. For example in the later 1930s, Noe and Gina Petroff bought a smaller house in the Junction not just to avoid the rising rent on their nine-room boardinghouse, but because they were left with only one rather than seven or eight boarders by then.

Few Macedonians sought to acquire Toronto property in the early part of the period under study. Sojourners did not want to own property; they did not wish to lay out large amounts of money; nor did they want the kind of commitment and responsibility in the new world that ownership caused. A group of Niagara Street sojourners had a chance at one time to buy the house they were living in for $700. They knew it was a reasonable and attractive offer. The men declined the offer on the grounds that the purchase would bind them to Canada and make them "forget home."

During the settler period, residential property ownership continued to lack the central importance it acquired for other immigrant groups. The reason was not lack of initiative, but rather the practical extreme of initiative. The guiding philosophy or set of priorities of many was summed up in the proverb: "A business is like a flour mill. A house is just like a barn." A business generated income and financial returns; it was a productive entity. Houses — unless boarders were added — demanded too much upkeep and attention to tenants, etc. Like barns they were always in need of tending and filling.[19] Both labourers and entrepreneurs among the Macedonians preferred to rent their accommodations. As we have seen, labourers and workmen tried to minimize the cost of rent by taking in boarders. In that sense, the easy distinction made between unskilled workers and entrepreneur by North American historians of mobility and labour historians is, at best, naive. Many families also chose to share living quarters and expenses with relatives and friends. Each family paid a rental fee of $10 a month. A Macedonian soap factory worker and his wife shared a house on Niagara at Wellington Street with their friends: two couples.

The successful establishment of a commercial enterprise, with families living in the rented quarters above the store or restaurant, was seen as a shrewder way to live and work in the city than mere ownership of a family homestead and a daily trek to work as a labourer for someone else. Such entrepreneurs also tried to share the burden of rent with boarders, relatives or business partners and their families. A King Street East haberdasher and his family shared the three or four rooms above the store with boarders. Two energetic partners in a Keele Street restaurant business shared their living quarters above the restaurant with at least ten men. Only a very subtle eye could notice and understand the difference in contractural terms, which made those quarters neither a boardinghouse nor a hotel, but merely a shared rental.

As in the boardinghouse, this sharing of housing and of living quarters brought on human tensions and personal disagreements. Three couples who shared a house in the west end disbanded when the women "started [acting] kind of funny; [they] never got along together." Sometimes splits occurred when their children did not get along. An angry Mr. and Mrs. Steve Gemandoff left the bungalow they had shared with Noe Petroff and his wife after their young sons fought and proved sadly incompatible: "the kids will kill each other." Maybe as the young acculturated, they simply could not feel or understand the same mutual need and ethnic bond that their parents did.

Despite their limited urge to own their own domiciles, the acquisition of property by Macedonians in the period before 1940, symbolic of the new attitude toward remaining in Canada, was extensive. Both small businessmen and labourers — where that distinction can be made — became property owners. The process began about seven or eight years after the first wave of migration. In 1913 merchant Tipe Tipouloff and his partners secured the property on which their east end store stood. By 1915 Naum Phillips, one of the community's steamship agents, also purchased property. After renting two locations, a restaurant and a dry-goods store on King Street East, Phillips purchased the property and buildings where he had his dry-goods store. By 1927 businessman Dimitre H. Paul and Jovan Nicoloff appear as the freehold owners of a lunch room on St. Clair Avenue West and a confectionery on Mulock.[20]

Businessmen generally purchased property both as a place to live and as a place from which they would develop their business. Purchase of a building, especially in less residential areas, freed an entrepreneurial man or family to use the rooms and building space to maximize income in any way they saw fit. You could work all day for a packinghouse, at night running a smokehouse and sausage factory of your own, preparing *sojuk* for favourite customers. The Petroff family, for example, bought a small bungalow with a big front on Keele Street. The big front could be and was effectively converted into a storefront. Mrs. Petroff offered a rationale for the purchase: "We bought them [the house] for the front and not for the house . . . if we were going to buy a house we would have bought a home in Baby Point [a well-to-do neighbourhood]."

By the 1920s Macedonians of a great variety of occupations and of incomes had bought property in all three settler areas. Both businessmen and labourers were pushed by ever-increasing rents to make property purchases. Rent increases forced one Macedonian worker and his family to abandon a house in the King-Sumach Street area. In their effort to accumulate a small pool of capital for later use in Toronto, they moved down to less attractive quarters, first to Wascana Avenue and then to Trinity Street. Their effort succeeded and the family eventually bought a house in the east end.

Macedonian decisions about buying or renting obviously were made in much the same way as those of their neighbours from other ethnic backgrounds, but there were typically Macedonian considerations as well. Several factors affected the Macedonians' residential choice and location inside or outside the settlement areas. The structure of anti-immigrant prejudice served to define their choice of lodging and the availability of housing. One of the early Macedonian women settlers in Toronto recalled with some bitterness her lengthy search for a house to rent: "Many places told me. They said, 'You said you a foreigner.' They slam door." In the Niagara Street district, angry Anglo-Canadian renters, on more than one occasion, protested when landlords sold the building in which they were renting to Macedonians: "Why should the foreigners come and take our house?"[21]

The choice and purchase of a house sometimes was affected by the commercial and residential jostlings of other ethnic groups in the Macedonian settlement areas. One respondent recalled her family's aborted purchase of a house in the east end: "He [father] bought [a] house from English people but was rented to Italians. They would not go because they used to keep bananas downstairs to [go] ripe." Landlords' objectives played a role in the pattern of the Macedonians' acquisition of housing and property. Some oral sources cite the unwillingness of owners in existing settlement areas to sell while property values were rising. Many landlords, it seems, were prepared to retain their holdings for the lucrative rewards or rumoured commercial redevelopment and institutional expansion. Corporate landlords such as the Union Stock Yards and the Swift Canadian Company in the west end and the Canadian Northern Ontario Railway in the east seemed equally unwilling to sell to interested individuals. Lands held by the big firms on Keele Street, St. Clair Avenue West and Eastern Avenue were withheld from the market at least for a time for company development projects.

In the late 1920s, the gradual acceptance of buying a residence for residence's sake began to appear. An agreeable home became a status symbol. The importance of residence also played a role in the group's movement to the peripheries of the settlement areas and beyond. The movement of immigrants above Queen Street East and east of the Don River; of the Junction residents to Fisken, Priscilla and Willard avenues, for example; of Niagara Street residents to the area above Queen Street West and to Parkdale help to demonstrate the Macedonians' own movement away from industry, of their growing willingness, even desire, for distance between the home and workplace. This willingness to separate residence and commerce marked the passing of one aspect of the village mentality brought from the Balkans.

Some men began to acquire property in the manner of Turkish beys and pashas back home. Property became a commodity not a patrimony. By 1913 the community banker, grocer and one-time steamship agent, Hadji D. Peroff, certainly understood that. He bought homes at 18 and 20 Eastern Avenue and a rear residence at 24 Eastern Avenue. By 1915, in partnership with Simo Velianoff, he was also a property owner and landlord on Parliament Street for fruit-dealer Natale Catalino and various Macedonian tenants. That same year merchant Tipe Tepouloff and his partners became landlords in a budding housing business with an Anglo-Canadian, George F. Dowson, a confectioner at 472-474 King Street East.[22]

By 1940 confidence and experience, ambition and nerve put

small entrepreneurs and restaurateurs in the forefront of the movement away from the original settlement areas. Some opened businesses outside of the neighbourhoods, but continued to live there.
While always maintaining his residence in the Niagara Street settlement district, Alex Martin, a barber, established beauty salons at
Carlton and Jarvis streets, at 1182½ Queen Street East, between
Jones Avenue and Curzon Street in the area east of the Don River.
Martin also was the owner of the Metropolitan Lunch, which was
located at 3481 Yonge Street, the site of the TTC radial station at the
city limits with North York. Other merchants chose to move their
families along with their business ventures out to the new areas.
When a former King Street East butcher, Nako D. Grozdanoff, set
up home and shop east of the Don River on Jones Avenue, he succeeded in attracting a diverse non-Macedonian clientele. His
customers, in the words of his daughter, were "Educated people . . .
government people, insurance [agents], policemen [and] detec-
tives — no factory workers." The process continued. Tina Vassil
and her restauranteur husband moved out of the Macedonian settlement areas because they felt that their very survival depended on it.
Mr. Vassil opened a restaurant on Danforth Avenue (at Coxwell)
where most of his patrons were Anglo-Canadians. It was imperative
that they do business in non-Macedonian areas because "in the thirties [you] couldn't get rich serving Macedonians." The depression
merely served as a culmination of a process whereby Macedonian
working men, as more and more families were formed, ceased to eat
out, or provide the restauranteurs with a basic clientele.

Macedonians and their families made an impact in these new
areas of the city both as employers and customers. They came more
in contact with other ethnic groups as customers, employers and
workers. A Macedonian shoeshine and cigar-store operation at
Yonge and Wellington Street West, outside the Niagara Street district, employed Italians as shoe-shine boys. The spread of Macedonian families throughout the city meant opportunity and adjustment
for non-Macedonian business as well. One Bloor Street Italian fruit
and vegetable merchant was shrewd enough to learn the Macedonian words for a variety of foodstuffs including rice, peppers and
grapes from his neighbour, a Macedonian shoe-shine operator.[23]

The original Macedonian settlement areas can barely be discerned now. Commerical and industrial development has destroyed
many of the little streets of working-class housing, which characterized the Macedonian east end. The growth and development of
housing projects such as Regent Park pushed most of those who held
on out of the area. Two Macedonian churches stand as lonely sen-
tinels over the northern boundary of a once thriving neighbourhood.
Even they are on the northern fringe of the old settlement; SS. Cyril
and Methody's, built in the 1940s either to stem or to keep up with

the flow northward, was a miscalculation. The community's first and second generation were being drawn by opportunity and acculturation out to the suburbs as much as they were leaving the old Trinity Street matrix because of its industry and decline. With the closing of the Lake Ohrid boardinghouse on Eastern Avenue, no visible Macedonian presence remains.

Macedonian neighbourhoods were then never as visible as Chinatowns or Little Italies, but in each of the three settlement areas, networks of loyalty from the old world villages and shared new world conditions were elaborating an ethnic group. Toronto's Macedonian colony was one of the two largest in North America; it was a centre of nationalist politics and religious ferment. Few outside the group could understand how large these humble neighbourhoods loomed or the mental landscape of Macedonians everywhere in the world.

Notes

1. Interview with Mrs. Gina Petroff, 29 June 1975, Multicultural History Society of Ontario, Toronto. (An extensive collection of Macedonian oral testimony, of which the above interview is a part, is held by the Multicultural History Society, henceforth cited as MHSO. All interviews have been conducted by myself unless otherswise cited). SS. Cyril and Methody Macedono-Bulgarian Orthodox Cathedral (henceforth cited as SS. Cyril and Methody), *National Calendar 1916 and the 1914-1915 Financial Report* (Toronto, 1916); Macedonian Political Organization (henceforth cited as the MPO), *15th Annual Convention Almanac* (Indianapolis, Indianapolis, Ind., 1936), p. 95.

2. In *Rails from the Junction,* James V. Salmon focused on the growth and impact of the Toronto Suburban Railway upon the city's western neighbourhoods. The emergence of the area as a railway and meat packing centre and the settlers who came to live and work in it received only cursory attention. The challenge of learning and writing about an ethnically diverse area has never been taken up. Displaying a similar indifference to North American community life, Macedonian scholars both here and abroad have mostly chosen to study political and nationalist topics. Immigrant group historians such as F.S. Tomev are only now beginning to follow up their moving accounts of partisans and village social life with Toronto community studies. For writing on early immigrant history, see the following: J.E. Middleton, *The Municipality of Toronto: A History I* (Toronto: The Dominion Publishing Company, 1923), p. 402; G.P. de T. Glazebrook, *The Story of Toronto* (Toronto: University of Toronto Press, 1971), pp. 201-5; R.F. Harney and H.M. Troper, *Immigrants: A Portrait of the Urban Experience, 1890-1930* (Toronto: Van Nostrand Reinhold Ltd., 1975); James V. Salmon, *Rails from the Junction: The Story of the Toronto Suburban Railway* (Toronto: Lyon Productions, 1976); this booklet was prepared for publication by John F. Bromley and Mike Filey. It is on file at the City of Toronto Archives: see the article in it, Andrew A. Merriless, "A History of the Town of West Toronto Junction", pp. 3-4.

3. Unless otherwise indicated, information on the Macedonians of Toronto is obtained from *Might's City Directory*, 1903-1940, and the City of Toronto Archives, *Tax Assessment Rolls*, 1903-1940, on deposit at the City of Toronto Archives and Central Records.

4. F.S. Tomev, "Memoirs," Macedonian Collection, MHSO, Toronto; MPO, *16th Annual Convention Almanac* (Indianapolis, Ind., 1937).

5. Unless otherwise indicated, all church records cited are from SS. Cyril and Methody (Toronto); see my M.A. thesis, "The Macedonian Community in Toronto to 1930" (University of Toronto, 1976); Toronto Department of Health, *Report of the Medical Health Officer Dealing with the Recent Investigation of Slum Conditions in Toronto, Embodying Recommendations Amelioration of the Same* (Toronto, 1911), on deposit at the City of Toronto Archives; C. Nedelkoff, *English-Bulgarian and Bulgarian-English Letters* (Granite City, Ill.: Elia K. Mircheff and Company, 1911); A.C. Yovcheff, *Various Bulgarian-American Letters* (n.p., 1917); D.G. Malincheff and J. Theophilact, *The First Bulgarian-English Pocket Dictionary* (Toronto: D.G. Malincheff and N.D. Velcoff, 1913).

6. See the following: *Might's City Directories*, 1903-40; *Jack Canuck: A Weekly Review of What the Public Say, Do and Think* I (Toronto), 29 July 1911, on deposit in the City of Toronto Archives, p. 17; Interview with Mr. Vasil Dimitroff, 26 August 1976, MHSO; memorandum of an unrecorded conversation with F.S. Tomev, 5 February 1981, Macedonian Coll. See Richard Bebout, ed., *The Open Gate: Toronto Union Station* (Toronto: Peter Martin Associates, 1972), pp. 15-26; the Great Fire of 1904 destroyed most of Toronto's manufacturing and wholesale district south of King Street and west of Yonge Street. In the long block of Front Street between Bay and York Streets, where Union Station now stands, all was rubble except for two or three buildings. Toronto, *City Council Minutes* (1912), p. 990, on deposit in the City Archives: "The Board recommends that the City Architect, Property Commissioner and Medical Health Officer be authorized and instructed to forthwith prepare plans and specifications for the erection and establishment of a municipal abattoir and cooling plant."

7. 1910-1927 *Tax Assessment Rolls*. Toronto, Department of Health, *Report of the Medical Health Officer Dealing with the Recent Investigation of Slum Conditions in Toronto*, pp. 2-12. Interview with Mr. Tony Phillips, 22 July 1975, MHSO; interview with Mr. N.S. Telmelcoff, 8 July 1975, MHSO.

8. Tomev, "Memoirs," Macedonian (Mac.) Coll.; Interview with Mr. Dono Evans, 2 August 1975, MHSO; memorandum of my unrecorded conversation with Mr. Chris Mitanis, 10 October 1975, Mac: Coll.

9. Yovcheff, *Various Bulgarian-American Letters*, pp. 97, 155; Nedelkoff, *English-Bulgarian and Bulgarian-English Letters*, pp. 28-29, 115; Malincheff and Theophilact, *The First Bulgarian-English Pocket Dictionary*, pp. 390-410; memorandum of my unrecorded conversation with F.S. Tomev, 5 February 1981, Mac. Coll.

10. F.S. Tomev, *A Short History of Zhelevo Village Macedonia*, pp. 25, 79; Interview with Mr. Vasil Trenton, 19 July 1978, MHSO; Interview with Mr. Dono Evans, 2 August 1975, MHSO. Tomev, "Memoirs"; memorandum of my unrecorded conversation with Mrs. Gina Petroff, 10 October 1981, Mac. Coll.

11. 1903-1940 *Tax Assessment Rolls*; Stoyan Christowe, *The Eagle and the Stork* (Harper's Magazine Press, New York: 1976), p. 146.

12. Malincheff and Theophilact, *The First Bulgarian-English Dictionary*, back pages; Christowe, *The Eagle and the Stork*, pp. 185, 212.

13. *Might's City Directory*, 1915-40; memorandum of my unrecorded conversation with F.S. Tomev, 25 February 1981, Mac. Coll.; interview with Gina Petroff by R.F. Harney, 21 January 1977, MHSO; memorandum of my unrecorded conversation with Mrs. Gina Petroff, 12 February 1981, Mac. Coll.; R.F. Harney, "Boarding and Belonging: Thoughts on Sojourner Institutions," *Urban History Review*, no. 2 (1978), pp. 8-37.

14. Interview with Mr. N.S. Temelcoff, 8 July 1975, MHSO; interview with Mr. Mike Tallin, 25 August 1975, MHSO.

15. Interviews with Mrs. Fanche T. Nicoloff, 15 August 1975; Mrs. Donna Spero, 29 November 1975, MHSO; Mrs. R. Pappas, 23 January 1976; Mrs. Sophie Pandoff, 30 March 1977, MHSO; Mr. Louis Mladen, 24 October 1976, MHSO.

16. Interview with Mrs. Helen Petroff, 17 July 1975, MHSO; interview with Professor B.P. Stoicheff, 28 January 1976, MHSO; memorandum of my unrecorded conversation with Mrs. Gina Petroff, 12 February 1981, Mac. Coll.; interview with Mr. Louis Mladen, 24 October 1976, MHSO; interview with Mrs. Gina Petroff, 29 June 1975, MHSO; memorandum of my unrecorded conversation with Gina Petroff, 10 February 1981, Mac. Coll.; interview with Mrs. Gina Petroff, 12 October 1976, MHSO.

17. Interview with Mrs. Helen Petroff, 17 July 1975, MHSO; interview with Mrs. Gina Petroff, 12 October 1976, MHSO; interview with Mrs. Gina Petroff, 13 October 1976, MHSO; Interview with Mrs. Gina Petroff, 21 January 1977, MHSO; memorandum of my unrecorded conversation with Mrs. Gina Petroff, 12 February 1981, Mac. Coll.; interview with Mrs. Gina Petroff, 29 June 1975, MHSO; memorandum of my unrecorded conversation with Mrs. Gina Petroff, 1 August 1980, Mac. Coll.

18. Harney, "Boarding and Belonging," pp. 8-37; interview with Mr. Louis Mladen, 24 October 1976, MHSO; MPO, *16th Annual Convention Almanac* (1937), p. 55; interview with Mr. Ted Vangel, 24 November 1975, MHSO; memorandum of my unrecorded conversation with Mrs. Gina Petroff, 10 May 1980, Mac. Coll.

19. Malincheff and Theophilact, *The First Bulgarian-English Pocket Dictionary*, p. 400; 1920-1940 *Tax Assessment Rolls*; interview with John Spero, 29 November 1975, MHSO; Memorandum of my unrecorded conversation with Mrs. Gina Petroff, 12 February 1981, Mac. Coll.; interview with Mr. Vasil Trenton, 19 July 1978, MHSO; Memorandum of my unrecorded conversation with F.S. Tomev, 5 February 1981, Mac. Coll.

20. Interview with Peter Floroff, 1 August 1975, MHSO; interview with Mr. Tony Phillips, 22 July 1975, MHSO; interview with Mrs. Helen Petroff, 17 July 1975, MHSO; interview with Mrs. Gina Petroff, 29 June 1975, MHSO; interview with Mr. Tony Phillips, 22 July 1975, MHSO; 1919-1927 *Tax Assessment Rolls.*

21. Interview with Sophie Pandoff, 30 March 1977, MHSO; interview with Mrs. Gina Petroff, 21 January 1977, MHSO; memorandum of my unrecorded conversation with Mrs. Gina Petroff, 12 February 1981, Mac. Coll.; interview with Mrs. Hope Paliare, 15 July 1975, MHSO; interview with Mr. Tony

Phillips, 22 July 1975, MHSO; interview with Mrs. Gina Petroff, 21 January 1977, MHSO; interview with Mrs. Mara Kercheff, 25 November 1975, MHSO; interview with Mrs. F. Nicoloff, 15 August 1975, MHSO; interview with Mrs. Donna Spero, 29 November 1975, MHSO.

22. Interview with Mrs. B. Markoff, 9 December 1975, MHSO; See my interview with Mr. Mike Tallin, 25 August 1975, MHSO, for example; see the 1903-1940 *Tax Assessment Rolls.*

23. Interview with Mr. Anastas Petroff, 6 December 1975, MHSO; interview with Mrs. D.K. Thomas, 25 February 1978, MHSO.

Tailor-Maid: the Finnish Immigrant Community of Toronto before the First World War

Varpu Lindstrom-Best

On the cold evening of January 1, 1907, Mayor Coatsworth was waiting for the results of the municipal election in Toronto. He was confident of victory, since his aides had assured him there was virtually no opposition. As the evening progressed, the mayor became more concerned. Who was this James Lindala winning so many votes? Where did he come from? Mayor Coatsworth's aides were puzzled, for Lindala was a stranger to them and to 95 per cent of the voters, who had never even heard his name until a week before the nomination. Those who did not wait for the results that evening read the shocking news in the headlines of the morning *Globe*: "Unknown Socialist Polls a Large Vote for Mayor." Torontonians were surprised to find ". . . that an unknown Socialist tailor of foreign birth should poll over eight thousand votes for the Mayoralty of Toronto against a barrister of irreproachable personal character. . . ." The victory had lost some of its sweetness for Mayor Coatsworth.[1]

Not far from the mayor's office, in the centre of Toronto's immigrant community, James Lindala was celebrating with his fellow Finns, who had helped him campaign, with members of the Journeymen Tailors' Union, who had supported his candidacy, and with this friends in the Socialist Party of Canada. The mayor and the tailor could have been separated by miles rather than by a few city blocks. The differences between the two men extended to their backgrounds, lifestyles and world views. Much has been written about Mayor Coatsworth's Toronto; it is time now to study that of James Lindala.

Every ethnic community has a founder, a pioneer bold enough to settle in an unknown territory. James Lindala (Jaakko Lintala) can claim that distinction in the Finnish community of Toronto. He hopped off the train on October 13, 1887 and walked slowly toward the mish-mash of warehouses and narrow buildings near Spadina and Queen Street, wondering if this place could give him the opportunity to work and finally to settle down.[2]

Lindala was only one of the 350,000 Finns who emigrated to North America before the First World War. In many ways his migration route and his search for work was similar to the other optimistic, curious young emigrants who had chosen the promise of the new world instead of the old familiar surroundings. Lindala originated from Ostrobothnia, an agricultural area in western Finland that was the largest source of overseas emigrants. His search for work began at the age of eleven when he first left this quaint, but overpopulated village of Vähäkyrö, and moved to the coastal city of Vaasa to be a tailor's apprentice. He was fortified with a few cups given by his tinsmith father and two weeks of formal education. Still, like 98 per cent of the Finnish emigrants, he was literate, having learned to read in the village Lutheran church.

In Vaasa Lindala met returning or visiting immigrants from America. Many told stories of adventure, described exciting frontier towns, some even displayed dollars and gold watches hanging from their pockets. Of course Lindala had also heard of mining accidents, illness and other misfortunes, but the young mind could easily discard these. America became an inescapable dream, a place where one would at least have a chance. Little was known of Canada, Toronto was unheard of. Until 1891, according to the calculations of Reino Kero, only 1 per cent of the Finnish emigrants gave their final destination as Canada. Michigan was the state where most Finns started their search for work, among them the young tailor, James Lindala.[3]

He travelled alone although the ship was full of other youthful emigrants, most of them male. Before the First World War, two-thirds of the Finnish emigrants were male. Their reasons for emigrating were varied: family feuds, broken hearts, debts, and desire for adventure could encourage some to leave it all behind. Others escaped the political harassment and oppressive atmosphere created by the despised Russian bureaucrats who ruled the Grand Duchy of Finland until 1917. Compulsory conscription to the Russian army was an added incentive to seek out the "freedom" of the new world. Nevertheless, the greatest motivating force for overseas emigration was the promise of better economic opportunities. Except for a handful of socialists, emigration for the Finns was an entirely voluntary act. They came — as the familiar proverb states — to carve gold with wooden knives.

Although Upper Michigan offered some economic opportunities to the general workers — 90 per cent of Finns falling into this category — it was not a haven for an ambitious tailor; miners' clothes presented no challenge for a creative artisan.[4] Thus, Lindala decided to leave once more, to seek out better prospects in Toronto, a booming commercial city inhabited by "gentlemen in tweed suits." In Toronto, he had heard, tailors were in demand.

Lindala was not disappointed and decided to make Toronto his new home in North America. Work was plentiful but the life of "the only Finn in town" was desperately lonely. When his landlady, at 115 Adelaide Street West, surprised Lindala speaking in Finnish to the mirror, Lindala realized that it was high time to entice a friend to come and join him. This decision marked the beginning of a Finnish community that was to grow around James Lindala.

A brief portrait of the first nineteen immigrants known to have settled in Toronto before the end of 1901 helps us to establish the role that kinship, letters and word-of-mouth played in the recruitment of immigrants, as well as the founder's influence on the character of the community. Lindala's first recruit was Reinhold Mikkonen, a tailor whom he had befriended in the copper country of northern Michigan. Mikkonen arrived in 1889 and promptly started work at Biltmore Brothers where Lindala had earned a good reputation for Finnish tailors. Together they moved to 11 Trinity Square.[5] Mikkonen was born in Hyrynsalmi in Oulu province. Other tailors were told of the employment opportunities in Toronto through letters from Lindala to his sister Mathilda, and from Mikkonen to his wife Anna, a Finn-Swede who joined her husband with their two children in 1891. Both Anna and Mathilda were residing in Upper Michigan. Other tailors soon followed the pattern established by Lindala. Johan Latva arrived in Toronto in 1891 and his wife Sigrid arrived in 1897 (her migration route is not known).[6] Heikki Heinonen, born in Lieto, Finland, in the province of Turku-Pori, and his wife Johanna, arrived in 1892.[7]

In 1893 James Lindala travelled to New York to attend a design course. A year later he returned with his seventeen-year-old wife, Charlotte Irene Leineberg, who had come to North America at the age of fifteen from the coastal town of Pori to work as a maid. She ran out of money in New York and, searching for her relatives, decided to place an advertisement in a Finnish-American newspaper. Lindala saw this advertisement and sought Miss Leineberg out. They fell in love and together moved to Toronto.

Johan Ranta, a tailor from Lindala's neighbouring village of Isokyrö and a childhood friend, had married Lindala's sister Mathilda. Ranta claimed that he married Mathilda because she was the only girl Lindala would not steal away from him. In 1894 Ranta moved to Toronto from Michigan, and Mathilda followed in 1896.[8] Thus, the first five founding families of the Toronto Finnish community had followed a migration route from Finland to northern Michigan to Toronto. They were one another's friends or relatives, and the men were all tailors.

More were to follow. In New York, Lindala had spoken to Gustaf Nyros, living in Brooklyn with his wife Frederika and their six children, two of whom died of diphtheria before the family moved to Toronto in either 1899 or 1900.[9] Nyros was originally from Pyhämaa, a small coastal village south of the city of Rauma. Before settling in Brooklyn, Nyros had tried his luck in San Francisco. One more family (there is very little information about them), Tuomas Rappee and his wife Ida, arrived in Toronto in 1899.[10]

In addition to these seven couples, three single men and two single women had settled in Toronto before the end of 1901. Aati Saarimäki, a tailor from Keuruu, is perhaps the first Finn to have come directly to Toronto. According to his son Paul, in 1899 he came to Toronto "because he knew Lindala."[11] Väinö Paananen, a tailor from the village of Kinnula in Ostrobothnia, emigrated first to California and in 1899 moved to Toronto.[12] Julius Nyysänen, also a young tailor, arrived in Toronto in 1901, most likely from northern Michigan. The two single women, Paananen's sister Toini, who arrived with her brother in 1900, and Anna Rönkkä, who came in 1901, were maids.[13]

The growing community was markedly different from the other Finnish immigrant communities in North America. First, there was a high ratio of couples and twenty-one children, fifteen of whom were born in Toronto before the end of 1901. The females made up 47 per cent of the adult (over sixteen years of age) population, which is far above the average for Finnish emigrants in North America.

The second main difference was the occupational structure of the Finnish men. Instead of general labourers, all were tailors. That so many tailors from Upper Michigan should move to Toronto is even more remarkable in light of a study done of the Finnish labour force in Houghton and Keweenaw counties in northern Michigan in 1890. Out of a sample of 409 males, only two were tailors.[14]

All the Finns clustered in the south-central area of Toronto, within walking distance of each other, the railroad and the tailoring shops on King Street. By 1901 Lindala owned a house at 20 Markham Place, where he lived with his family. The Lindalas did not take boarders, but their home in later years was always full of visitors and relatives. The Mikkonens owned a house at 35 Nelson

Street, where Pekka Hartikainen, a young Finnish tailor, boarded for a few months in 1901. The Heinonens, or rather Johanna, kept a rooming house at 25 Nelson Street. Among her tenants were the Latvas (lodgers) and Aati Saarimaki (rented one room). The Nyroses either owned or rented a house a 115 Chestnut Street, and the Rantas owned a house at 31 Kensington Avenue. The two single women lived in their places of employment in the Rosedale area. The Rappees and Nyysänens are not listed in the city directory until 1904, at which time they were still lodgers.[15]

By 1901 a pattern for housing in the immigrant community was being established. Four of the five founding families owned their own homes, and one family either owned or rented a house. The later arrivals, the maids excepted, either boarded with or rented from the already established group. A community spirit, in the form of social gatherings and mutual help, began to take shape. The children played together and occasionally gathered at the Heinonens for Sunday school. James Lindala became the community leader through his fluency in English, knowledge of the Canadian way of life, material success, and status as the first Finn in Toronto. This small nucleus was to have great sigificance in the development of the community when the mass immigration from Finland began in 1902. The patterns that the founders established were still evident in 1913.

At first Finns had generally bypassed Toronto, but in 1902 the trend changed. In that year alone, at least 57 settled in Toronto and in 1903 their number had increased to at least 128.[16] By 1905 it was estimated that the community had about 400 members,[17] and by 1910 it had risen to 766.[18]

Finnish immigration to Canada increased rapidly after the turn of the century. The lean years and poor harvests in Finland during 1902-3 gave added impetus to emigration. By 1901 Toronto had a stable, established community of Finns who could help to attract others. Many of the new arrivals were relatives and friends of those already settled in Toronto. As will be demonstrated, an overwhelming majority of those staying in Toronto were skilled artisans. A large city offers better employment opportunities, and Toronto was growing and industrializing rapidly.

In October 1903, some of the tailors decided to take a census of the Finns in Toronto "because such a document would be of great value to future historians.[19] The original questionnaire had ten questions, but in the final census only the name, occupation of males, date of birth and date of arrival in Toronto were listed. Not all the information was collected for each individual, which accounts for the difference in the size of the samples used in this paper. The 1903 *Väestönlaskenta* has an advantage over national censuses and city directories in that no Finns were excluded through ignorance of foreign names or indirect migration patterns. The two men in charge of the project, V. Holmsten and F. Syrjälä, were respected members of the community; Holmsten was a volunteer English teacher and Syrjälä was a candidate in a municipal election. They divided their area into districts and took great care not to miss the many lodgers and live-in maids. Despite the socialist views of the two collectors,[20] there is no indication that any "church Finns" were ignored.[21] In 1910 the 1903 *Väestönlaskenta* was updated; unfortunately, the original documents have not survived, although they were published in summary form.[22]

The sample I used for 1913 relies entirely on city directories and membership lists of Finnish organizations and congregations. Judging the percentage of Finns in the city directories as compared to the Finnish Society's 1913 membership list, about 50 per cent of the heads of households are missing from the directories.

Information on women is more scanty because wives were not listed in the directories and they were less likely to appear in membership lists in order to avoid paying a double fee; moreover, female occupations were not recorded in the detailed 1903 Finnish community census, although they do appear in the revised Finnish community census of 1910. Some of these gaps in information have been filled by matching the names in the 1903 census with information found in collection lists, membership lists and city directories.

Information on the occupational status for Finnish men and women in Toronto shows the continuing dominance of tailors in the male labour force and of maids in the female labour force. In 1903, out of a sample of 109 males, 75 per cent were skilled workers (mainly artisans), and 43 per cent were tailors. This trend continued and in 1913 fully 80 per cent of the Finnish men were artisans and 40 per cent of them were tailors. In 1913, out of a sample of twenty-five women, ten were maids, one was a cook and the rest were needle-workers: five tailors, five finishers, two seamstresses and two operators. Personal interviews indicate, however, that most of the women worked as live-in maids. This is confirmed by the 1910 summaries showing that out of 263 women, 119 were working outside the home, 66 per cent of whom were maids, 25 per cent were seamstresses and tailors and 9 per cent were laundresses.

Thus the Finnish community was working class; in 1913 there was only one professional — an engineer. Although tailors occupied the top of the Finns' occupational and social hierarchy, moulders were the highest-paid skilled workers. In 1910 the average annual salary expectations for the Finns were as follows: moulders, $849; tailors, $752; metal workers, $750; carpenters, $730; steel (iron workers), $698. Maids could expect to earn $205 annually, plus room and board.

Many enterprising Finns began their own small businesses. In 1903 the largest employer of Finnish men in Toronto was the "Iso-Paja" (Big Shop) at 159 York Street, owned by Lindala. This cooperatively run shop had room for fifty tailors who could rent space and the use of machines for 25 cents per week, and work in an atmosphere of camaraderie. All had to join the Journeymen Tailors' Union, and socialist doctrines were actively promoted at Iso-Paja. The tailors listened to selections from working-class papers, socialist literature, Marx, Engels, Kautsky and Finnish authors such as Aleksis Kivi, or from English authors such as Shakespeare, read by a paid reader during the busy times and by one of the tailors during the slower season. In the front of the store Mrs. Lindala sold groceries, and downstairs there was a large public sauna. James Lindala also arranged for prepaid tickets for relatives at home, exchanged Canadian and Finnish money and acted as the official court interpreter. Before the Finns had their own community hall, Iso-Paja functioned as the unofficial community centre.[23]

Other tailors started their own businesses; for example, the Kuosmanen Brothers and the Grondahls had shops on King Street and occasionally hired Finnish apprentices. Canadian tailoring firms such as the House of Hoberlin also employed Finns.

Until the long strike of journeymen tailors in 1912, they enjoyed steady and relatively well-paid employment. This increased their ability to buy their own homes and lessened their geographic mobility, making tailors the backbone of the community. (James Lindala had speculated quite successfully in real estate and owned several properties.[24]) Working hours were long, however, and the job often tedious. They made up many songs and poems about their situation. The following is the ending of one song, composed by a lonely tailor's wife at Iso-Paja:

Siis räätälit rakkaat mä toivoisin
että heittäisitte yö työn helkottiin
sillä yö on luotuna levolle,
ja päivä työn teolle.

[Therefore dear tailors I sincerely suggest
that you throw your night work to hell
because the night was created for rest
and the day for work.][25]

For those who did not do tailoring, McGregor and McIntyre Company was a likely place of employment for moulders and iron workers, who constructed ships and bridges. In 1913 at least nine Finnish men were working there under a Finnish foreman. Similarly,

Polson Iron Works hired moulders as well as "helpers," and seven coppersmiths found jobs at Booth and Coulter Copper and Brass Company. The Finns, when possible, helped their countrymen to find jobs and worked in groups to ease the problems of coping with English.[26]

For the women who did not wish to work as live-in maids, Eaton's was the biggest employer. At least eight women worked there in various needle-trade jobs in 1913. Iso-Paja also employed tailors and finishers, but usually there were no more than five women in Iso-Paja at one time. The owners of the Parisian Laundry, a "sweat shop," employed Finnish girls "almost exclusively for two decades."[27] The Laundry was first located in the heart of the Finnish community, on Adelaide Street, and later moved to Spadina Avenue, where it still operates. Five women were cleaners at the Toronto General Hospital.

The married women found several ways to supplement family income. Many of them helped at night with their husbands' tailoring. Others took lodgers and roomers into their already cramped quarters. The more enterprising women ran rooming houses with complete board; Widmer Street was soon full of them. Home restaurants were started for those without families and Holm's restaurant on the corner of Widmer and Richmond streets became the meeting place for single men. At least four of the founding families — the Heinonens, Saarimäkis, Mikkonens and Rantas — engaged in these kinds of businesses. In addition to supplementing the income of their families, the women hired newly arrived Finnish girls as helpers, cleaners, cooks and babysitters. Many women, especially widows with children, specialized in running "Koiratorppia," illegal liquor outlets, where in addition to alcohol they sold home-made beer. By the Firt World War a dozen such establishments flourished within walking distance of Widmer Street.

Mrs. Anderson operated the largest female employment service, specializing in placing Finnish maids in Rosedale area homes, and Frederika Nyros was the community's midwife.[28]

In addition to the work done by these women and the tailoring done by their husbands, Finns owned bakeries (Löppönen's was the first and Miettinen's the second) and invested in building enterprises, especially in the construction company of Mr. Hill, a Finn whose firm was large enough to employ several carpenters and painters.

Some other instances of occupational upward mobility are evident during the ten-year period, 1903 to 1913. Men listed in the 1903 community census as labourers later became painters, carpenters and iron workers. Carpenters specialized further in cabinet- and piano-making. Nevertheless, occupational structure between 1903 and 1913 remained essentially the same. Although many succeeded in operating small businesses, the majority were in blue-collar trades. The high percentage of artisans and the Finns' entrepreneurial spirit earned them the reputation of a working-class "artistocracy"; as a tailor described it, "We are not ragged beggars but the cream of the working class."[29]

The geographic distribution map for 1903 indicates that the Finns continued to live in south-central Toronto, where the original settlers had arrived. The heaviest concentration was in the rectangle bordered by Queen Street on the north, King Street on the south, Peter Street on the east and York Street on the West. Soho Street also had a number of families, and at the corner of Soho and Queen streets was the "Soho Hotelli," where Finns could quench their thirst. Few families had moved to Kensington Avenue and William Street by 1903, but the heaviest distribution outside the rectangle was on Teraulay Street, where tailors owned rooming houses. No addresses for Finns could be found outside of Wards 3 and 4.[30]

The 1913 map shows considerable decentralization of the Finnish community during the previous decade, although the heart of the community remained within the rectangle.[31] Toronto was spreading to the east and west, where new housing was built to accommodate the growing population. Finns followed the trend and moved to the largely working-class area east of the Don River and to western Toronto. North of Bloor Street, on Alcorn Avenue (called Wickson before 1908), we find an unusual concentration, because prosperous tailors and leaders of the Finnish community followed when Lindala moved there. The area became known as the "Korvenloukku" (Boondocks), because of its distance and isolation from the centre of the community. Among the residents of the Korvenloukku were the Ahlqvists, Lehtos, Latvas, Sailas, Grondahls and Hellsbergs. It is not clear if the establishment of the Korvenlukku involved a deliberate attempt at residential segregation by those "who had made it," or whether it reflected confidence in James Lindala's real estate investments in the area.

Stephen Thernstrom found, in his study of Newburyport in *Poverty and Progress*, that home ownership was higher among Irish immigrant workers than among native Americans, and he believed that property served as a substitute for a lack of occupational mobility.[32] Owning property was also important to the Finns in Toronto. A comparison of residence status in 1903 and 1913[33] shows a dramatic increase in home ownership and house leasing, and a decline in lodging, boarding and rooming. In 1903, only 35 per cent owned or leased their own homes, while in 1913 this figure had nearly doubled to 62 per cent.

It is, of course, possible that their homes were a substitute for limited occupational mobility, but the Finns had other reasons for owning property. An article in *Toivo*, a handwritten Finnish newspaper in Toronto issued in 1902-4, noted that ten families owned their homes in 1904 and concluded: "This confirms, because all of our house owners belong to the working class, the skilful art of living among us." The principles of the "art of living" were hard work, thrift and temperance.[34] By 1910 the number of property owners had risen to seventy-four.[35]

Property ownership was also a sign of stability within a community, and during an age of limited welfare legislation, it was considered security. Because many of the Finnish immigrants had experienced the hardships suffered by displaced agrarian workers, home ownership meant that they need not fear eviction. In one decade, the number of home owners or lessees doubled proportionately, which indicates remarkable upward social mobility, as far as material success is concerned. The homes they owned or leased were usually quite small, however. A typical home on Widmer Street housed up to fifteen adults. Single lodgers shared the attic, while couples were given their own rooms on the second floor. The downstairs front room and dining room were often separated by a curtain, giving some privacy to two more families. Sometimes more communal arrangements were made; for example, a lodger might be given a couch or corner of a room and so lived as a member of the family. There were virtually no backyards.

Thus, living conditions were, in most cases, very crowded, but not dirty.[36] Many rooming houses were known to have strict rules about cleanliness and order. The occupants interviewed also praised the quality and the substance of the meals. Often these standards were achieved by the eighteen-hour work day of the maids, who, as a result, preferred to work for the less demanding *kieliset* (tongued — meaning English-speaking) families.

In a study of the geographic mobility of the people of Hamilton, Canada West, Michael Katz found the proportion of population persistence over a decade (1850-60) to be between 35 and 40 per cent.[37] This is comparable to Steven Thernstrom's findings for American cities such as Boston.[38] These results indicate an "astonishingly high" internal movement in North America.[39] The Finnish community showed similar signs of fluidity. Two samples for different time periods indicate that, of those Finns who had resided long enough to join an organization, over 30 per cent moved within a two-year period.

My first sample is based on the Finnish Society membership list from 5 October 1902, to 1 June 1905.[40] The total number of members was 154, and of these, thirty-six males (35.6 per cent) and seventeen females (32 per cent) moved. Only two married women had moved, while fourteen married women stayed, indicating that single people were the most mobile. Out of the total sample of thirty-seven single women, fifteen, or 40.5 per cent, had moved. From the second sample, based on the Presbyterian Church membership register, we can calculate that between January 1907 and June 1909, out of a total of fifty-five, 30.9 per cent moved.[41] The congregation was largely made up of single women, of whom a staggering 53.6 per cent, out of a sample of twenty-eight, had moved away.

Neither of these samples indicates organization strength, however, because many names have been deleted for such reasons as non-payment of dues. Since only those actually listed as having moved were considered, the real figure is likely even higher. We can conclude that the mobility rate was about 15 per cent yearly and that the persons most likely to move were single. Of the women who indicated their destination, all had chosen to move to other large cities such as New York, Detroit, Chicago and Cleveland. The wages for maids were higher in the United States and the border crossing was relatively trouble-free. Only twice was the purpose of the move listed as "returned to Finland."

If this general geographic mobility is compared to the founding members of the community, we see a distinct contrast. All of the married Finnish couples who had come to Toronto by December 1901 were still there in 1913.[42] Of the single men, Saarimäki had married a Finnish girl in 1902 and later became the first Finnish consul in Toronto.[43] In 1904 Julius Nyysänen had the distinction of being the first to marry "an English-speaking person"[44] but continued to take part in the Finnish community despite his "handicap."[45] Väinö Paananen is the only male among the founders who could not be traced in 1913; his sister Toini died in a train crash in 1903 on her way to London, Ontario.[46] Anna Rönkkä is the only female that cannot be found from my sources; since she was single in 1901, she probably married and would, therefore, be listed under a different surname. There were many other Rönkkäs in Toronto in 1913. Since this is an uncommon Finnish surname, it is possible they were her relatives. Thus, of the nineteen original settlers, sixteen were still in Toronto in 1913, one had died and two could not be located twelve years later. The foundation on which the Finnish community was built was very stable indeed.

In addition to the resident Finns, Toronto had many transients. Because of its good and numerous rooming houses and cheap restaurants, it had become a stopover, mostly for general workers on their way to northern Ontario. According to Tyyne Latva, who worked in Holm's Restaurant in 1913, and Martta Kujanpaa, who lived on Widmer Street in 1911, there was a continuous flow of human traffic. "As soon as you would catch a good-looking Finn fellow, he disappeared to the bush,"[47] lamented Martta. The fluidity of the population created some difficulties for organizations trying to develop a stable membership. For example, the sports organization, Yritys, was hampered by "this devilish system which exists in this country — that people must forever keep moving."[48]

With the population in such a state of flux, those who stayed for longer periods naturally gained importance. Thus, any of the founding members rose to positions of dominance and leadership. Their continued presence gave the community stability and permanence. The Finns, then, followed the patterns of North American fluidity studied by Thernstrom and Katz, and, in many instances, their geographic mobility surpassed that of their Canadian neighbours.

We noted earlier that the original Finnish settlement in Toronto differed from other Finnish-American communities because it had a high number of women. The close sex ratio continued throughout the period of this study.

Using the 1903 Finnish community census, we find that out of a total sample of 188 adults, 79, or 42 per cent, were women. The 1910 *Väestönlaskenta* indicated that the total population of Finns in Toronto was 766, of whom 229 were children, 274 were men and 263 or 49 per cent of the adult population were women. The same survey found 113 families; therefore, only 42 per cent of the adult Finns were married.[49] According to the 1911 Canadian census, out of a sample of 545 Finns (children included) 256, or 47 per cent, were women. Thus, the 1911 sex ratio was exactly the same as that of the first settlers in 1901.[50]

Examination of age structure reveals that in 1903 community members were mainly in their twenties. From the 1903 census, it is also possible to calculate the ages of the Finnish immigrants who arrived from 1887 to 1903, and to conclude that they were even younger, on the average, than the earlier immigrants to Toronto. When these figures are compared to Kero's quantitative study that indicates the average age of all emigrants from Finland to be 24.1 according to the passport lists, and 23.5 according to the passenger lists, it becomes evident that the Toronto Finns were younger than the average Finnish immigrants in North America.[51]

This could be due to the fact that, in 1903, most of the members of the community had lived in Toronto for such a short time that they lacked the economic stability to bring over aged relatives. In 1903 James Lindala's mother Maria, aged sixty-seven, was the oldest member of the community and its only senior citizen. Because the adult population was so young, most of the children were less than five years old. Just as there were almost no people over forty, there were very few teenagers. Unfortunately, no accurate sample exists from which calculation of the average age of Finnish immigrants in Toronto in 1913 can be made.

Kathleen Neils Conzen has argued in *Immigrant Milwaukee, 1836-1860: Accommodation and Community in a Frontier City*, that one ingredient for a successful immigrant community, such as that of the Germans in Milwaukee, is a large enough population to allow for diverse occupations, skills, culture and neighbourhoods.[52] If the Finnish community in Toronto is judged by this criterion, then it did not have the "building blocks" for a strong community. After all, by 1913, there were probably less than one thousand Finns.[53] Geographically, they were distributed in clusters around the city. The 1911 census reveals the following distribution in Toronto: south, 239; east, 177; west, 80; centre, 49.

A community, however, is based on much more than is revealed in studies of its quantitative factors. Such studies provide only the background and framework for understanding the other, more human functions of the community. The Finnish community of Toronto certainly had its difficulties, but, as is demonstrated in the following two sections, what it lacked in numbers and concentration, it made up for in community spirit.

If the immigrants were in fact "human cargo," muscle power for industrialized North America, they would not have had problems assimilating. But the people we are dealing with had deep-rooted emotional attachments to the land of their birth that could not easily be wiped away by "Canadianization." There is no magic formula of assimilation; no one can instantly adapt to a new society, and that is why the support of countrymen is so important.

The Finnish community of Toronto helped its members cope with the new surroundings, helped to soften the cultural shock and to develop their sense of belonging to the new society. It has been argued that immigrant communities retard the process of learning the law and language of the new society. This might well be true, but one must wonder how many immigrants would survive in Canada if left entirely on their own. The community was able to provide assistance and its newspapers kept them informed, not only about Finland, but about events in Canada. The Finnish Society made every attempt to give English instruction, provide citizenship information, and encourage participation in unions and political activities; it did not, however, try to deny the members their heritage and culture.

In Finnish Society meetings and in the newspaper *Toivo* the problem of torn loyalties was discussed. The following quote is a typical example of the general sentiment:

> It is doubtful that anyone would disagree, that we are, having moved to this country, living here, and leaving our descendants

here, responsible not only to respect the laws of this country, but also to help to improve them. In order to accomplish this we must have an understanding based on facts about the conditions of the country and its development. A Finnish proverb states: "Live in the country as the countrymen do or leave the country!" The Americans feel the same way when they declare: "In Rome do as the Romans do!" . . . I have noticed that the motto of young America is going to be: One language, one mind. When we remember how sweet that sounded in Finnish and even now echoes in our ears, we certainly can't scorn its nationalistic concept here in America.

The author's loyalties, however, were obviously divided. He continues: "We are not going to leave mother Finland, especially now when other countries generously help her. . . . Wretched is the man who does not love his mother, remember her, help her in her worries, troubles and needs, and guard her with tenderness.[54] The rate of return to Finland has been estimated to be only 15 per cent; thus, compared to southern Europeans, the Finns were, by and large, permanent settlers.[55] They regarded Canada as their new home and wanted to improve their living and working conditions here. Nonetheless, the immigrants could not help but be homesick. A touching poem written by a young Finnish immigrant, Juho Rietti, expresses the nostalgia and concern felt by many for their land of birth.

Kaunis synnyinmaani, kallis,	My dear beautiful land of birth
Tuonne jää nyt merten taa,	Is left behind the seas
Toivon etta Herra sallis,	God willing
Että sen vielä nähdä saan.	I'll see it once more.
Vieraat olot, vieras kieli,	Strange land, strange language,
Tunnu kotoisalta ei	Does not feel like home
Lemmetön on outo mieli,	Without love is my queer mind
Se, se rinnast rauhan vei.	The peace has gone from my heart.
Kaukana siell' äiti Suomen	Far away mother Finland
Kärsii sortoo, sorrontaa.	Suffers from opression
Milloin koittaa vielä huomen	When will the tomorrow come
Jolloin Suomi kukoistaa.	That Finland can blossom.
Vaikk' mä lennän lehden lailla'	Even when I fly like a leaf

Maissa vierais kuljeksin,	Wonder in strange lands
En tunteita mä oo vailla,	I am not without feelings
Ain' Suomen onnee	Always wishing happiness
toivoisin.	for Finland
Sanat muut jos vaihteleekin	Even if other words change
	their meaning
Loppu aina kuuluu näin	the end sounds always like
	this
Herra siunaa	God bless my land of birth
synnyinmaamme	
– Se on summa virrestäin.	– that is the sum of my
	hymn.[56]

The conflict of loyalties was also evident in the organized activity of the community, for example, the financial assistance given by the community and the Finnish Society to various causes:

1903	Starvation victims in Finland	
1904	Strikers' families in Voikka, Finland	$ 66.66
1905	Viapori uprising victims in Finland	
	"Tyomies" (Finnish-American newspaper)	21.75
1906	Social Democratic party of Finland	122.61
	In aid of the Russian revolution	
	Rockland, Mich. strikers trial fund	
1907	Cobalt Miners Union, local 146	22.00
1908	For unemployed Finns in Canada	
1910	Fedorenko Defence League (Winnipeg)	56.60
1912	Eaton's strike fund	25.55
	Lawrence, Mass. strike fund	20.80
	Socialist candidates election fund	38.60
	Agitation work	34.58[57]

These are random samples taken from the many collections made in the community. During 1903-5 Finland received most of the funds, but towards the end of the first decade, the community concentrated on aiding working-class struggles in North America. They also spent "thousands of dollars" to keep *Työkansa*, published in Port Arthur since 1907, afloat.[58] This left-wing newspaper finally succumbed to its financial difficulties in 1915.

In 1910, during a discussion about the allocation of funds, Emil Tigert, a tailor and executive member of the Finnish Socialist Organization of Canada, protested: "Therefore, it is comical for us to even think that we *Canadians* would go to Europe, even to Finland, to fight against capitalism at a time when the same enemy haunts us within Canadian boundaries. Of course we can find exceptional cases such as general strikes, work stoppages and other large confusions whether they be political or economic in nature.[59] In the tug-of-war between Finland and Canada, Canada seemed to emerge the winner.

The life of the Finnish immigrants in Toronto was not easy and occasionally a member of the community would face insurmountable difficulties. The Finnish organizations — both left and right — and private citizens joined forces to help. They took up collections to pay hospital bills and arranged and paid for funerals for those who could not. The very ill were sent home to Finland to "recuperate" and were often provided with clothing for the trip. For example, when Mr. K. Lindell started to speak to telephone poles, the community arranged for his return to Finland,[60] which cost them $64.30.[61]

There were few early deaths among the first generation of immigrants; the population was in its prime and their employment in Toronto was seldom hazardous. Therefore, there were very few orphans to take care of or elderly people in need. The mortality rate among children, however, was high. In 1940 *Toivo* stated: "This year six children were born to Finnish families and seven children have died, the oldest of whom was about six."[62]

"Mamma" (Lyyli) Anderson's home for maids took care that there were not many illegitimate children, either. While Mamma did not perform the abortions herself, she made the necessary arrangements with a "real doctor" and looked after the girls during their convalescence. This service was not only for single women, but also for all who wished to practise family planning. According to Tyyne Latva, "You didn't get a bad reputation if you visited Lyyli, the issue of abortion was quite openly discussed. No one that I knew of was ever hurt, except some who had gone to Cleveland to have it done."[63]

The Finns lacked professional people and thus had to rely on English-speaking doctors and funeral directors. However, the community provided interpreters. All used the same doctor (Elias Clouse) and funeral parlour (Thompson's).[64]

The community was especially helpful to the newly arrived; according to tradition, a "bunch of Finns would always meet the immigrant trains and find out if there were any Finns aboard who needed assistance."[65] The immigrants then walked to Widmer Street rooming houses and were given a hearty meal. If relatives or friends had room to spare, they would initially live with kin.

The most pressing problem was obtaining a job. Channels of communication between employers and immigrants were created by Finns who specialized in finding jobs and providing interpreters and transportation. The payment for these services was not fixed and was often totally voluntary. Others would try to place the new arrivals in their own places of employment.

Once an immigrant found work, he could then look for more permanent housing. The community was of immeasurable help, because the Finns gave reasonable rates to their countrymen. Sylvester Svensk, a tailor and the founder of Sarastus Temperance Society, owned one of the many Finnish rooming houses. Information in Mr. Svensk's notebook reveals that the average weekly "hyyry" (rent) ranged from fifty to seventy-five cents. Between 10 August 1903 and 14 April 1906, the Svensks had not less than forty-four different roomers, of whom only five were women. Some of their roomers stayed only a week, while others remained for several years.[66] The collection of rents indicates that newcomers were given the chance to get employment first and worry about rent later. Rooming houses such as the Svensks's played a vital role in allowing the immigrants to get a good start. The community also provided organized activity. Cultural and sports events and social occasions were arranged by the Finnish Society, Taimi, Sarastus, or the Mitchell Avenue Church.

The problem of shopping was eased by the presence of Finnish groceries, bakeries, travel services, saunas and restaurants. Even a Jewish grocer located in the heart of the community, on Widmer Street, had to learn Finnish in order to survive, and Mr. Jasney became familiar to all.[67]

The maids did most of their shopping at the T. Eaton Co., where the products were clearly displayed. The Finnish women were very particular about their dress and appeared as if "they were part of the labour aristocracy because they wore hats."[68] In a community dominated by tailors, much attention was given to dress. In photographs taken on social occasions, it is difficult to see that inside the fancy and stylish clothing were working-class immigrants, sometimes struggling to survive. When these photographs, often taken in studios against elaborate backdrops, were sent home to relatives, they served to perpetuate North America's image as the "land of gold." What was known in E.P. Thompson's England as one's "Sunday best" became, for the maids in Toronto, their "Wednesday best."

The community enforced a strict code of social behaviour: "The Finns did not dare to get in trouble with the law for fear of the embarrassment to the community that was sure to debase the image of the Finns."[69] The community was not always as judgemental as it might appear from this description, given by a court interpreter. For example, the Finnish Society rushed to the aid of a fifteen-year-old youth who had stolen a bicycle, providing assurance to authorities that a good home and guardianship would be provided for him.

The community functioned with the understanding that "the Finnish reputation should be held in high esteem." Therefore, when the first minister to reside in Toronto, Reverend Matti Hirvonen, suspected that there had been an attempt to poison him in a Finnish restaurant, he "kept the information between himself and God" so as not to give outsiders a bad impression of the Finns.[70] The most common conviction was for rowdy behaviour while drunk. Despite the two temperance societies, the *koiratorppas* (illegal liquor outlets) were a lucrative business. The temperance societies were forced to forgive their fallen members time after time in order to keep fighting what seemed to be a losing battle.

The Finnish immigrants in Toronto then were not lonely, helpless creatures, exploited at every turn, for they could rely on their community to help them in day-to-day life as well as in disaster, thereby making the accommodation process less painful and less traumatic.

According to Gabriel Kolko, the "Americanization" of the working-class immigrants produced "a working class that was to a great measure both *lumpen* and insecure, accommodating but not assimilating in America, uncertain of its ultimate destination in the case of most, cut off from the larger society and even, to an increasingly remarkable and painful degree, his own ethnic community and family." This insensitive characterization of the working-class demonstrates the need for more detailed study of immigrant communities. Was it in fact true "that the mass culture which most immigrants brought was simply a knowledge — often very minimal — of their language and the conventions of their rural societies." Kolko further assumes that they were uninterested in the new country and so did not bother to learn English because they intended to return to their homeland. For this same reason, the immigrants are seen, in general, as politically inactive: "Such marginal socialist ethnic groups as arose, above all among Jews, Germans or Finns, were scarcely efforts to escape their particularist culture but rather a transitional assertion of values temporarily useful in the diaspora and thereafter to become almost exclusively social and ethnic in function."[71]

Herbert G. Gutman, on the other hand, attempts to see beyond Kolko's "lumpen people in a lumpen society," and argues that because the emigrants' cultures were pre-industrial, their communities often became centres of radicalism.[72] If Gutman's argument is considered with Ryan Palmer's assertion — that the skilled "élite" of the working-class was the radical group — then we can more realistically begin to study the vibrant immigrant community of the Finnish Torontonians, rather than dismissing it as "lumpen."[73]

The political character of many of the Finnish communities in

North America before the First World War was socialist. According to George Hummasti, "theirs was an immigrant socialism, shaped both by their belief in socialist doctrine and by their position as strangers in an alien land."[74] The nature of their political beliefs and actions were shaped in Finland as well as in North America.

Many emigrants declared that they had left Finland for political reasons, that they were fleeing tsarist Russia. Of course, it may have been more romantic to believe that one was fleeing an oppressor rather than escaping economic hardships, but the notion is so persistent that it cannot be discounted. For example, we can examine Vilho Säilä's account of his reasons for emigration: "In the beginning of this century a considerable number of Finns began to come to Canada. The reason was the Russian tsar's oppressive policies towards Finland. Because of this, many who had the opportunity traveled to America's "land of gold" in the hope of obtaining a better and freer opportunity to live."[75] Furthermore, a 1905 article in the *Mail and Empire*, entitled "Why Finlanders come to Canada," indicates that the Finns were political refugees. The article is also interesting because it shows how Toronto society perceived them:

> By the thousands Finns are fleeing from their country as from the land accursed. A despatch on Saturday announced that a great immigration to Canada will take place in the spring. In the past thousands of Finns have found homes here. They have become good citizens, and Canada is glad enough to be the refuge for those who are to follow. The Finn makes an admirable settler, and is as freely assimilated by the English-speaking community as a German or a Frenchman. He is industrious, sober and peaceable invariably, and is mentally more active than the average Swede or Norwegian. He is not a fighting man, the Finn. If he were, he would be in Helsingfors with his back to the wall, or plotting with the nihilists in London. Yet he has a passion for freedom equal to that of the Englishman, Irishman, Scotchman or American. To tyranny and injustice he opposes passive resistance. This has failed with the Russian, whose stolidity equals that of the Finn, and who is supported by ferocity unknown to the other. So it comes that the Finns are deserting their country wholesale, seeking in Canada and the United States those common places of justice and equality unknown in their own country . . . . This much is sure — if a Finn wishes to live with comfort in his native land he must bow his neck to the Russian yoke. His alternative is emigration. Those thousands who will pour into Canada next spring have chosen exile rather than submission.[76]

The Finns were so delighted with this account that they sent a thank-you letter complimenting the editor for his accurate research. In addition to being flattering, the article did mention the political nature of the "exiles," bringing with them their socialist beliefs.[77]

The overwhelming majority, however, came from the rural area of Ostrobothnia, the least socialist province of Finland. Many of them had never heard of socialism or, if they had, they considered it anti-religious. All immigrants had to be confirmed as Lutherans in order to obtain an exit visa. The Finnish Lutherans were conservative, and many belonged to even stricter sects, such as the "Laestadians," a common sect in Ostrobothnia.

But in Toronto there was no state-run church to influence political thinking. William Hoglund has written a revealing article in which he notes the resistance immigrants showed towards the state-run Lutheran Church in the old country, with its compulsory taxation and authoritative leadership.[78] The Toronto Finns "resisted" until 1931, when the first Lutheran congregation opened its doors.[79]

There were, of course, religious Finns in Toronto; however, their numbers and organizations were too small to make a significant impact on the community before the First World War, especially because the new community lacked a traditional, conservative base. A survey taken in 1910 showed the following breakdown of political views among the adult population: Socialists, 57 per cent; Christians, 13 per cent; uncommitted, 29 per cent; other, 1 per cent.[80] The "Socialists," therefore, outnumbered the "Christians" more than four to one. This can be partially explained by the many "conversions" to socialism. Iso-Paja was especially successful at spreading socialist doctrine. Mr. Ranta, whose wife "was the pillar of the first Finnish Presbyterian congregation in Toronto,"[81] and who belonged to one of the founding families, explains his conversion in the following manner: "I was listening to this preacher, and it dawned on me that he was really on the other side, he was backing all those capitalists that you fellows were always ranting about. Here I was [Halifax], in this strange city, far away from home [Toronto], because the bosses wouldn't settle in Toronto. 'Perkele,' I said to myself, 'I'm in the wrong camp.' "[82] The Finnish Presbyterian Church records contain notations such as "turned to socialism."[83]

Political thought was not only imported from Finland, but also influenced by conditions in Canada. The immigrant, dependent on his ethnic community, was easily influenced by it. Its members were the "elite" artisans, the tailors, who ran the Finnish organizations and encouraged support for the Socialist party.

Their position as aliens, suffering from language difficulties, often made their work situation more difficult than that of native Canadians. With able socialist leadership, the Finns ultimately increased and clarified their class consciousness.

Their "associative" spirit, so evident in the many communities established in North America, had its first expression in Toronto on 5 October 1902, when the Finnish Society was formally founded. The idea was born in Iso-Paja, and it is no wonder that of the forty-seven founding members, thirty-eight were tailors and their wives. Most of the original settlers were present; James and Irene Lindala, as well as Henry Heinonen and Toini Paananen, became part of the first executive and played an important role in shaping the character of the society.

The society was based on "free thought." Ideally, it was created for all Finns, whether they supported socialism or churches or neither, or whether they spoke Finnish or Swedish. The intent of the society is clearly explained in its declaration of incorporation.[84]

Article I

The object of the Finnish Society of Toronto (herein referred to as the Society) is to form a bond of union between Finlanders of Toronto and the vicinity, so as to unite them into cooperation, to develop their intellectual powers and to assure their material advantage as much as possible.

Article II

The most important functions of the Society shall be:
a) to maintain a library and a reading room to the extent that means may be found for its purpose:
b) to introduce intellectually elevating amusement for Finlanders and also to procure courses of instruction and discussion on the diverse spheres of human existence;
c) to increase the means for the purchase and maintenance of buildings and grounds for the use of the Society.

It is clear from the articles that the intent of the society was more far-reaching and intellectually oriented than one might expect from such a "lumpen society." What is more, the society did fulfil its intended function. It promptly set up a library and stocked it mainly with scientific books, socialist literature, immigrant newspapers, Finnish novels and dictionaries. In addition, the society arranged debating and discussion groups to teach Finns public speaking and to develop their confidence. Among the topics of debate were such issues as: are women equal to men; what is tolerance; Hellenic civilization; unnecessary spending on luxury goods; the merits of socialism.[85] The society also arranged meetings before elections, explaining the issues and candidates involved, arranged citizenship information and provided application forms.

The most staggering obstacle to successful assimilation into Canadian society was learning English. The Finnish Society was able to negotiate with the board of education for a free English teacher and a class room at the John Street Public School twice a

week. The classes commenced on 4 October 1904. The first teacher
was a Mr. Bell, assisted by V.S. Holmsten, a tailor. All together,
seventy-one pupils started the first course, a remarkably high
percentage of an adult population that numbered approximately three
hundred and fifty. Of the students, only twenty-two were female.
Since most of the working women were maids whose only day off
was Wednesday, they were unable to attend the classes, which we
held on Tuesdays and Thursdays. A small compensation for the
maids was the regular "piika tanssit" (servant dances) held every
Wednesday by the Finnish Society in honour of the maids' free
day.[86]

Only thirty-three successfully completed the course; eleven
moved away, sixteen withdrew, and twenty-seven had missed too
many classes. Long working hours and a general lack of education
made study difficult. Although the Finns' high literacy rate is praised in many studies, their knowledge of grammar was limited. The
teacher lamented "We must take note that scarcely three per cent [of
the students] knew anything of even Finnish language structure and,
therefore, it had to be taught in order to make the teaching easier to
comprehend, alongside with English grammar.[87]

If to historians, immigrants appear unwilling to learn the
language of the new country, it is often because they found it difficult. As the case of the Finns in Toronto demonstrates, they were
eager to learn and knew the benefits of knowing English. Other difficulties with which the immigrants had to contend, while learning
the new language, should not be underestimated. Inability to speak
English slowed their social mobility and increased their dependence
on the Finnish community.

In 1907 the Finnish Society realized its dream of owning its own
premises. They purchased a property at 214 Adelaide Street West
for $5,000. The building was renovated by a cooperative effort. The
carpenters built a stage, the tailors made the curtains, each member
bought a chair, and the women collected money by sewing and by
holding bake sales. With their own building, cultural and social
clubs could put forth more ambitious schemes.[88]

The Finns had their own bands, "Visertäjät" and "Kanteleet,"
which provided entertainment at dances and picnics, and gave concerts with the choir. The theatrical group performed a new play
every second week. The quality of the plays, of course, suffered
because the people involved were amateurs; however, the group attempted to produce a variety of serious, as well as entertaining
works, many of which were written by the immigrants themselves.

In 1906 the Finnish Society started "Yritys," a sports club.
From its modest beginnings, in a sand lot at the rear of 246 Richmond Street, the club developed into a nationwide amateur sports
federation and participated in many national events. Perhaps the

most famous Yritys athlete was E. Löppönen, a bakery owner and the national heavyweight champion in wrestling from 1908 to 1912, and a member of the Canadian Olympic team competing in Antwerp. Yritys held regular sports meets and practice sessions for gymnasts, wrestlers, boxers and track and field athletes, male and female.[89]

The society's social activities included picnics at High Park, a yearly excursion across Lake Ontario to Niagara, and dances.[90]

Ideologically, the society did try to maintain its ideal of "free thought." Meetings might begin one week with H. Heinonen speaking on the "miracles of Jesus Christ," and the next, with James Lindala lecturing on "Tolerance and Unity." After 2 August 1903 an increasing number of the lectures were delivered by Frans Syrjälä. On the day Syrjälä arrived in Toronto, he was at the debating meeting,[91] delivering a lengthy speech "On the conditions in Finland." Syrjälä, a participant at the founding meeting of the Social Democratic Party of Finland, had left the country because of political harassment.[92] His favourite topics centred on socialism, about which he wrote numerous articles for *Toivo*, and he gave hundreds of speeches on socialist thought and radicalism in the Finnish community. To men such as Frans Syrjälä, the society was not radical enough, because it attempted, at least on the surface, to appear non-political. On the 24 April 1904, a group of socialist Finnish tailors founded a temperance society, Taimi (Seedling), which was based on "working class ideals and abstinence from alcohol."[93] Although the Finnish Society prohibited the use of alcohol on its premises, it did not demand absolute temperance. A united Finnish community seemed an elusive goal.

The society and its membership continued to lean towards the left and on 25 November 1903 it openly declared its support for the newspapers founded on the principles of the Social Democratic Party, which were, it stated, the foundation of the society's social and political thought.[94]

The absurdity of two separate organizations, so similar in nature, became evident when both the Finnish Society and Taimi began to collect funds for the purchase of their own hall. Economically, this would have been disastrous, and so a compromise was reached in April 1905: the two societies agreed to unite under the name Toronton Suomalaisten Yhdistysten Liitto (League of Finnish Societies of Toronto). This was done with the understanding that the league would select a group of fifteen people who would join the Socialist party in order to learn about the alternatives it offered. The ultimate goal, however, was to affiliate with the Socialist party. When the two societies were formally united on 1 June 1905, the name was again changed, to Toronton Suomalaisten Socialisti Liitto (League of Finnish Socialists in Toronto); however, they continued to use its English name, the Finnish Society. On 18 November 1905 the Finnish Society took one further step and joined the Socialist party as one of its foreign-language groups.[95]

About the time that the society abandoned its position of neutrality, a group of conservatives decided to start their own organization because the largely socialist membership had made their situation difficult. Those who were religious, such as Saarimäki and Heinonen, had been dropped from the executive and left with very few decision-making powers. On 11 May 1905 August Svensk founded the Sarastus temperance society and purchased a house at 44 Mitchell Avenue for their meetings.[96] This temperance society soon became the centre of religious activity; temperance activity decreased and was replaced by the sermons and the church. In 1906 religious Finns purchased the building and started the first Finnish congregation in Toronto. Initially, they were Congregationalist, but soon became part of the Presbyterian Church, and, with the unification of the Presbyterian and Methodist churches, became part of the Church of All Nations of the United Church of Canada. They also rented their premises to a small group of Laestadians.

By June 1909 the Finnish Presbyterian Church of Canada had only twenty-nine members and Sarastus had stopped all its activity. At the same time, the Finnish Society had more than one hundred and fifty paying, adult members.[97] These figures, along with the society's own survey taken in 1910, confirm that the vast majority of Finnish Torontonians identified with the Finnish Society and the Socialist party, even after the church Finns had provided an alternative. After 1905 the Finns made a conscious choice "to join the working class."[98] They were not an apathetic group who ignored their present condition because of rosier dreams of a future in Finland and allowed politicians to take advantage of their ignorance. Instead , they sent representatives to Socialist Party of Canada (SPC) meetings, provided interpreters, and put forth Board of Education candidates, such as Emil Tigert and Frans Syrjälä. They also supported James Lindala in 1907 in his bid for the mayoralty of Toronto.

The artisan elite successfully encouraged other socialist-oriented Finnish communities to organize locals within the SPC. When the Toronto Finns were kicked out of the SPC because of their "revisionist" attitudes, other Finnish locals also left, and all joined the Social Democratic Party (SDP). By 1914 the Finns made up 55 per cent of the SDP membership and had sixty-four locals across Canada with 3,047 registered members.[99]

They became avid union supporters and participated actively in labour struggles. When the journeymen tailors' union went on strike in 1912, its Toronto local had 104 Finns, fourteen of whom were women. Finns realized that in order to improve their living and working conditions they must actively partake in Canadian politics. As J.W. Ahlqvist, a Toronto tailor and a long-time Finnish Society spokesman expressed it, ''as socialists we must be members, and advance *this* country's economic and political revolutionary movement.''[100]

The community of Finnish tailors that mushroomed in Toronto after the turn of this century was strongly influenced by its original members. The nucleus of the community grew up around the residences of the first settlers. The Finns were primarily artisans and nearly half of the men were still tailors by 1913. Because of the limited number of studies of urban Finns in North America, it is difficult to conclude whether this situation was unique. We can only speculate on what would have happened if the first Finn to immigrate to Toronto had been, for example, a shoemaker and lived on Parliament Street. Throughout the period studied, the founding members continued to exert their influence and guide the community by holding executive positions in Finnish organizations; James Lindala's Iso-Paja had a profound influence on the development of Finnish-Canadian socialism. The character and stability of the founding members gave the community a sense of permanence and leadership.

Compared to other Finnish communities in North America and to Finnish emigrants in general, the urban experience of Toronto Finns differed most strikingly in occupational structure and sex composition. The relatively well-paid artisans created for the community a prosperous image perpetuated by their immaculate dress, the high percentage of home ownership and their generous donations of money to various causes.

The high percentage of women in the community allowed for more normal family situations. Married couples were less geographically mobile and provided the community with a solid core, while single persons, especially the women, moved from city to city.

Structurally, the community was not self-sufficient. Its demographic patterns reflect the newness of the society and its immigrant character. The Finns were all drawn from the working class and had to go outside the community for professional services. Geographically, the Finns dispersed; by 1913 less than half of them still lived within the ''rectangle.'' The dispersal of residences, however, signifies only a physical break-up within the community. Psychologically and emotionally, the Finns continued to support the community's organized activities, providing mutual aid, entertainment and intellectual fulfilment. The bond that held together the community was the immigrants' memory of their homeland, its culture and language.

The community was of invaluable help to the newly arrived immigrant, assisting him with immediate needs such as employment and housing, as well as learning the language and customs of his new country. Socially, the community provided its members with a sense of familiarity and belonging in an otherwise strange land with alien customs, it provided a buffer against harsh realities and gave support to the immigrant for as long as he needed it.

The Finnish community of Toronto paid particular attention to making the immigrant's life more meaningful by encouraging intellectual activities and political participation. A prime example of the Finns' desire to be part of the decision-making process in Canada was James Lindala's mayoralty candidacy. It could be said that the large vote polled by Lindala — 8,286 as opposed to Mayor Coatsworth's 13,698 — was a victory for immigrant advancement. It was not. Six thousand voters were protesting against the sluggish performance of Mayor Coatsworth. The *Globe*, after recovering from its initial shock, explained away Lindala's votes: "It is quite evident that some six thousand electors cast their votes for the socialists as a protest against the policy carried out by Mayor Coatsworth during the past year."[101] The *Western Clarion*, a socialist paper, did not revel in the victory either, but quite soberly wrote:

> The election of 1907 developed a surprise. For the first time the Socialist Party nominated a candidate for mayor, comrade Lindala, an unknown Finlander, who possessed considerable property. A manifesto full of revolutionary fire was issued, it drawing sharp attacks from the capitalist press for its dangerous doctrines. . . . Comrade Lindala received a monster vote of 8,200, fully 6,000 non-socialists voting for a socialist as a protest against the weak capitalist mayor.[102]

A disastrous blow to the enthusiasm of aspiring Finnish-Canadian politicians was dealt by their "friends" within the Socialist party. The party refused to support their nominations in 1908, dropping Lindala and Sundsten from the ticket. The *Western-Clarion* editorialized:

> One regrettable feature, however, is the fact that two Finnish comrades were "cut" by hundreds of sympathizers who evidently are too capitalist-minded and jingoistic to overcome the prejudice against a "foreigner." But all the lessons for this non-class conscious vote were not to be found outside the party itself. Comrade Lindala's big vote a year ago encouraged hundreds to say: If Simpson had been the candidate he would have

won — Simpson being a popular Methodist, Orangeman, Unionist, Son of England, and Lindala an unknown foreigner.[103]

Although such an attitude might make political sense, it also demonstrates the prevailing suspicion and prejudice towards foreigners. Even though the Finns "were admirable settlers" and "most welcome to Canada,"[104] they were judged by their place of birth rather than their ability. Precisely for these reasons an immigrant community is so important to its members. Within it, at least, exists a clear hierarchy, a set of social rules and functions understood by its members, an intricate and highly developed set of organizations and cultural activities that enable the immigrant to maintain his old culture while trying to learn the new. To an outsider all this might seem very meaningless and "lumpen," but to those who understood and benefited from the community, it was a valuable stepping-stone in the process of assimilation. The immigrant's problem of trying to assimilate to the new country seems to be as difficult as having the new country accept the "foreigner." Ultimately, the first-generation immigrants remained "foreigners" forever, for their place of birth was beyond their control.

Notes

This article is a revised version of *The Finnish Immigrant Community of Toronto 1887-1913* originally published as Occasional Paper number 8, 1979 and reprinted in May 1981, by the Multicultural History Society of Ontario.

1. The *Globe*, 2 January 1907.

2. Information on James Lindala and his family has been gathered through interviews in 1978, 1979 and 1982 with his two surviving daughters Saimi Hormavirta and Aili Piton. The interviews and Lindala family archives, including photographs, are deposited in the Multicultural History Society of Ontario (hereafter cited as MHSO) Archives. All interviews, used in this article are in the possession of the author or deposited at the MHSO. The latter is indicated separately.

3. For information on Finnish emigration see Reino Kero, "Emigration from Finland to Canada before the First World War," in *The Finnish Experience*, special issue of the Lakehead University Review 9, no. 1 (Spring 1976); also his *Migration Studies C1* (Turku, Finland: Institute for Migration, 1974); and Keijo Virtanen, *Settlement or Return: Finnish Emigrants (1860-1930) in the International Overseas Return Migration Movement, Migration Studies C6* (Turku, Finland: Institute for Migration, 1979).

4. Matti E. Kaups, "The Finns in the Copper and Iron Ore Mines of the Western Great Lakes Region, 1864-1905: Some Preliminary Observations," *Migration Studies C3* (Turku, Finland: Institute for Migration, 1975); see also A. William Hoglund, *Finnish Immigrants in America 1880-1920* (Madison: University of Wisconsin Press, 1960).

5. The addresses for this section of the paper are from Might Directory Ltd., *Toronto City Directory* (hereafter cited as *Might's Directory*) (Toronto, 1890).

6. From the 1903 census *Väestönlaskenta*, gathered by the Finns in Toronto. It is part of the Finnish Organization of Canada Collection (hereafter FOC) in Public Archives of Canada.

7. For information on the Heinonen family, see: 1903 census; Finnish United Church of Canada Records (MHSO); interviews with Saimi Hormavirta and Aili Piton (MHSO).

8. For information on the Ranta family, see: Saimi Hormavirta and Aili Piton collections held at the MHSO archives; Finnish United Church of Canada membership register; Alina and John Flink, "Muistelmia," in *Canadan Viesti* (Canadian Messenger), February 1956; Akseli Rauanheimo, *Kanadan Kirja*, (Porvoo: Finland, 1930) p. 218; 1903 census of the Finnish community.

9. For information on the Nyros family, see: 1903 census of the Finnish community; interview with Julius Nyros' granddaughter, Alma Ruth Toija, (MHSO). According to the census, the Nyroses arrived in Toronto 14 October 1899, but Alma Toija was quite certain that they did not arrive until "late in 1900, when her mother Ruth Nyros was six months old. She was born in Brooklyn on 14 June 1900."

10. 1903 census of the Finnish community.

11. For information on Aati Saarimäki, see: interview with his surviving son, Paul Saarimäki, 1978; Finnish United Church of Canada records; Akseli Rauanheimo, *Kanadan Kirja* (Porvoo: Finland, 1930), p. 218; 1903 census of the Finnish community.

12. For information on Väinö and Toini Paananen, see: interview with Väinö Paananen's nephew Arvo Paananen, 1903 census of the Finnish community; interview with Saimi Hormavirta (MHSO).

13. 1903 census of the Finnish community; interview with Saimi Hormavirta, Tyyne Latva and Martta Kujanpää (MHSO).

14. Kaups, "Finns in the Copper and Iron Ore Mines," p. 63.

15. *Might's Directory*, 1901.

16. 1903 Census of Toronto Finns.

17. V.S. Holmsten estimated in October 1904 that "the number of Finns in Toronto was more than 400." See: "Kielikurssi 1904-1905," FOC collection PAC.

18. *Airue* (Port Arthur: Työkansa, 1910), pp. 74-75.

19. Minute books of the Finnish Society (hereafter cited as FS), 4 October 1903, FOC collection.

20. V.S. Holmsten and F. Syrjälä were both members of the Socialist Party of Canada (SPC).

21. Finns who later became members of the "Mitchell Avenue Church" were listed in the census.

22. *Airue*, pp. 74-75.

23. Information on Iso-Paja is derived from interviews with Saimi Hormavirta and Aili Piton (MHSO), and employees of Iso-Paja: Vilho Säilä, Nicholas Flink (MHSO), John Lievonen.

24. According to Aili Piton and Saimi Hormavirta, in 1912 James Lindala sold his York Street property for $35,000 and took his wife and three children for a three-month tour of the old country, precisely twenty-five years after James Lindala had left Vaasa, penniless.

25. *Toivo*, no. 2, January 18, 1903, p. 28, edited by Paulina and Matti Penger. *Toivo* is available at PAC for the years 1903-4, and is part of the FOC collection.

26. Interview with Tyyne Latva, whose husband worked at McGregor and McIntyre Co.

27. Although *Might's Directory* did not list any Finnish women as working in the Parisian Laundry, all the women interviewed testified to its importance as an employer of Finnish women. For example, see: Alina Flink interview MHSO.

28. Interviews with Tyyne Latva, Sulo and Aino Aijö, Martta Kujanpää, and Alma Ruth Toija (MHSO).

29. Annual minutes of Yritys, 1906, FOC collection. To avoid confusion, the following is a breakdown of occupations:

1903

Tailors	47	Turners	1
Labourers	26	Wood-turners	1
Moulders	15	Coppersmiths	1
Carpenters	7	Shoemakers	1
Machinists	5	Tanners	1
Iron-plate workers	2	Bicycle repairmen	1
		Unemployed	1

1910 Men

Tailors	83	Shoemakers	2
Moulders	36	Painters	2
Labourers	36	Furriers	2
Carpenters	20	Tanners	2
Iron-workers	20	Machinists	2
Metal-workers	6	Mechanics	2
Filers	4	Smiths	1
Bakers	3	Stone-cutters	1
Coppersmiths	3	Bookbinders	1
		Turners	1

1910 Women

Maids	78
Seamstresses	22
Laundresses	11
Tailors	8

1913

Tailors	56	Erectors	2
Labourers	14	Foremen	2
Moulders	9	Engineers	1
Helpers	8	Builders	1
Carpenters	6	Shoemakers	1
Coppersmiths	4	Chippers	1
Painters	3	Machinists	1
Piano-makers	3	Press FDR	1
Bakers	2	Messengers	1
Cabinet-makers	2	Apprentices	1

30. The 1903 map indicating Finnish residential areas in Toronto is compiled from information available in *Might's Directory* of 1903 and 1904. If the address given differed from 1903 to 1904, the 1903 address was used. The city directories have been complemented with information derived from various collection lists, which give some addresses, as well as some membership registers of the Finnish Society. FS archives, FOC collection.

31. The 1913 map is compiled from *Might's Directory* of 1913 as well as from the FOC membership and collection lists. The 1903 map of Toronto is provided courtesy of the Metropolitan Toronto Library. The maps for 1903 and 1913 do not indicate the number of Finns living on each street, but merely the areas where they lived.

32. Stephen Thernstrom, *Poverty and Progress: Social Mobility in a Nineteenth-Century City* (New York: Atheneum Press, 1975). The topic is discussed in chapter 5.

33. *Might's Directory* for 1903-4 and 1913-14.

34. *Toivo*, no. 7, 1904, p. 158.

35. Airue, p. 75.

36. Historians often depict the living conditions of the immigrant community as squalid. See, for instance, Gregory S. Kesley, *Hogtown: Working-Class Toronto at the Turn of the Century* (Toronto: New Hogtown Press, 1974).

37. Michael B. Katz, *The People of Hamilton, Canada West* (Cambridge: Harvard University Press, 1975).

38. Stephen Thernstrom, *The Other Bostonians* (Cambridge: Harvard University Press, 1976).

39. Katz, *Hamilton*, p. 119.

40. The time period is the first thirty-two months of the society's existence.

41. The Presbyterian Church membership register (the Mitchell Avenue Church) is available from the MHSO. The time period studied is the first twenty-nine months in the registry.

42. They were all listed in *Might's Directory* for 1913.

43. Interview with Paul Saarimäki.

44. This notation was found in the margin of the Finnish Society membership list.

45. This term was used by Saimi Hormavirta.

46. Interview with Aili Piton (MHSO).

47. Interview with Martta Kujanpää (MHSO).

48. Yritys annual report, 1906-7, FOC collection.

49. *Airue*, p. 75.

50. The 1901 figures are calculated from *Väestönlaskenta*, 1903; 1911 figures are from the Canada census.

51. Kero, *Migration Studies C1*, p. 92.

52. Kathleen Neils Conzen, *Immigrant Milwaukee, 1836-1860: Accommodation and Community in a Frontier City* (Cambridge: Harvard University Press, 1976); see especially chapter 2, ''Building Blocks of Community.''

53. This is an estimate based on the average yearly growth of at least 100. In 1910 the total number of Finns, according to their own calculations, was 766.

54. *Toivo*, no. 4, 1 March 1903, pp. 63-65.

55. Keijo Virtanen, ''Problems of Research in Finnish Re-emigration,'' *Migration Studies C3* (Turku, Finland: Institute for Migration Studies, 1975).

56. *Toivo*, no. 5, 1903. The surname of this amateur poet is unclear in the hand-written paper. It could read Riettinen, Riettimaa or Rietti.

57. These samples are collected from various files and minute books of FS archives, FOC collection.

58. In an interview, Vilho Säilä told how the tailors of Iso-Paja alone secured a thousand dollars in one day, to keep the doors of Työkansa open. For the history of *Työkansa* see: Arja Pilli, *The Finnish Language Press in Canada, 1901-1939, Migration Studies C6* (Turku, Finland: Institute for Migration, 1982).

59. Letter from Emil Tigert to the executive of the Finnish Socialist Organization of Canada (FSOC), 1910, FOC collection.

60. Interview with Saimi Hormavirta (MHSO).

61. Minutes of FS, FOC collection.

62. *Toivo*, no. 1, 9 January 1940, edited by Bertta Heikkinen. See "Finnish-Torontonians during the year 1903," p. 92.

63. Interview with Tyyne Latva (MHSO).

64. The illness and death of Mandi Grondahl is a good example. The society paid for her doctors' bills, funeral costs, sent flowers and paid for the cost of sending the casket home. This young Finnish maid had been in Toronto for two days when she became ill with "flying tuberculosis."

65. Interview with Aili Piton (MHSO).

66. August Svensk's note and account book for his rooming house at 25 Nelson Street, Toronto, 1903-6, August Svensk collection, MHSO.

67. Interview with Martta Kujanpää (MHSO).

68. Based on Allen Seager's studies of Blairmore, Alberta. See also Edna Ferber's short story, "Every Other Thursday," about the life of a Finnish maid in New York City.

69. Interviews with Aili Piton and Saimi Hormavirta (MHSO), both of whom acted as court interpreters in the absence of their father James Lindala or their brother George.

70. Letter from Reverend Matti Hirvonen, March 24, 1947, Finnish Canadian Historical Society Collection (FCHS), MHSO.

71. Gabriel Kolko, *Main Currents in Modern American History* (New York: Harper and Row, 1976), pp. 95-99.

72. Herbert G. Gutman, *Work, Culture and Society in Industrializing* America (New York: Vintage Books, 1976).

73. Bryan Palmer, "Most Uncommon Common Men: Craft and Culture in Historical Perspective," *Labour/Le Travailleur* I (1976).

74. Paul George Hummasti, "Finnish Radicals in Astoria, Oregon, 1904-1940; a Study in Immigrant Socialism," (Ph.D., University of Oregon, 1975).

75. Vilho Säilä, "Canadan Suomalainen Järjestö Kunnialla 60-vuotiaaksi," *Vapaus*, 28 September 1971, sec. 2, p. 6. This edition marked the sixtieth anniversary of the Finnish Organization of Canada.

76. The newspaper clipping can be found in the FOC collection. It is most likely from the *Mail and Empire*, summer 1904.

77. Minute books of the Finnish Society, 4 September 1904, FOC collection.

78. William Hoglund, *For the Common Good* (Superior, Wisconsin: Työmies Society), pp. 23-64.

79. Yrjö Raivio, *Kanadan Syomalaisten Historia* (Vancouver, 1975). This was not the

first Finnish congregation but the first Lutheran Finnish congregation in Toronto.

80. *Airue*, p. 75.

81. Interviews with Aili Piton and Saimi Hormavirta (MHSO). See also Alina and John Flink, "Muistelmia."

82. Satu Repo, "The Big Shop: Finnish Immigrant Tailors in Toronto," *This Magazine* 9, no. 5, 6 (November-December 1975), p. 31.

83. The Finnish Presbyterian Church records appear under the Finnish United Church of Toronto records, available at MHSO.

84. Minute books of the Finnish Society of Toronto, 14 September 1902, FOC collection.

85. Minute books of the Debating Club of the Finnish Society of Toronto, 17 April 1904, FOC collection.

86. Finnish Society of Toronto language course, 1904-05, FOC collection, PAC. This file contains a year end report by the teacher and a detailed account of the progress of his pupils. The estimate of 350 was made by V.S. Holmsten, the Finnish grammar teacher, in his report on the language course.

87. Ibid. V.S. Holmsten sent the following letter to the Board of Education. (The spelling, grammar and punctuation are the same as in the original).

Toronto, Ontario 3/x-04

To the Board of Education,

The Society of "Finlanders" of Toronto do wish to know, if you can advise us. We wish to be educated in the English language. By these reasons we have resolved in our Society to ask you 1) John st. School room at night. we say about two nights a week, and 2) an English teacher to teach us in the reading of English languege one night a week.

We will get a finlander teacher, who will teach us the English grammar.

Here is about 350 finlander now and that number will increas every day.

Senserling hoping you will look into this matter at once and waiting an early answer I remain yours respectfully.

V.S. Holmsten
Correspondent sect., of the
Society of Finlanders
290 Adelaide St.

88. Frans Syrjälä, "The History of the Finnish Society's Hall," 20 October 1907, FOC collection.

89. *Canadan Suomalaisten Urheilukirja*, a fortieth anniversary publication (Sudbury: Vapaus Publishing Co., 1965).

90. The Finnish Society Archives contains an invoice for tickets for one hundred adults and four children from Niagara Navigation Co. Ltd., dated 9 July 1910. This indicates that the excursions were popular and well attended.

91. Minute books of the Finnish Society, 1903-4, FOC collection.

92. Elis Sulkanen, *Amerikan Suomalaisten, Työväenliikkeen Historia* (Fitchburg, Mass., 1951), pp. 500-1.

93. Minute books of Taimi, Finnish Society archives, 24 April 1904, FOC collection.

94. Annual report of the Finnish Society, 1904, FOC collection.

95. Agreement between the Finnish Society and Taimi Temperance Society, signed 23 April 1905, FOC collection. See also J.W. Ahlqvist, Järjestömme Toiminta Vuoteen 1920," in *Canadan Suomalainen Järjestö, 1911-1936* (Sudbury: Vapaus Publishing, 1936).

96. *Canadan Viesti* 26, no. 2. See also letter by Reverend Matti Hirvonen, March 24, 1947, FCHS collection, MHSO.

97. The annual report of the Finnish Society for 1908 listed 156 members.

98. Interview with Nicholas Flink (MHSO).

99. SDP report of the six months ending 31 December 1914, vol. 91, File 55, p. 5, FOC collection. The report contains a semi-annual report of the Finnish Socialist Organization's SDP membership: on books, 3,047; good standing, 2,044; locals, 64, total contributions, $3,867.92.

100. J.W. Ahlqvist, "Iso-Paja," in *Canadan Suomalainen Järjestö, 1911-1936* (Sudbury: Vapaus Publishing, 1936).

101. *Globe*, 2 January 1907.

102. *Western Clarion*, 8 February 1908.

103. Ibid.

104. *Mail and Empire*, "Why Finlanders Come to Canada," a newspaper clipping in the FS archives, FOC collection.

For additional information on the Finnish community of Toronto see: Varpu Lindstrom-Best, "The Unbreachable Gulf: The Division in the Finnish Community of Toronto, 1902-1913" in Michael G. Karni, ed. *Finnish Diaspora I* (MHSO, 1981); and her article "The Socialist Party of Canada and the Finnish Connection, 1905-1911" in Jorgen Dahlie and Tissa Fernando eds., *Ethnicity Power and Politics in Canada* (Toronto: Methuen, 1981).

Preface

The most distinguished and renowned Polish immigrant, and at the same time one of the most outstanding residents of Toronto, was Kazimierz Stanisław Gzowski. A Polish political exile, he arrived in Canada from the United States in 1842. He was later knighted and has entered our historical annals as Sir Casimir Gzowski. He was an immigrant of noble birth, a highly talented and successful businessman, a civil engineer and builder of roads and bridges. Gzowski belonged to the social elite of Toronto and submerged himself totally in Anglo-Saxon Protestant society. The only symbol of his ethnic origin was his surname, since he even converted to the Protestant faith when he married.

Before his arrival in Toronto in 1845, Gzowski had lived in London, Ontario. Later on, as his company Toronto Rolling Mills (established 1859) was flourishing in the city, local directories also recorded — beginning in 1865 — other inhabitants with Polish surnames.

Andrzej and Maciej (Andrew and Matthew) Hubaszek were also businessmen. Unfortunately, we do not know their fates, nor the whereabouts of any of their offspring. Their company was established as the Toronto Vinegar Works in April 1865. The Hubaszeks were partners with A. Rondenstrauch. The company produced forty barrels of vinegar per week.

A rather extensive family, registered from 1868 on, was the Kupetz family. In some registries and annuals the name is entered as Kupitz. The proper spelling is most likely Kopeć. Since the Christian names entered were Edward and Juliusz, it can be assumed they came from Silesia, where Kopeć was a popular surname. Edward and Juliusz were butchers and tradesmen. Both brothers ar-

rived at the same time and set up neighbouring shops on Queen Street until 1872, at which time Juliusz moved to 124 York Street.

The Kopeć brothers had more than just butcher shops; they also sold household goods: "crockery, dry goods, fancy goods and glassware." Mrs. Edward Kopeć is also registered as the owner of a "crockery and dry goods" shop at 33 Queen Street West. Some time around 1890, Juliusz Kopeć died. The City Directory subsequently lists Mary Kopeć, widow of Juliusz, residing at 28 Camden Street. (The last record of Mary Kopeć is entered in 1913.)

Alfred Kopeć, possibly a younger brother, but more likely a son of either Edward or Juliusz, is entered in the directory as: "Kupitz and Enright, Butchers, 166 York Street." Alfred did not remain in the business long, however, since in 1903 he was registered as a "driver" and in 1909 as a "paper hanger." After that there were no more entries for him.

In 1893 Edward Kopeć Jr. is listed. In 1896 Robert appears, but it is not certain whose son he was. Robert was a carpenter, residing at 60 Dundas Street. He is last entered in the directory in 1902. The female representatives of the Kopeć clan are recorded only as long as they remained unmarried. In 1901 Lizzie, a hairdresser with W. T. Pember, lived at 10 Maud Street, along with Edith, a seamstress, who moved to 307 Grace Street in 1909. Elizabeth, residing at 1 Givens Street, was registered in 1907. (The last entry of the Kupetz (Kopeć) surname occurs in 1913.)

The Kusiar family (occasionally registered as Kusia) settled in Toronto somewhat later than the first Kopeć representatives. The original Kusiar recorded was Francis, a shoemaker. There was also Franciszek, his son, also a shoemaker. The elder Kusiar had his workshop first at 55 Ann Street, then at 101 Ontario Street. Franciszek worked for F. J. Weston and Sons. Charles Kusiar, also a shoemaker, was registered in 1892 as a resident at 101 Ontario Street. The following year he moved to 50 McGill. Charles, along with another member of his family, and William Brown and R. Stewart, were owners of a company that made "fine boots and shoes" at 13 Adelaide Street. Ethel, Artur, Edna and Frederick Kusiar were employed by the T. Eaton Company.

The first Polish physician is recorded in Toronto in 1890. Jakub Zieliński lived and practised medicine at the following addresses: 136 Simcoe Street, 4 Beverley Street, 21 St. Patrick Square, 11 Soho, 284 Queen West and at 120 Brunswick Avenue, his last known address, from 1908 to 1913. According to the local tax assessment roll, in 1894 Dr. Zieliński was fifty-six years old, his family consisted of three members, and he supported the separate school board.

In 1885 Paul Szeliski was a bookkeeper for the Heintzman Piano Manufacturers Company. His name was entered with "von" before it, which indicates he came from the Prussian sector of partitioned Poland and felt it necessary to emphasize his noble background. Szeliski changed occupations several times. He sold real estate, then insurance, and in 1913 he was president of Szeliski and Stone Limited.

Another land and real estate agent, co-owner of a company as early as 1878, was Edwin Brokowski. A Miss P. Brokowski, residing in 1879 at 39

Howard, was registered as a "vocalist." There were other Brokowski's as well. Joseph, the last member of the family entered in the directory — in 1897 — was a student.

In the small group of earliest (from the 1860s) Polish settlers in Toronto, we find also Henry Chałaupka, most likely Chałupka, a bandmaster for the Queen's Own Regiment, residing at 141 York Street during 1867-68; A. Knowsky, a grinder for the Philips Richard Company; W.C. Pulaski, a pattern-cutter for the Hughes Bros. Company from 1867 to 1869, later a partner with a man named Martin in a "dry goods and clothing" establishment at 147 King Street East.

While Henry Chałupka was a bandmaster, William Labitzky, a resident of the village of Yorkville from 1867 on, was registered as a "music teacher." The city directory from 1885 lists a William J. Labitzky as "painter and tobacconist." His last known address, in 1910, was 50 Oxford Street. The local tax assessment roll (Ward 2, Division 1B), recorded the following in 1907: "Labitzky, William, age 47, franchise freeholder, painter, owner of the house; value of land $820; value of building $300; Roman Catholic, Separate School supporter; number of children between 5-21 years — 5; number of children between 5-16 years — 3; total number of residents — 8."

The nobleman "von Szeliski," sometime bookkeeper, real estate agent and insurance broker, was not the only member of the Polish aristocracy recorded in the early city directories. In 1893 "F. Karol de Stasicki, professor of modern languages," resided at 24 Ross Street. Among other early Polish surnames recorded in the city directories, we cannot overlook Ernest J. Zablocki, "artist penman," residing, from 1884 , at 142 Ontario Street, later, from 1896, at 16 Sheppard's Lane. He disappeared from the registries in subsequent years.

One more person warrants mention among early Polish settlers in Toronto, although the surname appears only at the beginning of this century, in 1901 to be precise — Mary Livinski, palmist, living at 391 Church Street. Some further information was given: "Know Thyself — The scientific interpretation of the palm rendered by Mme Mary Livinski. Hours 2-9pm. Fee 50 cents." It seems that the returns from "scientific interpretation" were not adequate, since the city directory also informs us that at the same address Mme Livinski ran a business: "Paper Bag Manufacturers."

From this numerically modest account of permanent or temporary Toronto residents with Polish surnames — Polish immigrants — we are struck instantly by the wide variety of occupations. This is quite remarkable, since all sources and documents relating to the later mass immigration from Polish territories indicates a vast majority of peasants and farm labourers. From the random data of the Toronto city directory and other archival records, which preceded the mass Polish immigration, it is easy to ascertain the social and professional diversity of the émigrés. There were noblemen like Gzowski (von Szeliski and de Stasicki), musicians, music teachers, piano-tuners, a bookkeeper, insurance agents, pattern-cutters, gilders, shoemakers, tradesmen, butchers, cattle traders, factory workers, etc. Each of these residents in his or her own way helped develop and enrich this city, not only in a material sense.

BENEDYKT HEYDENKORN

The Polish Community in Toronto in the Early Twentieth Century

Zofia Shahrodi

At the turn of the century the successful settlement of the prairies became an important objective for the Liberal government of Wilfrid Laurier. World economic conditions were in Canada's favour: food prices were rising quickly; European industry provided a large market for Canadian grain. The agricultural settlement of the prairies would bring profits from grain exports, as well as provide a market for the industry developing in eastern Canada. To benefit fully from these conditions, Canada needed more settlers on the prairies. The most desirable immigrant was "a stalwart peasant in a sheepskin coat, born on the soil. . . ."

Eastern Europe — particularly partitioned Poland — was full of ideal prospective immigrants. Poverty and lack of available land in Galicia and the Congress Kingdom forced local peasants to seek a better life abroad. Thousands of peasants accepted Canada's "invitation" and arrived to settle and work the fields in Manitoba. There were also many who, despite the official policy discouraging "labouring men and mechanics," came in search of employment in industry. Canada was, after all, a "land of opportunity" and rapid economic growth. Between 1896 and 1914 railway mileage doubled, mining production tripled and wheat production increased tenfold.[1] Ontario emerged as the most industrialized province in the country. Toronto became an important industrial and commercial centre. Immigration from eastern and southern countries provided a steady flow of labour to capital.

Toronto was one of the cities immigrant Poles were drawn to in search of employment. There are no statistics available to specify the exact number of Poles living in Toronto at the beginning of the economic mass migration. The Canadian census registered Poles as Russian, Austro-Hungarian or German subjects; furthermore, not all of these immigrants were even aware of their national background. They often identified themselves with the region or village they came from. They were attached to their families, villages and traditions.

A large majority of the Polish immigrants who came to Canadian cities prior to the First World War intended to return home. They treated their participation in Canadian life as temporary. One of those early arrivals recalled: ". . . I am one of the oldest Polish immigrants in Toronto [he said during the celebration of the fortieth jubilee of St. Stanislaus' parish, in 1951]. I came to Toronto in 1904, forty-seven years ago. Then, there was six of us Poles, we gathered together. It was sad to live here because no one of us could understand English. Every one was thinking of collecting some savings and returning home. In 1905 some more of our countrymen came. We gathered together and talked where we could find a church for ourselves."[2] The first Polish religious gatherings took place in St. Patrick's church on McCaul Street, where the immigrants recited the rosary in Polish and sang the Little Hours to the Virgin Mary.

Since that time, the Polish presence in the city has been registered in church statistics. Polish names have appeared in the registration books of St. Patrick's Church, St. Mary's Church on Bathurst and St. Michael's Cathedral. In 1906 a Polish priest, Father Paul Sobczak came to Toronto and performed services for the Poles at St. Michael's Cathedral. Later, he visited occasionally and offered services at St. Mary's Church on Bathurst and St. Patrick's Church. From one of his visits, which took place in March 1907, Father Sobczak reported back to Archbishop O'Connor. It was in a letter written by Rev. Schweitzer from Berlin, Ontario, where Father Sobczak was a member of the Congregation of the Resurrection. The report mentions that about 150 Poles and 12 Macedonians received the sacraments at St. Mary's Church just before Easter. These people had to live reasonably close to St. Mary's Church. The above-mentioned Macedonians, who approached Father Sobczak to hear their confessions, were in fact Lithuanians who, if not fluent in Polish, at least knew the basic language. Father Sobczak himself could speak some Lithuanian. The visiting priest was also approached by the Ruthenians — the Uniates and other Slavic people. He expressed his concern about them, especially the Poles in his report:

With regard to the moral standing, Fr. Paul states that according to what he was informed, it must be worse that what he has found among the lowest class of Poles even in Chicago. There are several reasons for this. First, the poorer and lowest class of people usually come to this country, with but few exceptions; second, in Toronto they are herded together into small quarters, so that frequently several families live, where one family would be poorly housed; third, the Poles are fond of strong liquor; fourth, the unscrupulous Jew takes advantage of them, and uses all means to degrade them in order to get their money from them. They also persuade them not to approach the priest, for fear that he would help them to get rid of them; fifth, because so far they had no spiritual guidance of any kind in Toronto.[3]

Polish immigrants, prior to 1914, were characterized by a high rate of illiteracy. They were of peasant background and came from poor and backward regions of partitioned Poland. They were totally ignorant of western culture and the English language, and emotionally attached to their customs, tradition and families back home. The alien environment, the language barrier and the absence of educated people among them, made the situation very difficult. The transition from a village community in agricultural Galicia or the Congress Kingdom into life in an industrial city was indeed a hard process. There was no Canadian agency to help the newcomers, nor was there an official Polish representative. The immigrants were forced to rely on their own resources.

In 1907 a handful of Polish immigrants organized the first mutual benefit society in Toronto, with the help and inspiration of Stefan Adalia Satalecki who had arrived from Chicago in 1906. It was called the Society of the Brotherly Aid of the Sons of Poland, under the Protection of the Holy Mother of Czestochowa, the Queen of the Polish Crownlands, and offered mutual help in case of sickness and death. According to its 1907 constitution, each member of the society who paid his initiation fee ($1 for men between eighteen and forty years of age and $2 for those between forty and fifty-five years old) and 25 cents each month for at least six months, was eligible for financial assistance in the amount of $4 a week in case of sickness. The society also provided financial help in covering medical expenses.

A member of the Sons of Poland could be a Pole, Ruthenian and Lithuanian, as these nations inhabited the Polish crownlands. The society was responsible for organizing national holiday celebrations and preserving Polish culture among the immigrants and their children. The first constitution of the Sons of Poland stated that the society would try, by all possible means, to establish a Polish parish, but prior to that, would try to bring a Polish Roman Catholic priest to the community at least twice a year.[4] It appears that by 1907 there were enough Poish immigrants in Toronto to constitute a parish and to take up financial responsibilities for it. The annual statement sent by the Sons of Poland to the Department of Insurance for Ontario, at the end of 1908, showed that the society had twenty-two members; that no sick or funeral benefits had been paid to its members; and that the total assets of the organization to date were $39.50.[5]

Toronto city directories give a broader picture of the Polish population in the city. Although they did not register all the Poles living in Toronto, they remain one of the fundamental sources for information on the community during the first decade of the twentieth century. The 1904 volume registered only a few Polish names in the city, from that time on the number of Poles steadily increased. The earliest immigrants were registered as labourers employed, for the most part, in the city's heavy industry. A vast majority of them lived in boardinghouses on Chestnut, Elm or Elizabeth Street in the Ward, or in other locations in Toronto.

In 1907 only a few of those registered actually rented entire houses; even fewer were listed as owners. These were men with families in Toronto. Church statistics show that in 1906 and 1907 these immigrants baptized their first children born in this city. They were men in their thirties and forties, who worked as labourers and also took boarders into their homes. The 1907 tax assessment roll shows that in 1906, at 399 Adelaide Street West, there was a house occupied by a Pole, aged thirty-two; he was a labourer, and owner of the house with another Pole. He was Roman Catholic, had two children between five and sixteen years of age and there were sixteen residents in the house. Usually, there were only three or four boarders living with a Polish immigrant family.

As the number of Polish immigrants increased, by the end of the first decade of the twentieth century they began settling in different parts of the city east of Yonge, on Church, Jarvis, Seaton and Ontario Streets, and others west of Yonge. Still the Ward was the district where many boarders from eastern and southern Europe could find a place to live. Some immigrants were already moving farther west along Richmond and Adelaide over to Niagara Street. College Street to the north and King Street to the south formed the other boundaries of Polish settlement. There was also a group of Polish immigrants in West Toronto between Davenport and Dundas Street West, on Uxbridge, Pelham, Perth, Franklin and Kingsley Avenue in Ward Seven. Both of these locations were inhabited not only by Poles but by other ethnic groups as well. Poles usually chose to live as close as possible to their place of work and changed residences often if there were better wages to be had in other places.

Nonetheless, by 1911 Polish immigrants were among the dominant ethnic groups in the area around Bathurst and Queen.

Niagara, Richmond, Adelaide, Portland, Wolseley and Denison Streets were all heavily populated by Poles. For the most part, these were rental properties transformed by the Poles into boarding-houses. According to the 1910 tax assessment rolls, at 143 Niagara Street there was a tenant with a Polish surname, thirty-eight years old, a carpenter; he had three children between five and sixteen years of age and there was a total of eleven residents in the house. The following year he had thirteen residents registered and he continued to keep boarders over the years. The 1912 tax assessment roll shows that at 498 Adelaide Street West a Polish immigrant rented a house in 1911 from Jacob Singer. He was employed at the Massey plant, had no children between the ages of five and twenty-one, and had eight residents in his house.

West Toronto — the Junction — was another area of Polish concentration. There several Poles owned houses and also took in the boarders. As early as 1909 one of the Poles owned a grocery store on the corner of Pelham and Uxbridge Avenue, as well as seven houses, two on Uxbridge and five on Pelham Avenue. Tax assessment rolls registered the occupants of his houses as various tenants, occupation: Poles. At 76 Uxbridge Avenue in 1909 there were nine tenants registered; their occupation: Polanders. A few streets west, at 150 Cawthra Avenue, there was another Polish freeholder who worked as a piano-maker at the nearby Heintzman piano factory. He was forty-four years old, had three children between five and twenty-one years of age and thirteen residents in his house. He kept boarders for a few years. The Junction attracted many immigrant settlers with its employment opportunities. The iron and steel industry could absorb a large number of male labourers. It was also a high-wage industry.

The Ward was a heavily populated city district with a mixture of almost all immigrant groups. Poles were not as numerous as Jews or Italians but there were over thirty families living in the area in 1911, as well as a large number of individuals. There, as in any other area in the city, the practice of keeping boarders was popular. The houses of the Ward were characterized by their high number of occupants. Polish boardinghouses were not registered by the city directories as official boardinghouses in Toronto.

Today, these boardinghouses can be examined, albeit indirectly, through a report on slum conditions in the city submitted to the Board of Health in Toronto in 1911 by Dr. Charles Hastings. The term slum, in the report, applied to poor, unsanitary houses, characterized by overcrowding, insufficient lighting, bad ventilation and unsanitary, filthy yards.[6] Poles inhabited three out of six districts investigated by Dr. Hastings' inspectors: the Ward, the Niagara Street district and the Bathurst and Queen area.

Overcrowding and unsanitary living conditions were reported

as major problems in every district examined. The report states that:

> in one of the houses 19 men sleep in three rooms, seven in one room, another room is very small, the cellar is unsanitary and a place of filth. In another place, 13 people live in five rooms. These are 11 lodgers paying $3.00 a month, each lodged as follows:
> room 9 12 - 3 beds, 6 men
> room 9 10 - 2 beds, 4 men
> room 7 10 - 1 bed, 1 man, who does shoemaking eats and sleeps in the one room.[7]

In 1911 there were many houses in the city transformed into lodging houses for foreigners. A migrant-labourer who was totally unfamiliar with conditions in this country and unable to communicate in English was at the mercy of his landlord; the latter, as a rule, was his fellow countryman who had arrived some time earlier. A boardinghouse was a profitable institution, whether rented or owned. As the Hastings' report mentioned, each man paid from about 75 cents to $1.25 a week for lodging and washing. These were not poor men; they were in receipt of good wages of $1.75 to $2.00 a day and some even as much as $3.25 and $3.50 a day.[8]

High wages were paid in the iron and steel industry. By 1911 the iron and steel industry was a major employer of Polish immigrant workers. A large majority of them worked in the foundries as moulders. The minute book of the Sons of Poland registered the new members, who entered the society in 1908, as follows:

18 Sept. 1908	Wojciech Bednarek,	age 43, married, moulder
	Jan Zegzula,	age 26, married, moulder
	Piotr Spiewak,	age 26, married, moulder
	Jan Kadzik,	age 31, married, moulder
	Jakub Skrynik,	age 20, single, moulder
	Andrzej Zajac,	age 25, single, moulder
18 Oct. 1908	Ludwik Toltarz,	age 30, married, moulder
	Jan Konopka,	age 28, single, moulder
15 Nov. 1908	Pawel Bilewicz,	age 22, single, tailor

There are no sources available to specify the number of working hours spent by Polish immigrants in the foundries, nor is there any information about their wages. Department of Labour Statistics on wages and hours of labour between 1901 and 1920 show that, in metal trades, workers were employed 54 hours per week, almost up to the First World War and the nine-hour day remained a general practice well into the war years.[9]

Working conditions in early twentieth-century industry were poor, particularly in the foundries. The Inspectors of Factories often described working conditions in the foundries as critical, even unacceptable. The moulders were exposed to extreme heat and "in some cases cold, obnoxious and dangerous gases, fumes and smoke etc., all of which are offensive, unpleasant and injurious."[10] Accidents at work were frequent and a man's health would deteriorate after only a few years. One of the reports says: "There is no class of work more laborious and subject to such extreme temperatures as that of the moulder. And it is not surprising that each year the class of labour is becoming more scarce. The young men of today prefer to select an occupation that is easier . . . ."[11] However, there were no difficulties in replacing these men with strong, Polish immigrants, eager to work.

A large number of the Polish workers joined Polson Iron Works, engine and boiler manufacturers and builders of steel vessels. They were employed, for the most part, as helpers and boiler-makers. The company was located on the Esplanade East at the foot of Sherbourne Street. Another company employing Poles as helpers and blacksmiths was McGregor and McIntyre, located on Pearl Street. This company manufactured fire escapes, iron stairs, anchors, jail cells, balconies, automatic fire shutters and other iron works. Phillips Manufacturing Company, makers of mouldings, mirror plates and cornice poles also employed many Polish labourers. In West Toronto, the CPR employed Polish workers in its workshops and Heintzman used some Polish immigrants as carpenters and piano-tuners. There were also Polish workers, men and women, employed in the needle trades, some men in shoemaking, some became peddlers for a short time.

These workers were generally of peasant background and usually constituted an unskilled labour force. A few of them were craftsmen, but their training did not match the fast-developing industry in Canada. Alfons Staniewski, who came to Toronto in 1910 and became one of the early activists in the Polish community, describes these Poles:

> Then, the Polish colony was small, no more than 500 people, the majority of them were single men, or men with families left behind in Poland. The emigrants in Toronto constituted one class of people, they came here to work. Many of them were from small villages and small towns, from the regions of Kielce, Radom, eastern and southern Poland, from the areas of Krakow, Skala, Boryslaw and Sanok. They were either peasants or sons of peasants from small holdings, they came here hoping to improve their living conditions back home. Very few of them were skilled workers from big cities like Kraków, Warsaw, Łódź or Lwów. There were not at all any professional people in the whole city of Toronto. There were no people with any organizational experience either.[12]

There is no reliable information on the number of Polish residents in Toronto at this period. The 1911 census shows 622 persons of Polish origin in Toronto, 438 males and 184 females, 240 of them lived in the central part of the city, 15 in East Toronto, 8 in the northern part, 221 were living in the south, 138 in West Toronto. The census has a separate column for persons of Galician, Bukovinian, Ruthenian origin, as well as Russian, Austrian, Hungarian and German.

Polish immigrants in Toronto, above all else, desired their own church with a Polish priest. Church authorities were seriously concerned with this matter. When in January 1909 Rev. B. Jasiak arrived from Pittsburgh, a permanent service was offered to the Poles at St. Michael's Cathedral. The church's registration books give detailed information about the Polish people enrolled in the church. Rev. B. Jasiak specified the village they came from, their home parish, religion, occupation and present address. Most of these immigrants came from Russian and Austrian Poland; they were registered as labourers or farmers, and very few of them were skilled. Some of the Ruthenians registered as Roman Catholics of the Latin Rite, some as of the Ruthenian Rite. The marriage register shows that married couples were usually from the same or nearby village at home. It was a busy missionary post for the Rev. Jasiak, as he sometimes married three or four couples a day. Thus, when he left Toronto in 1910, the archbishop's secretary, the Rev. John Kidd, was anxious to find another Polish priest. In the meantime, by June 1910 the members of the Sons of Poland had collected $500 for the establishment of a Polish church.[13]

The history of the first Polish church in Toronto begins with Eugene O'Keefe, a papal chamberlain and generous benefactor. One Sunday morning he saw from the chancery window a large group of people going to church. They attracted his attention, these women dressed like babushkas, with long skirts, big scarves on their head and shoulders. The priest told him that these were Poles, a very deeply religious people; they come to church long before the priest comes to celebrate the mass, and they sing Little Hours to the Virgin Mary.[14] When in April 1911 Archbishop McEvay negotiated the purchase of the Western Presbyterian Church, on Denison Avenue, for the congregation of Poles, Eugene O'Keefe bought the church and gave it to the Polish people. O'Keefe's daughter, Mrs. Helen French, put up the money for refitting the church, and it was named St. Stanislaus' Kostka.[15]

The Rev. Joseph Hinzmann, who came from Pittsburgh in early 1911, became the first pastor of St. Stanislaus' Kostka. Working previously among the Polish immigrants in the United States, he used some of his American experience in this parish. He organized the first school in the city for teaching the children the Polish language and became its teacher. In 1912 Rev. Hinzmann established a mutual benefit society in the parish, the St. Stanislaus' Kostka Society. The society provided financial help for its members in case of sickness and misfortune. The first society's constitution was prepared in March 1916, but the minute book tells us that, already in 1912, each member had to pay a $1 initiation fee and 50 cents every month. After five months he was eligible for financial support of $5 a week. For those who could not pay 50 cents a month there was an option to pay only 35 cents, but the benefit received then was only $3.50 a week. The society could not offer funeral benefits to its members in 1912; it was decided first to build up a cash basis of $1,000.[16]

The St. Stanislaus' Kostka Society, like the Sons of Poland, had as one of its aims the preservation of their culture among the Polish immigrants. Members of the society participated in all national activities. At St. Stanislaus' Church national and religious holidays were often combined together. The Society's first report in 1915 states that the society had eighty-five members; five members received sick benefits, during the year, and the society also paid for its members medical attention. At the end of 1915 the total amount of standing cash was $543.13.[17]

Since the Polish parish was established on Denison Avenue more people moved closer to the Bathurst and Queen area. Denison, Augusta, Wolseley, Portland, Richmond, Adelaide West, Niagara, Bathurst and Queen Street West comprised the area of the developing Polish neighbourhood. Again, it was not an area inhabited only by Polish immigrants. East European Jews had small shops along Queen Street West, Lithuanians were also to be found in the area. Some of the latter attended St. Stanislaus' Church, some went to nearby St. Mary's Church on Bathurst. In the late 1920s, the Slovaks living in the area made up a large portion of St. Stanislaus' parishioners. The church became the nucleus of the Polish neighbourhood and a centre of all community activities. The role of the priest as organizer of the centre and leader of the community was significant. In the early period of its existence St. Stanislaus' pastor was one of the few educated men among Polish immigrants in Toronto. The priest was often their advisor, interpreter, teacher in the parish school, and someone who could get them financial assistance in times of crisis.

St. Stanislaus' parish constituted a closed community, and local residents began to call the area Stanisławowo. There were several parish-oriented organizations operating, both religious and lay. The parish had its own White Eagle brass band of forty-eight musicians and its own gymnastic association, Sokół. The report sent by Rev. Hinzmann to the Chancellor of the Archdiocese in January 1914 mentions two religious societies existing at St. Stanislaus' Church, the Holy Name Society and the Holy Rosary. According to information in this, the only existing report from the early years of St. Stanislaus' church, in 1913 St. Stanislaus' parish consisted of two hundred families, making some fifteen hundred souls. The report mentions the existence of the parish school, although class attendance was low — only fifteen children out of the seventy-five expected. In 1913, the report states, the parish priest performed sixty-seven marriages, 115 children were baptized and six people died.[18]

By 1914 over 250 families of Poles were living in West Toronto. Rev. Marian Wachowiak, a visiting priest, occasionally performed religious services for them in the lower hall of the Ukrainian church on Franklin Avenue. In 1915, the Polish families started a collection for their own church, and a committee was set up with the responsibility for overseeing the building of the church. It was to be the second Polish church in Toronto under the name of ''Nativity of Blessed Virgin Mary of Czestochowa.'' The church was opened for service in October 1915 at 2014 Davenport Road, with Rev. Marian Wachowiak its first pastor. The parish served its religious purpose, but constant financial difficulties affected its cultural activities. The parish had incurred a big loan to pay for the church buildings, which later was paid off by Archbishop McNeil.

The outbreak of the First World War changed the life of the Polish community in Toronto. The united effort for the restoration of independent Poland became a first priority. North American Polonia joined in all activities to gain independence for Poland and to help their countrymen at home. In cities across Canada committees were formed to help hungry people in Poland and support the Polish army in France. Publicizing the Polish cause in North America contributed to the final outcome in 1918.

On 25 November 1917, the Citizens Committee was formed in St. Stanislaus' parish. This committee included St. Stanislaus' parish, St. Mary's parish, St. Stanislaus' Kostka Society and the Sons of Poland. They organized a united body to carry on the war effort and be responsible for financial contributions to the war. Collections were organized in the city to help people in Poland with money, food and clothing, to support the National Treasury and the Polish army in France. The Citizens Committee took strong action against declaring the Polish immigrants enemy aliens, and placing them in internment camps. Several letters were sent to the Canadian press, a number of meetings and demonstrations were held in Toronto to clarify and explain the position of the Polish nation in the world conflict.

The Polish Military Commission's headquarters in New York established a new recruitment centre in Toronto for the Polish army in France. Recruitment Centre No. 39 was located on the corner of

Queen Street and Spadina Avenue, and a second, unofficial, recruitment centre was at St. Stanislaus' Church. The volunteers for the army were coming mostly from across the boarder, to the camp situated at Niagara-on-the-Lake. Canadian Poles constituted about 10 per cent of the total volunteers.

In 1918 Poland regained her independence and Polonia's new efforts were harnessed to help restore the country. Before the Polish government established its first consulate in Montreal, the Polish parishes became its first consular agencies. St. Stanislaus' and St. Mary's parish organized a "Polonia Council" under the presidency of Rev. Joseph Chodkiewicz, with the offices installed in these two churches. The council took care of Polish immigrants, issuing passports and visas for those who intended to return home.

In 1920 the Citizens Committee organized support for Poland, which was involved in a war with Communist Russia. A separate body was formed, responsible for selling Polish government securities. The Polish Bond Committee worked from June till December 1920 organizing collections and meetings in Toronto. Cooperation with the Polish government started with the opening of the consulate in Montreal. The new pastor of St. Stanislaus' Church, Rev. L. Blum, strongly supported action for Poland and tried to involve the whole community in this endeavour.

The war effort ended with the action of the Polish Bond Committee; the Citizens Committee decided to dissolve itself in 1921. From then on, Toronto's Polish community turned its attention towards its internal life. The year 1921 brought the unification of two major Polish organizations, 'the Sons of Poland and St. Stanislaus' Kostka Society, into the Polish Alliance. The Polish Progressive Union, which was organized in 1918 by the Polish radicals in Toronto, joined the Alliance in 1923. Polish Alliance was, like its predecessors, a mutual benefit society oriented to the preservation of Polish culture among the immigrants and their children.

After the First World War a second wave of economic migration from Poland to Canada arrived in the 1920s. By this time the organizational structure of the Polish community in Toronto was well established. The city had two Polish Roman Catholic parishes with numerous organizations, the Polish Alliance, and a tradition of cultural and political activities. The new arrivals strengthened the Polish presence in Toronto. They settled in the neighbourhood of St. Stanislaus' Church or other areas of already established Polish settlement.

Toronto, presently the "Polish Capital" in Canada, had inauspicious beginnings. Polish immigrants who entered the city prior to the First World War did not intend to stay here premanently. They came in search of employment, ready to take any job, under practically any conditions if there were better wages. The majority of

Poles entered Toronto's iron and steel industry where higher wages guaranteed fast savings. They lived in boardinghouses, which lowered the cost of living and provided them with the company of their own people. These men wanted to return home as soon as they would have enough money to pay the travel expenses and to improve their living conditions back home, which often meant buying their own farm. To help each other in case of sickness and accidents, which occurred frequently at work in the foundries, they organized their own mutual benefit society. This society also took responsibility for maintaining "Polishness" among the immigrants and their children. The establishment of a Polish parish gave them protection and assistance to succeed in an alien environment. The war forced many of the immigrants to stay in Canada. After the First World War a new wave of migration began to arrive and the Polish community strengthened its presence and esteemed position in Toronto.

Notes

1. Donald Avery, "Continental European Immigrant Workers in Canada 1896-1919; from 'Stalwart Peasant' to Radical Proletariat,'' in *Canadian Review of Sociology and Anthropology* 12 (1975), p. 55.

2. *Złote Pokłosie Parafii Św. Stanisława Kostki, Toronto, 1911-1961* (Toronto: Parish Committee, 1961), p. 81.

3. Letter of Rev. Schweitzer C.R. to Archbishop D. O'Connor, dated April 12, 1907. (Archdiocese of Toronto Archive, Archbishop O'Connor file), p. 3.

4. *Złoty Jubileusz Związku Polaków w Kanadzie, 1907 1957* (Toronto: Editorial Committee, 1957), p. 5.

5. Report of the Inspector of Insurance and Registrar of Friendly Societies for the year 1908 in *Ontario Legislature Assembly Sessional Papers*, 1909, XLI, part IV, p.C 211.

6. Charles J. Hastings, Medical Health Officer, *Report of the Medical Health Officer Dealing with the Recent Investigation of Slums Conditions in Toronto Embodying Recommendations for Amelioration of the Same* (Toronto, 1911), p. 3.

7. Ibid., pp. 13-14.

8. Ibid., p. 8.

9. Michael J. Piva, *The Condition of the Working Class in Toronto — 1900-1921* (Ottawa: University of Ottawa Press, 1979), p. 90.

10. Ibid., p. 104.

11. Robert Harney and Harold Troper, *Immigrants: A Portrait of the Urban Experience, 1890-1930* (Toronto: Van Nostrand Reinhold, 1975), p. 53.

12. *Księga Pamiątkowa Związku Polaków w Kanadzie, 1906-1946* (Toronto: Polish Alliance Press, 1946) p. 33.

13. The Sons of Poland Minute Book 1908-1921 (Toronto, Archives of Ontario, microfilm).

14. Interview of Rev. Felix Kwiatkowski by Zofia Shahrodi (Toronto, MHSO oral history collection, 1983).

15. Records of Archepiscopal Acts, Book II, p. 29 (Toronto, Archdiocesan Archives).

16. St. Stanislaus Kostka Society Minute Book 1912-1921 (Toronto, Archives of Ontario, microfilm).

17. Report of the Registrar of Friendly Societies' transactions for the year 1915 in *Ontario Legislature Assembly Sessional Papers*, 1916, XLVIII, part IV, p. 302, no. 11.

18. Report of Rev. Hinzmann to the Chancellor of the Archdiocese, dated January 1914. (Archdiocese of Toronto Archive, St. Stanislaus' Church, parish history).

The Elusive Community: Greek Settlement in Toronto, 1900-1940

Lia Douramakou-Petroleka

They were full of sadness at their parting.
They hadn't wanted it: circumstances made it necessary.
The need to earn a living forced one of them to go far
   away — N.Y. or Canada.

Before Time Altered Them
- a poem by Cavafy

Although the "push" factors of Greek emigration are varied and complex, differing from region to region, for the emigrant setting out from his home village, whether his destination was other Greek communities in Egypt, Asia Minor, Africa or across the Atlantic to the New World, his purpose was quite simple: to make money in order to improve his economic and social status in his home village. As one such emigrant has stated, "We all came with the idea that we would stay two or three years and then we would go back; I wanted to make money to buy a whole bunch of sheep." This type of reasoning dominated the thinking of the majority of immigrants to America. This is clearly seen, in the way they moved around within North America from cities to small towns looking for more promising places and fields of employment, and in the large number of remittances sent home.

This emigration was mainly a movement of young males between the ages of 15 and 45. It was typical for men in many regions of Greece to migrate, whether it was to neighbouring regions as itinerant pedlars or master craftsmen, or further afield to communities of the Greek diaspora. Consequently their emigration to North America was only an extension of this migratory pattern which throughout the nineteenth century was mainly confined to Greek communities or urban centres within the Mediterranean littoral. Although their emigration to places beyond Gibraltar broke with the traditional pathways of their wanderings, the patterns of migration remained intact.

Greek immigration and settlement in Canada, unlike its counterpart in the United States, is generally regarded as a fairly recent occurrence, commencing only after the Second World War. There are two reasons for this view: first, in contrast to the abundant literature on the prewar Greek immigration south of the border, there is a dearth of writings on the experience in Canada; and secondly, the large postwar flow of migrants and the problems created in their wake blotted out the previous immigration. Hence, not only did sources of knowledge about prewar Greeks in Canada die out, but the surviving physical traces of what had been an elusive and dispersed community began to disappear.

However, remnants of an elder Greek immigrant presence did still exist and continued to cast shadows upon postwar developments in ways which still await clarification and elucidation. It is, in fact, with the origins of these remnants and the history behind their formation that the present paper will deal. Its purpose is not to make a testimonial offering to the evolving Greco-Canadian ethnicity of the postwar arrivals, or to engage in an exercise in antiquarianism. Rather, the hope is that it will stimulate further inquiry into the multiple, unseen and hitherto unrecorded links that joined these prewar ethnic clusters with the more recent arrivals. More importantly, it wishes to enrich, in a Greco-Canadian context, the wider historical understanding of how the continuum of the migratory chain, then as well as now, articulates itself.

The endeavour to achieve these tasks is based on an attempt to record the life and internal developments of one of the many Greek migrant communities which appeared in North America between 1900 and 1940 — that of Toronto. It will do so by means of an historical mapping of the residential, occupational and societal patterns of its early members that lie behind the individual and collective shifts from migrant to immigrant to ethnic.

Toronto not being a port of entry or close to a port of entry initially had very few direct emigrants from Greece. The majority of Greeks who came were migrants from other North American towns and cities. One observer of pre-World War II Greek emigration had stated that immigration to Canada was largely an offshoot of Greek immigration to the United States[1] as the table below indicates:

	Canada[2] No. Arrivals	U.S.[3] No. Arrivals
1900-1910	3,210	167,519
1911-1920	5,600	184,201

The majority of Greek immigrants came through New York and Ellis Island. Many of these immigrants, if they did not have any previous knowledge of or ties with other cities beyond New York, would initially settle in this vast city of opportunity and in time fan outwards to other towns and cities in search of employment.[4] They learned of these opportunities by word of mouth, through letters from friends or relatives, employment agents or from their own ethnic newspapers. A large number of immigrants were hired by labour contractors (*padroni*) and taken west to work in labour gangs on railroad construction, in lumber mills and in the mines.[5] Others moved to cities in the northeast such as Boston, Worcester or Lowell, Massachusetts finding employment in the mills and factories as previous immigrants had done. Still others moved on to Rochester, Buffalo, Detroit and Chicago. From these American cities many Greeks eventually crossed over to Canada, most of them unaware that they were entering another country. To them North America was one vast region — a new land without boundaries.[6] Those from the northeastern towns of the United States found it relatively easy to migrate to urban centres in eastern Canada, a large number settling in Montreal. However, there were many who also migrated to Ontario, settling in its small towns, usually employed in the service trades, others finding work in the lumber camps and mines in northern Ontario or as navvies with the railroad companies. A few drifted into Toronto.[7]

Toronto, as a large urban centre that had expanded quickly in the last decades of the nineteenth century, offered many opportunities for the more enterprising immigrants. In many ways it was virgin territory to the Greeks; not only did it offer opportunities for entrepreneurial expansion but it lacked some of the strict business restrictions which were being enforced in the United States.[8] For instance, by an act passed in February 1907, it became possible to institute criminal proceedings against any *padroni* for conspiring to commit an offence against the United States. This made it increasingly difficult for *padroni* to control the supply of labour.[9] Consequently, many moved north to Canada to exploit the possibilities there. One such person who was credited with having more than one hundred shoeshine parlours under his control in the United States eventually opened a number of these establishments in downtown Toronto and brought many young boys from Greece to work in them.[10]

Initially, however, Toronto, like Montreal and several other towns in northern Ontario, was a base camp during periods of unemployment for many immigrants who worked as seasonal labourers in the nearby mines, lumber camps or on railroad construction.[11] These men drifted into nearby urban centres where they passed their time idly in the company of their compatriots in similar situations or attempted to find temporary employment until they moved to the bush again. Many of those who were successful in obtaining work in the city did not return to the harsh working conditions of the bush, preferring the security of the urban environment which offered more opportunities for quick profit. As one contemporary observer in Chicago noted about Greek labourers:

> Their apprenticeship [in the gangs that do railroad and general construction work] is shorter than with most nationalities. A labour agent who supplies two or three thousand foreigners a season for this sort of work says that the Greek seldom "ships out" more than once or twice. In that time he has learned some English or accumulated enough money to venture on a small commercial enterprise for himself. He becomes a peddler, perhaps later owns a fruit-stand and finally an ice-cream parlour.[12]

Information on the first Greek immigrants in Toronto is fragmentary. One must rely on such sources as city directories, census reports and other city records (i.e., police records) which may refer to their presence. However, the reliability of these sources is suspect since, due to the nature of early Greek immigrant occupational and residential patterns, they were not accurately enumerated. Men who resided in the city only during periods of seasonal unemployment in the lumber and mining camps may well not have been included in the census counts or city directories.[13] Furthermore, new immigrants tended to be very mobile even within the city, so that a change in residence could occur many times in the year, usually following a change in one's place of employment. However, through a cross-reference of various sources one can arrive at a reasonably safe estimate and description of the early Greek presence in the city.

Compared to other North American cities where Greeks had settled in increasing numbers since the early 1890s, the Greeks did not arrive in Toronto until after 1900. No Greek names are to be found in *Might's City Directory* until 1905. With the exception of one man of Greek origin who had come in the mid-1860s to study medicine at the University of Toronto and subsequently remained, the first recorded immigrants were Basile Karapanagiotis (Karry), who came in 1901 from Chicago, and Chris Jannopoulos

(Johnson).[14] Both of these men had stores in the city centre, the former a stationery shop and later a billiard hall and bowling alley, and the latter had a hat cleaners and shoeshine parlour. Other sources, however, reveal the invisible immigrants who are often missed by the enumerators. Between July 1904 and November 1905 there were at least thirty-nine Greek peddlers residing in the south-central part of the city.[15] Since the names of these men did not appear in the city directory one can only assume that by 1905 Greek immigrants had started to drift into the city, but due to their small numbers and probable transiency their presence went unrecorded.[16]

It is not till 1907-8 that the Greek population in Toronto appears in the records. *Might's City Directory* lists approximately twenty Greek-named residents. A number of Greek-owned establishments had been opened. There were four restaurants all located within a very short distance of each other on Yonge Street; there was a fruit store; two confectionery shops, one at 226 Queen Street owned by James and William Moskakos who in 1905 were listed as peddlers, and another at 468 Yonge Street. There were also six shoeshine parlours or stands located in the downtown area and owned by the same person — Peter Smirlies. Finally, there was a grocery store at 130 Yonge Street which sold Greek foods. One other establishment was opened in this period — a Greek coffeehouse (or *cafeneion*) at the corner of Elizabeth and Queen streets.[17] The appearance of a coffeehouse and Greek grocery store substantiate the Greek presence in Toronto and reflect a more permanent and expanding population in the city.

The number of Greek-owned businesses more than doubled between 1907 and 1912.[18] The most common enterprise seems to have been restaurants. More than nineteen were situated in the downtown area on Yonge, Queen and College streets. Many Greeks were also engaged in the confectionery business of which at least nine Greek-owned shops existed at this time. In addition there were a number of fruit stands situated over a wide area of the city, shoeshine parlours in the city centre and two billiard halls and a bowling alley. At this time also another importer/merchant, Roubanis and Company, opened a store at 111 Queen Street West selling a variety of Greco-Levantine products and later added a travel agency and Greek bookstore.

The majority of shop-owners and businessmen had lived for some time in other North American towns or cities.[19] This explains the large number of establishments set up within a short period of the immigrants' arrival in Toronto. These men would already have established themselves in business and been able to speak some English. However, these businesses represented only the tip of the iceberg of the Greek presence in the city. Underlying this were large numbers of transient male labourers who worked as peddlers, bootblacks or in Greek stores and in local manufacturing industries.

The first official enumeration listing the total Greek population in Toronto was that of 1911. According to this census there were 484 males and 35 females in the city.[20] However, this included only those people born in the Kingdom of Greece, and thus excluded immigrants from Asia Minor and the northern Helladic lands (at the time unredeemed Greek territory) who considered themselves Greek.[21] These immigrants were listed as Turkish nationals of which, according to the census of 1911, 564 were males and 39 females.[22] Although it is not possible to say what proportion of these people identified themselves as Greek (for they may have included a large number of Armenians and Jews from the Ottoman Empire) sources indicate that a large number of Greeks from Asia Minor and present-day Macedonia had settled in Toronto. Therefore, an approximate number of Greeks living in Toronto at this time would be between eight hundred and one thousand.

The main concentration of Greek immigrants was in the downtown core of the city and particularly Toronto South. This area, close ot the major transportation networks, had accomodated most of the new immigrant arrivals in the late 1890s and early 1900s.[23] Once a prosperous middle-class residential and commercial district, it was gradually abandoned by the more affluent residents with the building of the railroad yards and the encroachment of industry during the latter part of the nineteenth century.[24] By the turn of the century the area was a conglomeration of low-cost housing, small-scale commercial establishments and manufacturing industries. It was particularly the presence of these factors — low-cost housing close to prospective places of employment — that initially attracted foreigners into what was a dilapidated and overcrowded part of the city.[25]

As the majority of these early Greek immigrants were single males, the boardinghouse was, initially, the predominant institution of settlement.[26] Several men of the same nationality or from the same region would live together. This type of accommodation was well-suited to their needs, providing them with inexpensive room and board. The premises would either be rented on a cooperative basis or from a house boss, who was sometimes also responsible for preparing meals. In other cases an employer would provide accommodation for his employees near or within the premises as his business. This type of boarding arrangement was usual with boys employed as bootblacks, or in restaurants and other shops.[27] In these cases the employer usually forbad them to live anywhere else, their expenses for room and board being deducted from their wages. Under this system these boys were often grossly exploited.[28]

Within the boardinghouse life was highly organized despite the outward semblance of disorder and overcrowding. Household chores were strictly distributed and rotated between the boarders, expenses were shared and an individual's property (even when he was away for long periods) was respected. The description of one immigrant of the organization of boardinghouse life is characteristic:

> When I arrived in Toronto I went to 153 Niagara Street. That is where my brother had lived before [returning to our village] and had left some of his furniture there, a bed and a chair. That is where all our people lived. In the house (three storey building) there were twenty-eight people; in each room there were two double beds with two people in each bed.
>
> Everyone had a duty. One day a month I had to clean the house and one day to cook. One guy was the representative of the men who lived there — he was the "boss" — he collected the rent from all of us to pay the landlord. We did not know the landlord. We let the boss worry about affairs between the men and the landlord.[29]

The younger men in the boardinghouse were often strictly guided by the elder boarders, particularly in their moral obligations. For instance meat was not served on Wednesdays and Fridays as dictated by the Greek Orthodox faith. As one immigrant pointed out: "The old men would punish us if they caught us eating meat on those days."[30] Thus, underlying the overt chaos was a sense of order and responsibility often with a strict hierarchy of duties.

The Greek immigrants were able to find their ethnic food in shops that catered to the needs of other southeastern Europeans. Despite their limited population as compared to other immigrant groups, by 1907 a few grocery stores and a coffeehouse catering to the Greek sojourners were established.

The coffeehouse — an important gathering place for the male inhabitants of every village in Greece and the Middle East — was also an important element of community life of the Greeks abroad, providing a focal point in the embryonic years of community development. Within the immigrant's environment the coffeehouse, besides the atmosphere of familiarity and security it transmitted, provided different types of services — a centre of information, a post restante, a centre of recreation and entertainment. For immigrants it was a refuge in a strange and often hostile environment.[31]

In the period from 1910 to 1920 the Greek community underwent a transition from simple clustering of lone males to one of a more defined entity. From a community of transient men, it slowly increased in population and developed formal institutions which reinforced its existence. Greek business establishments mushroomed, particularly in the central core of the city and eventually extended north along Yonge Street and further east and west along Dundas (Agnes) and College streets. Since the majority of these enterprises serviced the needs of the host society, many Greek entrepreneurs began to venture out of the initial settlement area, establishing shops in residential and commercial districts throughout the city.

Economy in time and money were two vital factors influencing an immigrant's choice of residence. Thus, they tended to live close to their place of employment.[32] Since the majority of Greek businesses were located in the downtown district, a small cluster of Greek immigrant settlement developed here, later reinforced by the location of the Greek Orthodox Church in the same area.

A reflection of the development of permanent settlement and the increasing prosperity of some immigrants was the formal establishment in 1909 of the Greek Community of St. George with a governing council of "symvoulio" to overlook the affairs of the community.[33] The establishment of a community organization always preceded the founding of a church. Thus, in 1910, having set up the administrative and legal basis, the St. George Greek Orthodox Church was founded and housed in a former warehouse at 170 Jarvis Street.[34] This acted as a cohesive element and provided a focal point around which the Greek community was to develop. Furthermore, it endowed the Toronto community with a special and predominant position vis-à-vis other Greek communities in nearby towns. Until the founding of the church, religious ceremonies and services were held by itinerant priests. After the establishment of the church many Greeks from nearby towns also attended church services in Toronto. The attraction of the Greek population from the city's hinterland infused new vitality into the life of the Toronto community and led to the expansion of enterprises which provided specialized services to the Greek immigrants.

Chain migration, either indirectly from other North American towns and cities or directly from their villages, was eventually the main source of the increase in the Greek immigrant presence in Toronto. Very quickly three regional groups predominated: those from the Peloponnese, particularly the districts of Laconia, Archadia, and Messinia; from Macedonia, especially from the district of Florina; and from the coastal towns and cities of Asia Minor, particularly Smyrna.[35] Underlying the regional distinctions were cultural and political differences which, in time, were to play an important role in the evolution of social and communal relations.

The immigrants from these three groups displayed occupational and residential patterns. The list of business establishments mentioned earlier shows the wide range of activities in which they were employed. However, a closer examination of occupational patterns reveals a close correlation of occupation to region of origin. The most obvious example of this is between those immigrants coming from northern Greece and those from the Peloponnese.

The majority of men from the Peloponnese and also from Asia

Minor were mainly employed in commercial establishments, the catering trade and other service-related occupations.[36] Thus, many of the establishments located in central Toronto on Yonge Street and its periphery such as restaurants, confectionery shops, shoeshine parlours, grocery and fruit stores, and Greek coffeehouses were operated by and employed Greeks from these regions. This same occupational trend has also been noted in other Greek communities.[37] For instance, the Greek immigrants in Chicago, of which the majority were from the districts of Laconia and Archadia, were mainly employed as "independent peddlers and merchants instead of employees in some large factory."[38] Similar patterns are also to be found in many other cities. This of course does not mean that Greeks from these regions did not work in factories and industrial plants, but they represented the minority.[39]

On the other hand, the majority of men from northern Greece were mainly employed in the industrial and manufacturing sectors. Thus, there was a high concentration of these men in boarding-houses near these factories and plants in areas such as in the Junction and the southeast district of Toronto, whereas Greeks from the Peloponnese and Asia Minor mainly lived in the centre of the city and later dispersed throughout Toronto.[40]

The reasons for these occupational patterns are complex. Although they can partly be explained by chain migration whereby men helped their compatriots to find similiar employment as themselves, this is not in itself a sufficient determinant of occupational trends. Despite the fact that law immigrants were restricted in their choice of employment by their own inexperience, insufficient knowledge of English, and prejudice by the host society, they were still able to exercise a certain amount of choice. Nevertheless, each regional group showed a definite preference exhibited in its own particular field of occupation.[41] Consequently, the main reasons for this must be sought in the particular socioeconomic conditions which predominated in the various regions from which these immigrants came.[42]

Concurrent with the geographic and institutional establishment of the Greek presence in Toronto was the increase in the number of family households. This was reflected in the increase of the female population, particularly after 1914.[43] Men, particularly those who had established themselves economically, brought over their wives and families or other female relatives.[44] The influx of female immigrants reinforced the permanent character of the community, particularly with the formation of family groups. Although females represented a small minority of the Greek population, their influence was quite pronouced. The transition from a predominantly migrant collection of men to a stable community was due mainly to increased female immigration. Residential patterns were altered accordingly. Men without women relatives or families rented separate quarters in houses or flats near or above their places of employment.

Furthermore, the female element in the community increased the demand for various services and products with which they were familiar at home and thus made their availability more important. Many of these products could be found in shops catering to other immigrants with similar dietary tastes; however, difficulties of language and the desire to communicate with people of one's own background increased the need for Greek grocery stores.

Married women rarely worked outside the home, and the majority of those who were employed tended to be associated with the family business or worked in the shops of relatives.[45] Particularly in the early period, it was unusual for Greek women to be employed in factories, sweatshops, or as domestics as many other immigrant women were.[46] Their world was strictly limited to the familial environment as was the lifestyle back home.

The main social outlet for the women was the church. Their presence there added a new dimension to church activities. This was mainly in the realm of charitable and voluntary work. In 1921 their philanthropic activities were formally channelled with the establishment of the Ladies Philoptocho (Benevolent) Society.[47] The society's services were directed to Greek immigrants in difficulties (for example, by providing for and visiting lone sick men, assisting poor families with food and clothing, and on occasion paying funeral expenses). The society also looked after the needs of the church and helped to set up a day school for Greek children where lessons were taught in Greek and English. Besides administering aid, the society was also a medium through which the women of the community could meet and socialize, helping foster closer community ties.[48]

The women who were the most active in functions outside the home were usually the wives of businessmen and community leaders. If the founding members of the Philoptocho Society are taken as an indicator, they were women of an urban background, the majority from the Peloponnese and Asia Minor.[49] These women had greater freedom of movement and were familiar with extra-familial activities from their homeland which they sought to transplant in their new environment. This was particularly true of women from Asia Minor.

Thus, by the second decade of the twentieth century, appoximately twenty years after the first influx of Greek immigrants, a semblance of community life had evolved. In the period between 1912 and 1930 the population wavered between one and two thousand.[50] It seems to have reached a peak by the end of the first decade of the twentieth century. During the 1920s the size of the population stabilized and showed signs of decreasing as a result of restrictions which limited immigration to sponsored relatives and immigrants qualified to work as farm labourers or domestics.[51]

In fact during this time Greek immigration into Canada was strictly discouraged, as the following letter points out:

> . . . I may say that Canada has never encouraged immigration from Greece because Greeks seldom farm in Canada and agriculturalists are about the only class we require at present . . . only men who are coming to engage in agriculture and women coming for domestic service may now come as immigrants. Where a man has settled in Canada we of course arrange for the entry of his wife and children.[52]

Greek immigrants were regarded as unsuitable mainly because it was suspected that they would not remain as farm labourers for long but attempt to move to the cities as quickly as possible. This opinion is best expressed in the following facetious statement made by W.J. Egan, Deputy Minister of Immigration, in response to an inquiry made by the Cunard Line regarding the immigration of Greeks to Canada:

> I would suggest that the best way to develop [the movement of Greek farm workers] would be to secure application from bona fide Greek farmers in Canada who want to employ their fellow-countrymen on their farms. This would be the soundest method of encouraging the movement which otherwise will develop largely into a movement of candymakers and restaurant employees.[53]

However slighting the comment, it nevertheless seems to have been founded in fact. According to an advertisement in the *Greek-Canadian Business Guide* of 1922, approximately 60 per cent of all the restaurants and ice-cream parlours in Ontario were owned by Greeks.[54]

Underlying the semblance of harmonious community development were social and political rivalries compounded by inter-regional feuds. Due to the parochial world view of the immigrants and their strict regional loyalties, they tended to socialize and mingle only with people from their own particular village or district.[55] Anyone beyond these strict physical and mental boundaries was considered an outsider, a stranger. This was reflected in the founding of parochial clubs whose membership was restricted to men from a particular village or district and whose main concern was for the welfare of the people of the region they represented. Even in Toronto, despite the relative small size of the Greek community, a number of parochial clubs were established.[56] On many occasions regional rivalries and prejudices disrupted communal relations.

Community relations became especially tense and volatile with the outbreak of the First World War which had triggered an intense political conflict in Greece between the Royalist conservative faction and the Republican-Venezelist faction regarding Greece's position in the war.[57] The Greeks of Toronto as everywhere else showed particular concern over the role that Greece was to play in the war and aligned themselves with the same partisan factions as those in Greece.[58]

The Greek-language newspapers, especially the two largest dailies, the *Atlantis* and the *National Herald* (both published in New York) played an active role in the debates that ensued and added fuel to the conflict. As one writer noted "passions rather than reasons prevailed among the Greeks and the two journals helped to divide the Greek [communities of North America]. The succession of vituperative editorials contributed to coffeehouse violence, the termination of long friendships and the breakup of church communities."[59] This conflict soon overshadowed and undermined any semblance of communal harmony and cooperation in all Greek immigrant communities. In many cases the local authorities had to intervene to prevent bloodshed and rioting between rival factions.[60]

In Toronto the Greek coffeehouses were soon aligned politically. The predominance of political discussions in the coffeehouses and sometimes their catering to men of similar political and regional loyalties only was not unusual. However, the feud quickly exposed itself on a more serious front: in the church where due to the disagreement over the chanting of the "polichronion" (hymn for the King), the Venezelist faction withdrew and soon took steps to start a new church. Although a new church was not actually established, separate services were held for some time afterwards.[61] This conflict continued to poison relationships until well after the end of the war and actually intensified with the military defeat of Greece in Asia Minor by Turkey in 1922.

In addition to the intra-communal conflict, the policy of neutrality created problems for the Greek immigrants vis-à-vis the receiving society who resented the pro-German sentiments of the Greek state. Consequently this led to open conflict with verbal and physical attacks on the Greeks by the Canadian population. The war and the official Greek stand gave the host society a reason to openly vent their long-standing resentment and prejudice against the Greek immigrants.[62]

In Toronto material damage was inflicted on Greek-owned shops which became particular targets of anti-Greek sentiments. This came to a climax on August 2 and 3, 1918 (ironically well after Greece had officially joined the Allies) when a mob composed partly of demobilized Canadian soldiers vandalized and looted shops, mainly restaurants and cafés owned by Greeks. The riots were believed to have been instigated by a rumour that a returned soldier had been seriously assaulted in a café kept by a Greek on College Street. In the two days of rioting it was estimated that damages to Greek property totalled some $42,000.[63]

Close surveillance was also kept on Greeks' activities and on communications originating from Greece for fear of espionage. Concern regarding espionage activities was expressed on many levels and authorities were instructed to strictly censor any suspect communications: "Innumerable letters and telegrams are being sent to Greeks in Canada by means of German money. All such telegrams should be rigidly censored."[64]

The chief press censor for Canada pointed out that "enemy messages are being transmitted to and through Canada in the Greek language."[65] Consequently "all private telegrams addressed to and originating in Royalist Greece and all commercial telegrams other than those related to allied interests were to be stopped."[66] Innumerable telegrams were translated and examined before being delivered. Furthermore, attempts were made to monitor telephone communications on the suspicion that Greeks were used as go-betweens and agents in German spying rings in Canada. Instructions were given to operators on long distance circuits "to keep a special watch for connections to and from Greeks resident in Canada" in order "to obtain information which will lead to the disarrangements of the plans made by the enemy for communicating with enemy agents in Canada and the United States."[67] However, in order to successfully implement the surveillance of telephone communications it was found necessary to have a list of Greeks resident in Canada. Since no such list existed the Counsul General for Greece was asked to provide one.

Even Greek newspapers suspected of supporting pro-German views were banned by the Canadian authorities after complaints about them were made by Greeks with opposing (pro-Venezelist) loyalties. Consequently, the distribution of the *Atlantis* and the *Loyal*, believed to express anti-Allied propaganda, were forbidden to circulate in Canada.[68]

The Greek population for their part tried to reassure the host society and the Canadian government of their loyalty by public demonstrations of their solidarity with the Allied Powers. At a press conference in March 1918 on the occasion of a visit to Toronto by the Consul General of Greece, leaders of the Greek community expressed their bitterness at the hostility being shown to them by the Canadians and reaffirmed their loyalty to the Allied cause. Nick Speal, secretary of the Greek community, pointed out that "since the beginning of this war the sympathy of the Greek colony of Toronto had been with the allies. More than thirty Greeks from Toronto had enlisted in the first two years of the war while their country was neutral."[69] Furthermore, it was pointed out that Greeks with Turkish nationality were particularly treated with hostility and distrust by the authorities who regarded them as "enemies" because of Turkey's position in the war. Mr. Kilismanis, secretary of the Karteria Club, composed of Greeks from Asia Minor, stressed that they were "Greeks and intended to stay Greeks" and that they considered it a "disgrace and an injustice to be classed as Turks by their adopted country, Canada."[70]

In addition to the intra-communal political conflict, the Greek population was extremely concerned with pro-Bulgarian activities in Toronto (especially with its large Slavic-Macedonian population). Geo-political feuds in the Balkan peninsula over Macedonia were also transplanted to North America and were an additional undercurrent of political sentiments which influenced the development of intra-communal relations. In Toronto, a campaign to fight what was considered to be Bulgarian propaganda was actively carried out. Greek community leaders (the majority were usually Peloponnesian) were always on their guard against such propaganda and considered it their duty to keep the federal authorities (particularly the immigration authorities) informed.[71]

However, by the late 1920s and particularly during the 1930s political differences and inter-regional feuds subsided. As the ties to Greece loosened due to the effects of time and the decrease in new arrivals, and with the rise of political moderation in Greece in the late 1920s, the immigrants showed more concern for their own welfare and future in their new homeland.[72]

The 1920s was a period of maturity and consolidation for the Greek community. Many of the Greek business establishments had a stable clientele, while new concerns were constantly being set up. Some entrepreneurs who had confectionery stands or were restaurant keepers branched off and became suppliers for the trade. Others went into real estate. Although settlement was still largely concentrated in the south-central part of Toronto, many families, mainly those of shop-owners, had dispersed throughout the city.[73]

The depression of the 1930s brought hardship to many. A large number of Greek businesses were faced with bankruptcy. The population of the community was steadily decreasing as a result of out-migration, triggering widespread concern that they would soon be engulfed and assimilated within the fabric of Anglo-Canadian society.[74]

In this period Greek ethnic institutions became very important as a means by which the immigrants could retain their cultural identity. Offshoots of fraternal organizations founded in the United States were also established in Canada. Thus, the Lord Byron Chapter of AHEPA (Anglo-Hellenic Educational Progressive Assocation) was instituted in Toronto on October 29, 1928.[75] AHEPA initially espoused a doctrine of assimilation with meetings conducted in the English language and attracted well-established and middle-class Greeks.[76] As a reaction to AHEPA's policies, another organization was formed, GAPA (Greek-American Progressive Assocation), which stressed the retention of the Greek language and traditions and the Greek Orthodox faith.[77] A GAPA branch was also established in Toronto in the late 1920s, but it was not very popular and soon became inactive.[78] Social and cultural activities organized by these associations or by regional clubs and church groups gained new significance as an expression of communal cohesiveness, particularly for the younger generation who were most prone to stray from the cultural milieu. A Youth Association was established through the auspices of the church which became a medium of social intercourse for the second generation.[79] Above all, the Greek parish school became especially important as a means of keeping alive in the children their Greek identity and knowledge of the Greek language.

The inauguration in 1937 of the St. George Greek Orthodox Church in a larger building, with all the attendant fanfare, reflected a new pride and cohesion of the community.[80] It was an expression of the community's importance vis-à-vis other Greek communities in North America. It was also a reinforcement of their ethnic identity.

By 1940, although the population in the community had started to decline, it nevertheless reflected aspects of permanent settlement. The number of family groups had increased to 269 by 1941.[81] The influx of new immigrants had ceased and those who remained had established institutions to protect their ethnicity and yet, at the same time, to make themselves more acceptable to the host society.

The establishment of a mixed youth church choir, which is unusual in traditional Orthodoxy, and a drama society reflected tendencies of assimilation. Annual dances, sponsored by government notables, and public exhibitions which stressed the nobility of their heritage — ancient Greece — were expressions of a desire for cultural respectability and acceptance by the host society. All this reflected a desire to conform to and emulate the ways of the host society while at the same time preserving and glorifying their ethnic identity.

The crowning exhibition of communal unity and their acceptance by the wider receiving society as respectable citizens rather than undesirable immigrants was their indefatigable efforts for the Greek War Relief Fund in 1941.[82] This was in stark contrast to the virulent communal feuds, as well as to the xenophobic sentiments of the host society in the First World War.

Thus, in the four decades from 1900 to 1940, from a mere trickle of transient labourers, whose presence was overshadowed by the wider patch-work of immigrant settlement, developed a community which underwent the "rites of passage" from migrants to immigrants to ethnics. A community which despite its small population and relative insignificance displayed attitudes, patterns of residence and occupation similar to many Greek communities of the diaspora, whether these may have been in Europe, Africa, the Far East or North and South America. Even contemporary Greek emigration, whether it is to North America, Australia or Western Europe, is undergoing the same pangs of development and integration as those experienced by this small pre-World War II community in Canada.

Notes

1. G. Vlassis, *The Greeks in Canada* (Ottawa, 1942), p. 12.

2. These figures are from the Canadian census cited in H. Papamanolis, ed., *A Concise History of Canada and A Greek-Canadian Guide: 1921-1922* (Montreal: Reg. Greek Publication Co., 1922), p. 38.

3. T. Saloutos, *The Greeks in the United States* (Cambridge, Mass.: Harvard University Press, 1964), p. 35.

4. Taped interviews with: Mr. Diakopoulos; Mrs. P. Jannetakes.

5. Jean Morrison, "Ethnicity and Violence: The Lakehead Freight Handlers Before World War II" in *Working Class History*, pp. 143-60; H. Papanikolas, "Greek Workers in the Inter-Mountain West: The Early Twentieth Century" in *Byzantine and Modern Greek Studies*, Vol. 5 (Oxford: Basil Blackwell, 1979), pp. 187-215.

6. Taped interviews: B. Mergeles, Diakopoulos.

7. Papamanolis, *Canadian-Greek Guide*, pp. 341-74.

8. Saloutos, *Greeks in the United States*, p. 51.

9. Ibid., p. 49.

10. *Might's City Directory*, 1907, listed 6 shoeshine parlours run by Mr. Peter Smirlies. Also interview with Mr. Ted Paraskevopoulos, August 1977.

11. R.F. Harney, "Chiaroscuro: Italians in Toronto, 1885-1915" in *Italian Americana*, 1:2 (1975), p. 149; cf. R.F. Harney, "Toronto's Little Italy" in *Little Italies in North America,* R.F. Harney and J.V. Scarpaci, eds. (Toronto: MHSO, 1981), p. 46.

12. Grace Abbott, "A Study of Greeks in Chicago" in *American Journal of Sociology*, XV (November 1909), p. 386.

13. Harney, "Chiaroscuro," p. 149. ". . . the migrant and non-propertied were always under-enumerated." Also Abbott, *Greeks in Chicago*, pp. 379-80, points out that the Greeks were very transient. Many left in May for work in the bush, thus the population of the community declined significantly in the summer months until their return to the city in October.

14. Dr. Constantinides came to Toronto in 1864 to attend the University of Toronto Medical School. Upon graduation he remained, residing on Gerrard St. close to Church St. In due course he was to provide many important services to the Greek community both as a doctor and an intermediary vis-à-vis the Greeks and the host society. Regarding the first Greek emigrants to Toronto see Papamanolis, *Greek-Canadian Guide*, pp. 347-50 and 364.

15. Police Registry of Criminals, Division No. 1, 4, 5 Toronto City Archives.

16. Police Registry of Criminals. Since many of the names in the Police Records reappear during particular months of the year and also the number of offences listed fluctuated accordingly (i.e., the number of peddling offences increase during the winter season and decrease during the summer) it can be assumed that many of the men were involved in the peddling trade on a seasonal basis and most likely worked during the summer months in railroad construction, lumber camps, etc.

17. *Might's City Directory*, 1907 and 1908; Papamanolis, *Greek-Canadian Guide*, pp. 341-74.

18. *Might's City Directory*, 1907, 1908, 1909, 1910, 1911, 1912.

19. Papamanolis, *Greek-Canadian Guide*, pp. 341-74. Also verified through taped interviews.

20. Census of Canada, 1911, *Session Papers*, Vol. 47, 1913(B).

21. "Greeks Claim Ill-treatment," *The Globe*, Toronto, March 2, 1918, p. 8. See also, S. Zotos, *Hellenic Presence in America* (Wheaton, Ill.: Pilgrimage, 1976), p. 74; and Z.D. Ferriman, *Home Life in the Hellas* (London: Mills & Boon Ltd., 1910), p. 198.

22. Census, 1911.

23. R.F. Harney, and H. Troper, *Immigrants: A Portrait of the Urban Experience, 1890-1930* (Toronto: Van Nostrand Reinhold Ltd., 1975), p. 23; cf. Harney, "Little Italy," p. 43.

24. D. Ward, *Cities and Immigrants: A Geography of Change in Nineteenth Century America* (New York: Oxford University Press, 1971), pp. 105, 120-21. See also, Peter Goheen, *Victorian Toronto, 1850-1900: Patterns of Process and Growth*, Research Paper No. 127 (Chicago: University of Chicago Press, 1970).

25. Harney and Troper, *Immigrants*, p. 23; Tilly Charles, "Migration to American Cities" in *An Urban World*, C. Tilly, ed. (Toronto: Little Brown & Co., 1974), p. 352; also J. Zucchi, *Italian Immigrants of the St. John's Ward, 1875-1915* (Toronto: MHSO, 1981), p. 3.

26. R.F. Harney, "Boarding and Belonging," *Urban History Review*, No. 2-78,

p. 32: "Boarding provided for all the needs of the sojourners in the early period of ethnic settlement." It should be noted that even in contemporary emigration (e.g., migrant workers to Western European countries), settlement patterns and housing conditions reflect those of earlier emigrants to North America. This is shown in a study on migrant workers in EEC countries, *The Housing of Migrant Workers: A Case of Social Improvidence* (Brussels: EEC Publications, 1972).

27. "Often the owner of a restaurant, a fruit store or a shoe shine parlour furnished his employees board and room." Abbott, "Greeks in Chicago," pp. 390, 391-92.

28. L.B. Terhune, "The Greek Bootblack," *The Survey*, XXVI (September 16, 1911), pp. 852-54.

29. Taped interview, B. Mergeles, Toronto, August 1977.

30. Ibid.

31. See Saloutos, *Greeks in the United States*, pp. 78-79, for a good general description of the coffeehouse and its role in North American Greek communities.

32. Harney, "Toronto's Little Italy." Transportation compared to an immigrant's small wage was expensive. Also public transportation was not always accessible to the newcomer. See "Passengers Protest against Foreigners," *The Globe*, Toronto, March 7, 1918, p. 6. The main concentration of Greek immigrant settlement was in the area east of Yonge Street as far as Broadview Avenue and north of Front Street and south of Carlton Street.

33. Taped interviews of Greek immigrants and in Papamanolis, *Greek-Canadian Guide*, pp. 341-74. See also Vlassis, *Greeks in Canada*, p. 14.

34. Papamanolis, *Greek-Canadian Guide*, p. 341, and *The Greek Orthodox Church in Canada*, A Report given by His Eminence Athenagoras of Elai, Greek Orthodox Metropolitan in Canada, May 31-June 2, 1961, pp. 17-18.

35. Based on the St. George Greek Orthodox Church Records and taped interviews of Greek immigrants.

36. Papamanolis, *Greek-Canadian Guide*, p. 341.

37. Even in Athens internal migrants of the late nineteenth and early twentieth century tended to be involved in commerce or the catering trade. Many opened restaurants or grocery stores (bakals). From a contemporary nineteenth-century description of life in Athens the writer notes that ". . . the Greek easily turns restaurateur. There are many establishments of what may be called an amateur character . . . their clients always belong to the same province and the city is full of these little coteries." Ferriman, *Home Life in the Hellas*, p. 325.

38. Abbott, "Greeks in Chicago," p. 383.

39. Many Greek emigrants, particularly from the Peloponnese, were employed in the textile mills of New England.

40. L. Petroff, "Macedonians in Toronto: From Encampment to Settlement" in *Urban History Review*, No. 2-78, pp. 58-73. Also taped interview with Mr. B. Mergeles.

41. Taped interviews of Greek immigrants.

42. Succinctly the main difference between these groups was that those from north-ern Greece came from a peasant subsistence-oriented economy whereas those from the Peloponnese came from a more cash-based agricultural economy and were also more urban-oriented than their counterparts in northern Greece. Emigrants from Asia Minor tended to be urban residents. For a good analysis of this, see N. Mouzelis, ''Greek and Bulgarian Peasants: Aspects of their Social Political Situation During the Inter-War Period,'' *Comparative Studies in Society and History*, Vol. 18 (Cambridge: Cambridge University Press), pp. 85-105, particularly pp. 90 and 94. See also, K.D. Karavidas, *Agrotika* (Athens, 1931), pp. 125-36 and 201-68; M. Sivignon, ''Frontier Between Two Cultural Areas: The Case of Thessaly'' in *Annals New York Academy of Science*, Vol. 268 (New York, 1976), pp. 43-58, particularly pp. 46-53.

43. Many men who had returned to Greece to fight in the Balkan War of 1912-1913 brought their families with them on their return to North America. In 1922 ap-proximately 110 Greek families resided in Toronto; Papamanolis, *Greek-Canadian Guide*, p. 342.

44. In a contemporary study of the Greek community in Chicago it was noted that ''65% of the owners of ice-cream parlours and 75% of restaurant keepers belonged to family groups.'' Abbott, ''Greeks in Chicago,'' pp. 386.

45. The employment of female relatives helped to cut back on overhead costs of running a business or small shop.

46. Taped interviews of Greek immigrants. Also in a study of Greeks in Chicago it was noted that ''unlike the Italian women the [Greek women] do not work out-side their own homes or at sweatshop work. Of the 246 Greek women over 15 years of age only 5 were found to be at work.'' Ibid., p. 388. See also Saloutos, *Greeks in the United States*, pp. 86-87.

47. The Benevolent Society was formally established with a constitution in 1925; Mrs. P. Jannetakes, taped interview, August 1977.

48. Ibid.

49. Ibid.

50. According to figures given in an article in *The Globe*, Toronto, March 2, 1918, the Greek population in Toronto was 1,500 to 2,000. However, in Papamanolis, *The Greek-Canadian Guide*, it is stated that the population in the past had reached a maximum of 1,600 and now (1921) does not surpass 1,000. For 1930 the Greek population was estimated to be 1,200 according to an article in the *Toronto Daily Star*, April 5, 1930.

51. Memorandum from the Commissioner of Immigration dated January 23, 1929, ''Regulations Affecting the Immigration into Canada of Citizens of Greece,'' *Canadian Federal Archives*, Ottawa, File No. 998358.

52. Letter to G. Poulios, Manchester, N.H., from F.C. Blair, Secretary to Minister of Immigration and Colonization, dated December 17, 1923, PAC, File No. 998358.

53. Letter to Cunard Line, Montreal, from W.J. Egan, PAC Deputy Minister of

Immigration, Ottawa, January 5, 1929. See also, letter to K.A. Blatchford, M.P. for Edmonton, from Acting Deputy Minister of Immigration, dated September 10, 1929, ibid., File No. 427176.

54. Papamanolis, *Greek-Canadian Guide*, p. 373.

55. It is interesting to note that even the population of Athens in the late nineteenth century was a cross-section of various regions of Greece. These internal migrants tended to mingle and patronize shops and services of their own compatriots (i.e., men from their own region or village). One traveller in Athens at the time wrote that "when one has sojourned for a time in Athens it is interesting to note all these little worlds which make the capital a microcosm of Greece." In speaking of one grocery store he says that the owner is a Thessalian and "so are most of his customers. The grocery store owner at the next corner is from Eleusis and the people who frequent his shop are from that countryside." Ferriman, *Home Life in the Hellas*, p. 323. So it was also in North America, whenever a Greek community had been established the same attitudes were transplanted.

56. In Toronto parochial clubs were more broadly based: they tended to represent regions rather than villages. For example the "Karteria" had members originating from Asia Minor (in 1918 it had 100 members), and other clubs representing emigrants from various districts of the Peloponnese and Macedonia.

57. For a detailed description of this conflict and its effects on North American Greek communities, see Saloutos, *Greeks in the United States*, pp. 138-59.

58. Taped interviews of Greek immigrants resident in Toronto.

59. V. Papacosmas, "The Greek Press in America," *Journal of Hellenic Diaspora*, pp. 51-52.

60. Saloutos, *Greeks in the United States*, pp. 163ff.

61. Taped interviews of Greek immigrants in Toronto.

62. Saloutos, *Greeks in the United States*, p. 163.

63. Report of the Committee of the Privy Council Canada, dated February 26, 1921; and letter from the Foreign Office, London, dated April 11, 1921, No. C6637/2927/19; also letter to H.M. Secretary of State for Foreign Affairs, Rt. Hon. the Earl Curzon of Keddleston from the Greek legation dated February 5, 1921, PAC, RG6 A12, 1918, Vol. 10, File No. 2360 (Enquiry into Alleged Anti-Greek Riots in Toronto).

64. Correspondence of Deputy Chief Censor, Ottawa with Foreign Office, London, dated January 18, 1917 regarding a telegram received by the Foreign Office from the British Ambassador in Washington, Canadian Federal Archives.

65. Letter from the Chief Press Censor for Canada, January 19, 1917, Ottawa, PAC.

66. Letter to Deputy Censor, Ottawa, from the Foreign Office, London, January 18, 1917, PAC.

67. Letter from Chief Press Censor, Ottawa, January 22, 1917, PAC.

68. Correspondence regarding the distribution of these two papers and allegations against them in PAC, Vol. 136, File 370-G1, in particular: letters from C. Argyros to Chief Press Censor for Canada dated April 11, 1919, Montreal; from B.K. Salamis to Chief Press Censor of Canada dated May 5, 1919, Montreal; and latter to Thomas Mulvey, Under-Secretary of State from the Chief Press Censor for Canada, Ottawa, May 7, 1919.

69. The *Globe*, Toronto, March 2, 1918.

70. Ibid. It is interesting to note that one of the main reasons for Mr. Walsh, the Consul-General's visit to Toronto was to "take a registration of all Greeks in the City." This was most probably at the request of the Chief Press Censor for Canada.

71. Letter to Immigration Minister, Ottawa, dated September 4, 1929, from Vice-Consul for Greece at Toronto, N.K. Martin, PAC File No. 998358. See also letter to J.S. Fraser, Division Commissioner of Immigration Ottawa, from D.H. Chisholm, K.C., Port Hope, November 15, 1927, PAC File No. 998358. Also taped interview of Greek immigrants in Toronto.

72. Saloutos, *Greeks in the United States*, pp. 256-57, for similar trends in the United States. "By the mid-1920s, the intense Greek nationalistic feelings of the prewar era were disappearing. America had been changing the immigrants . . . it was eroding Greek customs, traditions, the old World Heritage . . . the political situation in Greece ceased to be the principal topic of conversation . . . the house lot in Milwakee, Chicago or St. Paul was beginning to mean more than the vineyard in Archadia." These same attitudes were expressed by the old Greek immigrants who were interviewed.

73. The *Globe*, Toronto, March 2, 1918, "The Greeks were dispersed throughout the city."

74. Many of the people interviewed stressed the fact that, especially by the mid-1930s, many members of the community were moving to other towns and cities as a result of the difficulties they encountered due to the depression. Members of the parish were constantly decreasing and people criticized the need for a larger building for the church since "our people are all leaving." Mr. S. Jannetakes, taped interview.

75. Vlassis, *Greeks in Canada*, pp. 14-15.

76. Saloutos, *Greeks in the United States*, pp. 246-50.

77. Ibid., p. 250.

78. Taped interviews: Ms. H. Baille, G. Marmon. Also see Vlassis, *Greeks in Canada*, p. 16.

79. St. George Young Ladies Association and the St. George Young Men's Association, taped interviews particularly H. Baille.

80. *The Greek Orthodox Church*, p. 18.

81. Vlassis, *Greeks in Canada*, p. 12.

82. Ibid., pp. 16-17. The headquarters for the fund was in Montreal. It was directed by the national committee headed by George Genetakes (president). The fund collected half a million dollars for relief work in Greece.

The Beginnings of Ukrainian Settlement in Toronto, 1891-1939

Zoriana Yaworsky Sokolsky

Among the first Ukrainians to visit Toronto (York) were the mercenary soldiers of the de Meuron and de Watterville battalions who fought in the War of 1812 and who for their services received land grants on the Rideau River near Perth, Ontario, and in the Red River valley at the present site of Winnipeg.[1] All were from Eastern Galicia in Western Ukraine.

The first Ukrainian to settle permanently in Toronto was Charles George Horetzky who in 1891 had a house built at 88 Bedford Street and lived there until his death. Horetzky was born in Scotland of a Ukrainian father and a Scottish mother and came to Canada in 1856. He worked for the Hudson's Bay Company in northern Ontario until 1871. Then, upon the recommendation of Sir Charles Tupper who was a friend of his parents, he joined a Canadian National Railway survey party searching for the most suitable mountain pass through the Western Cordilleras. As a result of this work, Horetzky left much valuable pictorial information not only of the Rocky Mountains and British Columbia but also of northern Ontario which he explored later.[2]

However, this cannot be regarded as the beginning of the Ukrainian settlement in Toronto; that had to wait until the beginning of the 1900s when large numbers of Ukrainians began to arrive in Canada.

The beginning of permanent settlement can be traced to the arrival of three young men, Panteleymon (Peter) Ostapowich, Wasyl (William) Neterpka and Joseph Strachalsky, who on April 15, 1903, arrived from Pennsylvania and had settled in Toronto. Born in Eastern Galicia, they first emigrated to the eastern United States where there was already a large Ukrainian settlement in the coal-mining towns of Pennsylvania. Dissatisfied with the hard work and low pay in the coal mines, the three men came to this fast-growing and industrializing city in search of better work.

In Toronto they found a Jewish population of about five thousand living in the Ward, of which a large segment came from the villages and towns of both Eastern (Russian) and Western (Austrian) Ukraine. Although ethnically and religiously different, they were their countrymen and thus it is no wonder that the first Ukrainians became boarders in Jewish homes. As the Ward was the primary immigrant reception area, it became the first reception area for single Ukrainian immigrants also. But not for long. As Ukrainians arrived and the first Ukrainian boardinghouses were established, settlement began to evolve west of the Ward, in the vicinity of Queen Street and Spadina Avenue, where the housing was better and the air cleaner. This area still contains many Ukrainian churches, institutions, stores and restaurants and is still inhabited by many Ukrainians of which a large percentage are old single men.

After 1905 many Jews emigrated directly from Ukraine to Toronto and this, too, must have influenced Ukrainians' destination as they heard of the fast-growing industrial city in Eastern Canada.

Another early concentration of Ukrainians evolved in the Junction area of West Toronto. The new industries locating around the Canadian Pacific Railway offered many jobs and the residential area was clean and pleasant. Already by 1909 it contained the largest number of Ukrainians and when in 1914 the St. Josaphat Church was built at 110 Franklin Avenue, the surrounding streets with their main commercial axis of Royce Avenue (now Dupont Street) became the heart of the Ukrainian settlement. By 1919 the area contained some 2,500 Ukrainians and most cultural activities took place there. Both centres were reached by the Dundas streetcar.

Ukrainian immigration to Toronto proceeded fairly quickly and by the beginning of 1911 there were some 2,500 Ukrainians.[3] It is probable that by the outbreak of the First World War the number of Ukrainians reached 4,000. During the war years it increased further, as industries changed to war production and there was a great demand for workers. Although the immigration from Europe was halted in 1914, many Ukrainians came from the mines and forests of northern Ontario and from the farms of western Canada as the life in cities was easier and wages were high. On November 1, 1920, the *Trans-Oceanic Herald,* which was edited by Paul Crath (Krat) in Toronto, reported that there were close to 40,000 Ukrainians in eastern Canada at the end of the First World War and Toronto led with 9,000. Although this figure could be inflated, these figures cannot be verified. The census of Canada enumerated Ukrainians as Austrians, Galicians, Ruthenians, Poles, Russians, Bukovinians, and others, and the Toronto city directories often listed them only as "foreigners."

Most of the earliest immigrants were young single people, predominantly men, whose prime purpose was to earn money to improve their financial position. In 1906 Volodymyr Anastazievsky wrote in the *Canadian Farmer:*

> Eastern Canada was merely a stopping place — a temporary way-station-for the Ukrainians who only stayed here long enough to earn sufficient money to take them 'farther into Canada,' to settle firmly on the farms. There were some of them who, having made enough money, would go back to Ukraine, gather up their family and return again to Western Canada, to settle on the farms — to be their own 'hospodar' (landlord). The soil was always like a magnet to the land-loving Ukrainian villager. There is not any problem of getting a job here as the "bosses" are very pleased with the way our people work.[4]

These young men moved continually in search of higher-paying jobs. The men often disappeared from Toronto to work in the forests and mines of the Canadian Shield, on the construction of railways in northern Ontario, and in the plants of other Ontario towns. Many reappeared again as the outdoor jobs stopped for the winter, hoping to find some other work to tide them over until spring. There were also many farmers from as far away as the prairies who hoped to earn the badly needed cash during the winter months and who returned to their farms in time for the spring sowing. Thus, the early community was transient in nature and did not stabilize until the outbreak of the First World War, when the War Aliens' Act was passed in 1914 requiring all men over eighteen to register and report regularly to the police stations.

While the earliest immigrants to Toronto might have come with the intention of making enough money to buy a farm in the prairies, this soon changed as they found life in cities easier and more comfortable than on farms. As they sent money to their families at home, they also wrote about the great work opportunities and their "good life" in Toronto; thus they instigated further immigration and soon surrounded themselves with relatives and friends. The earliest marriages began to take place by 1905.

Ukrainians arrived in Canada in groups and Toronto was no exception. During the peak immigration years from 1908 to 1912, groups of up to thirty people came, often from the same village or district. Their arrival was prepared for by relatives and friends who rented flats and often houses and sometimes took them in as boarders. By 1911 there were several Ukrainian boardinghouses in the vicinity of York and King streets, where the largest number of single men resided.

Most Ukrainians came from Eastern Galicia, in particular the districts of Husiatyn, Horodenka, Zboriv, Zolochiv, Ternopil, Brody, Tovmach, Terebovla, Dolyna, Chortkiv, Radykhiv, Zalischyky, Borschiv, Pidhaytsi, Kalush, from Bukovina (Chernivtsi) and from the central Ukraine of the Kiev region. As most came from the villages and towns, they formed a very homogeneous group culturally and since almost all were from farming families, most had had only a few years of elementary education. Domestic arts and crafts practised at home equipped them with the necessary survival skills, which they often used to good advantage in jobs in Toronto. Women worked in clothing establishments, in factories, hotels, restaurants and as domestics, while men were employed in construction, manufacturing of various sorts, shipping in Toronto harbour and at any other job available to them. Lacking a knowledge of English and specific skills, at first they often performed the most difficult and dangerous work.

Religiously, however, they formed a diversified group. While the greatest numbers were Ukrainian Catholics of Byzantine rite (Uniates) (75 to 80 per cent), a smaller number (15 to 20 per cent) were of the Latin rite, known as "Latynnyky," and a very few were Ukrainian Orthodox (of Byzantine rite) from the regions of Bukovina and central Ukraine. Being used to a well-organized church life at home, all found themselves without their own priests or any spiritual guidance, and from the beginning were exposed to the proselytizing efforts of Protestant churches.

In 1894 the Vatican prohibited married clergy (which was the norm in Ukraine) from leaving Europe with the emigrating Ukrainians. Further, since such clergy were not accepted by the Canadian Roman Catholic hierarchy, this led to a catastrophic scarcity of Byzantine-rite Catholic priests in Canada.[5] Thus, in the early settlement period Ukrainians in Canada had to rely heavily on visiting priests from the eastern United States where the number of Ukrainian priests was larger.

When the first Ukrainians arrived in Toronto, they found a small Syrian Greek Catholic (Melchite) church at the corner of Victoria and Shuter streets, then known as the St. Vincent Chapel and later renamed Our Lady of Assumption. It had been given to the Syrians for their use by the Toronto Roman Catholic archdiocese and it is quite probable that some Ukrainians of Byzantine rite attended there, although they did not understand the Arabic language.[6]

Ukrainians also relied on the Roman Catholic churches for the necessary religious services, although many did not attend regularly as they waited for their own priest. The church records of the Roman Catholic churches show that as early as 1905 Ukrainians married and baptised their children at St. Mary's Church and St. Michael's Cathedral in the city and St. Helen's Church in Brockton.

The first report of a visiting Ruthenian priest (as Ukrainians were called until the 1920s) dates from 1906, when Rev. J. Schweitzer, of Berlin (now Kitchener) reported to the Archbishop of Toronto, Most Rev. D. O'Connor, that:

> Last year a certain individual, whether he was a real or bogus priest is not known, had been in the city. Without the knowledge of your Grace or your jurisdiction he went from house to house hearing the confessions of those who were foolish enough to give him $1.00 beforehand — others he would not hear! Moreover, as many, among whom also Mr. John, state, he was smoking cigarettes while hearing confession. This makes the people suspect, that he was an enterprising Jew making use of the confessional for making money![7]

In April 1907 Rev. John Velyhorsky of Black Rock, N.Y. visited Toronto and his letter of introduction by the Most Rev. Charles H. Cullen, Bishop of Buffalo, is on file with the Archdiocese of Toronto.

In 1909 Ukrainians had finally succeeded in obtaining their own priest when in February 1909 Rev. John A. Zaklynsky arrived. He took up residence at 25 Edith Avenue in West Toronto where he converted his living room to a chapel. As the premises were too small to hold many people, the members of the newly formed parish committee approached several Roman Catholic pastors for permission to use their churches but were turned down.[8] After a few months Rev. Zaklynsky left Toronto and it was only by chance that some Torontonians visited Buffalo, and approached Rev. Leo I. Sembratowicz, the pastor of the Ruthenian church there, who during 1909 and 1910 commuted occasionally to Toronto.

In October 1909 Father Sembratowicz came in contact with Very Rev. Dr. Alfred E. Burke, the fiery first president of the newly created Catholic Church Extension Society of Canada and the editor of the weekly *Catholic Register*. This contact not only allowed the use of the St. Cecilia Church in West Toronto for religious services but also brought to the fore the plight of the priest-less Ukrainians and led to the creation of the first Ukrainian Catholic mission in Toronto. Thus, the Archbishop of Toronto, Fergus P. McEvay, personally wrote to the Apostolic Delegate to Canada, the Most Rev. Donato

Sbarretti, on June 16, 1910, asking for an "unmarried good Ruthenian Priest" who wrote to Cardinal Gotti, the Prefect of the Propaganda in Vatican who in turn had communicated with the Metropolitan Anrei Szeptycki, the prelate of the Ukrainian Catholic Church in Western Ukraine, who at that time was visiting all major Ukrainian centres in Canada and the United States, stating:

> . . . a letter has just come here from the Cardinal Prefect of the Sacred Congregation, in which His Eminence states that, having communicated the petition to Mgr. Szeptycki, Archbishop of Lemberg, he is happy to be able to place at Your Grace's disposition the Rev. Charles Jermy, a native of the Diocese of Stanislaopolis. He is 34 years of age, a celibate, and according to the attestation of the Bishop *a sacerdos integris moribus et valde pius*. The Sacred Congregation has written to his Bishop, in order that he may give instructions to this priest to leave as soon as possible for Canada.[9]

As Metropolitan Szeptycki (also spelt Sheptytsky) was in Buffalo visiting Father Sembratowicz, both came to Toronto on November 25, 1911, where together with Archbishop Fergus P. McEvay and Father Burke they laid the foundation for the formation of the Ukrainian parish and for the establishment of the Ruthenian rite faculty at the soon-to-be opened St. Augustine Seminary in Scarborough.[10] Two months later Rev. Dr. Charles (Carlo) Yermy, accompanied by the Lithuanian Byzantine-rite priest, Rev. Vincent R. Delianis of Philadelphia whom Bishop Ortynsky had sent to help Father Yermy get established, was already in Toronto. On February 5, 1911, he celebrated his first Liturgy at the old St. Helen's Church which was made available to the Ukrainian community until its own church would be built. For this purpose the Roman Catholic Episcopal Corporation for the Diocese of Toronto at the end of March purchased two building lots at the corner of Ossington Avenue and Harrison Street at a cost of $10,000.[11]

Father Yermy began to organize the parish which at first he intended to place under the patronage of St. Joseph but in May changed it to St. Nicholas. The old St. Helen's Church was renamed the Greek Catholic Ruthenian Church and its interior was beautified in the Ukrainian manner. The presbytery at 821 Dundas Street was furnished with the help of the St. Peter Women Auxiliary and the ladies of the Women's Auxiliary of the Catholic Church Extension Society of Canada began teaching English classes two evenings a week. Two socials were organized to raise money for the new parish and Father Yermy also he began to organize another parish in Oshawa. It seemed that everything was going well when in the middle of June Father Yermy, offended by some parishioners, abruptly left Toronto. This infuriated the good parishioners who called a public meeting to chasten the offenders. However, Father Yermy did not return.

To secure a new pastor, in January 1912, the new Archbishop of Toronto, Neil McNeil, wrote to Bishop Ortynsky in Philadelphia and Father Sembratowicz was asked to help. He commuted twice a month from Buffalo to Toronto while the Archdiocese helped to defray his travelling expenses. To aid the church financially, on November 25, 1911, he brought his parish's drama club (the Kotlarevsky Ruthenian Dramatic Circle of the St. Josaphat's Ruthenian Congregation in Buffalo) and its orchestra (the Alpha-Omega) which under his direction presented Toronto's first Ukrainian operetta "Natalka Poltavka" at the St. Patrick's hall on McCaul Street. In December the Immaculate Conception Society (Mariyska Druzhyna) was formed of some thirty girls and women who also looked after the church. Men formed an Enlightenment Society ("Prosvita") which met every Thursday and Sunday evenings in rented quarters at 40 Pelham Street.

At the beginning of February 1912, Rev. Joseph (Osyp) Boyarczuk, sent by Bishop Ortynsky of Philadelphia, had arrived in Toronto and on February 17 he was officially appointed pastor by Toronto's Archbishop Neil McNeil. The 32-year-old energetic priest at once began to enlarge his parish and collect money for the erection of the church. In May 1913 a house was purchased for the rectory at 143 Franklin Avenue in West Toronto and a building lot across the rectory at 110 Franklin Avenue, where on July 20, 1913, the cornerstone for the church was blessed in the presence of Archbishop Neil McNeil by the first Ukrainian Catholic Bishop, Nicetas Budka.[12] The church was finished nine months later at a cost of $30,785 — a debt which the Roman Catholic Episcopal Corporation for the Diocese of Toronto in Canada guaranteed — and on Palm Sunday, April 12, 1914. It was consecrated and opened for religious services by Bishop Budka. The parish changed its name to St. Josaphat and the church hall became the focal point of Ukrainian life, housing all Ukrainian activities in West Toronto until 1919.

On August 28, 1913, the St. Augustine's Seminary in Scarborough was officially opened and Rev. Dr. Ambrose Redkewycz was on the original teaching staff. He arrived with Bishop Budka in December 1912 and from 1913 to 1916 was professor at the faculty of theology and philosophy where he taught the Ruthenian rite Liturgy, ecclesiastical chant and cannon law to eleven Ruthenian theology students. It was hoped that the seminary would train and provide the Ukrainian Catholic community with the badly needed priests "to save the faith of these good people."[13]

If one takes into consideration the religious affiliations of

Ukrainians in the villages and towns of central Western Ukraine from where most Ukrainian immigrants came, it is probable that Latynnyky formed 10 to 20 per cent of Toronto's early Ukrainian community.[14] In the city they attended St. Mary's Church at Bathurst and Adelaide streets and St. Michael's Cathedral; in the west they worshipped at St. Helen's in Brockton and St. Cecilia's in the Junction. When in 1906 Rev. Paul Sobczak, began to commute regularly from Berlin to look after the Polish Roman Catholics, they joined the Polish congregation and later formed the basis of St. Stanislaus parish.[15] In 1909 Rev. B. Jasiak of Pittsburgh was assigned to St. Michael's Cathedral, where the St. John's Chapel was given to the Poles for worship and thus the foundation for the Polish Catholic parish was laid. When two years later, at Archbishop McEvay's request, Rev. Joseph Hinzmann came to Toronto from Pittsburgh, and Eugene O'Keefe in his great generosity bought and donated the Western Presbyterian Church at 12 Denison Avenue for their use, St. Stanislaus (Kostka) parish was officially formed. The parish was composed primarily of Ukrainian Roman Catholics (Latynnyky) and to a lesser degree of Poles, Germans (from East Prussia who spoke Polish) and some Lithuanians. As Latynnyky intermarried freely with Ukrainians of Byzantine rite, many of the latter also attended religious services there, and belonged to the parish. This was a constant irritation to Father Boyarczuk who complained about it often to Archbishop Neil McNeil.[16]

During Father Hinzmann's pastorship the relations between the Ukrainian and Polish parishes were close, as Ukrainians intermingled freely and the two priests were friends. However, after 1920 the two priests left and relations deteriorated as nationalistic feelings, brought out by the Ukrainian-Polish war in Western Ukraine, were awakened. The war ended with the Polish occupation and when reports of ever-increasing oppression and forced polonization of Ukrainians by the Polish government in the 1920s and 1930s reached Ukrainians in Toronto, the anti-Polish feelings were quite strong. Latynnyky, too, were exposed to polonization efforts in St. Stanislaus parish under the pastorship of Rev. John Joseph Dekowski, who was a Polish patriot decorated with the French Croix de Guerre and the Polish Cross of Virtuti Military for his services as the chaplain in General Haller's army which helped to overthrow the Western Ukrainian National Republic in 1920. The turmoil which resulted within the parish culminated in the establishment of the Polish National Church as many parishioners left. Those who remained wrote to the Archbishop of Toronto on September 13, 1934, complaining that Father Dekowski ''does not teach God's word.''

On May 24, 1935, they petitioned the Archbishop to establish another Polish parish and to send them a Franciscan father, as

''St. Stanislaus is made up of three different extractions of people, from Russia, Austria and Germany and there are two classes of people from Austria and Germany, these are in the one class and from Russia we have another class, and on account of these two classes there is no sympathy or affection to Rev. Dekowski.

Rev. Dekowski was ordered by Archbishop J.C. McGuigan to vacate the parish by June 30, 1935[17] and the new pastor, Rev. Stanislaus Puchniak, who was educated by the Oblate Fathers in St. Boniface, Manitoba, and who spoke Ukrainian well, united the parish.

In 1908 John A. Kolesnikoff, a native of Kherson, Southern Ukraine, and a Baptist preacher from Scranton, Pennsylvania, was hired by the Baptist Home Mission Board for missionary work among Ukrainians, Poles, Russians, Bulgarians and Macedonians, as he knew these languages. Soon he opened three missions in Toronto: one at 426 King Street East where he lived with his family and where his main activities took place; the second at $10^{1}/_{2}$ Alice Street, which was later moved to 38 Elizabeth Street and then to 124 York Street; and the third, opened in 1913, at 1546 Dundas Street in West Toronto. The last two were for Ukrainians, Poles and Russians, while the King Street mission was predominantly for Russians, Bulgarians and Macedonians who lived to the east of it. The main attraction of the missions were the evening courses in English and native languages which were attended by many people. Each mission was also equipped with a reading room, which Kolesnikoff called a "Prosvita," where native newspapers and magazines were available. The West Toronto Mission was also furnished with a modern kitchen where cooking, sewing, and dressmaking were taught. At the King Street Mission Dr. James Simpson conducted a free dispensary one evening each week and on Thanksgiving, Christmas and New Year's Day dinners were held there. There was also an annual picnic on Dominion Day with sports and food. While these activities offered educational and social opportunities, they all were accompanied by Bible reading, prayers and preaching, aimed at conversion. To recruit people, Kolesnikoff preached often at the corner of Elizabeth Street and on Royce and Franklin avenues in West Toronto and during the summer months at the corner of King and Trinity streets at 5:30 on Sunday evenings. This latter street meeting attracted more people; the Macedonian Brass Band played religious songs and it was hoped that the people would follow to the King Street Mission where a Gospel service was held.

To further his religious work among Ukrainians, Kolesnikoff

began publishing a religious four-page magazine, the *Good Friend*, in Ukrainian which next year was enlarged to sixteen pages and renamed the *Witness of the Truth*. In fact, it was the first Ukrainian publication not only in Toronto but in eastern Canada. The *Witness of the Truth* was co-edited by Andrew Mylanyn (a former teacher in Western Ukraine), Wladyslav Kryszynsky (a former student at the Lviv University) and Wasyl (William) Cwior (a printer) who knew the Ukrainian language better than Kolesnikoff. It was printed at the King Street Mission and mailed throughout Canada, the United States and overseas to Ukraine. This bi-monthly publication was published uninterruptedly till the autumn of 1917, when Kolesnikoff became seriously ill. Kolesnikoff also published *The Ukrainian Arfa*, a book of 125 religious songs many of which he himself translated from English and which he reprinted in 1912 in a smaller version under the name *Kymbaly*. His other publications in Ukrainian consisted of small religious pamphlets such as ''Baptists and Their Teachings,'' ''Who Are the Protestants?'' and others.

In April 1915 Kolesnikoff's Slavic missions consisted of fifty-three baptized Ukrainian and Russian members.[18] After his death in March 1918, the missions were cared for by his son-in-law, A. Ambrosov, and after the latter left Toronto, by Boris Kluchkov, a Russian who did not speak Ukrainian. Later the missions were united in the Beverley Street Church and have lost their Ukrainian character.

The Independent Greek Church, popularly known as the Ruthenian (Ukrainian) Independent Church and also the Independent Orthodox Church was formed in 1903 in western Canada as a result of the lack of Ukrainian Catholic clergy and to combat the proselytizing efforts of the Presbyterian Church. Ivan Bodrug and Ivan Negrych, both Ukrainian public school teachers in western Canada, were its chief promoters. Like other ministers of that church, both were trained at the Presbyterian Manitoba College in Winnipeg and were funded by the Presbyterian Board of Home Missions and Social Service. The Independent Greek Church formed a separate branch of the Presbyterian Church until June 1913.

A mission of the Independent Greek Church was established in the spring of 1911 in Toronto when Ivan Bodrug approached the Presbyterian Board of Home Missions and the latter agreed to its funding. It was known as the Chapel of the Holy Trinity and religious services were held by Rev. Volodymyr Kupczynsky in the church hall of St. Andrew's Institute at 80 Nelson Street every Sunday at 10:30 a.m. The mission had some one hundred Ukrainians attending, most of whom were probably the Ukrainian Orthodox who did not have their own priest until 1926. Rev. Kupczynsky left

Toronto at the end of the summer and his place was taken by Volodymyr Pendykowsky from Newark, who later worked at the Julian Kunikewich's International Steamship Ticket Agency and then opened his own agency.

In June 1913 a Presbyterian convention was held in Massey Hall in Toronto and was attended by all ministers of the Independent Greek Church, who at the same time held their own "sobor" (convention). As it was revealed that the Presbyterian Church was losing money heavily through its expenditures on the support of the foreign missions, the consistorium of the Independent Greek Church was given an ultimatum: either join the Presbyterian Church and thus avail itself of its financial help or else detach itself completely from the Presbyterian Church. As the majority voted to join the Presbyterian Church, the Independent Greek Church came to an end.

It is said that the first attempt at organizational life was made when in 1906 a group of Ukrainians met in a private home on Church Street opposite St. Michael's Cathedral to form a mutual benefit society, called the St. Michael's Society (Tovarystvo Sviatoho Mykhaila). In all probability it was the same society which was renewed on October 10, 1910, and which received a charter on November 27, 1911, under the name of the Ruthenian National Benefit Society in Toronto. Its purpose was to provide financial help in case of sickness or disability and "to unite in brotherly love all Ruthenians living in Canada and to spread enlightenment in Ruthenian and English languages among the members and to try for their social and spiritual well-being."[19] To raise money and provide a meeting place for young members, the society rented the Labour Temple Hall at 167 Church Street where dances were held almost every weekend. Sometime in 1913-1914 the society also engaged Humeniy Tymofiy, a choir master, who organized a small choir and a drama club which staged two musical performances, *Oh, Do Not Love Both* (Okh, ta ne luby dvokh) and *Horseback Riders* (Verkhovyntsi). Thus, the society became Toronto's first Ukrainian social and cultural organization.

In 1914 the society changed its patron's name to Taras Shevchenko and in the following years became a much more active organization. After Tymofiy left Toronto, Wasyl Burtnyk took charge of the drama club in 1916 and during the 1916-1917 season alone the society staged eight performances, nineteen dances and an excursion to a park outside the city. In June 1917 the society formed a literary association called Chytalnia Prosvity Imeny Tarasa Shevchenka (The Reading Room of the Taras Shevchenko Prosvita

Society) which became the first Ukrainian library in Toronto; Volodymyr Faryna and Dmytro A. Nykolak donated 134 books for its use. In the fall of the same year the society engaged Nicholas Ziombra from Winnipeg to teach music to the members of the newly formed brass band called the Mykola Lysenko Music Society (Muzychne Tovarystvo imeny Mykoly Lysenka) and to teach the society's choir. In 1919 a children's Ukrainian-language school was formed, where eighty-six children attended three times a week after regular school hours to study such subjects as Ukrainian language, history, geography, music, and culture. This school was in continuous existence till the 1950s.

The formation of the Ukrainian National Republic after the dismemberment of the Austro-Hungarian Empire and its subsequent struggle for survival had profound influence on all Ukrainians in Toronto. The Taras Shevchenko Society believed in an independent Ukraine and supported the struggling Ukrainian state. For this purpose it formed the Aid Ukraine Fund (Fond Pomochi Ukraini) which consisted of voluntary contributions and 10 per cent of all income from Prosvita's enterprises. This money was sent to Lviv, Western Ukraine, to support the cultural and educational institutions which had sprung up, such as the only Ukrainian newspaper, *Country and Freedom* (Zemla ee Vola) and the Ukrainian school, Ridna Shkola. The society also helped Ukrainian war invalids and political prisoners in Lviv and later flood victims in the Carpathian Mountains. In 1919 and again in 1922 it organized public protest meetings in the Star Theatre and Massey Hall against the Polish and Russian oppression in Ukraine and in 1921 and 1922 sent telegrams to the Supreme Council of the Peace Conference in Paris when the latter discussed the fate of Eastern Galicia (Western Ukraine).

In 1920 the Taras Shevchenko Society rejected the proposed union with the Ukrainian Social Democratic organization Zluka, as the latter was becoming increasingly communistic. Thereby it lost some of its active members, and the Mykola Lysenko Music Society fell apart as many of its members joined the Ukrainian Social Democrats. From then on all its public political meetings and national concerts were disrupted by the Ukrainian Social Democrats who supported Russian communism and later the Ukrainian Soviet Socialist Republic while the Taras Shevchenko stood for an independent Ukraine and spoke out against Soviet oppression in the Ukrainian lands.

In 1919 through its many activities which acquainted the Canadian public with the Ukrainian culture, the society began to emerge as the representative of Toronto's Ukrainian community. In this year, with the help of Paul Krat, it organized a Ukrainian corner at the Canadian National Exhibition where Ukrainian embroideries and folk art began to be exhibited every year till 1956. In 1922 its choir began to perform regularly during the Music Day at the CNE and in the 1924-1932 period, under the direction of Yuri Hassan, it achieved such excellence that it staged many concerts for the non-Ukrainian public in Toronto. In 1925 the society sponsored Vasile Avramenko's immigration to Canada who in 1926 with his Toronto folk dance students performed daily at the CNE's Grandstand.

In 1926 the Taras Shevchenko Society changed its name to the Ukrainian People's Home Association and in 1928 purchased its present home at 191 Lippincott Street. The years which followed, till the end of the 1940s, were the busiest and most productive so that the editor of the Toronto daily newspaper *The Evening Telegram*, C.H.J. Snyder, assigned a reporter to cover its activities.

The arrival of Rev. Joseph Boyarczuk in February 1912 signalled the beginning of Ukrainian cultural life in Toronto. Almost at once he organized a church choir and a drama club which under his direction in 1912-1913 staged three plays: *The Stolen Luck* (Ukradene Schastya), *The Betrothal in Honcharivka* (Svatannya na Honcharivtsi), and *The Conscience's Punishment* (Kara Sovisty). The first two plays were staged in St. Peter's Church hall, and the third in St. Mary's Church hall at Adelaide and Bathurst streets. A fourth play, a musical comedy, *Oh, Gregory, Do Not Attend the Soirees* (Oy, ne khody Hrytsyu ta na vechernytsi) was the first play to be performed in the parish's own quarters, St. Josaphat's Church hall, in 1914.[20]

The availability of a permanent meeting place led to the formation of various parish and secular associations. Among the first was the Markian Shashkevych Chytalnia Prosvita (Chytalnia Prosvita imeny Markiana Shashkevycha) which was a literary society with a reading room, a drama club, and a choir. It met every Monday and Thursday evening for rehearsals of plays but its members also sang in the church choir and met on Tuesdays and Fridays. When Semen Kucharsky arrived in Toronto, the first string orchestra was formed of young men who bought their own instruments and who met twice a week for practices at the hall. Unfortunately the orchestra disbanded after three months as an overzealous parish committee member insisted that only paid-up parish members may attend. This offended the young men, who left and who later formed the nucleus of the left wing of the Ukrainian Social Democratic Party, the Russian-Ukrainian Social Revolutionary Group, which in 1919 tried to take over the parish buildings.

In 1914 Father Boyarczuk organized the first Ukrainian-language school for fifteen children who studied the Ukrainian language, music, culture and religion three days a week after regular school hours. The teacher was the church cantor, Ivan Zvarych, later Stepan Prychoda and then Nicholas Yureskiw, whose other duties were also to teach the church choir and assist the parish priest.

As the 1913-1914 years were years of great unemployment and many Ukrainians suffered hardship due to loss of jobs, Father Boyarczuk organized a mutual aid society, The Brotherly Aid (Bratnia Pomich), in 1915 which at five cents a week attracted many members and helped others. The parishioners belonged also to the St. John the Baptist Brotherhood (Bratstvo Sviatoho Khrestytela), formed in 1912, which paid $5 a week in cases of sickness-and death. In 1916 its members joined the newly formed Ukrainian National Association.

In 1915 Father Boyarczuk also instituted two educational courses for adults: an English-language evening course taught by Wladyslav Kryszynsky from November till February 1916 and a course for cantors taught by Father Boyarczuk. The latter did not last long, as the interest of the participants waned. In 1917 the M. Verbytsky Music Society (Muzychne Tovarystvo imeny M. Verbytskoho), a brass band, was formed which in 1919 joined the Ukrainian Social Democrats.

While the parish hall was the centre of cultural life in West Toronto, the mortgages on the church and the rectory weighed heavily on the parish committee who had the additional task to finish and furnish the interior of the church. As a favour to Father Boyarczuk and the Ukrainians who worked there, the Gurney Foundry donated the whole heating system. The altar, which was imported from Lviv, was paid by a "rich English lady" — probably Mrs. Helen McLean French, the daughter of Eugene O'Keefe, who was a great philanthropist. Through the generosity of parishioners a large church bell (known as "Joseph" in honour of Father Boyarczuk) was purchased in 1915 and also a large chandelier, at a cost of $500. Later, a parishioner, Teodor Mushaluk, donated a smaller one and the St. John the Baptist Brotherhood bought two confessionals. In 1917 oak benches to seat seven hundred people were purchased, thus doing away with the burden of moving chairs from the parish hall to the church every Sunday. The church was further beautified in 1918 with eight large religious oil paintings but was not plastered inside until the 1920s. To deflect his parishioners' dissatisfaction with it, Father Boyarczuk in his sermons often compared it to churches in Christ's times.

Father Boyarczuk had a good singing voice and was an excellent orator, but he also had a sharp tongue. Thus, in 1919 at a parish meeting, when two parish committee members began publicly to settle their grievances, Father Boyarczuk, seeing that the meeting was getting out of hand, ended it and left. Sensing the dissatisfaction and an opportunity to take over the parish buildings, the members of the Russian-Ukrainian Social Revolutionary Group in Toronto (who were not members of the parish) jumped in and for three months fanned the flames and agitated against the priest and religion. Father Boyarczuk, seeing the pressure and ridicule exerted on his faithful parishioners, closed the church and suspended all religious services for several weeks. When the church was reopened by Bishop Budka, Father Boyarczuk declined to remain as pastor and Rev. Michael Ircha took his place. Quiet and dedicated, he renewed the church life and restored some of the former parish activities. The community, however, was permanently divided.

As the number of Ukrainians grew in the vicinity of Bathurst and Queen streets, a parochial Ukrainian-language school was instituted there in 1925 by Rev. Andrew Sarmatiuk, the then pastor of St. Josaphat's parish. A children's Liturgy was begun on Sundays at 9 a.m. at St. Mary's Church hall. It was so well attended that in 1928 the parish purchased the Missionary Tabernacle at 146 Bathurst Street for $24,500 and renamed it Our Lady of Perpetual Help Church. It, too, became the focal point of religious and cultural life in the city and on October 8, 1937, was instituted as a separate parish, with Rev. Peter Kamenecky (one of the first Ukrainian Catholic priests to have graduated from the St. Augustine's Seminary in 1915) as its first pastor.

In spring 1937 St. Josaphat's parish purchased another church in East Toronto which in June 1939 became Holy Eucharist parish, with Rev. Steven Borys as its first pastor.

Socialism in Western Ukraine began to take root in the 1870s where it originated as a force against the national and social oppression under Austrian rule. It was brought to Canada by former high school students who settled in cities and who in 1907 formed their first branches in Winnipeg, Portage La Prairie and Nanaimo. In 1909 these branches formed the Federation of Ukrainian Social Democrats which in 1910 joined with Jews and Latvians to form the Social Democratic Party of Canada. In 1914 the federation was renamed the Ukrainian Social Democratic Party and when the latter was banned by the Canadian government in September 1918, it continued legally under the new name of the Ukrainian Labor Temple Association which in 1924 became incorporated nationally as the Ukrainian Labor Farmer Temple Association. It was a centralized cultural-educational labour organization whose activities were directed to the promotion of the communist cause among Ukrainians. [21]

The first attempt to organize a socialist group in Toronto was made in 1911 but it was not until the following year when young men began to visit homes to recruit members that the first socialist organization evolved in the centre of the city. It did not make much progress, however, until the arrival of Ivan Stefanicky from Winnipeg in 1915 who became its leader and who began publishing a newspaper which promoted the socialist ideas.

The outbreak of the Russian Revolution and the formation of the Ukrainian National Republic divided the Ukrainian socialists into two groups: those who supported the Ukrainian National Republic (a non-communist independent state) and those who drifted toward international communism, supporting the Russian Revolution and later the Ukrainian Soviet Socialist Republic. The latter called themselves the Russian-Ukrainian Social Revolutionary Group in Toronto and collaborated closely with Russian, Jewish and Polish social democrats.

The events in Ukraine were of great concern to Ukrainians in Toronto not only because their families and relatives were there but also because most of them intended to return home. This concern was exploited by the Russian-Ukrainian Social Revolutionary Group who together with Jews, Russians and Poles staged "informative" meetings and dances where speakers informed the public about the events in their homeland and showed pictures of the war. As they attracted many people, large premises were rented, such as the Massey Hall, the Broadway Hall at 450 Spadina Avenue, the Lyric Theatre at Agnes and Terauley streets, and the Odd Fellows' Hall at 404 Bathurst Street. The meetings were the vehicle to promote socialism and were always begun with the singing of the "International," followed by speakers in Ukrainian, Russian, Polish, Jewish and English. The choir provided several appropriate songs (for example, the funeral march in remembrance of those who were killed by Tsar Nicholas ii) and the meetings closed with collections for some socialist cause, such as the Russian Revolution Fund, a purchase of a printing press for the *Labour Gazette* in Kiev, or a supportive telegram to the communist regime.[22]

There were also concerts and socialist plays by the group's drama club, such as *Sichynsky-Potocki, The Executors* (Ubiynyky), *The American Worker* (Amerykansky Robitnyk) and others. The Social Revolutionary Group called on workers to leave their jobs and march in the May Parade (1917), to donate money to the fund for the dissemination of the social revolutionary propaganda in Russia on "Red Sunday" (June 3, 1917), to come to the concert and ball in support of the Russian Revolution Fund (April 14, 1917) and others. The leaders responsible for the activities of the group were Ivan Stefanicky, Ivan Boychuk, Hryhory Mak (until his return to Russia in June 1917), S. Waskan, L. Barylsky, W. Portas, Ivan Malaszczuk, W. Sitek, J. Zradowsky and others.

The arrival of Ivan Stefanicky in Toronto in 1915 gave impetus to the Ukrainian Social Democratic Party in Toronto. He was a moderate social democrat who as the editor of the socialist newspaper *The Working People* (Robochy Narod) in Winnipeg, opposed the leftist views which the paper and the party were taking, so he left and began publishing a new socialist newspaper *The Conscious Strength* (Svidoma Syla) in Toronto. It began as a semi-monthly at the end of 1915 and its purpose was to enlighten and educate the working class. In April 1916 it was decided to change *The Conscious Strength* to *The Workers' Word* (Robitnyche Slovo) which was officially done at the end of 1916. *The Workers' Word* became a weekly newspaper of four pages which was published by the Workers' Publishing Co-operative Association at 516 Queen Street West every Saturday. Its editorial staff consisted of Ivan Stefanicky as chief editor, Hryhory Mak (till the end of June 1917) and Paul Krat (after H. Mak left) as co-editors, and M. Yeremiychuk as the administrator. All were former colleagues at *The Working People* with the same political views.

The Workers' Publishing Co-operative Association also published a series of small socialist publications in booklet form, many of which were translated from Russian by Stefanicky and Mak. Others were written by Paul Krat or translated from English and other languages.

The Canadian government was well aware of the Social Revolutionary Group's activities and as *The Workers' Word* waged war against capitalism, war and conscription, in June 1917 Stafanicky was charged with agitation to destroy the capitalist system. On June 10, 1917, the police raided one of the group's meetings and almost the whole Social Revolutionary Group (eighty-five comrades) were put behind bars overnight. They were released next day after Stefanicky intervened (he was a Canadian citizen) but future meetings were forbidden at risk of $5,000 fine and imprisonment at the internment camps. The following September (1918) the Ukrainian Socialist Democratic Party of Canada was banned and all Ukrainian publications were suspended. The Workers' Publishing Co-operative Association was promptly renamed The Workmen's Book and Publishing Company and the selling of the booklets continued. The Workmen's Book and Publishing Company was incorporated in 1918 with a capital of $40,000 divided into 4,000 shares at $10 each.

By the time the ban was lifted, Stefanicky had settled his differences with the Ukrainian Social Democrats in Winnipeg and did not renew the publication of *The Workers' Word*; instead the Winnipeg paper became the official organ of the party (by then it was the Ukrainian Labour Temple Association). In January 1920 the Workmen's Book and Publishing Company began publishing *The*

Trans-Atlantic Herald (Zamorsky Vistnyk) which was a semi-monthly educational journal. In November of the same year the company moved to its own premises at 504 Queen Street West.

As already mentioned, the Russian-Ukrainian Social Revolutionary Group tried to take over the St. Josaphat's parish property in West Toronto and during the agitation process it appointed a committee to begin a court action. The latter, however, was dropped when their lawyer advised the group that it could not win as the parish property was registered in the name of the Roman Catholic Episcopal Corporation for the Diocese of Toronto, which had guaranteed the parish's mortgage.[23] When the agitation stopped, a large group of former parishioners left the parish and formed a new organization called Free Ukraine (Vilna Ukraina). It consisted of 360 members who formed a drama club, a Ukrainian-language school for their children and educational courses for the illiterates. Politically, it stood against the Polish occupation of Western Ukraine. In 1920 the Russian-Ukrainian Social Revolutionary Group proposed a loose union with other existing Ukrainian groups Zoria, a drama club, and Free Ukraine became Zluka No. 1 (there were five such Zlukas). At this point many of its members left and when Zluka drifted toward communism, it lost many more of its adherents. In 1922 Zluka was officially renamed The Ukrainian Labor Temple Association and in 1924 it joined the Communist Party of Canada.

During the 1920s communist groups grew as the cultural and literary activities attracted new members. In West Toronto a children's mandolin orchestra was organized in 1923, a literary society in 1924, a women's group and a youth group in 1927. Although the official party membership was low (there were only thirty-two members), with the help of other Labor Temples in Canada they built their own premises at Royce Avenue in 1926. The group in the city centre also grew and in 1927 had built its own Labor Temple at 300 Bathurst Street, which later became the provincial centre of communist activities.

It is impossible not to mention the activities of Paul Krat in the early history of Ukrainians in Toronto.

Paul Krat was a well-known social democrat who fled from Ukraine as a result of his revolutionary activities during the 1905 Russian Revolution and in 1906 at the Lviv University. He came to Canada in 1907 under the assumed name of Paul Ternenko. As such he joined the Social Radical group in Winnipeg (composed of former high school students) and became the first editor of their newspaper, *The Red Banner* (Chervony Prapor). Later he became the editor of the socialist newspaper *The Working People* (Robochy Narod) but left the newspaper and the Ukrainian Social Democratic Party as they both were taking the leftist course. He came to Toronto in 1917 where both I. Stefanicky and M. Yeremiychuk were publishing *The Workers' Word.* Although Krat declared himself to have broken with the party and to be an independent international socialist, he joined the publishing staff of *The Workers' Word* and thus continued to be in the socialist milieu.

While on staff, in the fall of 1917 he organized the Aid Ukrainian Immigrant Committee in response to the anti-alien feeling which Ukrainians faced in 1917. This, as he and other Ukrainians felt, was the result of public ignorance and therefore it was the purpose of the Aid Ukrainian Immigrant Committee to provide better information to the Canadian authorities on the Ukrainian Community and to change government restrictive laws against them. Another purpose was to help the newly formed Ukrainian state by providing it with badly needed skilled workers at the end of the war, especially with those from Canada and the United States who wanted to return home. Thus, Krat invited the most prominent Ukrainians in North America to join in the formation of similar branches in their localities and to take a census of all Ukrainians in Canada and the United States. In Toronto I. Stefanicky, C. Waskan, M. Yeremiychuk and Paul Krat formed the executive of the Aid Ukrainian Immigrant Committee and on December 10, 1917, had it incorporated. They appealed to those who wanted to return home to register and for that purpose the Workers' Publishing Co-operative Association printed registration forms and asked for one dollar donations to cover its costs.

In November 1917 Krat opened a Ukrainian night school of higher learning, called the Ukrainian Free School (Ukrainska Wilna Shkola) but popularly known as the Ukrainian Free University (Ukrainsky Wilny Universytet). Michael Petrowsky, who attended the school, described it in his autobiography as extremely interesting and useful.[24] It offered courses five evenings a week in political geography, ancient history, sociology, evolution, English language, Ukrainian grammar and public speaking. The school was located at 516 Queen Street West in the premises of the Taras Shevchenko Society and in 1919 had fifty students.

In January, Krat renewed his former humorous publication *Kadylo*, which he tried to finance by forming the Kadylo Synod, based on five-dollar donations. The publication consisted of eight pages of satire in prose, verse and jokes. As its readers did not readily part with their money, *Kadylo* soon died.

In 1919, to everyone's surprise, Paul Krat became a Presbyterian minister and opened a Ukrainian Mission at 516 Queen Street West. This mission was later moved to 160 Dowling

Avenue, then to 175 Shaw Street, and to 48 Peterboro Avenue in 1923. In West Toronto he held religious services in the small Presbyterian church at the corner of Edwin and Royce avenues, which was also used as the Russian Orthodox church where the Ukrainian Orthodox from Bukovina and central Ukraine attended. The membership of his mission was small, as seen from the following table compiled from the *Acts and Proceedings of the (46-51) Assembly of the Presbyterian Church*:

	1919 -20	1920 -21	1921 -22	1922 -23	1923 -24	1924 -25
Preaching stations	1	1	1	1	1	1
No. of elders	1	1	1	2[1]	1	1
Families	6	10	7	14	29	23
Single persons	40	16	41	16	18	11
Baptism:						
infants	1		3	2	1	2
adults	0	0	0	0	0	0
Sabbath school teachers & officers	4	0	0	0	0	0
Scholars (pupils)	50[2]					
Total individuals under pastoral care	15			65	111	103[3]
Communicants received				16	13	7

[1]Mr. Wm. Davidson from Agincourt was a representative helper at 48 Peterboro Avenue Mission.
[2]Students at the Ukrainian Free School.
[3]60 on roll.

To increase his membership during the inspection of his elders, Krat often announced public lectures and debates which attracted a large number of Ukrainians.[25] In June 1923 he began to publish a religious magazine, *Faith and Knowledge* (Vira ta Znannia) which was printed in Wasyl Cwior's printing shop until 1925.

In 1922 Krat attended the Ukrainian Evangelical Conference at Rochester, N.Y., which was held by ministers who wanted to preserve the identity of the Ukrainian Reformed Church. The conference created the Ukrainian Evangelical Alliance whose main purpose was to further bring together all Ukrainians of the Evangelical Reformed Religions and to hold annual conferences either in Canada or the United States. In 1925 the conference adopted a resolution to send to Western Ukraine, then under Polish rules three clergymen who were to head the Protestant communities where they were active. Paul Krat was chosen to be the first of these missionaries, and having availed himself of the Presbyterian Foreign Missions Fund (which allocated approximately half a million dollars to promote Presbyterianism abroad), he went to the town of Kolomyia where he established a Presbyterian mission and a printing house (Vydavnytstvo "Vira ee Nauka").

In 1929 the Ukrainian Presbyterian (Reformed) Church was formulated by pastor Michael Fesenko who had arrived in Toronto from the Princeton Theological Seminary. In 1930 the church was formally accepted into the fold of the Presbyterian Church of Canada and before the outbreak of the Second World War its membership reached two hundred.

When the First World War broke out Ukrainians, like most Austrian citizens, found themselves in a precarious position as they were considered to be alien enemies. The passage of the War Aliens' Act required all Austrian citizen males over eighteen to register with the police where they were issued alien identification cards and had to report regularly to the police station. Those who at one time were called upon to serve in the Austrian army at home were required to report twice a week and if the sergeant was a difficult man, even daily. Alien identification cards were to be carried everywhere and were to be shown on request; those who could not produce one were sent to Stanley Barracks (the present Marine Museum at the Canadian National Exhibition grounds) and shipped to the internment camp in Kapuskasing or Petawawa where they worked at clearing the forest and building roads.

Being classified as alien enemies stripped Ukrainians of all rights. The smallest offence meant internment camp (where they were treated as prisoners of war), travel was restricted, jobs in war production plants (which paid high wages) were prohibited, and enlistment in the Canadian armed forces was closed to them. The anti-alien feeling, fed by the returning soldiers who were often wounded or disabled but almost always disappointed and resentful when the expected high-paying jobs and preferential treatment did not materialize, rose throughout Canada. Toronto was no exception. In April 1917 bands of soldiers roamed the streets of Toronto ransacking restaurants in search of aliens, frightening landlords who rented premises to aliens and dragging the latter from their beds at night, raided plants, factories and shops requesting workers to show their alien identification cards and taking them to the police station, demanded their dismissal from jobs and the disfranchisement of naturalized Canadians.[26] On April 12, 1917, the Board of Control, at the motion of Mayor Church, decided to send two petitions to Prime Minister Borden and the federal cabinet to dismiss alien enemies from jobs in munition plants and ". . . to disfranchise Austrians, Germans, and other aliens who had not been domiciled in Canada for a period of at least twenty-five years."[27]

When, however, on April 16, Mayor Church put the vote on disfranchisement of the aliens to city council, its members voted against it and the veterans decided to go directly to the government. The behaviour of the soldiers and veterans was soon curbed by police and their own organizations as public criticism and opposition to the frequent work interruptions and the lawless actions mounted. It took, however, many more years before the anti-alien feeling subsided. Nicholas Yureskiw, who lived in Toronto during the war years, aptly expressed the Ukrainians' attitude when he stated that "It was not joke — one had to be very quiet."[28]

Yet Ukrainians enlisted in the Canadian armed forces and went overseas. Being well aware of the public ignorance of their homeland, they listed false countries of their birth (for example, Russia, Poland, Canada, Australia) and even Anglicized their names. They joined various battalions including the Canadian Forestry Corps and by 1918 seventeen of them from Toronto had died in action.[29]

When immigration resumed after the First World War, Canada again was interested in Ukrainian settlers. Thus, in the 1920s large numbers of Ukrainians arrived in Canada and many of them settled in Toronto. As most were better educated and politically conscious, having served in the armed forces of the Ukrainian National Republic, they formed their own organizations and began new publications. The Ukrainian People's Home Association continued to be most active and to represent Ukrainians in Toronto. In 1926 the first Ukrainian Greek Orthodox parish, St. Vladimir's, was established when Rev. P. Bilon temporarily became its first pastor. The Ukrainian Labor Farmer Temple Association suffered a blow in 1931 as some of its leaders were imprisoned but its cultural groups expanded. In fact all Ukrainian organizations were culturally very active and their drama clubs, orchestras and choirs staged plays and concerts in their own premises almost every weekend.

The depression years of the 1930s, although they stopped the influx of Ukrainian immigrants, resulted in the continuing growth of the Ukrainian community as the industries of Toronto attracted unemployed Ukrainians from various parts of Canada, but especially from drought-stricken Saskatchewan. Thus, by 1941 the Ukrainian community had reached 10,423.

Notes

1. Julian, Stechishin, *History of Ukrainian Settlements in Canada* (Edmonton: Ukrainian Self-Reliance League, 1975), pp. 100-106. Among the 150 soldiers who settled in June 1816 on the Rideau River near Perth, Ontario, were 20 Slavic names of which at least three are Ukrainian. Among the 80 soldiers who settled in 1917 in the Selkirk Settlement, over 10 are Ukrainian names. All were born in Ukraine — predominantly in Western Ukraine from where most Ukrainians emigrated to Canada after 1891.

2. A.J., Birrell, "Horetzky — Pioneer in Canadian Surveying Photography," *Ukrainian Echo*, March 3, 1982.

3. *The Catholic Register*, March 2, 1911.

4. Michel H. Marunchak, *The Ukrainian Canadians, A History* (Winnipeg and Ottawa: Ukrainian Free Academy of Sciences, 1970), p. 180.

5. At the end of 1912 there were only twenty-seven Ukrainian Catholic priests in Canada serving some 170,000 Ukrainians.

6. Information from Rev. Edward J.R. Jackman, O.P., Archdiocese of Toronto Archives.

7. Letter from Rev. J. Schweitzer to the Archbishop of Toronto, dated April 12, 1907, Archdiocese of Toronto Archives.

8. Rev. John A. Zaklynsky was married but left his family in Western Ukraine to do missionary work in North America. As he left without permission from his bishop in Ukraine, he would never have received permission from the Archbishop of Toronto to use a Roman Catholic church.

9. Archdiocese of Toronto Archives, September 14, 1910.

10. *Catholic Register*, November 26, 1910.

11. Certificates are at the Archdiocese of Toronto Archives.

12. Rev. Dr. Ambrose Redkewycz was assisting. Other priests were Rev. Joseph (Osyp) Boyarczuk (pastor) and Rev. Joseph Hinzmann, pastor of the St. Stanislaus Polish Roman Catholic parish. The White Eagle band of the St. Stanislau parish was playing religious songs.

13. *50 Golden Years 1913-1963*, St. Augustine's Seminary, Toronto, p. 11.

14. Census of Canada, 1971, showed that the Ukrainian Roman Catholics constituted 14.05 per cent of Toronto's Ukrainian community and 15.3 per cent of all Ukrainians in Canada. *Ukraine — A Concise Encyclopaedia*, Vol 1. p. 232, states that Latynnyky, together with Poles, formed 21.1 per cent of village population (39.15 per cent in cities) in Western Ukraine before the Second World War.

15. The earliest marriage and baptismal records of St. Stanislau's parish consist almost exclusively of Ukrainian names; these were later Polonized.

16. Archdiocese of Toronto Archives, letter dated July 23, 1915.

17. Ibid, June 19, 1935.

18. Beverley Street Baptist Church Records, April 28, 1915, pp. 94-96.

19. Dmytro A. Nykolak, *Korotky Istorychny Narys Ukrainskoho Narodnoho Domu v Toronto* (Toronto: Ukrainian People's Home Association, 1953), p. 8.

20. Interview with Nicholas Yureskiw, September 15, 1979.

21. John Kolasky, *The Shattered Illusion, The History of Ukrainian Pro-Communist Organizations in Canada* (Toronto: Peter Martin Associates Limited, 1979), p. 3.

22. *Workers' Word*, 1917.

23. *Almanac TURFDim 1918-1929* (Winnipeg: Ukrainsky Robitnycho-Farmersky Dim), p. 93.

24. Michael Petrowsky, Toronto, personal papers, n.d., 2 reels microfilm No. 119, MSR No. 1040, 2575 at the Ontario Archives.

25. Interview with Nicholas Yureskiw, September 15, 1979. He attended such a debate.

26. *Evening Telegram*, "Soldiers in Small Riot," April 13, 1917; *Globe*, "Soldiers Invade German Apartments," April 13, 1917; ibid., "Alien Workers Are Rounded Up," April 14, 1917; and ibid., "Soldiers Ignore Truce and Raid 'Kemp' Plant," April 19, 1917, p. 8.

27. *Evening Telegram*, April 12, 1917, p. 15.

28. Interview with Nicholas Yureskiw, September 15, 1979.

29. V.J. Kaye, *Ukrainian Canadians in Canada's Wars*, ed. J.B., Gregorovich (Toronto: Ukrainian Canadian Research Foundation, 1983), pp. 31, 106-25.

Contributors

J.M.S. Careless is Professor Emeritus of the Department of History at the University of Toronto. His many books include: *Canada: a Story of Challenge* and *Brown of the Globe*. His most recent publication is *Toronto to 1918. An Illustrated History* (Toronto, 1984). Professor Careless is chairman of the Historic Sites and Monuments Board of Canada, former chairman of the Multicultural History Society of Ontario and has served as president of the Canadian Historical Association.

Lia Douramakou-Petroleka wrote her M.A. thesis at the Ontario Institute for Studies in Education on Greek immigration to Toronto before the Second World War. She currently resides in Athens and works for the United Nations High Commissioner for Refugees.

Robert F. Harney is Professor of History at the University of Toronto and co-director of the university's Ethnic and Immigration Studies Program. He is academic director of the Multicultural History Society of Ontario and currently president of the Canadian Ethnic Studies Association. Professor Harney is author of *Dalla Frontiere alla Little Italies* (1984) and is co-author with Harold M. Troper of *Immigrants: a Portrait of the Urban Experience* (1976).

Benedykt Heydenkorn is the former editor of *Zwiazkowiec* (The Alliancer) and an editor at the Polish Canadian Research Institute. He is the co-author with Henry Radecki of a volume in the Generations Series entitled *A Member of a Distinguished Family* (1976). He has written and edited many works on Polish Canadians including the recent volume *Memoirs of Polish Immigrants in Canada* (1979).

Daniel G. Hill, Ph.D., is the past president of the Ontario Black History Society of Ontario and author of *The Freedom-Seekers. Blacks in Early Canada* (Agincourt, 1981). He was recently appointed ombudsman for the Province of Ontario.

Varpu Lindstrom-Best is a lecturer at Atkinson College of York University where she is completing her doctoral dissertation on Finnish immigrant women in Canada. She is co-author with Charles M. Sutyla of *Terveisiä Ruusa-tädiltä, kanadan suomalaisten ensimmäinen sukupolvi* (Tampere, 1984).

Murray W. Nicolson completed his Ph.D. at the University of Guelph in 1980. His thesis is entitled "The Catholic Church and the Irish in Victorian Toronto." Dr. Nicolson teaches part-time at Wilfrid Laurier University.

Dora Nipp wrote her M.A. thesis at the University of Toronto on Chinese pioneer women in western Canada before the First World War. She is now a Commonwealth Fellow studying at the University of Hong Kong.

Lillian Petroff completed her Ph.D. at the Ontario Institute for Studies in Education in 1983. Her thesis is entitled "The Macedonian Community in Toronto to 1940." She is a postdoctoral fellow at the Multicultural History Society of Ontario.

Zofia Shahrodi received her M.A. from Jagiellonian University (Krakow) in 1977. She is now a Ph.D. candidate in the Department of History, University of Toronto. Her thesis is entitled "Development of the Polish Ethnic Communities of Toronto and Hamilton before World War II."

Zoriana (Yaworsky) Sokolsky is a geography teacher at David and Mary Thomson Collegiate Institute. She is writing a history of the Ukrainians in Toronto.

Dr. Stephen A. Speisman is director of the Archives of Toronto Jewish Congress and the Canadian Jewish Congress, Central Region, the archives of the Jewish community of Ontario. He is author of *The Jews of Toronto: a History to 1937* (Toronto, 1979).

John E. Zucchi completed his Ph.D. at the University of Toronto in 1983. His thesis is entitled "Italian Immigrants in Toronto: Development of a National Identity, 1875-1930." He is currently a postdoctoral fellow at Darwin College, Cambridge University.

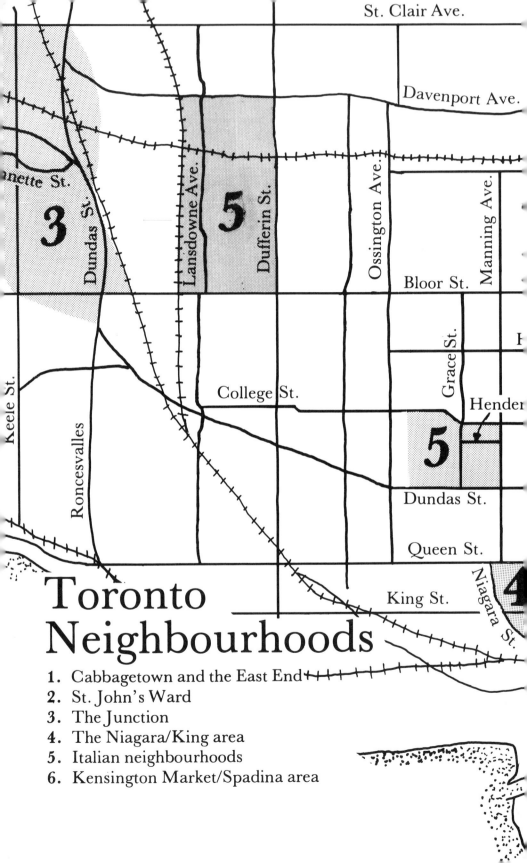

St. Clair Ave.

Davenport Ave.

anette St.

Dundas St.

3

Lansdowne Ave.

5

Dufferin St.

Ossington Ave.

Manning Ave.

Bloor St.

Keele St.

Roncesvalles

College St.

Grace St.

Hender

5

Dundas St.

Queen St.

Toronto
Neighbourhoods

Niagara St.

4

King St.

1. Cabbagetown and the East End
2. St. John's Ward
3. The Junction
4. The Niagara/King area
5. Italian neighbourhoods
6. Kensington Market/Spadina area

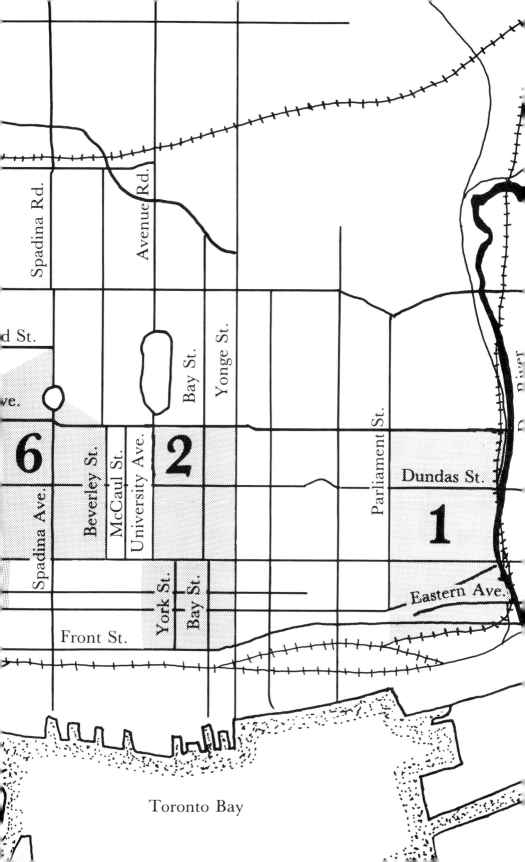

Spadina Rd.

Avenue Rd.

Bay St.

Yonge St.

d St.

ve.

6

Spadina Ave.

Beverley St.

McCaul St.

University Ave.

2

Parliament St.

Dundas St.

1

York St.

Bay St.

Front St.

Eastern Ave.

River

Toronto Bay

Printed in Canada

g